# SOUTHERN JOURNEY

*A Return to the Civil Rights Movement*

## TOM DENT

The University of Georgia Press
*Athens & London*

Paperback edition published in 2001 by the University of Georgia Press
Athens, Georgia 30602
© 1997 by Thomas C. Dent
Printed and bound by McNaughton & Gunn

The paper in this book meets the guidelines for
permanence and durability of the Committee on
Production Guidelines for Book Longevity of the
Council on Library Resources.

Printed in the United States of America

01 02 03 04 05 P 5 4 3 2 1

*Library of Congress Cataloging-in-Publication Data*

Dent, Thomas C.
Southern journey : a return to the civil rights movement / by Tom Dent.
p.   cm.
Originally published: New York : W. Morrow, c1997.
Includes bibliographical references (p. ).
ISBN 0-8203-2291-1 (pbk. : alk. paper)
1. Civil rights movements—Southern States.
2. Afro-Americans—Civil rights—Southern States.
3. Civil rights workers—Southern States—Interviews.
4. Southern States—Race relations.
5. Dent, Thomas C.—Journeys—Southern States.   I. Title
E185.615 .D47 2001
976'.043—dc21
00-061990

*British Library Cataloging-in-Publication Data available*

Published by arrangement with Basic Books, a division of
HarperCollins Publishers, Inc. All rights reserved.

Book design by Leah S. Carlson

To those who worked tirelessly and selflessly
to bring about a more just society in the
American South, this volume is dedicated.

# CONTENTS

Prologue

I

Greensboro

5

Orangeburg

79

Charleston

IOI

St. Augustine

I73

Albany

209

Selma

247

Mississippi

337

Afterword

373

Acknowledgments  383

List of Interviewees  387

Bibliography  393

MISSOURI

KENTU

ARKANSAS

TENNESS

ALABAMA

Mound Bayou

WEST POINT

GREENVILLE

INDIANOLA

MONTGOMERY

Lowndesboro

MAYERSVILLE

PHILADELPHIA

Eutaw

Marion

SELMA

CANTON

JACKSON

Meridian

LOUISIANA

Demopolis

Camden

Union Springs

Uniontown

MISSISSIPPI

MOBILE

NEW ORLEANS

Gulf

of Mexico

Oliver Williams

KY
VIRGINIA
EE
NORTH
CAROLINA
GREENSBORO
Durham
SOUTH
CAROLINA
ATLANTA
Aiken
ORANGEBURG
Denmark
CHARLESTON
GEORGIA
kegee
Leesburg
LBANY
Tifton
Newton
DORCHESTER
Brunswick
JACKSONVILLE
ST. AUGUSTINE
Gainesville
Daytona Beach
LORIDA
Atlantic
Ocean

*"I began to suspect that the great trouble and anxiety of Southern gentlemen is:—How, without quite destroying the capabilities of the negro for any work at all, to prevent him from learning to take care of himself."*

—FREDERICK LAW OLMSTED
*A Journey in the Seaboard Slave States* (1856)

*"Yesterday—an almost endless ordeal of reconstruction, colonial exploitation, caste and class divisions, segregation, isolation, poverty, depression, and wartime sacrifice—was finally on the wane, if not yet altogether finished. Tomorrow—an age of opportunity, growth, prosperity, recovered self-esteem, national parity, and full citizenship—seemed ready and waiting to be born."*

—JOHN EGERTON
*Speak Now Against the Day* (1995)

*"...the basis of culture lies in the folk, and that by folk we mean not in-culturated, static groups, giving little; but a people who, from the centre of an oppressive system have been able to survive, adapt, recreate; have devised means of protecting what has been so gained..., and who begin to offer to return some of this experience and vision."*

—KAMAU BRATHWAITE
*Contradictory Omens* (1974)

# SOUTHERN JOURNEY

# PROLOGUE

I was raised as a black youth in the city of New Orleans one generation before the maze of legal obstructions that delineated racial segregation in the South was dismantled piece by piece.

In those days, my family expected that I would seek my fortune elsewhere, because possibilities in the South were far too limited. The same expectation held for my brothers and my friends, those who were fortunate enough to share the benefits of education. The necessity that I leave the South for the sake of a more promising future was rarely explicitly stated, but it was strongly implied. The South, it was assumed by that generation of black elders, would eventually drop its racial barriers, but who knew when *eventually* would occur? Immense changes were not expected in their lifetimes, nor did they think the younger generation should depend too heavily on massive changes during our lifetimes.

I therefore began a rich dream life built around leaving for destinations so far from, so different from the South, the two worlds would never recognize each other. My first dreams were associated with the awesome Mississippi River, which always exercised a mysterious power over me, and ran right through downtown New Orleans. My fascination with the river began as a child; my father would pack us into the family car on Sunday nights for what became his ritual weekly drive to Canal Street, the main avenue of New Orleans, which runs from the river to Lake Pontchartrain. Downtown Canal Street was a concoction of decorative lights, dazzling store windows, and people waiting at bus stops for rides out to their isolated neighborhoods. Here was the mighty crossroads of the city and its largest marketplace.

Then my father would head for the river at the foot of Canal Street. Here, at the docks, right beside the Louisville and Nashville train station, he would park and we would get out. I always raced to the edge of the dock to stare at the strange muddy currents of the river, which was wide enough to be a lake. I would look upriver and downriver, to the very edge of its sharp bends, as if I might fathom the past hidden beyond the curve downriver, the future upriver. To me, the river was the oldest living person in New Orleans. It was the great highway out into the world beyond the street corners, beyond the limitations and boredoms of the world I was growing up into. The sound of austere ships' horns was enough to trigger my imaginary trips to more exciting places, for I knew the great river led to anywhere and to everywhere. So did the sound of train whistles—in my early dream world, trains always ran beside the river, leading to more certain and appealing destinations. For me and others like me, those dream roads—fueled by books, movies, and legends—led to a nonracial world, where we would find solace from the exclusively black world we were confined to, where the color of our skin, our racial heritage, did not matter. But then, that was truly a dream world—a world, I have come to believe, that does not exist.

Since my childhood, the American South has, against all odds, entered a new epoch. Our elder generation was wrong. Changes we hardly believed were possible have occurred, along with all the harsh trauma associated with a brief period of intense, highly publicized conflict. Doors that we thought would be slammed shut forever, barring a miracle, were kicked open.

As for me, I left the South for graduate school (after attending Morehouse College in Atlanta), finally settling in New York to work for a Harlem newspaper in 1959 and as press attaché for the NAACP Legal Defense Fund between 1961 and 1963. When I returned to New Orleans in 1965, I had no intention of remaining in the South. But somehow, I never did return to New York. This journey is an extension of that "never did."

A large part of why I remained in the South has to do with my experiences in Mississippi in the late 1960s. In Mississippi, I was able to experience more completely the civil rights movement, and learn what made it successful. The impetus for social change was rooted in a few courageous people, most of whom were black, some of whom were white, who were building upon the lonely spadework done by leaders from previous generations extending back to Emancipation. The sixties, including the civil rights movement, were an eruption of energy that had been building for some time.

My interest in the experiences of Mississippi veterans led me to want to interview and record their testimony of how they came to activism, though I had no idea how the interviews would be used. I did know their stories would provide counterpoint or detailed confirmation to the more broadly focused accounts of the South's most dramatic period of change since the Civil War.

When I completed the tapes, I wanted to expand my interviews to include the entire activist South, though I knew that would be taking on a bit much. I decided instead to undertake a long, and very possibly insane, leisurely drive through the South over a period of several months, if I could save up enough money to pay for the trip. My intent was to interview people in small towns or cities that experienced trauma over civil rights conflicts or racial disputes in the sixties or the period immediately following. I planned to work my way southward beginning in Greensboro, North Carolina, my choice as a starting point of the decade of change, and ending where I began two decades ago: in Mississippi.

I decided not to confine my interviews to civil rights history, but to search out people's impressions of their towns—as places to remain in, leave, or return to. I knew I would be talking mostly to blacks; they were the ones whom sudden change had most profoundly affected. I intended to talk to whites also, particularly newspaper people, who I believed were generally knowledgeable and relatively objective. I also knew that the views of southern whites on race had received, and continued to receive, considerable exposure.

I planned to avoid political officials, important administrators, pillars of the community, black or white, as I believed they would tell me little other than stories that confirmed their own importance. I also planned to skirt the large cities of the Deep South—Atlanta, Birmingham, Memphis, and New Orleans—for they were volumes in themselves, requiring resources I did not possess. On the other hand, I suspected that smaller towns would be more interesting, more resistant to change, more reflective of the South as a region. Following the same reasoning, I planned to avoid the interstate highways whenever I could, riding the old highways and, when there was enough time, circling around the towns I was visiting in the hope of updating my sense of what the South had become, entering the twenty-first century, or had not become.

This book is an account of that 1991 journey, which began in January in Greensboro, North Carolina, and ended in November at the Mississippi River in the Mississippi Delta. In undertaking this odyssey, I reversed the direction my life was expected to follow. Instead of leaving, I am, in a way that will unfold in more detail, returning.

# GREENSBORO

When the first sit-ins at a downtown Woolworth's took place on February 1, 1960, a new phase of black protest against racial injustice began. Four students from North Carolina A&T University, a black state school, went to a Woolworth's lunch counter reserved for whites only, sat down and ordered food, and refused to move until they were served. As customers, they might spend money in that store every day, but they were denied the convenience of the lunch counter—just one of the many inconveniences, small and large, imposed by racial segregation.

Word of the demonstrations quickly spread. That night, other A&T students pledged to continue the protests for as long as it took to bring down the racial barriers.

Durham, Charlotte, and other North Carolina cities where there were black colleges immediately initiated the same sort of demonstrations at dime store lunch counters in their downtowns. The national press and electronic media picked up the story and relayed it around the nation. These unique protests against segregation, dubbed the "sit-ins" by the media, marked the beginning of a new, activist phase in southern civil rights advocacy. It is important to note that the sit-ins were not initiated by racial leaders, but by college students who were virtually unknown.

Throughout the remainder of the 1960s, Greensboro continued to be the scene of energetic and innovative racial protests. I well realize that my choice of Greensboro as a point of origin for my journey into the South is an arbitrary decision, but I think Greensboro will be an extremely promising starting point. Greensboro represents an ideal geographic bridge between the upper South and the lower South, and a historical bridge between the earlier legal and individual forms of protest against racial segregation, and the more activist mass-movement phase. Greensboro was a vortex of racial conflict and change during the sixties, the most involved city in the upper South, and I wanted to know why that was so. What sort of town had Greensboro become since the sixties, since those tense days of protest and uproar?

I am driving on Interstate 85, heading for Greensboro. I've just left Durham, and finally, after months of preparation and planning, I am on my way. Lord knows how this trip will work out. I'm listening to the reports of the bombing of Baghdad, Iraq, by the U.S. Air Force on Cable News Network radio. It seems as if the U.S. government has jumped headfirst into war in the Persian Gulf. I was visiting old friends Leonard and Rhoda Dreyfus in Charlottesville, Virginia, when we heard of the first day's bombing. I don't like it. A military war over an interruption of the flow of oil to Western nations seems absurd.

The traffic on this highway is startling, particularly the truck traffic. It's as if I'm being propelled along faster than I want to drive; if I slow down, I'll be run off the road. I'm in the midst of the industrial South, not the sleepy South: textile mills, tobacco factories, clothing outlets, and all the related products.

I exit Interstate 85 to try the old highway between Durham and Greensboro, which is U.S. 70. The old highway is also loaded with cars. U.S. 70 leads me through the old-fashioned downtown of Mebane, decorated with a festive display of American flags. There is an air of excitement over this war; I can hear it on the radio stations, the talk shows. A prominent sign: GOD BLESS AMERICA. PRAY FOR OUR TROOPS.

At Burlington, a quite large town and a huge textile-factory center, there are numerous commercial outlets selling all sorts of clothing at cut-rate bargains. Then traffic begins to thin out, and there is hardly anyone on the road as I come to the village of Sedalia, which I have heard is basically an all-black town. I come upon the old Palmer Memorial Institute, once a prestigious prep school for elite black youth from all over the South, which I had always heard about but never seen. The school has long been closed, shut down after a devastating fire in 1971. I slow to see what I can; Palmer's empty buildings are maintained as a state historical site, a sign says, but the office is closed. I drive the few additional miles until I enter Greensboro.

At Greensboro, U.S. 70 becomes Wendover Avenue, which runs through an old section of town, continues through what looks to be a new section of town, and well, I'm lost. I'm looking for a motel but there aren't any on this road. I decide to head southward back to I-85 as it skirts the edges of Greensboro. I find an inexpensive motel, settle in, and make plans for the beginning of what I expect will be a long journey, almost a year on southern roads. It is January 22, 1991.

~

The morning after I arrived, I drove to downtown Greensboro to observe the old sit-in and civil rights demonstration area. Unfortunately, downtown Greensboro seems well on its way to becoming a ghost town. I felt like I had entered a movie set for an early-twentieth-century American town. Where once were department, clothing, hardware, and dime stores, there now stood a collection of small antique shops, the "economy" store, a billiard parlor, a television appliance shop, a large store selling cheap goods with the ubiquitous American flag in the window, and the United States bankruptcy court, all dwarfed by the huge Jefferson-Pilot office building, which towers over downtown like a majestic mountain amid small hills.

Greensboro's beginnings are traced to a 1749 Quaker settlement called New Garden, which was part of a substantial eighteenth-century Quaker migration southward from their Pennsylvania home into the Piedmont Carolinas, according to William H. Chafe in his excellent study of race relations in Greensboro, *Civilities and Civil Rights.*

By the time of the Revolutionary War, settlers moving westward from the Atlantic coast outnumbered the Quakers in what came to be known as Guilford County. Guilford County was the site of an important battle against the British during the War of Independence; the Revolutionary army in the Carolinas was led by General Nathanael Greene, for whom the town was named when it was incorporated in 1808.

Blacks were not as numerous in central North Carolina as on the coast, but the 1860 county census reported 4,000 slaves and 600 free people of color, a rather large number of free blacks. Following the Civil War and Emancipation, the first black settlement in Greensboro was established; it was called Warnersville in honor of the Philadelphia Quaker leader who purchased and donated the land. Apparently, for a while, freedmen were working and doing well. "Between 1870 and 1890, blacks constituted nearly 50 percent of all the skilled workers in Greensboro, serving as brickmasons, carpenters, foundry workers, and skilled railway workers," observes Chafe.

For blacks, the taste of freedom and economic opportunity turned sour at the turn of the twentieth century, not coincidentally, just as Greensboro's first textile mills and tobacco-processing plants were cranking up. Segregation laws were enacted and "employers fired blacks from lumber, woodworking, and furniture factories and replaced them with white men and boys.... White women replaced black women in the tobacco factories." Meanwhile, with the advent of the twentieth century, Greensboro was expanding: 2,000 in 1880 to 10,000 in 1890 to 53,000 in 1930. Blacks represented about a fourth of the population.

"In 1895 Moses and Caesar Cone arrived from Baltimore to begin construction of the giant textile factories on the outskirts of the city.... During the 1920s the Cone hegemony was challenged when Burlington Industries—later to become the largest textile firm in the world—started its meteoric rise in Greensboro.... Two of the largest insurance companies in the country, Jefferson Standard and Pilot Life, established headquarters in the city," according to Chafe. The two insurance companies later merged into Jefferson-Pilot.

Greensboro moved at a steady pace toward a remarkable textile and insurance prosperity, but the story for Greensboro blacks was one of continual struggle. To box the black community in, the city imposed a restrictive housing ordinance in 1914 that prohibited them from purchasing a home on any street where a majority of the homes were occupied by whites. Ninety percent of the black population lived in the southeastern section; the other black neighborhood was Warnersville, a tiny area descending from the original Reconstruction settlement. (This ordinance was revoked in 1929.) As for employment, Chafe points out that by 1950 nearly 40 percent of the Greensboro black labor force worked in *personal services*. Even so, in the thirties and forties, Greensboro blacks had a higher median education level than in Durham, and a higher median income, Chafe observes. This had to be due to the presence of North Carolina A&T and Bennett College, and a strong though legally segregated black public school system. By the time of World War II, textiles, machinery, tobacco, and insurance businesses were firmly established in Greensboro. Those businesses, particularly tobacco, were also prominent in the two cities, Durham, fifty-two miles to the east, and Winston-Salem, twenty-eight miles to the west, commonly associated with Greensboro, which is the largest of the three.

If the Jefferson-Pilot building symbolizes the financial affluence of Greensboro's industries, then North Carolina A&T, the state's black college, represents the aspirations of Greensboro's black community. These two symbols were often at odds during the post-World War II years.

⌒

I planned to visit A&T and the southeastern section that afternoon, but first I went looking for the Woolworth's where the famous sit-in took place in 1960, and, amazingly, it was still there. On the corner of South Elm Street, the main downtown street, there was a sign acknowledging the site of the "original" sit-ins, and in fact the name of the street itself had been changed to reflect the historic date, "February 1st Street."

This particular Woolworth's was definitely from another era, breezy with high windows, plenty of light; none of the narrow, crowded, merchandise-laden aisles of today's variety stores. The lunch counter was very much in operation—a long, L-shaped affair of the type I grew up with but could not eat at on Canal Street in New Orleans. It was about noon, and I decided to indulge in my own belated sit-in and eat something.

I ordered a hamburger and Coke. I was surprised at the amount of business the lunch counter was attracting. In fact, most of the customers entering Woolworth's headed for the lunch counter; no one seemed to be shopping. Maybe Woolworth's was the only place to grab lunch in downtown Greensboro. Some of the waitresses and short-order cooks were white, some were black; most of the customers were white. A group of dark-suited white men slid onto counter stools. I guessed they were from out of town, maybe doing business at the bankruptcy court. I shifted my glance to observe two gangly black teenagers. They were wolfing down their burgers and fries with a slightly guilty enthusiasm. They didn't have the hardened urban-ghetto look so familiar in the inner cities; their demeanor seemed more innocent, controlled. They may have been out-of-towners also, from some small rural place, and when one boy ordered "Another fries, please," he shot a smile at an older black man a few stools away. This is part of an athletic team, I imagined, and the man on the stool is their coach. They were soon gone, and my burger and Coke arrived. All I can say is it's a good thing I wasn't expecting anything special. And it's a good thing the sit-ins weren't about hamburgers and Cokes.

I then returned to my car and headed for the southeastern section of the city.

Market Street is the key thoroughfare leading from downtown into the black area. It looks like a street that was once busy with small commerce, but now it has become merely a major conduit for automobile traffic headed into and out of town, a mini-interstate. I noticed a few businesses scattered among several boarded-up structures: the African Boutique, Mitchell's Shoes and Clothing, Goodson's Curb Market, Cox Furniture, the boarded-up former Uhuru Bookstore, a beauty salon, and two buildings with FOR SALE signs on them. As you proceed away from town, the huge post office appears to be of recent vintage. A few blocks farther, there's the formidable Hayes-Taylor YMCA, and then the campus of A&T University.

The A&T campus is dwarfed by a massive, unattractive, and relatively new Engineering Building, which, as far as I could see, possessed no discernible entrance. Apparently, it was designed to imitate one of those brown-brick, tinted-glass office buildings where graduating students will be condemned to work, if they find work. Driving around the campus, it was my impression that structures had been erected haphazardly, with no sense of architectural symmetry.

Bennett College for black women only is a mere few blocks away. Bennett's buildings are imposing, apparently of early-twentieth-century vintage, the campus greens neatly kept. I got out of my car to walk around, but a security guard was eyeing me suspiciously. I didn't feel like explaining myself, so I returned rather quickly to my car. I then took a cursory spin around the entire southeastern area, the primary black business area. I observed sturdy houses of an older type with well-kept lawns, and only a few blocks away, clusters of run-down housing. To get to Dudley High School, the old black high school, I had to cross over an expressway. Surrounding the high school was a cluster of small modest shacks.

I decided to circle back to the A&T campus, park, and walk around. I strolled over to the library. Not terribly full of students for such a large school, but there were a few. I noticed one very young, very dark-skinned student whose skin color was what we used to call "blue gum"—a term blacks use among themselves to describe *very* dark-skinned people. Probably a freshman, he was bent over his note-book copying intently from a book, the title of which I would like to have seen. He had a small-town look about him; he was probably the first of his family to attend college and perhaps had dreams of becoming an engineering student ("They're pushing nothing but engineering now at A&T" was a complaint I heard more than once while I was there). He soon closed the book, shoved the notebook into his bag, and walked out. Forgetting his coat in the January cold, he was quickly back to retrieve it. When I left a few minutes later, I could see him striding toward his dormitory, in front of which stood a few students, one playing rap music on a boom box.

The dormitory was one of the older ones, probably dating from the 1940s, and as I walked back to where I had parked, I reflected that it was in these very ordinary looking dormitories, among kids like the one I just observed, that the drama of the sit-ins, the historical miracle that changed so much of our southern and national history, began.

That historical miracle of 1960, if we can call it that in this age so much less enamored with social change, was marked by a dramatic break with the racial past on the part of the younger generation of southern blacks. The sit-ins were deliberate acts of defiance against the segregation system, a psychological as well as physical act, an overcoming of long-standing fear within the race of the harsh consequences of defiance. In effect, they said, "Send us to jail if you will, but it won't stop us now." And they discovered, if they had not already known, that many of their peers were of the same mind.

I had grown up a generation earlier under the same system of complicated racial barriers in New Orleans. As a boy going to school in New Orleans in the late 1940s, I had had to sit in the rear of streetcars and buses behind a movable wooden barrier with the words FOR COLORED ONLY stenciled upon it as if some sort of privileged section had been set aside for us. We were to sit in the first car of trains, in the balcony of movie theaters, and on the main commercial street, Canal Street, we were waited upon at the side counters of restaurants like the one in Woolworth's.

We had to master a knowledge of where the "for Colored" bathrooms were at the downtown stores, and which businesses maintained them, however poorly; where the "Colored" water fountains were, which stores we might enter, which places we must never enter, certainly not through the front door. If a large auditorium or waiting room served the entire public, we must know, as if by special divination if no sign existed, exactly where we must sit. For fear of the ever-roving police, we had to know for our own protection which streets to walk, which never to tread upon, which never even to ride through on our bicycles. Growing up with this was a burden, but a little bit laughable because it was so ridiculous. Defying these rules and restrictions, if we could get away with it, increased our, and my, pleasure. This maze of restrictions created a certain psychological racial solidarity; for no matter how well off we were, or how poor, each of us was proscribed by the same rules.

We didn't think, or talk about, a mass rebellion, or active, deliberate, conscious resistance to these obstructions. Individuals, fed up or too egregiously insulted, did, from time to time, of course; they were jailed or worse. The attitude passed down from elders was: We should make out the best we could under the circumstances; someday a better time would come.

A few years later, when I was a student at Morehouse College, I experienced an Atlanta that was far more rigidly segregated than New Orleans. The college was located in a black world with its own institutions, businesses, and strata; the appearance of whites, unless they worked at one of the educational institutions, was akin to that of visitors from a foreign nation. Downtown Atlanta—Peachtree Street—was the counterpart of Canal Street in New Orleans. Peachtree Street was a great crossroads for blacks headed to work in white homes. I wonder now why at Morehouse in the early 1950s, we never thought about intentionally violating the segregation laws. I suppose, looking back, we did not think it would lead to anything productive. Had we decided to sit at the "wrong" counter and ask for a Coca-Cola, I don't know what would have happened; surely we would have been arrested. Parents would have been called. Our sanity would have been questioned. We would hardly have been heroes to other students, only fools to be made fun of and avoided. We would have, or we thought we would have, been derailed in our pursuit of promising careers as doctors, teachers, and preachers. If such protest actions were repeated, we would be expelled without explanation. In the fifties, our very education was designed to help us make the best of a restricted situation, and to overcome it via learning and accommodation, not confrontation. Change would come, we were sure, but we had no target date in mind. For postgraduate study, which was encouraged, we were to leave the South. Many of us dreamed of fulfilling our aspirations outside the South. I know I did.

In 1960 in Greensboro, somehow the time was right. It was as if the students had, in a single leap, crossed a psychological river that their elders had contemplated crossing for years without ever taking more than a step here, a step there. In Greensboro and other towns that followed in its wake, individual complaints against segregation became general. "I" became "we" as if through some unspoken communication of commonly and historically shared feelings; young people decided to take action. The generative force of this Movement was centered in Greensboro, specifically, North Carolina A&T. I wondered if that was merely a historical accident. Or was there something particular about Greensboro and/or A&T that made it likely the southern black activist Movement would spark to life there?

⌒

I decided to explore Greensboro a little further by driving around town, searching for areas other than the commercial downtown district and the southeastern black neighborhood. For a long time it has been my habit when arriving in a new town to feel the place out walking or driving, soaking up whatever might be of interest—architecture, neighborhoods, landmarks, parks, the shape of streets, particular smells and noises. For me these have always been meandering excursions with no set pattern or destination. Most people might consider such wanderings a waste of time, but I have found I am obsessed with the need to do this, maybe as a way of sensually capturing the feel of a place, even if I get lost or become confused. Sometimes such wandering/searching becomes a game—trying to discern where blacks live, or do not live. The less I know beforehand, the more interesting the game.

I think this ritual derives from riding with my father as a child during summer automobile trips to Houston, and from my first drive with my parents between New Orleans and New York when I was fifteen.

From my backseat window a South unfolded before me of abundant rolling fields and forests, a vista of great agricultural variety and expanse. The endless flatness of southern Louisiana and coastal Mississippi gave way to the foothills of Alabama as we turned northward toward Atlanta, negotiating the steep hills and winding roads, past the textile mills and tobacco factories of North Carolina that feed into the swift-paced, grimy grays of the densely populated Northeast.

On these trips through the segregated South, we were always conscious of our overnight stops. Hotels and motels were out of the question, so the respites were planned where my parents had friends who had been forewarned of our arrival. Because all restaurants on the highways and in towns were closed to us, eating was an adventurous mobile picnic filled with sandwiches, boiled eggs (with portions of salt and pepper wrapped in wax paper), fried chicken (because it can be eaten cold), and bags full of assorted fruit that my mother had prepared meticulously in New Orleans for the long journey. Locating restrooms required a sixth sense cultivated over many years by my father. Upon entering a likely service station, he would ask, just before ordering gasoline, "By the way, do you have bathrooms for Colored?" If the answer was no, we moved on. This might go on for several towns. Dad was aware of every speed limit sign, since the limits were often arbitrarily enforced by local police. If we were stopped, my father employed all his diplomacy and tact; he must never contest an officer's authority too strenuously lest he be perceived as "uppity." At the same time, he must not surrender his manhood. Almost always, it was necessary to find the black communities of towns along our route in order to gas up, locate bathrooms, get something to eat, and so forth. Dad seemed to have an unerring feel for locating "us," though he didn't say he was finding us. He was finding a place to eat, or to get gasoline. I watched him, silently fascinated. I was determined not to ask him how he did it. Finally, I figured out that his method was to look for railroad tracks—it was likely that blacks lived adjacent to them, or "across" from them, or in whichever direction the tracks led from the center of town. Black communities were little towns unto themselves, almost all of them separated from the white commercial and residential districts by natural barriers, like rivers or creeks, or by such man-made barriers as the legendary railroad tracks or highways. For me, the approach to the "Colored downtown" was always tinged with excitement and discovery, for here—in small restaurants and fish fry joints, bars and nightclubs, insurance companies, funeral homes, and the alluring, full-of-life barbershops where everything about everyone was known and wagered upon—here was a repository of secrets, extraordinary tales, and wondrous knowledge. And here were the ubiquitous churches, usually Baptist, some of them red brick with a cascade of steps leading to the sanctuary.

Black college towns usually looked more prosperous: better homes, better streets, a decent restaurant, sometimes a community newspaper. The colleges themselves and the areas around them were considered havens from the racial harassment that could occur anytime, anywhere, for any reason, or for no reason at all. They were havens, that is, as long as no challenge to the racial status quo issued forth from their campuses.

The families residing in those towns spanned a wide range of occupations and interests, their members having come in search of better conditions and good work— a twentieth-century quest that supplanted the forced, brutal, and arbitrary separations wrought by slavery. There were families who, like mine, anchored their lives in the church, who learned to read and write in schools that churches built and supported, education having become the religion of racial advancement after Emancipation. Education was the highway to status, the earliest professions bastions of community service: teaching, preaching, medicine, and law. Over time, in these separate towns across the tracks, the mind-set of successful blacks had settled into a delicately balanced accommodation of segregation. Forever after, I associated these southern black neighborhoods with trains and tracks, which bound them in, the sound of train wheels and the whistles and smoke of train engines. Those who wished to escape black neighborhoods were—and are—always trying to get as far away from the tracks as they could.

These were my own conclusions. My father was not one who enjoyed being asked "why" when it came to racial matters. You were supposed to become aware of the more subtle and unpleasant vagaries of race via osmosis. I eventually took to calling such undiscussed racial patterns "blues truths."

Lee Street leads away from A&T and the main black community. Just after passing the Coliseum, it becomes High Point Road. This road is the old highway leading to the town of High Point, about fifteen miles away, which can be reached much quicker now on the Interstate 85 expressway. High Point Road is a four-lane thoroughfare embellished by fast-food joints, an occasional moderately upscale restaurant, and a series of "Oriental Massage Parlors." Driving to the outskirts of town, I pass automobile dealerships and repair shops and then cross underneath the thunderously busy Interstate 40, which connects Raleigh, Durham, and Winston-Salem to Greensboro. To the left is a major shopping mall, conveniently located near the I-40 exit, then more retail stores and eating places, including an imitation-barbecue bistro I learned to like. From there on, the stores, shops, and chain restaurants thin out and the highway becomes just another old highway. If I-40 suddenly dropped out of sight, High Point Road would probably revert to a lonely highway leading out of town.

I made a U-turn back toward the center of town, then drove northward to explore two main roads leading from downtown, Battlefield Road and Friendly Avenue. Battlefield Road opens into a quite busy boulevard, the commercial spine of an upscale housing area, lined by restaurants, movie theaters, specialty shops, video rental stores, bookstores, yogurt shops, minimalls, and a newsstand with out-of-state newspapers and journals. And on, out to the huge Cone Mill. I saw few blacks in any of these places, not even shopping or working in the stores. High Point Road resembled Veterans Boulevard in New Orleans; Battlefield was a slightly less expensive Peachtree Road in the Buckhead section of Atlanta.

Friendly Avenue runs like a long, winding creek through well-to-do neighborhoods, though it is not as wide or as commercial as Battlefield. Friendly leads to the expensive-looking Guilford College, probably the most important legacy remaining from Greensboro's Quaker heritage. I planned to check it out more thoroughly later. Both Battlefield and Friendly left me with the feeling that the commercial and residential weight of Greensboro listed toward their direction, to the north. This area was so completely cut off from the main black section that the two areas and peoples might never intersect except in the now rather empty downtown area that still retains, however, offices of city and county government. It was almost as if there were two cities within one city limits, visual evidence of Chafe's observations in *Civilities and Civil Rights* that until the 1970s, the white well-to-do segment had so little contact with blacks (except for their servants) that they could live out their lives without ever knowing the black community of Greensboro existed, except in population statistics.

One person who could help me understand the racial aspects of Greensboro was Dr. George Simkins. I called and we arranged to meet at his office. Simkins, now in his early sixties, is generally recognized as the most important civil rights leader in Greensboro's history. He served as president of the Greensboro NAACP for two decades, and has for some time been a political power through his Greensboro Citizens Association. As a dentist, he follows in the footsteps of his father.

Simkins's office is located in the southeastern section near the A&T campus. His private office was stacked full of file cabinets, documents, books, photographs. Simkins is also known for his tennis *and* golf games (one usually plays one or the other, not both), so I was not surprised that he appeared to be very physically fit. Medium-brown skinned, and slightly balding, Simkins was direct, not overly friendly, and serious.

"We had to fight for *everything* in Greensboro, you need to remember that," he began. "This was a closed town for blacks. As for me personally, my involvement began in the mid-fifties with golf."

"Golf?"

"Golf. The golf course for blacks was absolutely horrible. See, at first we weren't trying to integrate, or revolutionize the South; we were just trying to get the city to fix up the black golf course. They never did anything. And in 1955, in the wake of the *Brown* Supreme Court decision, the city leased Gillespie Park Golf Course to a group of white golfers for one dollar so they could say it was privately owned, so the city wouldn't have to open it up to blacks. Anyway, on December seventh of that year six of us, all black golfers, decided we were going to go out to Gillespie and we weren't going to take no for an answer. Even if we went to jail."

Simkins and his friends arrived at the Gillespie course, startling the clerk. "We placed our fees on the counter before the clerk could blink. When we tried to sign the sign-in book, he snatched it away." They marched out to the course anyway, and proceeded to play. "The pro ran out after us and threatened us. I was so nervous I couldn't even hit a straight ball. I kept one club in my hand to use on the pro if he hit me. He called us a gang of black SOBs. I yelled, 'We're out here for a cause.' 'What damn cause?' he wanted to know. 'Democracy,' I yelled back. That's when he called the police."

They played nine holes and went home. That night a black policeman came by the Simkins home to arrest him for violating the segregation ordinance. "When the case came before the court, the judge begged me, 'Please don't pursue this. If you promise you won't appeal I'll just fine you'all a little bit and you can go home, that will be the end of it.' I said, 'No, that won't be the end of it, we're here for a cause. We don't think the city is right in this.' He fined us, and we appealed."

On appeal, at the state superior court, "the judge told us we had better not come out to *his* place trying to take over. He gave me a personal lecture. He told me I was beneath myself playing golf with a group of Negroes who were not professional men. He knew I was a dentist and he knew my father was a dentist. One of my golf partners was a barber, one was a chauffeur. Then he sentenced us to thirty days in jail."

Simkins and the group appealed to the federal courts, where the district court judge held that the city's one-dollar lease was a ruse. Gillespie was really city property; it had to open up to blacks. "Then just before the date set for us to use the course, *the clubhouse burned down.* In the wake of the fire, the fire marshal condemned the entire golf course, not just the clubhouse. It remained condemned for *seven years.* Now, that's Greensboro."

After the golf course case, Simkins became a staunch advocate of legal agitation against segregation. Simkins joined a suit to open a new city swimming pool to blacks. The city closed the pool rather than comply. He next became involved with an NAACP effort in the late 1950s to increase black voter registration that was extremely successful, and another to pressure the stalling Greensboro school board to take steps toward desegregation (there had been none). Simkins was also the prime litigant in a landmark suit against Cone Hospital, which banned black physicians and dentists from practicing even though Cone was the recipient of federal funds.

By 1960, Simkins had well established his activist credentials. It is not surprising that when Ezell Blair, Joseph McNeil, David Richmond, and Franklin McCain launched their historic sit-in on February 1, they called Simkins, along with other well-known adult community activists, to seek support. They received it immediately. Sit-ins had previously been held in other southern cities, but they had not continued long enough to take hold and become sustained demonstrations.

I asked Simkins whether he was surprised by the sit-ins. "No," he replied. "There had been a lot of talk. One of the people urging us to do something like that was Ralph Johns, a Market Street clothing merchant who sold to A&T students and was a strong member of the NAACP even though he was white. He wanted everybody to stage a downtown sit-in protest, including me. On February first, Johns called all excited, yelling over the phone, 'They're doing it. They're doing it *right now.'*"

That night Simkins went right to work to rally national support. "I had heard about the Congress of Racial Equality and their policy of nonviolent protest," he said. CORE, founded in the Midwest as a small religious group of social and interracial activists in the 1940s, had initiated nonviolent demonstrations for several years against restaurants that refused to serve blacks, mostly in Chicago, though this information was not widely known in the South. "I called them in New York to ask for assistance. Within two days they had a man here, Gordon Carey." Carey and Floyd McKissick of the Durham NAACP spent two weeks touring North Carolina, advising students at the various black state colleges who were taking up demonstrations in their towns, keeping the surge alive.

"Were you surprised how quickly the sit-ins spread?" I asked.

"Yes. But it was something students could do; adults didn't have the free time for that type of demonstration. And one other thing I think none of us anticipated: Because large numbers of black youth were downtown participating in and supporting demonstrators, all the businesses downtown were hurt. Their regular customers stayed away. The whites thought some sort of race riot was going on, so they stopped going downtown altogether. Once city officials saw their entire downtown suffering because of the demonstrations, they put pressure on Woolworth's to give in, hoping that would satisfy black demands. Of course it didn't," though Woolworth's made concessions and the city promised to take steps toward desegregation, bringing the demonstrations to an end.

"So how do you feel about Greensboro now," I asked, "after two decades have passed under the bridge?"

"We're in bad shape. With white flight from the city, the policies of the Reagan administration, and with this new Supreme Court, we're right back where we started. As far as Greensboro is concerned, this has always been a conservative town, and still is."

"How about black political achievement?"

"We have blacks on the City Council now, but for years the council operated under an at-large system, meaning only affluent whites were elected. It took *seventeen years* of battling to get the city to change to a district representative system. Durham, Raleigh, Winston-Salem, have long operated under district systems. But Greensboro is run by the corporate boys: the owners of the mills, the big insurance companies. They meet and decide what's best for this city. We don't have much say."

As Simkins was finishing the last sentence, his nurse ushered a patient past us into his dental office. The patient was a middle-aged black man; Simkins seemed surprised to see him. "Hold on, I've got to tend to this," he excused himself.

He quickly treated the patient and within a few minutes he returned with the patient, introducing me to attorney Walter Johnson, a member of the Greensboro school board for almost two decades. Johnson was a native of Greensboro, a graduate of the old black high school, Dudley, a student at A&T during the demonstration period, and the first black to graduate from the Duke University Law School in Durham. He had been a prominent member of the Greensboro school board. Johnson seemed in a rush to leave, but I squeezed in a few questions.

"What is Greensboro like in comparison to Winston-Salem and Durham?"

"The three cities are often associated as important textile and tobacco towns. Durham, Winston-Salem, Greensboro, are all very conservative," he replied. "In Durham, some blacks have long had money through their black insurance companies like North Carolina Mutual, and so forth; therefore they were able to exercise an economic independence we never had in Greensboro. But the white power structure in Durham is no more liberal than here. In Winston-Salem, R. J. Reynolds Tobacco Company hires blacks in blue-collar jobs paying good money. So Winston has always had a certain black economic strength."

"Why, then, did Greensboro have more civil rights activism than Durham or Winston-Salem? Or *did* Greensboro have more activism than Durham and Winston-Salem?"

"Greensboro had good black leadership, people who were willing to stand up," Johnson replied. He cited Simkins's advocacy through the NAACP. He mentioned Edward Edmonds, the NAACP leader who preceded Simkins in the late 1950s. Edmonds had been a teacher at Bennett College. "Many people feel that Bennett let Edmonds go because he was so aggressive, particularly on the school desegregation issue. We had a number of older blacks who supported the young radicals who emerged in the sixties. Our community backed the students. I don't know that that was equally true in the other towns."

Dr. Simkins now had patients waiting and Mr. Johnson, whom I was fortunate to have met, had to be on his way. So I bade them good-bye.

As I walked through town, I kept seeing the *Carolina Peacemaker* in street news racks. I was delighted to discover a black newspaper still surviving in 1991. Most black weeklies were a thing of the past thanks to television and the post-1960s coverage of black community news by city dailies. I decided to call *Peacemaker* owner John Marshall Kilimanjaro, who had taught drama and speech at A&T during the sixties. Kilimanjaro, then called John Marshall Stevenson, was known for his outspoken support of student activists. Kilimanjaro invited me to meet at his office.

The *Peacemaker* office was small, but well outfitted; there was a staff of about six, including Kilimanjaro's wife, Vikki. The paper had survived for more than twenty years as a weekly, no mean achievement.

Kilimanjaro turned out to be a large, formidable, dark-skinned man of gifted and purposeful speech. Friendliness and warmth oozed from him. I guessed he was about sixty. It was difficult for us to talk in his office, so we went to a restaurant in a shopping mall.

Kilimanjaro was born John Stevenson in Arkansas; he was raised in Little Rock and Fort Smith. His extended family was apparently exposed to considerable education; he mentioned his maternal grandfather, John Marshall Robinson, a physician and political leader in early-twentieth-century Arkansas, which was a very bad time for blacks. The old man, who lived until he was ninety, served as a beacon in Kilimanjaro's life, providing a sense of stability and achievement.

Unfortunately, the young Kilimanjaro's father was a railroad man "who wasn't home much. When he was, he wasn't much help." His mother raised him and his sister virtually by herself. When she died, tragically, from a botched operation while they were still children, none of the relatives could take them, so they were placed in a Methodist facility in Baldwin, Louisiana. Kilimanjaro was then ten.

Once his family somewhat recovered, they were able to return to live with relatives in Arkansas. Kilimanjaro completed high school there and, as a brilliant student, entered Tougaloo College in Jackson, Mississippi, on a scholarship. He didn't finish, however. He joined the Navy, where he served three years, the only black in his unit.

Upon discharge, Kilimanjaro entered Arkansas A&M in Pine Bluff. He finished college there, majoring in drama. He took his master's degree at the University of Arkansas at Fayetteville, which had just opened to black graduate students in the wake of *Brown* v. *Board of Education*. He was the only black student in the theater department.

With his M.A. in hand, Kilimanjaro applied to thirty-five colleges, with not a single positive reply. Except for A&T. "President F. D. Bluford of A&T called Arkansas A&M to see if I was real." On the basis of a solid recommendation from Arkansas, Bluford offered Kilimanjaro his first teaching job to begin in the fall of 1955.

Kilimanjaro arrived in Greensboro to discover he was the first and only teacher of a Speech and Drama Department that did not yet exist. "So I found a small room a block from campus and began classes. We had a way to go. I realized A&T was well overshadowed by North Carolina Central College in Durham and Bennett College in the liberal arts; they were private or quasi-private colleges with a traditional liberal arts curriculum. A&T, on the other hand, began in the 1890s [1891] with a farm, which was the 'A' for agriculture. Years later it acquired a glorified machine shop, which became the 'T' for technical. It used to be called 'A&M College for the Colored Race.' Making A&T the equal or the superior of its peers among the state's black colleges was Bluford's consuming dream. *All*-consuming. For thirty years he begged and scraped in an effort to build 'his' school into a powerhouse, and when I arrived he was on a roll."

I understood some of what Kilimanjaro was telling me. Nineteen fifty-five was a bountiful time for southern black land-grant colleges. Southern politicians were traumatized by the *Brown* school desegregation decision of 1954, and they were determined not to capitulate to the Supreme Court. But taking no chances, they decided to rapidly increase the budgets of the black land-grant colleges in the hope that the overwhelming majority of black undergraduate students would remain in black schools, and forgo applying to the then all-white state universities like the University of North Carolina. Facilities and funds black presidents had begged for for years suddenly, like magic, became available.

"Bluford's ambitious plans for A&T were to culminate in a magnificent series of Founders Day programs in November 1955, to be presided over by the president himself," continued Kilimanjaro. "As soon as I arrived in town, I was told to get involved in the preparations for Founders Day."

As the great day approached, it seemed extremely propitious that the heightened status of A&T among North Carolina colleges might be enhanced by the presence of the governor, Luther Hodges, at the Founders Day program. Hodges was up for reelection, and on a flying statewide campaign tour. However, black state leaders were just then very disenchanted with Hodges, whom they had originally thought would be a "progressive" governor. In the wake of *Brown*, Hodges had introduced a "voluntary segregation" program, which was based on the assumption that blacks really preferred to segregate themselves and the Supreme Court simply had no idea of the reality of the situation. Hodges was blasted by state NAACP officials. As Founders Day approached, Hodges was in the middle of a sniping war with the NAACP.

"The school band, the choir, the ROTC cadets sharp in their uniforms, were all there looking good on Founders Day," Kilimanjaro remembered. "The governor was late. When he entered, the ROTC unit shouted, 'Ten-*hut!*' and the uniformed boys sprang to their feet; then, not really knowing what to do, everyone stood." When it came time for the governor to speak, as Kilimanjaro explained, Hodges decided he would make two speeches. "The first speech went well. Then the governor paused, and said something like, 'Now I want to talk to you about another matter. Some of your leaders are taking you down the criminal's path.' Off he went, speaking in this vein, launching an attack on the NAACP. Then he said, 'And the *nigras*...' Feet started shuffling and I could hear a soft booooooo. Then he said '*nigra*' again. Well, that's something nobody liked because it sounded like nigger, and more students started shuffling their feet. So then Hodges turns to Bluford, asks him something, Bluford nods, and Hodges continues his impromptu speech. But by that time it was too late; we didn't want to hear what he had to say. The governor and his party quickly departed the auditorium before the program was over. After Hodges left, Dr. Bluford tried to speak to us, but we saw his spirit sink before our very eyes. It was as if he saw everything he had dreamed for slipping away. There was no way A&T would get a thing from the governor now because the story would get out that the governor had been embarrassed, or insulted. The band played A&T's alma mater gloriously, but Bluford wasn't with it. That night Bluford collapsed and had to be hospitalized. Within three weeks he was dead of heart failure."

Kilimanjaro paused for a while. He spoke extremely dramatically, but I noticed that at times while he was speaking he seemed, disconcertingly, to suddenly fall asleep. Within a few seconds he would resume his story, speaking as dramatically as before. When I mentioned this, he said he suffered from a form of sleeping sickness, which is why he retired from teaching. "Bluford was a tragedy of outworn leadership," Kilimanjaro concluded. "He had set up everything perfectly, but, you see, his time had passed. When I was leaving Arkansas, one of my friends remarked, 'You're going over there to North Carolina under Dr. Bluford, the last of the handkerchief heads.' It was the first time I had heard that expression. But Bluford hired me. He hired me for my first job when I didn't even know how to fill out a roll book. And he hired many, many others like me. So I see it as a generational tragedy: Today's firebrand becomes tomorrow's Uncle Tom. In the twenties Bluford would have been considered a racial radical simply for maneuvering to build up A&T."

In Greensboro, Kilimanjaro wasted no time becoming active in the NAACP. In 1958, NAACP leader Edward Edmonds invited Martin Luther King, Jr., to speak in Greensboro. Edmonds had known King when King was a student at Boston University. "It was a case of 'no room at the inn,' " remembered Kilimanjaro. "None of the churches would host King. Finally, Bennett College, where Edmonds taught, agreed to let King speak in their chapel. It was a momentous occasion. Classrooms were specially wired so the overflow crowd could hear King speak. There was still fear, but, you see, we were building a communitywide consciousness and activism here in Greensboro.

"Two weeks after King spoke, an A&T student, Joseph Cross, was killed by the police. Cross," Kilimanjaro explained, "was a Korean War veteran. It was known he was going with a white woman. He would meet her at a certain spot in town, signaling by blinking his headlights. On the fated night, he signaled, the other car blinked back, and when Cross emerged from his car, he was shot down like a dog in a police trap."

Dr. Warmoth T. Gibbs, who was dean under Bluford, was named A&T president after Bluford died. "Gibbs was concerned. Our students were so irate he thought they might create an incident. There was always that fear of a racial explosion, an outburst that would cost the school and staff everything. At a faculty meeting, Gibbs appointed me chairman of a committee to seek 'justice'; no one knew what to do or how to win justice. Meanwhile, the policemen who killed Cross were tried, acquitted, and after a year it was obvious nothing would be done about the killing. During this period I had raised about six hundred dollars for our justice committee though no one knew how it would be used.

"Meanwhile, there was a move on by Gibbs to commission a bust of Bluford. This was in the spring of 1959, late in the school year. During a faculty meeting, I learned it would be proposed by one of Gibbs's people that the Cross money be used to help toward the cost of the Bluford sculpture. In the meeting, when the motion was made, I responded that the funds—we're not talking about a lot of money—should be used in a way consistent with the cause for which they were raised. I wanted to donate the money to the NAACP Legal Defense Fund. President Gibbs ruled me out of order. Now I was young and headstrong, so I got carried away and demanded that the ruling of the chair be put to a *vote*. I knew my parliamentary rules, but of course this kind of thing was not done. Ordinarily, my gambit wouldn't have worked, but faculty meetings were then attended by the entire school staff—faculty, maintenance people, cafeteria workers, janitors—everyone. Had Gibbs been thinking, he would have asked for a hand vote so he could see who was voting against him. But he made a mistake and called a voice vote. He lost.

"Well, a month later I received a brief letter from Gibbs informing me my contract would not be renewed. They had decided they needed someone with 'more experience, training, and maturity.' By then I had married, and we had *three* children. But I was flat out of a job, and I didn't know what to do. Finally, I decided to go back to school and work on my Ph.D.'"

In 1963 new president Lewis Dowdy invited Kilimanjaro to return to the A&T staff, an offer he accepted despite his earlier experience. Returning from graduate school to a Greensboro that had undergone the sit-ins of 1960 and resumed demonstrations in 1963, Kilimanjaro quickly established himself as an independent and influential voice in the community, and a consistent supporter and adviser of student and community activists. However, by 1970, because of his worsening sleeping sickness disability, Kilimanjaro retired from the Speech and Drama Department.

During the late sixties, Kilimanjaro said he became interested in the Black Muslims, which had extended their organizing efforts southward to North Carolina. The Muslims published a newspaper, *Muhammad Speaks*, which sparked Kilimanjaro's interest in starting his own newspaper, which became the *Peacemaker*. "We started without any money and we've survived for two decades without any money," he laughed. Around the same time, he decided to change his name to Kilimanjaro, after Mount Kilimanjaro of Tanzania, the highest peak in Africa. Many African Americans were taking African names at that time as a symbol of identification with African liberation and their African heritage.

" 'What's the matter with Stevenson?' my wife and children wanted to know. 'We've been Stevenson all our lives, now we have to change because you want to change?' But I think they finally, after some time, realized I was serious and they accepted the change."

When we returned to his offices, he gave me a tour. I was introduced to the staff, including the editor, Hal Sieber, who is white. Another surprise. Sieber, though not a native Greensborian, was public relations director for the Chamber of Commerce in the early seventies. According to Chafe, Sieber worked tirelessly to open up the Chamber to professional blacks, though not all blacks were responsive to his efforts. But in the late seventies, Sieber either was fired or decided to quit Greensboro. Hardly expecting to find him back there in 1991 working at the *Peacemaker*, I made an appointment to interview him at his earliest convenience.

My conversation with Kilimanjaro had lasted the entire afternoon, but it was worth it. I was impressed that Kilimanjaro, a native of Arkansas, had found a home in Greensboro, or the black community of Greensboro, which allowed him the freedom to explore his ideas and expand his career in such enterprising and non-conformist ways.

Dr. Simkins and attorney Walter Johnson mentioned former A&T president Dr. Warmoth T. Gibbs as a hidden key to the success of the sit-ins. "He's an interesting person," added Johnson. "You ought to make an effort to talk to him. He still lives here in Greensboro. But don't wait too long because he's ninety-eight years old. If he'll talk to you, be prepared for an experience."

I called Dr. Gibbs, reached his gracious daughter, Mrs. Elizabeth Gibbs Moore, with whom he lived in the southeastern section, and she arranged for me to come over. They lived on what we used to call "a nice street": several blocks of comfortable pre–World War II homes, probably the most prestigious core of the old black neighborhood, a sort of enclave. Actually, it wasn't that far from the railroad tracks. (Speaking of those tracks, they run right by the A&T campus, paralleling East Market Street, I discovered, separating A&T from Bennett College.)

When I arrived, I was greeted by Mrs. Moore and shown to the porch. Gibbs entered the porch walking with some difficulty; he was a dark-skinned man, thin, dressed in suit and tie; friendly but wary. Once I explained to Dr. Gibbs the concept of my journey, and that I wanted to speak with him about the sit-ins, it became obvious that I would have to be interviewed by him first before we went any further.

"Do you want dissertation or conversation?" he inquired.

"Just conversation," I replied, as politely as possible.

"Where are you from?"

"New Orleans," I answered. His demeanor brightened.

"That's good, I'm from Louisiana myself. But you've probably never heard of the place. I'm from a little town called Baldwin." I knew a little about Baldwin. It's a hamlet about one hundred miles west of New Orleans on U.S. 90 at Bayou Teche. More important, it was the location of the black Methodist orphanage where Kilimanjaro was sent as a child, and the first site of Gilbert Academy, a Reconstruction black Methodist school.

In the first decade of the twentieth century, Gilbert Academy relocated to New Orleans on St. Charles Avenue, sharing the campus of New Orleans University, a Reconstruction black Methodist college. When New Orleans University (*not* the same as the current University of New Orleans, a state university founded in 1960 as part of the higher education system) closed in the 1920s, Gilbert continued at the St. Charles site until it was closed in 1950. I attended and graduated from Gilbert in the late forties. Gibbs and I attended the same high school, but at different places and certainly different times.

My father, Albert Dent, had moved to New Orleans from Atlanta to become the new superintendent of Flint-Goodrich Hospital. In the late thirties, New Orleans University and Straight University, a Congregational Church Reconstruction college located on Canal Street in New Orleans, merged to form Dillard University, the school that my father was president of for twenty-eight years, retiring in 1969.

Dr. Gibbs wanted to know who my parents were. I explained who my father was, that he had died in 1984. "My mother, Jessie Covington Dent, is from Houston," I added. "She was a musician." It turned out Gibbs had known of my father, so we were off to a decent start. When I told him I also attended Gilbert Academy, we were off to a very good start. As I had anticipated, his family was one of those that settled in the village of LeTeche, now Baldwin, the old Methodist project established right after Emancipation. His parents, virtually his entire family, had attended Gilbert.

In 1906, Gibbs left Louisiana to attend Wiley College in Marshall, Texas. He spent several years in St. Louis, then found his way to Boston and Harvard, where he received his B.A. degree in 1917. In 1991 he is the oldest living black graduate of Harvard. During Gibbs's senior year at Harvard, with World War I an imminent possibility, Monroe Trotter, the famed editor of the influential black *Boston Guardian*, along with leaders of the newly founded NAACP, were pressuring the White House to establish a training school for black military officers. The four black units in existence since Reconstruction, the 24th and 25th Infantry Regiments, and the 9th and 10th Cavalry Regiments, were commanded by white officers. In response to the pressure exerted by the black community, the War Department established a Colored officers' training camp at Des Moines, Iowa, in the summer of 1917. Gibbs applied and was selected for training along with students in black colleges and outstanding noncommissioned officers—there were about twenty-five hundred applicants. As a young lieutenant, Gibbs served in France with the 92nd Infantry Division, returning to Harvard in 1919 to work on his master's in education and government. In 1926 he was hired by President Bluford to come to A&T to teach history and direct their new ROTC unit. Eventually, Gibbs became dean of education. As a faithful supporter of Dr. Bluford, he had steadily advanced through the ranks at A&T. When Bluford died suddenly in the wake of the Founders Day fiasco, Gibbs succeeded him as president.

After Dr. Gibbs had recounted these facts of his career, I asked him if he was surprised by the sit-ins. What was his reaction?

"I was surprised," he replied. "But not too surprised, because I had *studied* it." Then Gibbs's mind flipped back to Des Moines, Iowa. Once again he began to tell me the story of the agitation for Negro officers. Then he added information I was not familiar with: "While I was at Des Moines, the Houston Riot of 1917 happened. The Adjutant General came. . . ." I thought he had misheard my question. "No, Dr. Gibbs," I interrupted. "I was asking about the *sit-ins of 1960*. Not the officer training school of 1917."

"But that's what I mean," he continued. "While we were in Des Moines in 1917, the Houston Riot happened, over segregation on the streetcars." He described the movable signposts on the streetcars in Houston that marked a special section for blacks in the rear, the same as I had grown up with in New Orleans. "The Colored soldiers hated the barriers, and threw them out the windows. It turned into a terrible problem. There was a riot. The soldiers killed some Houston police officers. The Adjutant General came from Washington and lectured *us*. He yelled at us about what happened in Houston. But we knew all about it. He said, 'You are representatives of the U.S. Army. You have to follow whatever local laws exist, you can't embarrass the Army.' We knew he meant the segregation laws of the South. 'If you cannot do that, I would suggest you turn in your equipment and go back home now.' We had been in Des Moines five or six weeks. We were so disgusted by his remarks, five hundred of the two thousand men left. I stayed, but it went down hard with me, what he said."

~

I understood what Gibbs was saying, but I still didn't quite know how it related to 1960. My problem was, I had no knowledge of the Houston Riot of 1917. Even though my mother was from Houston and our family visited her parents regularly while they were alive, I didn't recall anyone ever mentioning this trouble. I knew there had been several riots in towns where black troops were stationed during both world wars. I knew that at Brownsville, Texas, on the Mexican border, a black unit was accused of shooting up the town in retaliation for the abuses and insults they suffered in 1906. They were court-martialed, adjudged guilty by the Adjutant General, and issued dishonorable discharges. Years later they were exonerated.

A month or so after I left Greensboro, I came across Robert V. Haynes's fascinating *A Night of Violence: The Houston Riot of 1917*. It seems that the 3rd Battalion of the 24th Infantry, one of the four existing black regiments dating back to 1869, was transferred from Columbus, New Mexico, to Houston in July of 1917. It was just at the time the Colored officers training camp was being established in Des Moines. The 3rd Battalion was assigned, as it turned out, to perform menial duties during the hurried construction of a new base, Camp Logan, which was to be a training ground for national guardsmen being called to active service.

For most of their existence, the black units had been stationed in western states in an effort to keep them away from large white urban areas. The idea of investing black males with the uniform, weapons, and authority of the U.S. military seemed to make white Americans extremely uncomfortable. Nevertheless, the black units posted a solid military record. According to Haynes: "The 24th had the lowest rate of desertion in the Army, and fewer courts-martial than most white units."

During the Spanish-American War all four black units were involved, though they endured such hostility when they were stationed in Tampa, Florida, that a small riot ensued in 1898 in which twenty-seven of the soldiers were seriously wounded, more than were wounded in the war itself. At the turn of the century, the 24th was shipped to the Philippines to assist in suppression of an insurrection there. "Despite the courageous and dependable service of these black troops, William Howard Taft, the first civil governor of the Philippines, arranged for their removal from the islands for fear that the close rapport which existed between the two colored races might later prove embarrassing to the American government," Haynes observed. The 24th was back in the Philippines in 1906 to help quell another uprising. In 1916, the 24th was sent to the Mexican border to protect General Pershing's supply lines in the wake of a raid by Pancho Villa. The 3rd Battalion of the 24th left its base at Columbus, New Mexico, to journey to Houston on July 26, 1917.

It so happened that twenty-five of the 24th Infantry's top noncommissioned officers were chosen for the Des Moines officer training program, which helped me to understand the meaning of a comment Gibbs made when I interviewed him: "We knew what had happened in Houston."

What happened in Houston is that the black soldiers, delighted to be in an urban area with a large black community, flocked into town, where they were constantly abused and humiliated by racist Houston policemen and streetcar conductors. They were not accustomed to such treatment; the history of the unit had been one in which they were the policers, even if they were relegated to policing third world peoples.

On August 22, a black corporal was arrested, beaten, and thrown in the Houston jail. A rumor quickly spread back at Camp Logan that he had been killed. Throughout the day of August 23, anger mounted among the troops, with no sense among their white officers of the seriousness of the situation. That night, 75 to 100 men mutinied. They marched, fully armed, into town in search of any policemen they could find. Under the leadership of a veteran first sergeant, and in a rage, the soldiers, within two hours, killed 15 whites, including 4 policemen.

The War Department was stunned and outraged. The whites of Houston were dazed and horrified. The Houston black community was terrified of the reprisals sure to come. The 3rd Battalion was quickly disarmed, placed under guard, and transferred back to Columbus, New Mexico. There, after intensive investigations during which the black soldiers were accused of a "conspiracy of silence," sixty-three were charged with insurrection and mutiny. The result was the largest number of related courts-martial in American history.

The first of several trials was held in San Antonio. No testimony was permitted on the conditions that led to the violence. Thirteen of the black soldiers received the death sentence; they were hanged near San Antonio on December 11, 1917. After they were hanged, the sentences and executions were announced. The national NAACP protested vigorously to President Woodrow Wilson, as did several other black organizations.

"They have gone to their deaths," wrote W. E. B. Du Bois in the *Crisis*, January 1918. "Thirteen young, strong men; soldiers who have fought for a country which never was wholly theirs, men born to suffer ridicule, injustice, and, at last, death itself. They broke the law. Against them punishment, if it was legal, we cannot protest." However, Du Bois decried "the shameful treatment which these men, and which we, their brothers, receive all our lives, and which our fathers received, and our children await; above all we raise our clenched hands against the hundreds of thousands of white murderers, rapists and scoundrels" (as quoted in *A Night of Violence*).

Despite protests, the Army held two other trials, resulting in the hanging of six additional men in September 1918. None of the white officers was court-martialed. Sixty-eight men were confined in Leavenworth prison, all but five receiving life sentences.

I could well understand why so little is known of this story. Throughout the long struggle to better their condition since Emancipation, blacks have employed a range of options—from militant opposition to adjustments to the American "norm," whatever it is, in an effort to ease their passage into the mainstream. But the story of the Houston Riot encompasses *both* extremes. The unit had established an exemplary record as a shield of American imperialism for over half a century. Now these same soldiers had demonstrated that under extreme provocation they were capable of violence, despite the consequences.

To complete the story, the 24th was quickly abolished, along with discussion of the riot. Black Americans fearful of what had happened found it advantageous not to aggravate the fears of white Americans by reminding them of the Houston incident. Better not to mention the executions, either.

Dr. Gibbs never quite explained the meaning of the Houston Riot and how he related it to the sit-ins, but it must have had a profound impact on his thinking, or he would not have mentioned it. He may have thought it an example of the destructive violence that can occur when there is no legitimate avenue of recourse against grievances, or as an example of the painful insult levied when authorities do not recognize legitimate causes of complaint. He may have seen an analogy between black college students who could not be expected to become educated without desiring full rights in American society, the ability to use that education to the fullest, and black soldiers who were expected to defend their country but were denied equal treatment in the military. Black soldiers were, in fact, during World Wars I and II often treated as if they were the enemy. Such an analogy would have been very fitting for Gibbs, who was hired by A&T in the 1920s to head their new military ROTC unit.

A few days after the sit-ins began, Greensboro city officials requested a meeting with Gibbs. They met at A&T.

"Have you heard about the affair down at Woolworth's?" the mayor began.

"Yes," Gibbs said he replied. "I've heard about the affair, and I'm sure you have, too."

"Well, what do you plan to do about it?" the mayor asked, pushing forward. Most of the A&T students were poor and education was precious; the consequences of expulsion were not inconsequential.

Gibbs's response, as he recounted it to me, was sheer obfuscation. He has a step-by-step way of making a point; each thought is boxed in thoroughly on all four sides before moving to the next point. "You don't understand," he explained to the mayor.

"We have three thousand students. Some live at home, some live in dormitories. Some eat at home when their parents cook, some eat in town if their parents don't cook, some eat in the dining hall when they get here during the appointed hours. If they eat in the dining hall, they're covered by our regulations, and they must have meal tickets. But we really have no control over where they eat; we can't possibly control that. That's up to them. When they are on campus, that's our jurisdiction. What they do in town, that's out of our jurisdiction."

They went round and round for a couple of hours, Gibbs said, "but they didn't get what they wanted, and as far as I was concerned, that was the end of that." He laughed. "One kid asked the dining hall matron if she could make them sandwiches so they would have something to eat while they sat in at the lunch counters waiting for the dinner they never got. She called me. But I said, 'No, I don't think we can get away with that.'" Having refused to punish or suspend the demonstrators, Dr. Gibbs, already past sixty-five, was quietly retired at the end of the school year.

How black school administrators reacted to student demonstrations, which often culminated in arrests, became an increasingly difficult problem for them as the 1960s progressed into escalating protests. What to do? Black college presidents were under pressure from white political authorities to forbid student demonstrations from the moment the sit-ins began and as they spread like wildfire through the South.

Until then, black college campuses had been considered sanctuaries where even occasional interracial meetings and gatherings could take place without police intervention. The campuses were like tiny protected islands within the vast sea of the segregated South. To maintain this protection, the college authorities often went overboard in shielding their students from any sort of behavior that would draw the disfavor of white political and business leaders. Now, by deliberately challenging the segregation laws of southern downtowns, black students were destroying the theretofore unstated, across-the-color-line gentlemen's agreement between campus authorities and city political leaders.

Presidents of state-funded colleges had a much more difficult time of it than their compatriots at private colleges. At the state schools—A&T being a prime example—the presidents were almost directly answerable to their governors and legislatures. The same applied to black public high school principals. Local school boards were almost all-white until the 1970s, and those boards virtually uniformly acted to postpone or circumvent the *Brown* decision. As the decade wore on and black high school youth played a more active role in demonstrations, white superintendents expected their black school administrators to keep their students off the picket lines, but with little success.

On the other hand, black private college presidents, though answerable to their boards of trustees, enjoyed the luxury of a much wider range of options. Most black private colleges were funded by national church organizations from the time of Reconstruction as a sort of extension of church abolitionist activities; in almost all cases these were northern-based groups. Local moderate or liberal white business leaders were also considered desirable members of private college boards, but they were only rarely the most powerful members. When the students of private colleges joined the wave of demonstrations, their presidents could often afford to make no statement other than an expression of concern without receiving pressure from local white authorities on their own board.

I grew up overhearing discussions of how black colleges maintain a sense of educational integrity under the constraints exercised by the segregationist South. My father had been president of Dillard in New Orleans for two decades when Dillard students caught sit-in fever and demonstrated at the lunch counter of a nearby drugstore that they patronized all the time, but where they could not sit and eat like normal customers.

Dad was forever concerned with the image of Dillard and its funding needs. I don't think he would mind me saying that there were no extremely iconoclastic types teaching at Dillard; student behavior was also carefully monitored. As a poor but prominent product of the relatively advanced black educational and business world of Atlanta, and a protégé of John Hope, the president of Morehouse and architect of the Atlanta university system, my father possessed a starkly realistic sense of political and economic power. His racial strategies were based on the realization that blacks had very little of either. Racial progress, I remember him saying many times, could only ensue from education and measured pressure, with emphasis upon education. Active in city nonradical racial justice efforts, a lifetime member of the NAACP, and a staunch friend of Thurgood Marshall, the NAACP's top lawyer, he did believe in pressure, when properly applied.

When Dillard students sat in, I was living in New York, and working as press attaché for the NAACP Legal Defense Fund.

"How did you handle the students when they organized demonstrations?" I asked my father when I was visiting New Orleans a few months after these sit-ins. "What did you do?"

"I didn't do anything," he chortled. "I told them I would support them as long as they demonstrated peacefully, though the civil rights organizations would have to bail them out of jail. We couldn't pay that."

"Did you get pressure from city officials?"

"No. Just a lot of nasty and threatening phone calls from irate, ignorant whites I didn't know. Your mother and I took the phone off the hook at night, and kept it off."

My father didn't bother to mention conversations with Dillard board members which I'm sure took place as student protests continued and escalated. He, however, was able to steer a course around being forced to snuff out student activism, despite pressures.

In Greensboro, once the door had opened a bit, there was in the following years a crescendo of efforts to completely dismantle the city's FOR COLORED ONLY and FOR WHITES ONLY signs. In May and June 1963, students resumed downtown protests against still-segregated stores, those that denied ordinary courtesies to black customers, and those that hired no black employees though they enjoyed black patronage. In fact, during the spring of 1963 there were similar demonstrations by blacks and supportive whites in towns throughout the South, though the dramatic efforts in Birmingham led by Martin Luther King, Jr., and the Southern Christian Leadership Conference received most of the media coverage.

In Greensboro, marches and sit-ins were led by Bill Thomas of CORE and the Reverend Tony Stanley of A&T, both Greensboro natives, and A&T football captain Jesse Jackson, a native of Columbia, South Carolina, in what were his first civil rights activities. Students from Bennett notably participated in the 1963 demonstrations, as did students from Dudley High School. The jails of Greensboro proved insufficient to hold all those arrested; other city properties had to be pressed into service. Segregated theaters and restaurants were picketed. The NAACP under George Simkins demanded that the city get serious about the hiring of black policemen and sanitation workers, and initiate the process of hiring blacks in other city agencies.

Until this point, no effort had crystallized among city, business, or political leaders to even consider the demands of the black community, much less begin the process of substantive desegregation. If Greensboro authorities believed that the 1963 demonstrations were entirely the impudent and unrestrained actions of younger people, or "radicals" poisoned by ideas from north of the Mason-Dixon Line, such a notion was permanently dispelled by the events of May 22, 1963. On that night more than two thousand black adults marched downtown in a stunning demonstration of unity across class and age divisions. This "silent march" from the southeastern section included almost two dozen ministers, a small army of schoolteachers and principals, and every black physician in town. When I interviewed Angelina Smith, an esteemed former schoolteacher, and her husband, Samuel Cooper Smith, former director of A&T's Technical Institute, both in their nineties, they recounted with pride their participation in the march, a chance, finally, to express their pent-up resentment at being treated all their lives as second-class citizens.

The immediate result, however, of these marches was a statement by the mayor in June 1963 endorsing the principle of open accommodations and the urging of businesses to comply. The wave of marches gave way to negotiations between a committee of businessmen and a group representing the black community. The actual dismantling of the FOR WHITES ONLY signs, it must be said, only came about with the passage of the monumental Civil Rights Act of 1964, a response by President Lyndon Johnson and Congress to the extreme turmoil wrought on numerous southern cities where demonstrations had taken place, and the heightened worldwide media attention accorded those protests.

During the next few years the drive by blacks to open up Greensboro did not abate. With the stripping away of the outer core of racial discrimination, the focus of black leaders shifted to the more entrenched, less tangible, and more structural inequities inherent in southern society. Open accommodations in governmental facilities and the removal of racial barriers in restaurants or expensive clothing stores, for instance, meant little to those who lacked the money to take advantage of such newly available "rights." The Movement, as the civil rights thrusts were now referred to, had to dig a little deeper to benefit the great masses of poor and deprived people. Therefore, a demand for jobs became an extreme priority, particularly in businesses that blacks patronized but were prohibited from working in except as janitors or at other low-level positions.

Increasing the number of blacks voting was an imminent necessity. Without greater involvement in the political process, blacks, as a mass, could not begin to have a real impact on civic matters. Admittedly, removing southern legal and extra-legal barriers to voting was a more crucial and portentous problem in the heavily black-populated Deep South than in Greensboro. The potential political impact of mass black voting in the heavily black-majority areas was far greater. Greensboro was only 25 percent black (total population of about 160,000), so retribution via electoral politics would have its limitations. As it turned out, Greensboro blacks fought a long and hard battle into the 1970s to shift city elections to a district rather than at-large basis (as Simkins mentioned), in the hope that black candidates could benefit from the black vote concentrated in the southeastern area.

Second, and very important, in Greensboro the latter part of the sixties brought about an ideological change that emphasized the defining of and controlling of the Movement by blacks exclusively as part of a heightened consciousness of race and racial pride. Part of this thrust was a forsaking of interracial coalitions and, in fact, a move away from racial integration in itself as the prime goal of the Movement. These ideas were promulgated by younger Movement leaders, and they did create a fissure within the civil rights establishment locally and nationally, as well as con-sternation among sympathetic whites who had always considered themselves charter members of the civil rights leadership.

In Greensboro this new ideological direction was most notably represented by an organization called the Greensboro Association of Poor People. The A&T student government also played a key role. Both groups gravitated around the charismatic leadership of A&T student Nelson Johnson. Johnson's activities were brought to a tragic impasse in 1979 when, while leading a march of anti-Klan protestors, his group was ambushed, allegedly by Klan members, and fired upon, resulting in the death of five of the marchers.

I, of course, very much wanted to meet and interview Nelson Johnson. His career and extraordinary impact on Greensboro had been much discussed by Chafe in *Civilities*. When I asked Dr. Simkins and Walter Johnson what had happened to him, they said, "He's right here in Greensboro," to my utter surprise. "He's now *Reverend* Nelson Johnson, an assistant minister to Reverend Otis Hairston [a senior civil rights leader] at Shiloh Baptist Church. You should know," added Simkins, "that after his student organizing days, Johnson joined the Communist Workers party with the aim of organizing workers in the textile mills. Then, after the shootings and all that, he decided to go to divinity school. From nationalism to communism to the Baptist Church, that's a lot of twists and turns." To me, that made him all the more interesting.

It proved to be extremely difficult to arrange an interview with Nelson Johnson. Every time I called Shiloh Baptist Church, Johnson had just left, or was busy on the phone. I drove by the church several times, and considered just waiting in the church until I could catch him with some free time, but I decided it was better not to do that. Many ex-militants are now bitter and distant and don't want to talk about the past. I didn't know what Johnson's state of mind was, but I certainly didn't want to risk aggravating him by appearing to be overly aggressive.

Finally, one morning I did reach him. He said, "Listen, I'm very busy working on something right now. Why don't you talk to Lewis Brandon, a close friend who was a leader in the Greensboro Movement. After you talk with Brandon, I can probably give you some time." He was very polite, and I understood the unstated: He would speak to me if Brandon said I was all right. Johnson gave me Brandon's number. "He ran the Uhuru Bookstore during the old days." This must be the boarded-up bookshop that I saw on my first look around town. When I called Brandon, he agreed to meet me at a restaurant that very night.

Now a teacher in the public school system, Brandon turned out to be quite informal, low-key, and articulate. Of medium height, he looked to be in his mid- or late forties.

What about A&T's remarkable record as an incubator of black activism? Did he believe there was something special about A&T?

"Don't forget"—Brandon smiled—"A&T was considered a 'poor boys' school with a lot of military veterans. Black families sent their girls to Winston-Salem Teachers College. If the family had money or status, the school of choice for their daughters was Bennett College. North Carolina Central in Durham was coeducational, but was considered more of an upper-class school than A&T.

"I'm from Asheville, North Carolina, and my heart was set on Howard University in Washington. Just as I was about to depart, Dad said, 'Listen, I don't have Howard money. You're going to have to go to Greensboro.' Even so, I wasn't all that disappointed because I had heard about A&T students booing Governor Hodges in 1955; we even knew about the Greensboro golf course case, because it was widely publicized. Compared to Asheville, where nothing ever happened, Greensboro sounded exciting."

"How did the thinking at A&T escalate from the sit-ins into black radicalism?" I wanted to know.

"At first, during the early sixties, even after the 1960 and 1963 sit-ins, black kids came to A&T because they wanted to belong, to enter the mainstream. Most of them were from small, essentially rural communities similar to mine. They came out of Four-H Clubs, the Boy Scouts, and so forth. They really believed American society would open up for them if they were educationally prepared. But then, as the door did open a little, just enough for us to spend money where we couldn't spend money before, some students began to question the wanting-to-belong ethos they were raised with. Nelson Johnson was one of those."

"Then what happened?"

"The best way I can tell you is to tell the story of Claude Barnes. Claude Barnes was a brilliant student at Dudley High, the old black school prior to school deseg-regation in 1969. But Claude was also curious, a freethinker, and concerned with the issues of the day, even though he was still in high school. He joined a group called Youth United for Blackness in 1969, which was a youth wing of the Greens-boro Association of Poor People, GAPP. GAPP was considered very militant because it was challenging dilapidated and poorly kept up housing owned by absentee land-lords in the southeastern section through rent strikes, which were then unheard of.

"Claude's favorite teachers at Dudley were not amused by his association with GAPP. In particular, they didn't like the name Youth United for *Blackness*. The principal and teachers who ran Dudley were not interested in 'blackness' or the new racial boldness associated with calling ourselves 'black.' They thought of themselves as 'Negroes,' with a capital 'N,' and they had worked hard and long to get the 'N' capitalized.

"In early spring 1969, a faculty-student committee barred Barnes from running for student council president because of what they considered his radical community activities. He was already a member of the student council. Despite the ban, the students voted for Barnes through write-in votes, and he won easily. Then the committee, or the principal, disqualified the Barnes write-in votes and declared the runner-up the winner. In protest, Barnes and four other students walked out of school.

"Barnes immediately turned to Nelson Johnson and GAPP for support. GAPP members, led by Johnson spoke against Barnes's disqualification. One hundred ad-ditional students at Dudley then walked out in support of Barnes. The principal would not budge: It was his school and he controlled it, or tried to control it, in the manner of old-time black schoolmasters and college presidents. When Nelson Johnson attempted to speak to students on the Dudley school grounds, he was arrested. After picketing on May 21, stones were thrown at the police, tear gas was fired, the school was closed, and the students were sent home in confusion and distress. It was just a huge mess."

"Why didn't someone try to talk to the principal before the situation got out of control?"

"Most of the adult civil rights leadership did try to meet with the principal, but he turned his back on them. I was working with the NAACP at the time, and I tried to talk with the parents of the boy who had been defeated by Barnes in the write-in vote. They slammed the door in my face. It was just an unbelievable time. The black community splintered and crystallized into hardened factions. To show you how inflexible and personal the situation became, I was teaching at the same school as the wife of the Dudley principal, and because she knew I was close to

Claude and Nelson, she stopped speaking to me. Her *friends* wouldn't even speak to me."

Sitting in this fairly decent, not inexpensive restaurant where we were the only black customers, the tenseness and fears of that time seemed to have occurred light-years ago. Brandon pointed out that until this point, the dispute had been within the black community and its institutions, though it certainly touched upon larger questions of race and racial attitudes. Then the Greensboro school board appointed a white school official to "take charge" of the situation, superseding the authority of the principal. This move only succeeded in angering *all* the factions within the black community, while undercutting those who were attempting to negotiate a compromise.

"From that point on, the conflict worsened. Police were all over the place," Brandon lamented. Within a day or so, for reasons both understandable and difficult to understand, the brush fire raging at Dudley "jumped the fence" and spread onto the A&T campus. Militant A&T students had been unusually active that spring of 1969, and were already fired up. Just two months previously the student government association, with Nelson Johnson as a key figure (he was also student council vice president), had staged a two-day boycott of classes in support of a strike by the school's poorly paid cafeteria workers. During the previous year, in the wake of the assassination of Martin Luther King, Jr., A&T and Bennett students had burst forth from their campuses in angry marches downtown. Frightened, the mayor called in the National Guard. Now, a year and a month later, Brandon related sadly, the mayor called for the National Guard again, and sent police to patrol the A&T campus where infuriated students and some nonstudents were congregating. There were reports of gunfire coming from the campus, though both Chafe and Brandon point out that this was in response to reports of whites driving by the campus and hurling epithets.

On the night of May 21, just after midnight, an A&T student, Willie Grimes, was shot in the head and killed. It was never determined by whom. The next day, four policemen were shot, one seriously. It was never determined by whom. President Lewis Dowdy immediately closed down the university. The students were told to leave the campus, and it was fortunate they did, because the National Guard swept through the dormitories shooting locks off of doors, and firing into rooms. "All of this could have been avoided," Brandon lamented. "Nothing quite like this had ever happened in Greensboro. And the result was that black militants, especially Nelson Johnson, were blamed for the violence. They ended up blaming everything on Nelson."

In the wake of the explosion of 1969, the city authorities and media had a heyday examining and exposing the activities of GAPP, the Foundation for Community Development (the Durham foundation-funded organization that in turn funded GAPP), and other progressive or nonmainstream black community activity, as well as Johnson personally. The city officials seemed to believe that the assertiveness, bitterness, and resultant violence had ensued from a sudden attack of the always mysterious and lethal virus of communism, coupled with secret plans for black revolutionary war. Legitimate complaints, the general exclusion of blacks from the sources of power, and resentment of such alienation were hardly attributed as roots of the disturbances.

Nevertheless, black militants in Greensboro moved ahead to the point where the town quickly acquired the reputation of *the* center of black power ideology in the South. Malcolm X University, a private college espousing the black aesthetic and named for the assassinated New York Muslim leader, was launched in Durham in 1968 with bright hopes. Malcolm X University moved to Greensboro in 1970. Claude Barnes of the Dudley High School controversy became, fittingly, the first Malcolm X student. The school was located on the second story of a building on Asheboro Street (now Martin Luther King). The structure had originally been the Masonic Lodge building, but it burned down in 1990, Brandon explained. "People came to Greensboro from all over the country because of the excitement around Malcolm X University. When SNCC splintered into factions in the late sixties, several SNCC leaders headed for Greensboro." Though the school never had more than a few dozen students, I remembered that two or three high school graduates from New Orleans traveled to Greensboro to enter Malcolm X. "The black community across the board was supportive. It was an attempt to create something we felt was desperately needed. Volunteers arrived from everywhere to teach and help out. They worked for free. I worked for free. Meanwhile, Howard Fuller, the most influential leader at the Foundation for Community Development, campaigned nationally to raise funds to keep the school open. Students lived in the community and were also expected to work. The school owned a farm, a machine shop, and a pretty good library donated by friends. There was a preschool for children.

"Uhuru Bookstore, which I managed and where Nelson's wife worked, grew out of Malcolm X and GAPP. The bookstore became a meeting place, a kind of cultural center. We traveled to regional festivals and conferences to sell books and spread the word about our activities; those were the days! Nelson Johnson organized a national student group: the Student Organization of Black Unity. Black Unity published a newspaper, *Africa World*. In the early seventies we were at the center of ideas and organizations impacting young black people in the South."

There were now no traces of Malcolm X University or of the Greensboro Association for Poor People, or the Student Organization of Black Unity. "What killed all this activity?" I asked Brandon.

"There was a deep split which affected all the Greensboro-headquartered groups in the early seventies." Brandon explained that one faction was faithful to the ideology of black nationalism. "One of the dreams of Malcolm X University was to train people who would go to Africa and establish contacts between African Americans and Africans. That was rather idealistic. The other faction became Marxists, in the fashion of [President] Sekou Toure of Guinea and [President] Kwame Nkrumah of Ghana. Nelson Johnson became a Marxist.

"This split between Marxism and nationalism echoed throughout the black radical intellectual world. Now, the black intellectual world was really only a few people; an unmendable rift among their own group was enough to sink the whole effort. Then, too," Brandon continued, "there was too much theorizing, too much talk, and very little work. Meetings would go on and on all night long over the proper direction for our people. Some of the leaders were primarily interested in partying, having a good time. This is exactly where they got in trouble with Nelson because Nelson doesn't party. He has a puritan work ethic.

"And, of course, so much of our black nationalism and African identification during that period was too romantic. Finally, by the mid-seventies, particularly when funding for black community development dried up, things really fell apart. Now we've all grown older." He smiled.

Lewis Brandon's recollection struck a chord within me. Nineteen seventy sort of represented the apogee of black community activism and creativity, not only in the South, but nationally. In New Orleans, which was not noted for activism, I well remember the hopes and dreams of our storefront Free Southern Theater on Dryades Street and the audiences we drew. There was the bookstore down the street, the poetry journal, activist and political newspapers, the beginnings of a network of artists and political activists. There was the Nation of Islam, which was attractive to many ex-Movement people because of its philosophy of economic self-determination. In almost every southern town of any size, Muslims opened restaurants, and they were good restaurants. Travel to Africa was in the air, particularly the Africa of liberation movements. Previously, the only African Americans interested in Africa were religious missionaries and participants in the occasional exchange programs for young people, like Operation Crossroads (an annual work-study program that took young African Americans to Africa). Community work and volunteerism within the ghettos and housing projects were highly esteemed activities, particularly among blacks who were the beneficiaries of education or of fortunate economic circumstances. Music festivals and cultural programs with poetry readings, most of them political with a black nationalist slant, were common and drew large audiences. The development of small black cultural centers, even though underfunded and lacking in facilities, helped provide a place where these activities and interactions could take place.

Almost all of this happened within a black world with few white participants except for the most radical. Being shut off from the usual access to black activities, the traditional and conservative white community and its political leaders perceived these black-only activities as dangerous and threatening. Thus the demolition began. Those cultural activities considered too political were stripped of funding, where funding existed. Volunteerism among educated blacks became dangerous, and deleterious to one's career, and a new ethic of self-advancement and careerism became the vogue. Today, Dryades Street in New Orleans, once the center of so much of the activity in the late 1960s and early '70s, is a ghost town. Virtually abandoned. It is as if none of it had ever happened. As if we had been dreaming, only to wake up a few years later to a harsh reality of drug-infested housing projects, McDonald's restaurants, and suburban shopping malls. It seemed as if the same thing happened in Greensboro, though maybe a little later in the seventies. Malcolm X University and all of the dreams surrounding it came to a halt. Greensboro faded from consciousness as a center of radicalism in the South.

⁓

Now I was more than ever eager to interview Nelson Johnson. I was finally able to pin Johnson down; I would meet him at Shiloh Baptist Church; from there we would go to lunch. En route to the church, however, I had time to make a slight detour to the area that once had been Warnersville, the first free black community of Greensboro established in the hope-filled days following Emancipation. I was told by Brandon that the intersection of Ash and Florida streets would be about where Warnersville had been, not very far from the church. This site, if what I was told was accurate, is now a housing project. I might have guessed it. Actually, it seemed a very nice project, well kept up, without the demoralizing social deterioration that we associate with most projects. There was no sign that I could see, or business or establishment, that denoted the area as historic. I drove around and around looking for something, but there wasn't anything of that nature (except that a small park behind Shiloh Church is called Warnersville Park, I learned later).

Such is the way of most black historical areas or sites in southern towns; these areas are either ghost towns or have been absorbed by urban change, paved over by thruways, or converted into housing projects, like Warnersville. The only historical memory seems to be the memory of black elders, their stories of what once was, what transpired: the stories of blacks told by blacks I heard as a youth in barbershop conversations on Saturdays, punctuated by clipping scissors, the soft whir of ceiling fans, and memories of Joe Louis. Who lived where. Who had money. Times of trouble. Where the music, the nightclubs were. Who owned a business, and how they lost it. These are the ever-repeating themes of the stories.

Sometimes only the old churches remain, by themselves a reminder of an almost forgotten past. Searching for the remnants of old communities of blacks is like searching for remnants of Native Americans. In the isolated rural South one might come upon a strange out-of-place-looking ceremonial mound, the relics of an obliterated and defeated people. The churches of the black community surrounded by no living community are the mounds of black America. These churches, too, are an endangered species.

~

Shiloh Baptist Church is quite an establishment. Evidently a new brick structure, it is large enough to house a day care center, and offices for several ministers including the senior minister, the Reverend Otis Hairston. Hairston had been one of the adult group of supporters so crucial to the success of the civil rights movement in Greensboro, and he apparently inherited his obviously prosperous congregation from his father, who was minister before him.

While I was waiting for Nelson Johnson, Hairston, an impressive-looking, extremely dark-skinned man in his sixties, entered the waiting area. I tried to arrange a time to talk with him but he brushed me off, saying, "Talk to Nelson, he knows everything I know." Then Johnson appeared. He was rather short, stocky, with a smooth, youthful-looking face, and was dressed in a dark suit and tie. I was prepared to expect Nelson Johnson to be as serious a person as he turned out to be, but I was surprised, given his radical activist history, at how soft-spoken and rather conservative in his demeanor he actually was. Displaying an extremely dry sense of humor, he was careful never to overstep his claims for himself. My overall impression was one of a quite unusual person who was on a continual quest for meaning and purpose in life. Though friendly, Johnson was initially reserved. But the more we talked, the more freely he related his experiences.

"What motivated you toward activism?" I asked.

"I was always a believer," he began, "and I tried to act on the basis of my beliefs, no matter what others around me were doing. This brought me a lot of trouble," he added, wryly, as if speaking more to himself than to me. From a small town in Halifax County east of Greensboro ("Tobacco country; my father was a farmer"), Johnson is the fifth of nine children, all of whom, remarkably, are college graduates. "My family was a strong Baptist family." His father was "always talking politics," outspoken, and a founder of the county NAACP in the mid-1950s "right after the *Brown* decision, when things were tough. He instilled in me a sense of 'you've got to stand up for what you believe' that I never lost."

"So you sort of grew up an activist?"

"Not right away. Growing up, I believed in the glory, the mythology, you might say, of this country. Like a lot of black kids, I aspired to go into the military. So I joined the Air Force in 1961. I was eighteen and it was my first time away from home.

"In the service I wasn't a 'fast' person. I was shy. I was quiet, and I spent a lot of time off to myself. It was two years before I had a drink or smoked. As far as the military was concerned, I liked it. You'll probably find it unbelievable that I *volunteered* to serve in Vietnam in 1963."

I was astounded. "How did that happen?"

"The military was offering eighty dollars more per month to men who volunteered for Vietnam. During this time I was stationed in Massachusetts. My father came to New York to visit one of my older brothers, who was working there. I went down to visit them. When I mentioned Vietnam to my father, he just looked at me and said, 'I didn't know we raised such a big fool. What in hell is wrong with you? Those folks haven't done a thing to you.' He really hurt me. I was so embarrassed.

"Fortunately, at the time, early in the war, they were looking for people with experience. That disqualified me. I ended up assigned to Germany, where I grew up some. I became friendly with a group of blacks on the base." Johnson explained that he and his friends closely followed the progress of demonstrations against segregation. They debated the crucial issues and tactics employed by civil rights organizations. "We knew about the Muslims, too, and the militant speeches of Malcolm X. My friends were liking Malcolm. In contrast, I argued to my heart's end the virtues of nonviolent resistance to racism, even though my friends were derisive. I argued hard, but the assassination of Malcolm and the beatings on the Selma bridge hit me like a slap in the face. When I was discharged in 1965, I had left the positions of the NAACP and Martin Luther King, and had come to believe more radical action was necessary if there was ever going to be real change in America. I want to assure you, however, that I have always respected King as a person."

"So you returned to North Carolina to enter A&T?"

"Yes. In 1965. I always knew I was destined to go to A&T, even when I was in the service. My older brothers went to A&T. My father attended high school at A&T since there was no high school then for blacks where we're from."

Johnson's observations echoed Brandon's: A&T drew the children of working-class blacks, including a large number of military veterans who entered college on veterans benefits. He also mentioned the children of blacks who had emigrated to the Northeast; some of them sent their children back "home" to college. "I realized right away," Johnson pointed out, "that because A&T and Bennett were situated in the center of the black community, they were by necessity central to whatever happened to or within the community. The relationship between the Greensboro black community and these colleges is the key to understanding why the sit-ins 'took,' and why every single issue brought up by students during the sixties was relevant to the concerns of the surrounding adult community. And it helped that Greensboro didn't have a strong black upper class like Durham; the levers of control—what you could do, what you could not do—were *not* so strong here, the range of possibilities was wider. I didn't know all that then, but I realize that now."

"How did you get involved in community work?"

"While I was a student at A&T I volunteered to work in a tutoring program called Youth Educational Services. It was just something I wanted to do. The tutoring was done by student volunteers from A&T and Bennett who visited the homes of youngsters in the area; it was a racially integrated program. I wasn't thinking of myself as an organizer or anything like that, but this is when I began to know black families in Greensboro.

"Now, it bothered me that a lot of the black kids requested white tutors. I know it sounds crazy, but the children had fun playing with the hair of the white volunteers, and the white kids were enjoying the attention. They thought it was funny. I wondered what it meant, this preference for white tutors. As I began to talk about this with other black volunteers, I found that they were bothered, too. I wondered about the advisability of whites tutoring black kids in the first place. We thought it was perpetuating an already weak sense of black identity." Johnson, along with other blacks in the program, decided to bring the issue up for formal discussion as a policy matter.

"At the same time, there was quite a bit of interracial dating within the group.

Several black guys were going with white girls, which was greatly resented by the black females, we discovered. Anyway, when we brought all this to the floor, we were accused of separatism. The complaints were never satisfactorily resolved. Finally, our objections split the program."

His experience with the tutorial program led Johnson and his community-oriented friends to conclude that serious efforts to address the most acute needs of the black community had to be controlled by blacks themselves. "People needed power. They needed to define power themselves. And they needed to use power in a way meaningful to them." Out of this philosophy was born the aforementioned Greensboro Association of Poor People in 1968, funded by the Foundation for Community Development in Durham. "We didn't think we were all that radical. We had a lot of mainstream community help. The NAACP let us use their office space. We formed an advisory board consisting of community leaders like George Simkins and Kilimanjaro. We did this thanks to the insisting of Howard Fuller, who said to us, 'Don't get caught fighting your own people.' He had more sense than we knew."

"But GAPP quickly *came* to be considered radical, didn't it?"

"No doubt about it," Johnson agreed. "If for no other reason, because we employed rent strikes. Let me explain. There was a particular section of run-down tenements owned by a white realty company. I first became familiar with this area while I was in the tutorial program. I tutored some kids who lived in these houses, so I knew the conditions under which they lived, and I knew some of the families.

"We decided to try to get the company to fix up the houses. When they didn't, we set up a system to collect the rents from the tenants ourselves, and pay rents only when improvements were made. The realty company retaliated by evicting the tenants whose rents we were withholding. We then helped move those thrown out on the street, and we were able to find a church willing to help us locate new housing; we just got a tremendous response from people who were willing to help. Then we destroyed the houses from which people were evicted."

"Destroyed?"

"Yes, whatever destruction can be done with an ax. If we couldn't do it, someone in the community did. The idea was, you can't just throw people out on the street without paying a price."

"There was no retaliation?"

"Yes. I was arrested. But we did get the message across that we were serious. From that point on, when people in the community had a problem of that type, they came looking for us; we didn't have to go looking for them."

Claude Barnes and the Dudley students supporting him were one group that asked GAPP to intercede on their behalf.

"How did the Dudley dispute spread so quickly onto the A&T campus?" I was interested in hearing from Johnson's perspective. "How did you end up involved in that?"

"By 1969," he said, "I was vice president of the A&T student union. I had led several large student protests. I also knew Claude Barnes; I had known him since he was sixteen, as a youth leader for GAPP. Now, at the very time the Dudley situation was exploding, we were meeting at A&T in an effort to establish a national organization of radical black students. This was the organizing meeting of what became known as the Student Organization for Black Unity [SOBU]. While we were in session, Claude and the Dudley students marched over to A&T, entered our meeting, and asked for permission to be heard. They explained their situation and requested our support, which they received. Then we *all* marched back to Dudley. That's how I became involved."

"Were you surprised the conflict escalated the way it did?"

"I was. That escalation didn't have to happen. But we were treated like a dependent colony by the city authorities. No school board official would negotiate with anyone in the black community; we had to accept their blatant decisions. The media fanned the flames, distorting the truth. They simply didn't accept the legitimacy of black complaints, nor did they understand the dynamics of change.

"In this poisoned atmosphere whites started driving by A&T and shooting onto the campus. When gunfire was returned, the police and National Guard were brought in and a military occupation took place. And the fact that no one was ever charged for Grimes's death was outrageous.

"In the end, when the tear gas settled, the media and the city blamed us and me personally; there was just an unbelievable barrage of charges. I was arrested [for inciting a riot] and sentenced to two years in prison, though I was pardoned before I spent any real time in jail.

"I will say that even during this awful time we retained the support of black community leaders. President Lewis Dowdy of A&T didn't run for the hills. He understood what had happened, and why. He knew racism at work had helped bring his campus under siege. No authorities consulted him about how to deal with the situation. All of us, no matter which side we were on, resented that."

Unfortunately, we had run out of time. I had to shut off my tape recorder and drive Johnson back to Shiloh Baptist. However, a few days later we were able to meet at a virtually empty Howard Johnson's restaurant and continued our discussion over mindless Muzak that was driving me crazy.

"Somehow I came through 1969 moving full speed ahead. In the early seventies I was traveling all over the place, trying to build chapters of SOBU, so I dropped out of school." The SOBU effort and Malcolm X University were key aspects of Greensboro's radical profile in the early 1970s. And then the divisive debate between Marxism and nationalism emerged to overshadow everything.

Poet and essayist Amiri Baraka of Newark was the most prominent former nationalist leader to announce a shift to Marxism, and because he was so influential, Baraka's conversion sent shock waves through the nationalist community. Essentially, as I understand it, Baraka was saying that the advent of political and economic power among African natives and people of African descent did not in itself guarantee the betterment of conditions for those on the economic bottom. Extreme class divisions that solidified economic inequities continued, and must be taken into account. African liberation in several newly decolonized nations, as it was then disappointingly becoming clear, was too often producing neocolonialist dictators who were enriching themselves at the expense of their own people. European economic interests, now operating under the cloak of African officialdom, continued to dominate these nations.

On the other hand, nationalists, particularly cultural nationalists, believed that despite class economic divisions the most meaningful basis of unity among people of African descent was a common base culture, not to mention a shared history rooted in Africa and the devastating experiences of the slave trade and the struggle to overcome the continuing exploitation resulting from slavery.

Though Nelson Johnson was one of those who chose the Marxist path, he looks back upon the split with regret. "Both sides had a lot of right. It's a pity we couldn't learn from each other. The Marxists, including myself, did not sufficiently appreciate the depth of culture. For us, it was all economics. But people are more complicated than economic units. And the nationalists didn't always consider seriously enough the economic divisions among black people, and the poverty which crosses racial lines."

In the mid-1970s, in furtherance of his philosophical beliefs, Johnson was one of the organizers of an effort to establish independent unions in the tobacco and textile industries of North Carolina. It was an almost impossible task, because North Carolina, and the South generally, had always been extremely hostile toward unions, especially effective unions. The South was even more adamantly opposed to unions with an interracial membership and/or leadership. Yet, this was now their objective, and Johnson himself worked in several factories, including Cone Mills in Greensboro, toward this end.

Accused of being a Communist earlier when he wasn't, Johnson now joined the party, as he says, "openly." It wouldn't have been consistent with his psychological or moral makeup to have been deceptive about his political associations. But nothing caused Nelson Johnson as much trouble as his joining the Communist Workers party (CWP). He lost the support of the mainstream black community at this point, along with many of his friends.* "People wouldn't even sit on the same side of the

*While I was in Greensboro, I had hoped to interview Claude Barnes, the radical youth whose activism triggered the 1969 Dudley High/A&T incidents. In 1991, Barnes was in Atlanta, however, and I was not able to locate him and arrange a conversation until the fall of 1995, by telephone. The student radical is now associate professor of political science at—where else?— North Carolina A&T. Was I surprised? Somewhat. Cycles rarely complete themselves with such unerring symmetry. Brilliant sounding and smoothly articulate over the phone, Barnes filled me in on his details. "My parents were working poor. Dad was a waiter. Mom was a domestic; you know, three dollars a week. They were churchgoers. I can say they certainly were not happy with my participation in radical activities. But by the time I was sixteen, I was a youth organizer for GAPP, and I received as much of an education from them as at Dudley High, which, in hindsight, was a wonderful high school despite the validity of our protests at that time. The housing GAPP targeted because of poor conditions and called a rent strike against was very near where I lived (the landlord collected rent with a gun on his hip), so I knew exactly what they were complaining about. As for 1969, it was unreal. But the Greensboro white community had and has never come to grips with their racism. There's a legacy of paternalism. It's very had to make any progress." As a protégé of Nelson Johnson, Barnes followed Johnson faithfully through all of his various organizational phases during the 1970s, until Johnson joined the Communist

room with me," he recalled, sadly. No political activity was viewed more opprobri-
ously in the South than membership in the Communist party. Whites looked upon
the party as evil incarnate and southern politicians had red-baited the civil rights
movement to the point of ridiculousness; consequently, blacks were frightened to
death by mention of the CWP. Also, it didn't help that as Johnson shifted to a
more radical stance in his organizational activities, blacks were for the first time
seeping into the southern political and economic mainstream as a result of civil
rights successes—a few elected officials, a handful of appointed officials, a managerial
job here and there, and a rather fluid flow into low-level positions in retail businesses
and government, particularly in geographic areas where blacks represented large population percentages. There was renewed hope that the system as it was would be
more fruitful for blacks without the need for radical change. This was particularly
true in North Carolina, the wealthiest of southern states due to its textile, tobacco,
and insurance riches.

Though Johnson didn't dwell on this part of the story, or go into why he felt
it necessary to join the CWP, I remembered that he began our interview by explaining, "I was always a believer, and I tried to act on the basis of my beliefs, no matter
what others around me were doing. This brought me a lot of trouble."

Trouble appeared suddenly in the terrible form of flying bullets on November
3, 1979, on a street outside a Greensboro housing project. Johnson was one of the

---

Workers party. Barnes had entered A&T in 1974 after Malcolm X University closed for financial
reasons. In 1976 he dropped out of college to also join the Revolutionary Workers League in
the effort to organize textile mill employees, working at Greensboro's massive Cone Mills. "I
worked there two years, but I came to the conclusion that the idea was a mistake. When I told
one worker I dropped out of college to do this organizing, he looked at me in amazement and
said, 'You got to be out of your mind. I wish I had had a chance to go to school. Get the hell
out of here and go back to college as soon as you can.' I would have followed Nelson to the
ends of the earth, but I really didn't feel we were achieving what we set out to do, because the
company had its own pacified union well in place. So I returned to good ole A&T, and graduated
with a major in political science in 1979." He then went on to Atlanta University, earning his
master's degree in 1982 with a thesis on GAPP, and teaching stints at Morris Brown, Spellman,
Georgia Tech, and South Carolina State, among others. Barnes earned his Ph.D. in 1987. Married
to a girl he met in high school, he now has a daughter attending A&T, in the School of
Engineering. "I'm glad to be back home and glad to be at A&T," he said. "I've put my feet
down."

leaders of an anti-Klan march and rally that ended in a violent confrontation with alleged Klan and Nazi members. After shouts and the hurling of epithets between the two groups, the Klan members, who were armed, opened fire, killing five of the marchers.

I was attending a civil rights reunion at Tougaloo College in Mississippi when we heard this unbelievable news via radio and TV; it exploded upon us like a visitation from an awful past. We had come to think of the Klan as no more than a minor nuisance; a hooded anachronism more ludicrous than dreaded. Virulent racism in the South had long ago learned to attire itself in more drab and respectable clothing.

We watched a television tape showing several men jumping out of their cars, then calmly opening their trunks to withdraw rifles or shotguns, then opening fire on a group of people we could hardly make out in the distance. Was it a movie? There were no police on the scene, Johnson said with disgust, though the march had been prominently advertised with a taunting dare to the Klan to show their faces; trouble certainly could and should have been anticipated. Once again, much of the blame fell on Johnson ("I was the most visible spokesperson"), who himself was stabbed in the melee following the shootings. Why on earth was he leading a march called "Death to the Klan" in the first place, community people demanded? A march of godless Communists?

Twelve years later, it still isn't easy for him to talk about what happened that day, or the aftermath. "First of all," he said with more exasperation than anger, "the killings were portrayed as a shoot-out between two undesirable groups. I was portrayed as having lost my mind. I had come under control of outside forces. It was said in the community that I foolishly challenged the Klan, desired a confrontation, planned to get people killed, and hoped that it would be black children in the project, so that large numbers of people would join our organization to overthrow the government, or something. That hurt me."

"Did you know there was a likelihood of an attack by the Klan that might lead to fatalities?" I had to ask.

"No, I didn't. But I *should* have known. Others knew. The police knew. But nothing was done to interrupt an armed group from traveling to Greensboro from surrounding towns to where we were.

"The story of that tragedy is not understood, even by people in Greensboro. The starting point of discussing it is so unreal. Today, despite knowledge of the injustice, there is still the assumption of my culpability."

It was already painful enough for Johnson to talk about what had happened; there was no point in forcing him to reexamine every detail. I could hear the injury in his voice, as if we were probing a wound that would never heal, no matter what, though his voice only grew softer.

"After the shootings, you didn't try to get your usual support from the Greensboro old faithful?"

"I went to Simkins and Kilimanjaro and ministers I knew and asked them to hold a press conference. They agreed, but before we could do it the whole thing got derailed. I think Simkins received pressure from the national NAACP office to stay out of it," and of course Simkins was crucial. "We were able to hold a funeral march on November eleventh, 1979, which included about a thousand people. And on February second, 1980, there was a march of seven thousand, consisting of about one hundred fifty representatives from national groups. This was a memorial for the slain group and a commemoration of the twentieth anniversary of the sit-ins. A massive legal team rushed to Greensboro to represent us, but I hardly knew them, except Bill Kunstler, by reputation. All together, seven charges were brought against me, including contempt of court when I refused to stand when the judge entered the courtroom. I was dragged out of the court and out of sight and beaten. My bail was set at one hundred thousand dollars."

I asked Johnson if he, in hindsight, thought the CWP organizing efforts were able to achieve some success.

"Actually," he replied, "we were making progress in building strong unions in the plants. That's what the shootings were about, I'm convinced. The attack on us was connected to the fact we were making some headway, and to our interraciality. Of the five people killed—Dr. James Waller, Sandra Smith, Dr. Michael Nathans, Caesar Cauce, and William Sampson—four of them were white and four were involved in organizing. So a strong aspect of the shooting was union-busting, an effort to instill fear. These were not crimes of passion."

"How did your father deal with all this," I asked.

"My father was angry. He knew we were set up. He wanted me to move back home to Halifax County. But where is home? I can take care of myself better here, despite everything."

"And your wife, Joyce? How did she deal with it?"

"She stood by me through thick and thin. We married during GAPP days. When we were married, I was on my way to jail, so she *knew* what she was getting into. Really, Joyce has been more than a supporter, she has been a partner in all my causes."

⌒

For five years afterward, Nelson Johnson fought the legal charges stemming from the shootings. Finally, all were dropped except one, for which he served a short term in prison. As far as he knew, none of the attackers served time in jail. In the wake of the Klan tragedy, Johnson became a virtual outcast in Greensboro, where ten years earlier he had been the black community's most effective militant leader. "No one would hire me. No one needed me. No one valued my skills. I was beginning to wonder if I had any. I tried carpentry for a while, but it didn't take me long to find out I'm not a carpenter."

During this period "in the wilderness," a time of alienation, except for family and his closest friends, Nelson Johnson plunged into intense self-examination, reviewing again and again the progression of his life, and his life's decisions. This psychological and spiritual reevaluation, he says, helped him to come to terms with the inner person—the believer as well as questioner—he had always been. "No bolt of lightning hit me," he said, smiling. "I had always tried to be loyal to what I believed at the time. When I was working and organizing in the textile mills, I understood the need for unity between blacks and whites, plus the nature of imperialism. But I realized I was losing my sense of humanity in the process—*everything* we were doing was tactics and strategies—my sense of compassion was waning. During this time, after the shootings, I didn't see a way to keep going. And the enforced isolation hurt. People wouldn't meet with me, even though they knew me. This tried my faith. I had to move back to the people, who had always sustained me.

"I left the church in the late sixties because I felt religion was a lot of hot air. Churches weren't doing anything in terms of challenging the existing social order. People did not do the things they said they believed in. But later I realized I had mistaken

· 57 ·

the behavior of people for the ultimate beliefs of religious faith. Once I understood the difference, I could still be very critical of the church as an institution of men and yet respect a vision of a new social order. Let's call it a vision of the 'Kingdom,' where I feel the worth of persons is affirmed by the measure of 'the least of these.' This was the faith of Jesus. This is the faith I feel many of us grapple toward, even if we can't name it or define it. I came to understand that, in my own way, that's what I've always been trying to do, though I didn't always call it religion. But now I was willing to. I approached the Reverend Mr. Hairston, who had been there for me through thick and thin. At first he was shocked. But he promised to give me a chance.

In 1985, Johnson reentered A&T to resume his college work. In 1986 he graduated. That fall, he entered divinity school.

"Of course, some thought my going to divinity school was a ploy. People say to me now, referring to my new role—'since your conversion.' I hope people see me as more complex than that. My 'conversion,' if we use that term, has been a long, long process of self-discovery."

"From the perspective of the issues that were fought for in the sixties and the immediate aftermath, what worries you now, Nelson?"

"In Greensboro, or just generally?"

"Generally."

"I think the present period, as we enter the twenty-first century, is as bad as any we have known since slavery. I really do. There are greater divisions within the race along class lines. On the bottom there is a community of black folk who have nothing, not even *hope* that their condition will get better. On the other hand, there are black folk who are doing well, if not better than ever, as a result of openings brought about by the protests of the sixties.

"Secondly, this sort of economic widening *within the race* is occurring without a sense of alarm, with no awareness of national emergency, not even on the part of blacks. Successful blacks have become a part of the very world and worldview we fought against in the sixties. To the extent we wanted it, we have become a part of it, sharing the national lack of concern with the problems of those on the bottom. Concern only crops up when problems emerge in the form of crime. We don't have the societal instruments to reform our economic and social order—as for us, as a race, all our energy has gone into finding a way into the mainstream. There is no faith in our capacity to change this situation anymore, to change to a more equitable and humane society. That's a bleak view, I know, but that's what I see and feel."

⌒

That night, after my talk with Nelson Johnson, I decided to take a drive southeastward on Highway 421 headed in the general direction of Sanford, signs told me, about fifty miles away. I had no intention of going to Sanford; I was just driving while reflecting on Johnson's story.

Even though I was not religious, I could well understand the logic of Johnson's returning to the church, as long as he could return with his sense of mission intact, through a concept of an activist church. I sensed that though Johnson's passionate life work had been devoted to causes that were decidedly secular, the church had always lived within him, assuming the various clothing of his causes. It was no different now, except that now he was consciously working under the aegis of a religious institution. He seemed to be perfectly in tune with himself.

As I headed out on the narrow two-lane highway, which was called Liberty Road (probably because it originally led only to the hamlet of Liberty, about twenty miles away), the shopping centers became smaller, homes more scarce, as I moved away from the suburban housing developments. After about ten miles I was in hill country, a land of farms, sparsely placed homes, occasional autos, far from the big mill area and the heavy trucks. I was now in an area served by country stores, all of which were closed.

Somewhere in these hills reside the very active North Carolina Klan, made all the more real by several recent reappearances. I felt a quick stab of fear, an old fear of the unknown. I thought about turning around and making this exploratory tour during the daytime; then I thought, This is ridiculous, calm down. During the late 1960s, when I was commuting from New Orleans to northeastern Mississippi to teach, I had learned to swallow my fear of lonely roads at night. Then my wariness was not so much of the secretive Klan, wherever or whoever they were, but of marauding sheriffs and sheriff's deputies, that highly enthusiastic army that patrolled the Mississippi highways, primarily, it seemed to us, to keep blacks, particularly blacks connected to the civil rights movement, under control, and to monitor our movements. As a consequence, when I was driving on dangerous Mississippi roads with a Louisiana license plate, I instinctively concocted a story to explain what I was doing there should I be stopped: I was lost, or I was going to or returning from a visit to a relative in West Point, Mississippi (where I taught). Usually, it made sense to drive carefully, lie low, try not to call attention to myself.

During those years, I was friendly with Bob Analavage, a white civil rights journalist who was living in New Orleans. With his flaming, unkempt red hair and beatnik look, Analavage seemed totally out of place in the rural Deep South, though he did just fine in the French Quarter of New Orleans. I commuted to West Point in the middle of the week. Usually I drove, but once I traveled by bus. Just before I left to go back to New Orleans, Analavage said, "Listen, I have to come up that way for a story. Why don't I pick you up and we can drive back together." We had traveled through the Delta several times before, visiting civil rights projects. But when Analavage arrived to pick me up, he had his flamboyant girlfriend with him. In the rear seat was his huge German shepherd, "in case we run into trouble." The plan was to ride along the well-traveled but dangerous Highway 82 into the Delta, visit a civil rights project, then head down to New Orleans. I thought about it and said, "Bob, I don't want to insult you, but you, your girlfriend, a strange, mean-looking dog in the backseat, and me—I don't think it's going to work. I just don't feel like going to jail this weekend." I took the bus back to New Orleans.

Now, as I drove on through the darkness east of Greensboro, rounding curves and straining up hills, it occurred to me that though most whites in these areas would reject an identification with the Klan, the Klan, for them, did crystallize the poor white hostility to black and minority incursions into mainstream American society, an incursion they felt was unfair. The resurgence of the Klan in the 1970s was an omen of the national conservativism of the '80s, which air-braked an attempt to redress racial injustices, and adopted an approach toward the least fortunate, not as the most needy, but as victims of their own slothfulness.

I flipped on the radio and spun the dial to see what I could find. I was amazed at the tone of remarks on the proliferating call-in talk shows, clogged with people strongly in favor of the Persian Gulf war, attacking the protestors against the war, attacking Cable News Network broadcasters who remained in Baghdad to report on the American bombings, attacking Saddam Hussein as the devil incarnate, glorifying the technology of American weaponry.

If it wasn't the war, it was fundamentalist preaching, from one end of the dial to the other, a hermetic world of individualist religion, saving one's soul, devoid of any mention of responsibility for social conditions, devoid of a sense of otherness, of others out there besides us. As long as we are saved, we are right with God. This message was delivered in countless ways, depending on the style of the preacher, the words ricocheting through these hills, and across the land to the sea.

This road reminded me of rural northern Mississippi. You could live your entire life along roads like this one, and live and die by the laws of your fields and hills and the land you owned. If you didn't own anything, you were in trouble.

I had driven about thirty miles and it was time to turn around and head back to Greensboro.

I looked forward to a meeting both Hal Sieber and Nelson Johnson had invited me to at Shiloh Baptist Church on the night of January 31, which would commemorate the thirty-first anniversary of the sit-ins. The city of Greensboro and A&T both had planned events to celebrate the anniversary, and they were going at it in a big way. Now that the 1960s have receded into the misty past, Greensboro has incorporated the "disorder" into its own official past, and, in a public relations triumph, has decided to market the events that made the town famous, or infamous. Or so it seemed.

David Richmond, one of the four original student demonstrators, had recently died, but the other three—Ezell Blair, Joseph McNeil, and Franklin McCain—were brought back by the city to participate in the anniversary. A sidewalk sculpture of the footprints of the sit-in-ers was dedicated in front of Woolworth's. A&T held a large banquet/luncheon.

Nelson Johnson and a few other Greensboro leaders were unhappy with the purely celebratory nature of the anniversary. They, therefore, decided to hold a special interracial meeting in an effort to use the anniversary to address pressing contemporary problems and, hopefully, in the process, to revive the tenuous interracial coalition that had existed during earlier years. Apparently, this was the meeting Johnson was organizing while I was trying to get an interview with him. Hal Sieber was also an organizer of this session. Because of Richmond's recent death, the Shiloh session was dedicated to his memory.

I found this meeting to be rather strange. Everyone was dressed up (including the young folks; there was to be a youth meeting), a formality that seemed unnecessary for what was intended to be a hard-nails working session, though maybe it was natural in Greensboro to dress up for such occasions and it was my sense of appropriateness that was off. The gathering of about fifty people consisted of a spectrum of black establishment figures (though I didn't see Simkins, Kilimanjaro, or A&T officials), old-line white liberals from the Guilford College community and the University of North Carolina at Greensboro, and a few representatives from the business community.

We divided into smaller discussion units. I sat with the high school division. But they didn't seem to know what they were there for except to be there, so I moved over to the plenary session, which had now convened.

The suave chairperson was, I believe he said, a professor of sociology at A&T. With an air of tenseness and delicate politeness prevailing, a few black speakers introduced the issues they were concerned with. One of the reasons for the meeting, I had heard earlier as we were gathering, was the consternation caused among some whites when a black city councilman awarded Muslim minister Louis Farrakhan the key to the city on the occasion of his visit a few months previously. But blacks had long-standing complaints they wanted to air out also, and as it turned out, Farrakhan never came up in the discussion I attended.

There was, instead, testimony by blacks on their continued alienation from the mainstream economic power centers, now three decades after the sit-ins. Second, it was asserted that black businesses that thrived under segregation had expired under putative integration, one of the major reasons being that black entrepreneurs could not obtain loans from the major lending institutions. Black-owned banks were also under siege. David Dansby, a former president of the Greensboro NAACP, spoke on the disastrous results of the "redevelopment" of Martin Luther King Street (formerly Asheboro Street), in the southeastern section. "The various small black businesses that were there have been wiped out." As I noticed myself, nothing had been done to rebuild King Street. A black reporter for the *Greensboro News and Record* who appeared to be in his late twenties or early thirties, Allen Johnson, testified on the lack of self-confidence and assertiveness among too many black school youths. There were criticisms of the public school system, years after the plunge into desegregation. ("I'm sure you realize," former teacher Angelina Smith had loudly whispered to me when I interviewed her and her husband at their home, "that the teachers today aren't teaching our children what they need to know. It bothers me to death.") The county school system (85 percent white), which Greensborians can attend, is being used as a sanctuary for white flight from the city school system (55 percent black), it was alleged. There was considerable unhappiness with the school system, but I sensed from the discussion that the public schools were an issue that had been continually debated in Greensboro for at least two decades.

The response from some whites to these complaints was defensive, not to mention awkward. I'm sure they were thinking they didn't come to this gathering to end up being the targets of resentments and complaints from the black participants, complaints they probably felt they could not do much about anyway. "We'll have to get the Chamber of Commerce involved," one of the movers and shakers responded, while admitting that "black businesses surely have declined during the eighties." Sol Jacobs, a retired downtown delicatessen owner, bemoaned the absence of progressive white political leadership. Allen Johnson spoke again, offering that interracial dialogue in Greensboro is not genuine: too many forced smiles and too much artificial civility. "Maybe we need racial sensitivity sessions." Samuel Cooper Smith agreed, adding, "We dialogued during the forties and fifties. Why not now?" A black man who had said little so far declared that the problems voiced in this session would not change anything—"the real powers that be aren't here."

Nelson Johnson, who had been in and out of the plenary meeting, took the floor to state that the past decade had represented a stupendous polarization of the races. Racism was on the increase. "We definitely need community dialogues. Greensboro could serve as a model. If we don't do something, we're just stewing in our own juices." Then the discussion, which had gone on for about three hours, ended. Everyone shook hands and pledged to do something. The handshakes didn't shake my impression that this meeting didn't go well; something was missing. It reminded me of the strained interracial meetings of the 1950s.

The elderly Sol Jacobs was one of the people I met at the Richmond memorial. Hal Sieber informed me that Jacobs had run for mayor in 1980. "You should talk to him," Sieber urged.

I called the following day, and Jacobs agreed, and we set a time. Unfortunately, I arrived about forty-five minutes late. Jacobs appeared to have been pacing the floor waiting for me. Despite Jacobs's explicit directions, I got lost. He lived over in the northeastern section in one of those housing areas where you have to know where you're going in order to find it.

The diminutive Jacobs appeared to be in his seventies. He mentioned his family but he was alone that afternoon. Frankly, he looked sickly. (He said, of our conversation, "If this comes out in a book, I hope I'm still around to read it.") But he was fired up over conditions in Greensboro, and I had to slow him down until I could get my tape recorder working. He had left last night's discussion "disgusted." "Commemoration of the sit-ins is okay, but we need continuity to have a worthwhile discussion; we need to meet regularly, at least every month. When that guy mentioned taking issues brought up last night to the Chamber [of Commerce], I just laughed; those guys are going to hamstring things.

"Greensboro has suffered because of poor leadership on the part of whites. It looks like we reached a certain point in the seventies, then we never quite turned the corner."

Jacobs explained that he was part of Hal Sieber's group of Chamber members who had worked to bring in blacks. "Then when things settled down and the demands from the black community eased up, they chopped Sieber off." The Klan shootings followed, "which Greensboro blamed on outsiders," and nothing much happened in terms of interracial progress afterward.

"Are you a native of Greensboro?" I inquired.

"No. No." He smiled wanly. "I'm from Pittsburgh. Got here by accident. I'm one of five boys; four of us were in the military during World War Two. My parents came here to be with my older brother, who was stationed at the Greensboro depot." (Greensboro was a major departure point for troops headed for the European theater during World War II.) "While they were here, they opened a deli on Elm Street. I came in '49 to take them back to Pittsburgh. They were both sick. Once I got here, I told my brother, 'They'll never leave. They like it here.'

"Very soon after I arrived, my father died suddenly, and my mother was hospitalized, so I *couldn't* leave. I ended up running the deli, all the time thinking I was really dispensing with it. But that went on for twenty years."

"Why did you stay so long?" I asked.

"I don't know. This was a beautiful city."

I glanced out the window of his comfortable home, and I had to agree, from where he was living.

"Except, of course, for the black area."

"Yes," I agreed.

"My oldest child was a girl. Soon after we moved here we took a drive through the southeast end. 'Daddy, why do all the brown people live in poor houses?' she asked, and I never forgot it." Jacobs's mind flipped back to his Army days. "We were in New Guinea in the Pacific theater. I was an officer. We had heard a black company was being assigned to our base. I had never known any blacks. When I told my men a black company was coming, they all said, 'We don't have to eat with them, do we?' Well, within three or four days we were eating together and no one knew the difference. This was in New Guinea. Then when we got back to the States, everything changed.

"So I knew the racial situation in Greensboro could improve, and pretty quickly. Running a deli meant a lot of people hung around just to chat. Changes *could* be made if people who knew what had to happen had the courage to speak up. But speaking up for progress is hard to come by in Greensboro."

Jacobs shifted focus to Alma Adams, the black city councilwoman; I had also met Ms. Adams at the Richmond memorial. It seemed Jacobs was in the middle of a political skirmish with her. "She's naive," he declared, explaining that Alma Adams and the black councilman (two blacks are on the City Council) had attacked the city manager over an issue involving Coliseum contracts. Jacobs thought the city manager was doing the best he could, though I wasn't sure what he was talking about. He threw up his hands in mock resignation. "I know," he complained, "the only times we've *ever* had progress for blacks here there's been violence or the threat of violence, but we've just got to get to a point where we can sit back and recognize who is trying to do an honest job, and give them a little leeway."

In that case, how did he assess Nelson Johnson and his efforts through the years, I wondered.

He admired Nelson. "I understand what drove him to the Communist party; it was a natural progression of his commitment. But let me tell you, he is a leader. It's beautiful to see him operate. Really, he could even bring leadership to the white community, if they would let him." Jacobs was losing energy, coughing, and it was time for me to go.

"Remember," he said as I was departing, "check out the Quakers in Greensboro. I'm Jewish and I didn't know a thing about the Quakers before I came here, but I learned all about them at the deli. They're the people that make the Greensboro white community different. Different in the early days, and different in the sixties and the seventies."

⌒

As I mentioned, one of the people I met at the Richmond memorial was Council-woman Alma Adams. Because Jacobs referred to her, I was all the more eager to interview her. At the meeting she had spoken forcefully on the public schools, though I didn't know the details of the debate. I was also interested in Ms. Adams as a woman in politics, which is not a new phenomenon among blacks, but unusual, I thought, in male-dominated black Greensboro, which revolved around male-dominated A&T. When I called, she asked me to meet her at Bennett College, where she is chair of the Bennett Art Department, a rare combination—art and electoral politics.

Engaging, effusive, tall, light skinned, and in her forties though she looked younger, Ms. Adams enthusiastically related her story. As with so many of the Greensborians I met, she is not a native of Greensboro.

"I'm a native of Newark," she began, "but I *wanted* to come south for college, and major in art. I know that sounds strange. I had heard about A&T," she said, "and had relatives who lived near here, so I came. I knew it made sense to get out of Newark if I could."

Unfortunately, A&T proved to be a profound disappointment. "I was eager to learn about myself as an Afro-American, as an Afro-American artist, and I thought I would at least get that at a black college. Instead, we were taught everything *but* black art and culture; the focus was European art and its glories."

Nevertheless, she took to Greensboro. "People were very friendly. For the first time in my life, I felt strong. I got married early, lived in the community, became involved in activities at A&T. There was just an underlying feeling of black people in control at A&T. At home in Newark my high school adviser had said I wasn't even college material. My mother didn't feel that way. I didn't feel that way. A&T and Greensboro provided me with a nurturing community."

In 1981, Adams was awarded her Ph.D. in art education by Ohio State University. She returned to teach at Bennett College.

By 1982, Adams had divorced and was raising a son and daughter as a single parent. "That year several issues came up at the elementary school my daughter was attending. I became concerned, did my own research, and for the first time attended a parents-teachers meeting. When I spoke, the response from the audience was tremendous. I was so encouraged I decided to run for the school board in 1984.

"I won in '84 on the strength of the heavy national Jesse Jackson vote. Once elected, I focused on bringing more Afro-American teachers into the system, on the curriculum, and on negative teacher attitudes toward black children. The white community was alarmed by my vocalizing these concerns, and so I became a target, along with Mike King, another outspoken black board member. In 1986, when I came up for reelection, I won my primary, but they did a job on me in the general election. Mike King and I were accused of racially polarizing the school system. I refused to apologize for what I had said during my term. Some blacks criticized me also. 'Alma, you need to take it slow.' I didn't feel we had to 'take it slow.' I lost that election."

In 1988, Adams ran for the City Council seat vacated by Anna Simkins, the wife of Dr. George Simkins, with Mrs. Simkins's blessing.

Adams expressed pride in her political independence. "I'm not 'connected.' I'm not bound to any particular group. I don't feel anyone who contributed to my campaign thinks I would support them if I really disagree with them on the issues." Real independence in politics is hard to come by and only achieved with sacrifice, I knew that. I could see where Alma Adams might make some people unhappy, but, to me, just as an observer passing through, I could sense her well-grounded strength.

I'd been looking for a live music club. I hadn't found one. What I found was a disco near A&T. I thought I would go there on a weekend just to say I went, but when I parked my car in the lot outside and heard the booming electrical bass line, I said, "I don't think so." I know disco is a valid culture, or has become a culture for gathering and dance, but the scene is too loud for me and I have yet to understand the rituals. I had heard that Greensboro was once a good town for jazz, the music I like the most, that East Market Street, the tendon that connects the black community to downtown, was once replete with music clubs. The death of East Market Street commerce also meant the demise of the music clubs. I was informed by Alma Adams that Carl Foster, a native Greensborian, could tell me all about the old days.

While I was trying to meet Foster, I decided to check out the historical museum and cultural center in the downtown area. The soul of the museum turned out to be military history. Revolutionary War uniforms, Civil War muskets, Spanish-American War photographs (including pictures of a black company), World War I helmets and canteens, photographs of soldiers and military caps, as well as World War II photographs of Greensboro when the town appeared to have been transformed into a huge military camp. There was also an exhibit displaying regional culture—textiles (but no cigarettes)—and a video on quilting.

Life-size sculptures of the first four sit-in-ers at a life-size lunch counter joined this historical panorama, along with a bust of George Simkins, honoring his lifetime of service with the Greensboro NAACP, presented by the NAACP. I had once believed that museums were superfluous, because their collections bore little relationship to their locations, but now I view their collections for insight into what the ruling class of a place thinks worth preserving. Or what is seen as worth preserving from other peoples' past culture that the current ruling class esteems or identifies with.

Down the block from the museum is the cultural center, an attractively renovated nineteenth-century structure. The center rents space for shops, and contains a huge gallery that is presently exhibiting the artwork of Greensboro's school youth. This Sunday afternoon, at the other end of the gallery, a string quintet is offering a concert of classical music, everyone dressed to the hilt, the women in long black dresses, the gentleman violinist in formal attire. An audience of about seventy-five listens in absolute silence; a lone black woman sits on the edge of the front row.

I tiptoe across the hall to visit the newly opened African-American Atelier Arts Gallery, and exhibit of black artists. At the end of the hall, but closed that day, there is a collection of African art collected by an A&T professor. North Carolina is well-known in southern cultural circles for its funding of art centers and museums: all that textile and tobacco money. But I wonder how much folk art, based on the everyday experience of ordinary people, actually thrives.

When I asked Carolyn Coleman, the NAACP regional representative in North Carolina and a native Georgian, what she thought of Greensboro, she explained, "Greensboro isn't a place where there's a lot to do. Other than church. If you don't go to church, you're really rather isolated." Not a churchgoer myself, I knew I would be isolated if I lived in Greensboro. "This is a great place to raise a family," she quickly added. "But it's not for single people or younger people. Durham wouldn't be any better."

I was finally able to meet Dr. Carl Foster at his home on the outskirts of Greensboro. In his mid to late sixties, the laid-back, cautious, and soft-spoken Foster grew up in Greensboro ("My mother was a domestic, my father a handyman"), attended Dudley High, and went to A&T after having served in World War II military bands. Foster likes Greensboro and believes it to be "the most liberal city in North Carolina. Times were hard," he recalled, but "work was good." Foster has certainly done well, working his way up through the ranks of the school system. He has served as cultural director for the school system. He is currently principal of a "mostly white" elementary school. It was his musical background, however, that I was most interested in.

"Was A&T strong musically?"

"It certainly was," Foster replied. "A&T was famous for its band. Music students came down from New York in the forties and fifties just to be in our band." He mentioned that Lou Donaldson, the well-known saxophonist, had attended A&T. He said the former East Market Street music clubs—the Artists Guild, the Playmore Dance Hall, the Moose Hall—were regular stops on the southern tour for great bands like Count Basie's and Lionel Hampton's. "Hampton heard me play and begged me to leave school and join the band as trumpeter, but I was *so* close to finishing college I couldn't give up my education. Besides, those were hard days for bands—Birmingham tonight, Macon, Georgia, tomorrow, Atlanta the next night— I would have been dead by now!

"In those days, despite segregation, white kids came over to play with us, because we were where the music was. We couldn't go to their places but they could come to ours. We followed Bird [saxophonist Charlie Parker] and Dizzy [trumpeter Dizzy Gillespie] so closely you wouldn't believe it. Two weeks after their records came out, we had their arrangements down. We *lived* in the record store."

The more Foster spoke, the more enthusiastically he brought back the old days, and the inconveniences and insults of segregation faded into the background, as he told stories of eighteen-year-old high school student John Coltrane commuting over from High Point to practice and jam with them—"And he couldn't play our changes. Not yet." But then Foster's career had taken over, and by now "I hardly play anymore. Besides, the younger musicians here are not playing anything. Compared to what we were."

I had talked to Hal Sieber several times since I met him at the *Peacemaker*, and he had offered useful background on Greensboro. I usually met him at a decidedly unfancy coffee shop off an Interstate 85 exit. That was where Sieber did his writing. The Truck Stop, as I took to calling it, was a coffee shop, a small store with rental showers, and a refueling station for the mammoth trucks that roared up and down I-85 and I-40. Sieber, who was about sixty, maintained an authoritative, businesslike manner, smoking furiously when he wasn't coughing from the smoke.

Since working in Greensboro to transform the Chamber of Commerce, Sieber had served as a consultant on race relations in several cities and was on the board of the Martin Luther King Center in Atlanta, but it was obvious he really liked Greensboro, and he enthusiastically sold it to me.

He saw a city of enormous promise and growth. He cited the merged Jefferson-Pilot insurance company and its spin-off businesses, along with the continuing viability of the wealthy textile and tobacco industries. As a sign of sophistication, he pointed to the strong Greensboro and Guilford County support for former Charlotte Mayor Harvey Gantt, who is black, when Gantt ran for the U.S. Senate against conservative Jesse Helms in 1990.* Though Gantt lost by a narrow margin, Sieber was proud of the fact Guilford County did not buckle under the pressure of Helms's reactionary last-minute advertising. Greensboro now has four hundred black members of the Chamber of Commerce, he informed me, and a black police chief. There are now three black members of the school board, two aggressive City Council members, and a steady growth in total population to the current figure of approximately 185,000. Nevertheless, Sieber was quick to point out, the economic gap within the black community has widened, and was getting to be a major problem. Sieber's image of Greensboro as more progressive than, say, Winston-Salem or Durham, was based, to some extent, as was Jacobs's, on the town's Quaker roots.

"Greensboro, you know, was a *junction* on the Underground Railroad, a stop operated by the Levi Coffin family. Albion Tourgée, a nonconformist writer and leader during Reconstruction [1865–1876], was run out of Greensboro for his profreedmen convictions when Reconstruction was dismantled," Sieber added. "There was a Penn School in High Point. Warnersville, the original black Greensboro community, was named for a Philadelphia Quaker who purchased the land to establish the community."

Because of Sieber's views, I decided to make my long-postponed visit to Guilford College, the most prominent Quaker college in the South, where I hoped to find useful material on the original Quaker settlement. Guilford College was quite a drive (about ten miles) out West Friendly Avenue toward the airport; I entered the campus from the appropriately named New Garden Road. First called the New Garden Boarding School, Guilford today is a richly endowed college set in rustic greenery. The library is new and stunningly beautiful. I don't see how anyone gets any studying done in such a setting. Most of the students were white, but I saw a few blacks, and a goodly percentage of Asians.

The library was open; I discovered that North Carolina Quaker documents were maintained in a special room, and I was able to glean some information about the

*In 1996, Gantt opposed Jesse Helms again but was defeated.

early Greensboro settlement from a journal published by the college, *The Southern Friend*. The local Quakers, and what happened to them, had had a far more profound and reverberating impact on the condition and status of black folk in North Carolina than I ever knew.

The Quaker settlements were established in the Piedmont area of the western section of the original colony in the mid-eighteenth century. The first settlers migrated down from Pennsylvania, where original communities in North America were founded by William Penn in 1681. Penn, born in England, was an uncompromising leader of the Religious Society of Friends (their proper name) and had served time in prison in Ireland because of his early Quaker religious beliefs. His migration to America, along with that of his followers, was a quest for religious freedom. The New Garden village was the first settlement of the town that became Greensboro.

Opposition to slavery was a fundamental tenet of Quaker belief. North Carolina was a slave colony, however, and conflicts around the issue of slavery increased as the Quaker settlement took root and became permanent. The largest concentration of black slaves was located in the eastern part of the colony nearer the Atlantic coast, but there were slaves in the Piedmont. Despite their strong antislavery policy, some Quakers purchased and owned slaves.

In an effort to address this extreme contradiction between belief and practice, the North Carolina Meetings (their term for individual groups), or some of them, took the position that Quaker slaveowners must make concrete steps toward manumitting their slaves, a sort of early "with all deliberate speed" doctrine.

After the Revolutionary War, and after North Carolina became a state, in an effort to invent a way out of their dilemma, some of the meetings, including New Garden, established a board of trustees empowered to *purchase* slaves owned by their own members. The idea was to hold them until they could be legally manumitted, which could only be done by the North Carolina legislature. This didn't work. Once this practice became known, "group manumission" was bitterly attacked by proslavery advocates. They even sued the Quakers and eventually won a judgment in the state supreme court in 1827.

Another attempt at freeing slaves was made through the formation of the North Carolina Manumission Society in 1816; New Garden was a prominent member. Essentially, this effort was doomed before it started. A large and growing contingent of black freedmen was simply not wanted in North Carolina. The cost of transporting ex-slaves north to free states like Pennsylvania, Ohio, or Indiana was considerable. Finally, some northern antislavery moderates, along with some southerners who believed slavery to be morally objectionable thereupon advocated returning ex-slaves to West Africa.

This was the policy of the American Colonization Society (founded in 1816), which created the nation of Liberia in 1821 to receive ex-slaves. Strong northern abolitionists like William Lloyd Garrison were staunch opponents of colonization; they preached the complete eradication of slavery throughout the South. So did the antislavery wing of the North Carolina Quakers, including most prominently, the Coffin family of New Garden. Levi Coffin (1798–1877), along with others of his group, angrily split off from the North Carolina Manumission Society because Coffin believed the Society was really interested in removing free blacks from North Carolina, rather than limiting and suppressing slavery. Coffin instead resorted to helping slaves escape northward via the Underground Railroad, by which escapees were shielded and aided along a chain of "stations" or safe houses owned by sympathetic whites as they worked their way, by foot usually, northward to "free states." Coffin's New Garden home was one of the earliest stations; in his post-Civil War writing he mentioned a cave on his property that was used as a hiding place for black escapees.

But finally Coffin himself, coming to terms with the increasingly hardened defense of slavery in North Carolina and the deeper South, abandoned New Garden in 1826 and moved to Indiana, selling his homestead. Others who were like-minded followed. Not all left, however, and the settlement continued essentially as a self-contained religious entity. But Quaker antislavery agitation in North Carolina ceased.

I was fascinated by the story of the Quakers in Greensboro and North Carolina because I attended a Quaker high school in Poughkeepsie, New York, for one year after I completed high school in New Orleans. Traveling to Poughkeepsie by automobile from New Orleans with my parents (in 1947) was my first trip to the North and the entire business unfolded like a mystery to me. Why my father decided to send me to Oakwood School (along with my younger brothers, Ben and Walter, who also attended Quaker Haverford College), I never knew, though I'm sure it had to do with what he had heard of the Quaker beliefs on race.

I found the Quaker world difficult to adjust to: no formal church service, no preacher, no pulpit, no talking during service, no singing or instrumental music except on special occasions. There were group study periods at night; there was no talking. Having been raised in one of the noisiest and most musical cities in America, and living in a northern white world for the first time in my life, the Oakwood School required a major adjustment, which I never really made.

One of my strongest memories is the dean of men's scrapbook documenting the hardships of his "alternative service" as a pacifist and conscientious objector during World War II. These photographs depicted the harsh labor COs were sentenced to; their emaciated bodies resulted from intense fasting. I was most struck by the dean's pride in his self-sacrifice based on principle, even in the face of a uniformly patriotic war against Hitler. His unwillingness to bear arms under the circumstances and the suffering he and others like him endured were my earliest lesson in the cost of unpopular but principled behavior. I always remembered him when I later encountered others who made similar sacrifices because of their beliefs.

After leaving Guilford College, I decided to drive around the area to see what I could find of New Garden or the Coffin Underground Railroad sites. I tried to follow old maps, which led me to the woods behind Guilford, where it was rumored that caves that had harbored runaways might still exist. I didn't find anything of that sort. As far as I could determine, the Jefferson Standard Country Club now occupies the site of old New Garden. The country club had posted NO TRESPASSING signs for nonmembers, and I decided I would probably only end up on a golf course, and rather than repeat the George Simkins experience of thirty-five years ago, I decided to call it a day.

⌒

I'm at the truck stop restaurant near the I-85 exit again. I'm trying to piece together my notes on my last night in Greensboro. This is one of the few twenty-four-hour places in town, frequented by white and (a few) black drivers on their way to destinations north, south, east, and west. I have come to rather like the solace. The booths are spacious, each has its own telephone; the customers and waitresses don't stare at me as if I'm an alien from another planet; "aliens" are the crux of their business.

I could sit here in the restaurant, reflect on the day's discoveries, make notes, and though I might have aroused the curiosity of some, no one asked questions. For all they knew, I was writing letters home. From inside, I could actually hear the interstate traffic, a sort of music wrought from the growling of huge engines, the true music of Greensboro.

The restaurant seems to be owned, or at least managed, by white women. The cook is a middle-aged black woman who keeps up a lively chatter with the waitress-managers, a conversation that has nothing to do with food. A black youth of about twenty mops the floor, busses the tables, tends the shower stalls and bathrooms. This place reminds me of train depot restaurants of the Old South, with the same sort of blue-collar anything-goes atmosphere, only here blacks are present both as customers and workers and, as far as I can see, everyone seems to get along. This is the New South stripped to bare bones. Not that different from the Old South. Whites still own it. All the racial pushing and shoving of the past thirty or forty years has sort of come to this rather unglamorous adjustment, settled onto a tenuous peg of biracial accommodation.

Tenuous, because, as I reflected on my experiences during these past three weeks, I found it difficult to easily summarize the result, at that point, 1991, of Greensboro's remarkable racial struggles and troubles. On one hand, blacks have achieved the surface changes they had first fought for. Where once were FOR WHITES ONLY signs, explicit or implicit, now such racial proscriptions are only a memory, though a vivid one. Now blacks can go to any restaurant, and be seated anywhere. Whereas once blacks were treated like serfs at downtown clothing stores, now blacks can spend their hard-earned dollars at any clothing store, try on all the clothes one wishes, while being addressed as "sir" or "ma'am," quite possibly by a young clerk of color, male or female. Simkins and his friends had to sue to use the public golf course; now they can march around the course like they own it. Whereas sitting in a movie house, theater, or concert hall in the same section with whites was once considered unthinkable and at best foolhardy, in 1991 those old taboos aren't given a second thought. Whereas once the only employment men of color could find in white businesses was as handyman, janitor, elevator operator, or unskilled laborer in factories, and women worked most commonly as domestic servants, now a goodly sprinkling of well-dressed and well-spoken black men and women occupy managerial jobs in those businesses, provided they "get along," of course, and don't forget who signs their checks. School desegregation is well under way, though not without complaints—now from blacks.

Beneath the surface, however, change does occur more slowly than we wish, is more difficult to assess, and is not immune to unanticipated consequences and dismaying reversals.

In Greensboro, black-owned businesses are in obvious decline. That is not a small loss, for the economic strength of the entire black community, or any intact community anywhere, depends on the strength of economic institutions owned by those who reside, or identify with, that community. Businesses reinvest resources derived from whatever prosperity they enjoy. The death of businesses and the increasing limiting of middle- or high-income jobs to those with training and education is helping to drive a wedge between blacks who are able to take advantage of new opportunities and those who are spending their time rummaging through want ads in search of employment. This is a change of enormous paradoxical significance: Before southern society opened a bit, blacks could look at each other and say, "No matter how well-off or poor we are, we're all in the same boat because of the color of our skin," though that statement was usually made with more regret than pride. Now we're talking about two "boats" sailing farther and farther apart. A few blacks have benefited from a more open southern society, and the new opportunities for education and employment. But most blacks have not been in a position to take advantage of post-1960s opportunities.

Greensboro seems to have smoothly absorbed the protests of the sixties and seventies. The town has opened up just to a certain point. Then, as Sol Jacobs said, it "refused to turn the corner" toward an economically more equitable society.

One other thing about Greensboro that struck me as highly significant was how ineffective the old biracial coalition, if that's what the Richmond memorial represented, had become, when faced with issues of economic disparity. The once-effective protests, marches, boycotts, and so forth have become obsolete, for there is no concrete entity to protest or boycott. In Greensboro, you can choose to be aware of an underclass, or you can look away, not noticing any blemishes at all in what has become a smooth, bright mask of posttrauma adjustment to racial and economic conflict.

A black truck driver who seemed to be in his twenties entered the restaurant. He chose a booth with none of the old fear of the pre-1960s. I assumed the truck stop was part of his regular route. Within a few minutes, he was conversing with an older white man in the adjacent booth who I assumed was also a driver; just a conversation, without obsequious smiling or overpoliteness. I heard smatterings of their talk about the weather, the road, what they were trucking. Of course, this sort of conversation follows a certain etiquette of omission: no mention of race, the Klan, criticism of the Persian Gulf war or the national administration, homelessness, joblessness, or crime. Those issues remain submerged below the surface, lest there be an unpleasant polarization of ideas and perceived truths. On the jukebox, music alternated between rhythm and blues and country and western, a kind of musical separate peace.

This sort of conversation between blacks and whites existed in a half-light, but it was real, represented a small degree of change, a sort of unpaved road running underneath the superhighways of racial rhetoric and ideology.

Will the other towns I visit be this complex and tenuous and difficult to comprehend, I wondered? Tomorrow I am departing for the deeper South, for Orangeburg, South Carolina, and we can only see what we see.

# ORANGEBURG

Orangeburg, South Carolina, is the next stop on my journey southward. I chose Orangeburg because it was the site of one of the most blatantly violent reactions to student demonstrations during the period of intense southern black activism. Three young people were killed and twenty-seven injured on February 8, 1968, when state and local police fired onto the campus of South Carolina State University. Yet this tragedy drew little national attention. It was literally overwhelmed by ever more traumatic historic events in 1968: the assassination of Martin Luther King, Jr., in April; the murder of presidential candidate Robert Kennedy in June; the decision of President Lyndon Johnson in the summer to withdraw from the presidential election of 1968; and, finally, the election of Richard Nixon to the presidency in November. Few people outside of South Carolina knew where Orangeburg was; fewer still had even heard of South Carolina State University. The explanation that a "shoot-out" with the police had occurred, that three people lost their lives, and that the conflict began with a dispute over a segregated bowling alley seemed bizarre, totally nonsensical.

Never having visited Orangeburg, I was anxious to discover how much the town itself, and the school—South Carolina's only four-year college for blacks—had to do with the violence of 1968. And I wanted to know how the shootings are remembered if they are remembered) in the Orangeburg of 1991.

I am headed northward from Charleston on Interstate 26. I'm carefully plowing through a slashing torrential rain, debating whether to pull over and wait until it slacks up. Orangeburg is about twenty miles away.

It's been two months since I departed Greensboro on February 5. Instead of traveling directly to Orangeburg from there, I decided to take a detour to the biannual African film festival, FESPACO, in Ouagadougou, Burkina Faso. When I returned to New Orleans in early March, I ran into car trouble. I didn't feel it was smart to get back on the road until I was assured my 1988 Chevy Nova was working perfectly, so it wasn't until Saturday, March 30, that I left New Orleans for South Carolina.

Even though my destination was Orangeburg, I decided to detour to Charleston to meet my old friend from Mississippi days, Myrtle Glascoe. Myrtle is now director of the Avery Research Center at the College of Charleston. Since I knew no one in Orangeburg, I was hoping Myrtle could suggest interviewees. I planned to visit Charleston upon leaving Orangeburg; I was hoping Myrtle could help me there as well.

At the intersection of four-lane Highway 301, I exited and drove six miles westward until I arrived at the outskirts of Orangeburg. Mercifully, the rain had slowed to a drizzle, and before I settled on a motel, I decided to look around to see if I could get a sense of the place.

The town of Orangeburg, with a population of about thirteen thousand, struck me as an ideal location for a 1940s movie set located in the mythical small-town South. Freshly painted frame houses, generous front lawns, well-tended gardens, the main downtown street lined with shops that seemed to have existed as long as the town itself. Main Street was crowned by the obligatory statue honoring Confederate Army gallantry.

Driving to the end of the main street, which is called Russell Street, I arrived at the Edisto River, not much of a river, but a long one that winds southward through central South Carolina for about 150 miles. A city park and garden has been built on the banks of the river, a pleasant park that sort of completes Orangeburg's image of itself as a pleasant southern town.

Returning along the five- or six-block commercial downtown, I arrived at an intersection of double-bed railroad tracks. Across those tracks is located the quite considerable campus of South Carolina State University. Also fronting the tracks and adjacent to South Carolina State is Claflin College, a Reconstruction black

Methodist school, from which State was created in 1896, though they are separate colleges.

As a state university for blacks, South Carolina State is not nearly as large or well funded as North Carolina A&T in Greensboro. But I thought State's campus was more attractive than A&T's. Claflin appears worn and seems in decline. There is a black neighborhood across the tracks from the campuses, and what appears to have been a small black commercial area. Near there I located an inexpensive motel, and settled in.

~

My first contact was photographer Cecil Williams, who is related to close friends in New York. With directions precise to the tenth of a mile, Williams invited me to his studio located in a housing development of substantial black homes on the outskirts of town. A native of Orangeburg, and in his early forties, the gracious Williams spoke of his love of photography since his early teen years (an interest I share with him), and his work, which began while he was in high school, for the state NAACP photographing blacks who had been beaten up or killed as a result of racially motivated assaults or police abuse.

"How did three people end up getting killed in 1968?" I asked.

Williams responded that the events of 1968 were the culmination of a long series of protests waged by blacks in Orangeburg, "a town with a history of being *extremely* racially divided." Orangeburg was also, Williams made sure I knew, a town of considerable black achievement because of its universities and educated professional elite. Be that as it may, Williams added, the black elite was as cut off from the controlling white economic and political leaders as the poorest blacks in the county.

~

The town of Orangeburg was settled in 1732 in central South Carolina. It is the second oldest town in the state after Charleston. Once the Native Americans were "removed," Orangeburg County, the largest and most central in the state, thrived on the acquisition of land and slaves, though not as many slaves were imported as were along the Carolina coast. Isolated from the aristocracy that developed around Charleston and the Sea Islands, the planters in central South Carolina raised cotton, pecans, soybeans, and cattle. Once the colony became a state, the Orangeburg planters continually fought Charleston for control of the South Carolina legislature.

Orangeburg was a leader in the repression of the considerable black political activity that followed in the wake of Emancipation. It is important to remember that for a period of about ten years, there were more blacks in the South Carolina legislature than in the legislature of any other southern state. Then, when Reconstruction was overthrown in the South in the 1880s, Orangeburg County was as repressive as any other in central South Carolina in suppressing the black vote and economic independence through violence.

In the post-World War II period, Orangeburg was the state headquarters of the archconservative John Birch Society, and later, the White Citizens Council. In the wake of the 1954 *Brown* decision, the South Carolina Association of Independent Schools was created in Orangeburg, designed to foster private schools for whites (seg academies) if and when public school desegregation ever began. When public school desegregation didn't begin in the wake of *Brown*, about fifty black teachers signed a petition to the school board demanding implementation. The petitions were summarily denied, and many of the black petitioners lost their jobs.

In retaliation, the black community imposed a selective buying campaign on downtown Orangeburg. James Sulton, a tall, light-skinned patrician gentleman whom I visited later while in Orangeburg, was one of the leaders in this effort. "Our boycott was effective," he remembers, "because those businesses depended on our patronage." In an effort to sink the boycott, the Orangeburg White Citizens Council exerted pressure on the boycott leaders, including Sulton. "They cut off my supplies and my credit. During this period, when we were virtually at war, the publisher of the newspaper called me in for a chat. My family is one of the oldest black families in the county; his family was one of the oldest white families. I suppose he thought all he had to do was call me in and tell *me* to call off the boycott, and it would be done. I didn't know him. He acted like he thought I should identify with his economic interests. I walked out of there without saying another word. We kept right on going."

In 1963 students from State and Claflin inflicted sit-ins upon downtown Orangeburg, emulating black students in southern towns everywhere. Finally, as a result of the 1964 Civil Rights Act, by 1968 just about all the Russell Street businesses had desegregated, though this did not mean there was any real interracial communication.

As we discussed this history, Cecil Williams told me that South Carolina State was ignored by the white political and economic establishment. "Most towns would have seen the school as an asset. Not here. Except for patronage of downtown businesses, State was treated as if it didn't exist. No wonder the situation turned nasty when State students became aggressive and defiant in 1968."

In 1967 and early 1968 a group of State students attempted to use a bowling alley in a small Russell Street mall, not more than four blocks from the campus. All-Star Lanes happened to be the only bowling alley in town, but it boldly displayed a window sign reading FOR WHITES ONLY. The owner, Harry Floyd, contended that All-Star Lanes was a private business, which was like a private club not a public business; therefore, he was not subject to the open-accommodations provisions of the 1964 Civil Rights Act, and if he didn't want black customers, that policy was up to him. State students complained, and an attempt was made by State University officials to determine *if* the lanes indeed came within federal regulations. But they never obtained a definitive answer. There were attempts to negotiate a weekly night or two when blacks could use the facility. However, by February 1968, the owner still had his FOR WHITES ONLY sign prominently displayed in the window.

John Stroman, a senior at State, was the driving force behind the effort to desegregate the bowling alley. An experienced bowler, he had pointed out time after time that the closest lanes available to blacks were in Columbia, a forty-mile drive. None of this may have mattered to those who didn't bowl, which was the overwhelming majority of State students. But it mattered to Stroman and his friends who did bowl, and they wouldn't let the issue die. Disgusted that no progress had been made, Stroman and a few of his supporters decided to force a confrontation. On Monday, February 5, 1968, about forty students, led by Stroman, pushed their way into the bowling alley, demanded service, and were refused. The owner then closed the alley for the night.

The next night Stroman returned to the bowling alley with a far larger group of students, an estimated 300 to 400. That night virtually the entire Orangeburg police force was waiting for them along with a contingent of state highway patrol- men. The police arrested one young man who tried to force his way into the bowling alley; then they turned on the crowd of students and began to beat them.

Two aspects of this police action particularly incensed the students. Women students were beaten along with the men, and just as harshly, which was thought to be unnecessary. Second, in the midst of the melee, the police called a fire truck, which though not used against the students, invoked memories of the 1963 student sit-ins, when demonstrators were hosed.

Angry and suffering from the beatings, the students retreated across the railroad tracks to the campus in an ugly mood. Some of them vented their rage against businesses along the way, smashing windows and inflicting damage. What had begun as a protest against a bowling alley, a dispute that might have easily been settled by city authorities, or any authority, had now opened up a far more serious wound, involving virtually the entire State student body, along with sympathizers from Claflin.

Making matters worse, on Wednesday, February 7, Governor Robert E. McNair called in 250 national guardsmen to help control the situation. Almost all the guardsmen were white. Efforts by college officials to negotiate with the city au- thorities and the governor were unsuccessful. Instead, city officials made one of their rare trips to the State campus to attempt to address the situation, and possibly to make a belated attempt to explain themselves, but in a scene reminiscent of the Governor Hodges fiasco at A&T, they were hooted down when it was obvious they had come with no solutions or adequate responses to what by now had become a growing list of grievances against segregation in Orangeburg. The bowling alley was just a beginning. That night, throughout the night, bottles and rocks were thrown at the police, who hovered along the railroad tracks and the street fronting the campus.

On the morning of February 8 the railroad tracks in front of the campus were occupied by a phalanx of police—highway patrolmen as well as city police—and national guardsmen. The campus had been cut off from the downtown area. Acting president M. Maceo Nance, Jr., tried to calm students and restrain them from going to the front edge of the campus. The students were fired up, however, and Nance's warning had little effect. Throughout the day, a group of students taunted the police and guardsmen. That night it was cold and some of the students decided to build a bonfire in the street in the front of the campus, with the police lined up along the tracks. By 9:30 P.M. the bonfire was ablaze. The police thereupon decided to put it out. They called for the fire truck once again.

When the firemen arrived, they were afraid to extinguish the bonfire without police protection, so a squad of highway patrolmen moved up on the sidewalk directly fronting the campus, which was marked by about a six-foot grass embankment. At that point, the two hundred or so students who were congregated at the front of the campus and on the sidewalk quickly retreated to the rear, grumbling and cursing the police. They gathered at a men's dormitory about four hundred feet deep into the campus. (The dormitory was the building closest to the front.) While they were retreating, someone in their group threw a banister toward the huddled policemen. The banister had been extracted from a vacant house on the left side of the campus, though the house was not part of the campus. (Most of the wood to make the bonfire had also been torn from this structure.) The banister hit a patrolman (who never saw it coming) in the face and knocked him out. He was bleeding profusely. A rumor quickly spread among the other patrolmen that the injured officer had been shot in the head.

Reacting within seconds to the felling of the patrolman, a squad of highway patrolmen moved right up to the grass embankment at the front of the campus, raising their weapons. At the same time a few students, apparently angry at themselves for having run away a few minutes earlier, began to drift back toward the front to resume taunting the policemen, the nearest of them about one hundred feet from the embankment.

A few seconds later, at about ten-forty, several patrolmen from two positions opened fire. Terrified, the students tried to run back to the safety of the dormitory. The shooting lasted eight to ten seconds.

Three students were killed—Henry Smith, Sam Hammond, and Delano Middleton, a high school football player whose mother worked as a maid on the campus. Twenty-seven were wounded, "all but two or three from the rear or side," reported Jack Bass and Jack Nelson in their book on the shootings, *The Orangeburg Massacre.*

"I knew the police were capable of opening fire, but I was still surprised," remembers Jack McCray, who was then a student at Claflin College, and among those on the State campus that night. McCray is now a reporter for the *Charleston News-Courier.* I interviewed him in Charleston at the newspaper office before my drive to Orangeburg. McCray said he was standing toward the rear of the campus and was not hit, but he will never forget that night. "It sounded like the shooting lasted forever," he said. "I thought I saw tracer bullets, which the police denied they used. I could hear the bullets going by.

"After the shooting stopped, everyone ran to the school infirmary. Those who had been hit were carried in by other students." At the infirmary the one nurse on duty did the best she could to patch up the wounded, then she sent them on to the town hospital emergency room. "Even so," said McCray, "we felt we were cut off. The police had sealed off the campus so that city ambulances couldn't enter. Students drove those wounded to the hospital in their own cars.

"We thought the police were going to invade the campus later that night and shoot us in our dormitories. There was just a fear, and we were concerned about defending ourselves. We felt we were totally unprotected. The electricity was turned off in the dorms; so were the utilities. The telephones were off. There was no way to get word out to our families about what had occurred.

"That night an Orangeburg radio station went on civil defense. We heard the announcer thanking the National Guard for protecting 'us' from 'them.' We were the 'them,' of course. That night all the racial masks fell off. We were to be suppressed at any cost."

In the immediate aftermath of the shootings, local and state political officials were quick to blame Cleve Sellers, the former program director of SNCC, for radicalizing and inciting the State students, in the way that Nelson Johnson was blamed for the 1969 violence in Greensboro. Sellers had moved to Orangeburg in October 1967 in the wake of SNCC's bitter factional disintegration. Once there, he organized an Afrocentric student group at State, called BACC (Black Awareness Coordinating Committee). As a native of nearby Denmark, South Carolina, Sellers felt quite at home in Orangeburg, a town he had visited many times as a youth. He had returned with his family to live in his native Denmark in the wake of the death of his parents, and I arranged to interview him at his home there. Denmark is only twenty miles from Orangeburg. Now about fifty, and having earned his Ph.D. in education, Sellers vividly recalled that time twenty-three years ago. "All I did was try to help the students broaden their horizons, mostly through lectures and discussions, which they desperately needed, because they weren't getting much at State. I certainly was not interested in bowling. So I didn't have anything to do with the original protests.

"When the students were beaten at the bowling alley two nights before the shooting, however, I thought I might be able to help because of my experience with SNCC demonstrations. You wouldn't believe the violence in the air; we desperately needed to defuse the situation. But there was no viable outlet for student anger at State, or in Orangeburg.

"On the night of the shootings I was on the campus, where, foolishly, I thought I would be safe. My first thought when I saw the bad scene at the front of the campus was to ask the students to move back. Then the shooting started. Like everyone else, I ran away from it toward the rear. We could only see the top of the state patrolmen's heads, because they were firing from behind the grass embankment. I was hit in the left shoulder. I really felt I was lucky not to have been killed.

"When the firing stopped, I ran to the infirmary. The nurse did all she could for me and others who were hit. Everyone was in shock. I was shocked because I felt we were well within our boundaries. After Henry Smith was fatally wounded, the police dragged him downhill themselves and took him to the emergency room. He was dead before they reached the hospital."

Because Sellers was considered one of the leading SNCC radicals, he was a marked man when he moved to Orangeburg in 1967 to organize State students. "The nurse in the State infirmary insisted I go to the hospital. I didn't want to go because I was worried about being recognized. Finally, we found a player on the football team to drive me to the hospital and act as my bodyguard. When we arrived at the hospital, the deputies pointed a gun at my bodyguard and told him he couldn't enter the emergency room. While I was in the emergency room being worked on, a black deputy recognized me, and within a few minutes the sheriff was there with his men. They bandaged me in a hurry, rushed me to the county courthouse, and charged me with, can you believe this, arson, inciting to riot, assault and battery with intent to kill, destruction of personal property, damaging real property, house-breaking and grand larceny." The city magistrate set bond at $50,000.

"Then," he laughed, "they let me have a telephone call. I called my attorney Howard Moore in Atlanta and told him, 'Howard, I'm in a little trouble up here in Orangeburg.' Then they rushed me to Columbia at one hundred fifteen miles per hour, called the warden at Central Correctional, and threw me in jail. I remained there until Howard Moore and Matthew Perry [then an NAACP attorney; now federal district judge] arrived and bailed me out."

I was amazed at how similar the Orangeburg conflict was to the pattern of racial hostility that exploded into violence in Greensboro a year later. The Orangeburg shootings were also a prototype for similar police shootings at other black state college campuses in the South during the following three or four years. Students were killed at Jackson State University in Mississippi, Texas Southern University in Houston, and Southern University in Baton Rouge. This was a total reversal of the policy of accepting black college campuses as a sanctuary. It was as if there was a conscious or subconscious attempt to directly attack the youth of the black community, who were seen (properly) by the authorities as the heart and soul of ever-escalating protests.

I wondered why the administrations of such institutions were not able to prevent violent confrontations. Cleve Sellers pointed out that at Orangeburg, as the situation worsened, there was no viable mechanism for the expression of grievances, which hopefully might lead to resolution, or at least a cooling-off period. Also, I felt, since the advent of the sit-ins in 1960, black college presidents had adopted a hands-off policy toward off-campus student demonstrations. They couldn't control or stop demonstrations anyway; besides, they wanted to avoid being held responsible by the controlling white governmental officials if there was any way to legitimately do so. Most black state college presidents were simply impotent, or baffled, when it came to protests against segregation, or even protests against them as presidents. It didn't help that when students engaged in town protests, local authorities too often ignored the influence the college administrators might have had; instead, they brought in a large police presence, which almost always made things worse, particularly if the police were inexperienced in handling demonstrations.

It should have been possible for the president of State to call up the mayor of Orangeburg, or someone in authority, and say, "Listen, we've got a bad situation developing here. The last thing we need is the National Guard, which only serves to infuriate my students. Can't you tell this guy he's got to open up the bowling alley whether he likes it or not. If he doesn't, close him down and take his license and let him go to court if he wants to. But we can't have one man creating a situation where a lot of people might get hurt."

The president of South Carolina State in February 1968, M. Maceo Nance, Jr. (actually he was then acting president), had retired in 1986, and was living in Orangeburg. I called him, explained what I was doing, and Nance was quite willing to talk. I was able to see him early on the following Saturday morning.

We met in the den of the comfortable Nance family home. Relaxed, easygoing, and soft-spoken, Nance gave me the impression he was a natural-born politician without the crassness of so many natural politicians. A native of Columbia, Nance served in World War II, entered State in 1946, graduated in 1949, married an Orangeburg girl, the daughter of the State business manager, and worked in the business office where his father-in-law was chief financial officer, a job that he inherited. In 1967, when President Benner C. Turner was retired as a result of a barrage of student protests, Nance was named acting president, and finally, president. Without directly addressing my question concerning the impotence and alienation of black state college presidents, Nance began by saying, "Everything that could go wrong went wrong.

"Orangeburg is so conservative, Tom, that for a long time there were *no* inter-racial contacts. The presence of a black intelligentsia here created fear among whites, not pride. They never took advantage of what the colleges had to offer." That is what everyone else had said. "The bowling alley was the straw that broke the camel's back. What made it so bad was that every other business in that shopping mall was open to us, was aggressively soliciting campus business, and getting it. To put up a FOR WHITES ONLY sign was just asking for trouble. The city *could* have closed the bowling alley if they had been on top of the situation. But when we tried to communicate, we just fell on deaf ears. There was no marriage of town and gown, except, of course, when local businesses wanted our patronage.

"As for the shootings, every time we thought we had defused the situation, something else happened to throw more fuel on the fire. Like, for instance, the police bringing the fire trucks in on the night of the shootings. That was so stupid, the fire didn't have to be put out; it wasn't much anyway, and once they did it..." His voice trailed off. "There was never a shot from the campus that anyone has ever proven. But the troopers opened fire from a prone position like they expected to be fired upon. I had just come home from the office when the shootings occurred. Someone called me. I rushed back to the campus. From that point on, it was a real nightmare. I remember spending most of that night trying to calm down students, because many of them were trying to find weapons to retaliate. We would have had a bloodbath.

"Now, remember, for black college presidents there were no precedents for the kinds of demonstrations that occurred in the sixties, or for the kinds of police action that followed. We just had to play it by ear. We were buffeted from one end to the other by insistent and extremely contrary demands, hoping we were doing the right thing."

Following the tragedy, Nance adopted a redemptive policy, putting his political skills to work building support for State. To accomplish this end in the state legislature he found, or converted, a former segregationist state senator, the late Marion Gressette of the nearby town of St. Matthews, into a key ally and advocate. "Clemson and the University of South Carolina had their backers in the assembly. We would never have gotten anywhere until we had someone to carry our banner, and there were not enough blacks in the legislature in the seventies to do it, so we had to put together a coalition, and Gressette played a key role."

During Nance's tenure as president the State campus grew steadily, including the addition of a handsome new structure dedicated to Martin Luther King, Jr., located near where the thirty students were shot (three dead and twenty-seven wounded).

Nance instituted a memorial program for the three slain youths, which is held each February 8. The memory of Delano Middleton, Henry Smith, and Samuel Hammond, Jr., is also enhanced by an impressive and beautifully maintained monument at the center of the campus, and the naming of a new athletic center for them. So, on the State campus at least, there is a quite considerable effort to memorialize the victims of 1968, though students in 1991 may not know exactly how or why these memorials exist. "I served as president of State for *eighteen* years," Nance stated passionately. "During that time I wasn't a handkerchief head and I could have been. I didn't forget anything. Of all the things I accomplished I'm most proud of that."

Maceo Nance thought it would be helpful to speak with Dean Livingston, the editor/publisher of the *Orangeburg Times-Democrat*. I called Livingston, and after a couple of misses, we met at the newspaper's offices in downtown Orangeburg. They were modern offices. "We're completely computerized," Livingston proudly pointed out, as we walked to his private desk. Though not a native, Livingston seemed to have found a situation he liked in Orangeburg and had done well. My impression was that though he views the society he lives in with a firm sense of reality, he is not the kind of person to lead a crusade for social change.

When I asked about biracial bridges in Orangeburg, or the lack thereof, Livingston was unstinting in his praise for Nance's efforts. "Nance put together a successful legislative coalition after the shootings," he echoed, "and that was the only way to do it, because everything in this state is moved by politics. Even the governor became more aware of State and its needs." On the other hand, Benner Turner, the previous president, didn't make such an effort. "He didn't want State to be part of Orangeburg. I met with him on many occasions and had difficulty figuring him out." No one who spoke of Turner had anything good to say about him; he was a man reputed to be unusually stiff and elitist. But I didn't see where it was the sole responsibility of blacks to bridge the racial divide, or how they could do it with segregation as strongly in place as it was. Turner's world, as described by Livingston, and earlier by Jack McCray and Cecil Williams, was one of a separate, small, black professional elite. Theirs might have been a bitter reaction against exclusion from the surrounding white society, I thought, taking out their frustration on other blacks they felt superior to. Shunning civil rights activism when it occurred, and mirroring the race and class prejudices of the controlling white society, they constituted a phenomenon that is not uncommon in southern towns.

"Has there been significant movement toward biraciality recently?" I inquired of Livingston.

He mentioned the new municipal Hillcrest Golf Course, "which is the first integrated golf course," a project Nance and Livingston worked together to bring about.

"Is that all?" I asked.

"That's about it. But don't forget"—he smiled—"this is golf country." As golf goes, so goes racial progress, I joked to myself. "Of course, blacks are hired now in all sorts of jobs, where they weren't before. But this is a county of old families with old money, and the town has always been a center of commerce. I came here as a poor boy, and I never would have been accepted except for the fact I was in the newspaper business, which gave me special credentials.

"State has gained more influence, no doubt about it, but the city's nonaffiliated blacks are not well represented in the political equation, and they resent it. In fact, no one is looking out for poor whites or poor blacks. That means the next big social eruption is going to come from them. Unless there's some change, that's sure to happen."

Livingston was an eyewitness to the shootings in 1968. I asked him what he remembered about that night now.

"Fear. I was very fearful, and surprised. I was moving around between the patrolmen and the students. With all the firepower the police had, it wasn't going to take much for an eruption to happen. When I was a student, I saw kids lose control—then it was panty raids. They were students being students. No one could conceive of anyone being shot.

"I'll tell you one thing. This was a frightened community after that, even the encrusted whites were frightened, because they learned there was an awesome force of violence they could be confronted with."

~

The official version of the shootings put out by the governor was that the state patrolmen returned fire in self-defense when fired upon. The first information to hit the press about the death of the three students implied they were killed during a "shoot-out" with police. Later, when it was clear no shooting by students had precipitated the firing by officers, and there was conclusive evidence that most of the students had been shot from the rear or while on the ground, the account was modified to include the story of the patrolman being hit by the banister, which was considered "life threatening." Therefore, the patrolmen had opened fire in self-defense.

After a long investigation by the Justice Department, which included testimony from the officers and the wounded students, all of the patrolmen who fired were acquitted in March 1969. No further prosecution was attempted. Cleve Sellers notes that the highway patrolmen who fired their weapons were also eventually promoted.

~

Myrtle Glascoe of Avery Institute in Charleston suggested I talk to Dr. Rickey Hill of the South Carolina State Political Science Department, citing his studies on race and politics in South Carolina. I called him and we set up a time to meet at his office on the campus.

I decided to go early, however, in order to examine the campus more closely. First, I took a close look at the embankment from which the shootings took place. The embankment was still there, but lowered, and a parking lot is now situated just beyond it. Behind the parking area is a new administration building. Facing the campus, to the left of the administration building, is the new Martin Luther King, Jr., Auditorium. To the rear of the administration building is Lowman Hall, the dormitory to which the students retreated when the firemen arrived to put out the bonfire. The short street in front of the campus is still there, but the new structures and parking lot obscure the site of the shootings. The railroad tracks, of course, are still there, and trains still run in front of the campus.

Walking toward the rear of the campus, I came across the stone memorial to the three slain students, surrounded by circular shrubbery at an intersection of walkways. It was impressive and well designed. To the rear, more dormitories, a library, and the gymnasium, named the Smith-Hammond-Middleton Athletic Center. This is an attractive campus.

While I was on my walking tour, I wandered over to the library, where I met Barbara Jenkins, the head librarian. Cecil Williams had recommended her as extremely knowledgeable about State and Orangeburg. Ms. Jenkins was indeed knowledgeable, though unsmiling. Born in Union, South Carolina, her family moved to Orangeburg when her father became state supervisor of agricultural extension work, with offices on the State campus. Attending Orangeburg public schools, graduating from Bennett College in 1955, and after that earning her M.A. in library science, she then returned to State to work. Ms. Jenkins has served as head librarian since 1962.

"As far as changes since the sixties are concerned around here," she began, "society has opened up for those who can afford it. For those who can't, there has been no change." She cited the poverty and hardship of most State students who live in primarily rural areas. "The loss of federal benefits hurts our students tremendously; a very high percentage of them are on financial aid. There are too many from broken homes and so forth. The high schools they finish from aren't good, so we're getting a large percentage of students who aren't really prepared for college work. And then there's a general lack of discipline."

As for Orangeburg itself, Ms. Jenkins was equally caustic. "Blacks have jobs in town now, but you have to look at the level of jobs—very few managers. Okay, black physicians and nurses work in the hospital. We have black policemen. As far as school integration is concerned, there is a new comprehensive high school for blacks and those whites who don't go to Orangeburg Prep. But in the process black teachers and principals lost out. Black students are not doing well academically. And there's a movement away from the teaching profession on the part of younger blacks with talent, just when they're needed."

In this same vein, Mr. Nance, commenting on what blacks lost as a result of limited desegregation, had said that State was "suffering from a brain drain—we're not getting the top black students" who could win scholarships to the bigger universities. "Black Ph.D.s want to work where they can get the highest salaries, so I had to hire foreign teachers because we have to have a certain number of Ph.D.s, and I was criticized for that. We're caught between a rock and a hard place. On one hand, we have to address students at their learning level when they come here. On the other hand, we have to keep up academic standards no matter where the students are; otherwise we can't call ourselves a college."

From the library I went to meet Rickey Hill at his office. I was surprised to learn he is from Bogalusa, Louisiana, a town located north of Lake Pontchartrain on the Pearl River very near the Mississippi state line. Bogalusa is one Louisiana town that has experienced strong racial and union organizing. Hill said he was "raised in activism," though a bit too late for the civil rights movement of the early 1960s. Now in his early forties (I guessed), he came of age just in time for the black power/black consciousness phase of the southern movement, almost exactly paralleling the experiences of Claude Barnes in Greensboro.

Kicked out of Southern University in 1972 for his protest activities, Hill, like Barnes, bounced back with enough drive not only to complete college but to earn his Ph.D. in political science. He wrote his dissertation on the Bogalusa Movement, mirroring Barnes, whose dissertation analyzed the Greensboro Movement.

Dark skinned, youthful in spirit, harshly realistic, and without humor, Hill ran down his assessments of Orangeburg and State for me. I asked him, for fun, how he would compare Orangeburg and Bogalusa. Both towns are about the same size—Bogalusa may have a thousand more than Orangeburg's thirteen thousand. "Orangeburg is ripe for development," he replied quickly. "Bogalusa is not."

I remembered that Dean Livingston mentioned attempts by Orangeburg County to induce industries to relocate in the area, "now that air conditioning has made industrialization in the Deep South feasible." American Outdoor Products, Ethel Corporation, Hughes Aircraft, and Allied Signal, among others, are all companies that have existed or have recently located in the county.

Hill made me see Orangeburg as not so isolated as I had first thought. With its close proximity to Interstate 26 (five miles), which runs between Charleston and Columbia, and to Interstate 95 (about twenty miles), which runs from Florida to the northeast, Orangeburg is very accessible to major commercial transportation. "But none of this changes the fact that blacks are apathetic around here. The whites are politically and culturally conservative; so are the blacks." Blacks have achieved some political gains (three of seven on the County Council), "but there is no state-wide community political organization to develop issues or monitor the black electorate. Once elected, black political officials are responsible to no one.

"As for the students, they are very conservative. They even feel good about being ignorant and intolerant. It's a puzzle to me. They want jobs, but not in terms of developing a career, just money.

"They are very uncritical, unquestioning. They'll wear red, black, and green [the old Marcus Garvey colors of black liberation], but it doesn't mean anything. They'll wear clothing with Malcolm X's image on it, but I can't get them to read Malcolm. The ignorance is so overwhelming it's almost audacious. I have a struggle just to get people to want to pursue knowledge." Which must drive Hill half-crazy, since his consciousness and desire for education are direct products of a politically and racially activist background.

As for history, or knowledge of the State shootings, students are not interested. " 'We're past that. Let's not go back,' they say. There's an awful lot of interest in athletics and ROTC [military training]. That's about it."

Both Hill and Ms. Jenkins pointed to the infiltration of hard drugs into rural South Carolina as a new and ominous reality. In Orangeburg County, the easy access made possible by the interstate highways provides the same opportunities for the entrance of illegal drugs. In addition to the addiction, health problems, and violence associated with drugs, they cited the high incarceration rate among blacks, particularly young black males, the people usually involved in the low-level drug trade. "There're more black males in prison than in college," Maceo Nance had bemoaned.

While in Orangeburg, I visited a literary conference held in Columbia. While there, Myrtle Glascoe suggested I talk with Marjorie Hammock, who is the social welfare director of the South Carolina Department of Corrections, with programming responsibility for thirty-two prison facilities.

A native of Connecticut who had worked for twenty years in New York, Ms. Hammock had recently moved to South Carolina with her husband and two daughters.

"What's happening," she said, "is there is a remigration to southern states like South Carolina, because conditions in the northern cities poor blacks traditionally migrated to are worsening. One of the groups returning are those into drugs. What they're doing is creating a pervasive drug culture here. There are crack houses all over this state." I mentioned the grandfather recently arrested for drug dealing near Greenville, which I read about in the Columbia newspaper. "Older people are targeted by dealers. 'I know you're having trouble with your arthritis,' they say, 'and you don't have any money coming in. This won't hurt. All we need you to do is hold it. We'll give you a little money every week.' Innocent-looking grandmothers get caught up in this. Barbers. Undertakers. I'm amazed at the kind of people who get involved. There are just no guarantees anymore."

During our talk I mentioned the curious academic major called "criminal justice," which seems to be very popular at black colleges. "To me," she exploded, "that's a perfect example of the exploitation of those students. I resent 'criminal justice' as a degree. For one thing, it's not really taken seriously. In the way it's taught I don't see anything that involves a commitment to the black community. It's not the fault of the kids, but they're being prepared to become our own oppressors. It's the plantation all over again. For instance, the social work students I'm seeing are not being prepared to deal with people with problems. I'm not coming across innovative or interesting projects.

"This whole thing has become about jobs, and that's about it. They're told if you major in this field, you'll always work because there'll always be prisoners and prisons. That really bothers me, it really does."

⁓

"Criminal justice," I thought, sounds suspiciously like a program being pushed upon black students, probably fueled by federal money. Such programs may be fashionable now because, as Ms. Hammock pointed out, the population explosion of the incarcerated has made prison management a big business.

The development of sociology and the broader concept of "social work" among blacks were the outgrowth of an early-twentieth-century movement that emanated from settlement houses, primarily in Chicago and New York, designed to ease the passage of Eastern European immigrants into the American mainstream. Important investigative work on the status of the black community set a high standard of racial analysis and criticism. I was aware of the studies of E. Franklin Frazier, Charles S. Johnson, Ira D. A. Reid, St. Clair Drake, Gunnar Myrdal, and Kenneth Clark, among others, which profoundly impacted the defining of and direction of the African-American struggle for social justice. It was this crucial matrix that I thought Marjorie Hammock was saying was missing from the new criminal justice programs. She saw basic knowledge of social work as absolutely necessary if the new courses were to have any meaning, particularly with respect to deeper problems in the black community. "In discussing personal problems with prisoners," she had said, "and listening to the stories of how they got into trouble, I sensed that no one had ever taken the time to listen to them before, and they couldn't believe it was happening now."

My first awareness of the frightening depths of the psychological black hole that prisoners, usually at an early age, had slipped and fallen into was in the early 1960s in New York, when poet David Henderson and I placed a small advertisement in *Writer's Digest* soliciting material for our literary magazine, *Umbra*—a new journal, we noted with pride, of "racially relevant material." We were astonished at the amount of material that poured into our tiny post office box, especially from prison writers—poems, stories, novels, and autobiographical material. It was as if these people had ended up in jail, many of them for life, with absolutely no sense of what had happened to them or why. It was only now, through these elementary writings, that they hoped to connect with someone who was "listening." Reading their offerings was like listening to one mournful blues song after another day after day.

It was definitely a blues that I was hearing from those who were honestly attempting to address the basic problems in South Carolina. I came away with a feeling that they were weary and slightly overwhelmed. And yet, with its large black population, South Carolina and Orangeburg, as a symbol of its rural core, have tremendous potential for creative biracial productivity, if they will opt to use their black strength. But that would mean freedom from fear of that black strength, education for the masses, and freedom from fear of competition generated by those newly educated.

There is no indication that the majority population is ready for that. Better even to have apathy and crime than social change that upsets our age-old beliefs.

When the slightest of racial interactions did occur, even with me in my few days there, I felt like treading lightly, as if we were walking on eggs. What should I make of the overpoliteness and arched friendliness of the young white waitresses working at the coffee shops in Orangeburg? It was as if they almost believed (and were preparing to cope with by smiles) that the black aggressiveness that resulted in a smattering of racial integration was really fueled by an overwhelming desire for what has always been called, pejoratively in the South, "social equality," rather than by a desire to open the doors of opportunity. To them, "racial mixing," another pejorative code word, signified a desire for relationships across the racial line, or more. It was always blacks who wanted to racially mix, of course. These restaurant smiles were preemptive-strike defenses, and I would say the same about a noisy black waitress at a similar highway restaurant in Columbia—in both cases, the behavior was designed to defuse any hint of interracial tenseness or uncertainty.

It seemed that nightmares of slave rebellion plots still burned brightly deep in the subconscious of white South Carolina. Not to mention strategies for keeping blacks under control, the suppression of questioning even among themselves, and the romantic martyrdom of the "War Between the States" intertwined with the bitter-as-brine mythology of a horrendously evil black Reconstruction. All of this was profoundly related, I thought, to the events of 1968 in Orangeburg, which was a case of students going too far that was seen as a modern slave rebellion that must be put down as all slave rebellions must be put down, violently and suddenly, so as to render the futility of such rebellions into a lesson.

Somehow, Orangeburg and South Carolina State had survived the shootings and were moving forward at a slow but steady pace. For me, the place never lost its feel of rural isolation. I felt I was in the country, even when I was in the town. I was ready to move on to Charleston, which, though still in South Carolina, possessed a patina of romantic southern history and visual attractiveness that I was now prepared for.

# CHARLESTON

It was time to leave Orangeburg and head southeastward to Charleston and the Atlantic coast. I liked Charleston, though I had been there only for occasional visits in 1977 when I was staying at the Penn Center on St. Helena Island.

What really attracted me to Charleston, however, was its virtually unique contribution to southern civil rights history: the hospital workers' strike of 1969, a protest of immense potential consequence. Now, twenty-two years later, the strike and the massive civil rights–organized labor coalition forged to support it are barely remembered when the civil rights movement in the South is discussed.

The Charleston hospital workers' strike was important because it was such a classic example of the secondary phase of the movement, addressing fundamental economic inequities at the core of the racial and class structure of southern society. Basic civil and voting rights, the first phase—the dismantling of the walls of segregation—had essentially been accomplished by 1969. The Charleston strike was also significant because it was an attempt to gain union recognition by nonprofessional women workers aligned against a state-owned hospital, thus challenging the power of the state of South Carolina, a state in which labor unions were considered anathema. If such an effort by poor black women had succeeded, Charleston would have been a precursor for similar attempts in the Deep South. The Charleston strike also contained the potential realization of one of the most fundamental and far-reaching philosophical tenets of the civil rights movement: Once activated, powerless people will be unafraid to define their own interests and act on their own behalf, throwing away the shackles of oppression and apathy.

This particular strike was also remarkable because, in support of the striking workers, the temporary alliance between the Southern Christian Leadership Conference and organized labor was formed, though SCLC was still reeling from the assassination of its founder and leader, Martin Luther King, Jr., and Local 1199 of the Hospital and Nursing Workers of New York City had never tried to organize in the South. Such a working partnership between nationally prominent civil rights and labor organizations excited advocates of southern social and economic change because if it succeeded, there might be a bright future for agitation around issues of employment and wages.

After four months of picketing and demonstrations, in 1969 there was a settlement that provided small raises and a grievance procedure, but no clear recognition of the union was achieved. Charleston was the first and last instance of a labor–civil rights coalition in the South. In addition, since 1969 little or nothing has been heard about the eventual outcome of the Charleston strike, the fate of the key organizers, or how Charleston, which is not known for social and economic ferment, has accepted the story of 1969's troubles.

On the hour-long drive southward from Orangeburg, I rolled down both my front seat windows. It was now mid-April, and getting warm.

There are really no towns of consequence along I-26 south; everything leads to Charleston. Though Charleston is one of the South's oldest cities, it isn't a really large city; it has a population of just 80,000. North Charleston, technically a separate town, has an additional 70,000, making a total of 150,000 not including the barrier islands—greater Charleston is about the size of Greensboro.

When I reached North Charleston, I couldn't figure out which exit to take. I knew there were several inexpensive hotels in south Charleston, across the Ashley River on Savannah Highway, but it took me a while to figure out how to get there. Actually, Savannah Highway, I discovered, is U.S. 17 running north and south, a highway that cuts an awful swath right through town, which is a peninsula. When I found U.S. 17, it took me across the bridge, changing its name to Savannah Highway, which is where I found a motel only fifteen minutes from downtown. Savannah Highway is almost an exact replica of High Point Road in Greensboro, an old highway laden with the same chain restaurants, auto dealerships, service stations, and small shopping malls.

The Charleston peninsula is formed by the Ashley River on the southwest, and the Cooper River on the northeast. The two rivers converge at the tip of the peninsula, creating Charleston Harbor. James Island and Sullivan Island are barrier islands that protect the harbor. Between them lies a channel that opens into the Atlantic Ocean, providing Charleston with a natural protection from the open sea. These favorable natural attributes are the reason why the site was selected for settlement by the British in 1680.

The morning after I arrived, I headed for the Avery Research Center, where Myrtle Glascoe is director. The center was at 125 Bull Street, and was in the process of settling into a freshly renovated three-story wooden structure, which, I was told, was the main building of the former Avery Institute, Charleston's black college. Avery closed in 1954, but its alumni were instrumental in having the state save this structure and convert it into a research center under the aegis of the College of Charleston, one of the oldest private colleges in the United States, which has just recently become a state institution.

Myrtle was her usually gracious self, suggesting interviewees, pertinent written material, and offering the use of the center as a temporary office. I had known Myrtle from the days when we were friends in Mississippi. I was teaching there in the late 1960s, and she was working for the Head Start program. Later Myrtle taught at Tougaloo College in Jackson, and since then had received her Ed.D. in education from Harvard College.

First, I wanted to read as much about the strike as I could. I had already heard quite a bit of the story from my old friend Andrew Young, former mayor of Atlanta and UN ambassador, who was vice president of SCLC in 1969 and played an active part in every phase of the strike campaign once SCLC entered the picture. I was also able to garner basic outlines of the story from Jack Bass's "Strike at Charleston" in *New South*, Jack O'Dell's "Charleston's Legacy to the Poor People's Campaign" in *Freedomways*, and "Charleston Hospital Workers' Strike, 1969" by Steve Hoffious in *Working Lives: The "Southern Exposure" History of Labor in the South*, edited by Mark S. Miller.

The strike began on March 20, 1969, when approximately 325 women walked off their jobs at the State Medical College Hospital in Charleston. This was a walkout by nurses' assistants and other low-level personnel to protest the firing two days earlier of twelve workers, including nurses' assistants, who were attempting to meet with the hospital director to bargain for improved wages (they were paid a minimum of $1.35 per hour) and working conditions. Their goal was to have the hospital recognize the union they had just joined the previous year—Local 1199-B of the Hospital and Nursing Home Workers (now the Drug, Hospital and Healthcare Workers). The twelve fired workers were led by nurses' assistant Mary Moultrie, who was chairperson of the unrecognized Charleston local. Almost all of the nurses' assistants, kitchen workers, and clean-up workers who went on strike were black; the hospital administrators were white.

This confrontation had been brewing for several months. We could set a beginning in late 1967, when five black employees were fired over a dispute with a white supervisor who, they alleged, refused to let them see the health charts of patients on their watch. The women turned to Mary Moultrie for help. In only a year at the hospital, Ms. Moultrie had built up a reputation for fearlessness. Moultrie contacted Isaiah Bennett, a cigar factory worker and an organizer for the Retail, Wholesale and Department Store Workers, and William Saunders, an organizer from Johns Island known for his militance, for advice. Saunders was working as a foreman in a Charleston mattress factory. Apparently, both Bennett and Saunders knew someone who worked for the Department of Health, Education and Welfare, from which the Medical School Hospital received funds. HEW regulations included job protection provisions, and through the intercession of HEW the workers were able to win reinstatement.

But the firings opened a floodgate of additional complaints by employees. Moultrie and, now, a few other like-minded workers arranged with Bennett to use his union hall to hold weekly meetings to continue to hear complaints. Those meetings produced a barrage of testimony about perceived abuses. There was a general consensus among them that *something* needed to be done. The group then decided to seek out a union that could effectively represent their interests. They were all quite aware that winning union recognition would not be easy; South Carolina had always been adamantly opposed to organized labor. Furthermore, as employees of the state's medical school, they were technically government workers, and the idea of governmental employee unions in the South in 1969 was virtually unheard of. Moultrie and the hospital workers asked Bennett if his union could represent them. That was not possible, but Bennett had friends who were organizers for Local 1199 of the Hospital and Nursing Home Workers in New York, and they agreed to look into the Charleston situation.

Local 1199 was well known in New York City. After a long, grueling struggle, they had won unionization of hospital workers at Montefiore Hospital in the early 1960s. By 1968, more than thirty thousand hospital employees in the New York area were represented by the union. Because so many workers who belonged to Local 1199 in New York were black, the leaders of the union, especially president Leon Davis (who was not black), became avid supporters of the southern civil rights movement, particularly the campaigns of Martin Luther King, Jr., even though the union was not active in the South.

I well remember those first hospital strikes when I lived in New York in the early 1960s. Hospital administrators had argued that unionization could not be tolerated; medical work was an essential public service. This same argument was used in Charleston. Most of the low-level, nonprofessional workers in New York were black and Puerto Rican, and they were generally paid the allowable minimum wage. The same conditions prevailed when I returned to New Orleans in 1965; I had many friends who worked in nonprofessional roles in hospitals. These hospitals were not unionized, the pay was awful, and workers were constantly "written up" for petty offenses.

As a response to the overture in Charleston, Henry Nicholas, an official of Local 1199, was dispatched in the fall of 1968 to hear complaints from the group and assess the situation. By then the regularly meeting workers group had expanded to include a few aides from Charleston County Hospital. Their problems—poor conditions, low wages—were the same as those at the Medical College. As a result of Nicholas's recommendations, a Charleston branch was established, Local 1199-B, with Mary Moultrie as chairperson from the Medical College, and Rosetta Simmons as chair from the smaller group of County Hospital workers. Ms. Moultrie and Ms.

Simmons instituted efforts to meet with their respective hospital administrators, but the president of the Medical College, Dr. William McCord, categorically refused to meet with anyone representing the union.

By the end of 1968 the complaints of the hospital workers and their unsuccessful attempt to meet with the hospital's management had become public knowledge. In early 1969 the standoff was worrying Charleston political officials. At the urging of Charleston's mayor, Dr. McCord finally agreed—or seemed to agree—to meet with Ms. Moultrie and eleven of her associates on March 17. However, when Ms. Moultrie and her group arrived at the designated meeting room, they discovered, to their surprise, several other black employees waiting to attend, who, as far as they knew, were not part of the unionized effort, and who they suspected were invited to the meeting to demonstrate support for the hospital position on wages. Dr. McCord was not present. At that point, Ms. Moultrie and her group left the meeting room and marched to Dr. McCord's outer office. He sent word that he would not see them, then left his office through another door. After a while, Moultrie's group burst into the director's office and when they discovered he had left, they staged an impromptu sit-in. They remained until the Charleston police chief arrived and threatened them with arrest if they didn't leave, which they did.

The next morning when Ms. Moultrie and her group of twelve arrived for work, they were handed notices of termination. The news of the firings spread like wildfire. Two days later, in support of those fired, the walkout of over three hundred nurses' assistants occurred. They were supported a week later by a walkout of sixty workers from the Charleston County Hospital.

From that point on, what lifted this strike far above the ordinary labor dispute was the introduction of the SCLC as a full-fledged partner in strike planning and activities, and in the negotiations for a settlement. Andrew Young and Dorothy Cotton of SCLC knew Septima Clark and Bernice Robinson of Charleston through their work together in SCLC's Citizenship Education Program in the early 1960s. When the two women informed Young about the efforts to organize a union in late 1968, Young sent one of SCLC's top organizers, James Orange, to appraise the situation. When the walkout occurred on March 20, SCLC was hardly surprised.

There were several reasons why SCLC wanted to become involved. SCLC had recently undergone a major shift in focus from the pursuit of basic civil rights to a focus on achieving economic parity and jobs for the poor. They reasoned that once public facilities were desegregated and the Voting Rights Act was passed, no further gains could be made until more blacks were brought into the job market. Part of Martin Luther King's rationale for opposing the Vietnam War had been that the war not only was destructive in itself, but was siphoning away funds that could be used to bring the poor more fully into the mainstream economy.

SCLC did not come to this position through pure abstraction. Andrew Young, during the course of our several conversations, explained, "In the early sixties it was the masses who provided the human fodder for the fill-the-jails strategy of demonstrations in Albany, Birmingham, and Selma. Through this approach we were able to successfully address and remove the legalities of public segregation, opening up southern society a bit. But only a bit, because only those with training and education were in a position to take advantage of new opportunities. By 1966 and 1967 the masses, the economically deprived, were saying, 'Now you've got to do something for us!'"

Other national civil rights organizations were hearing the same message. Thus began the advocacy for the opening up of corporate America: Civil rights groups began to address "institutional racism," designing and arguing the validity of affirmative action programs for minorities, demanding the desegregation of trade unions and jobs in governmental agencies, particularly in urban areas with large minority populations.

In 1967, SCLC drew up plans for a massive demonstration in Washington, to be called the Poor People's Campaign, a more intensive effort than ever before to pressure the White House and Congress to deal more effectively with conditions of domestic poverty. As part of this campaign, SCLC planned a multiethnic encampment in Washington during the summer of 1968 to use as its ongoing organizational base. Apparently, the contemplated Poor People's Campaign angered the beleaguered President Lyndon Johnson, according to Andrew Young. The campaign also drew a barrage of criticism from members of Congress.

The White House was initiating its own Antipoverty Program, but Johnson and Martin Luther King, Jr., were on different wave lengths, and not necessarily headed for the same destination. "At one time the White House called our office very frequently," remembers Young. "But by 1967, Johnson wouldn't talk to Martin." A powerful reaction against mass-action civil rights was settling in. For many whites, increased employment opportunities for blacks and other minorities threatened their exclusivity in the hiring halls, promotion lists, and training programs.

In February 1968, with King under heavy fire from conservatives shouting "Enough is enough," and from black militants screaming "Your method of non-violent protest is a thing of the past," a call came from the Reverend James Lawson imploring King to come to Memphis to speak on behalf of the garbage workers of that city. Jim Lawson was an old King ally, a serious theoretician and practitioner of nonviolent protest who had been recently assigned to a Methodist church in Memphis. He was the chairman of a communitywide committee to support the garbage workers, who began a wildcat strike in January 1968.

The Memphis situation was an almost direct precursor of the hospital workers strike in Charleston a year later. In Memphis the lowest-level garbage collectors, all of whom were black, struck because of chronically low wages, horrible working conditions, and no representation. The event that ignited the strike was the accidental death of two workers in January. A continual problem for the garbage collectors was that when it rained they were unable to find a secure place to protect them-selves—a seemingly trivial problem, but a very annoying one. Since there were no provisions made for them, some took to sheltering themselves in the rear of their trucks, along with the garbage. One day in January 1968, the compacting machinery of a truck was accidentally activated, and two workers were crushed to death. Since there were no worker benefits, a collection had to be taken up to pay for their funerals. At the funerals, which were attended by many fellow workers, the talk was of *strike*, though they had not yet contacted a union. Once the wildcat strike began, the national office of the American Federation of State, County, and Municipal Employees union was not enthusiastic about taking on their case; the real sustenance came from a sympathetic black community. The Memphis city government would not yield, contending that it could not recognize a union of city workers, as was the policy all over the South.

King was in the midst of a whirlwind speaking tour, attempting to drum up support for the summer Washington campaign, but he agreed to include a stop in Memphis as part of an organizing trip to Mississippi. His mid-March appearance that night was received with such heartening enthusiasm that he agreed to return to

Memphis to lead a march to city hall. In late March, after a postponement due to an unseasonable blizzard, King and the Reverend Ralph Abernathy returned to Memphis. However, their long-awaited march was ill-fated; it was spoiled by violence perpetrated by bystanders in the rear. The march disintegrated into frightening disorder as the police waded in swinging clubs; blacks who were on the sidelines then attempted to retaliate by stoning the police.

King was vilified with a hail of criticism by the national press for being unable to lead a peaceful march. The next week he pulled his entire staff back to Atlanta for a long meeting, then sent them to Memphis to organize a peaceful march, which he felt he had to have if he was ever going to make the Washington campaign work. It was while he was in Memphis waiting for a court order to approve a march that he was killed on April 4. Many members of the SCLC staff believed the disorganization in Memphis and the ill-fated first march, organized by the Memphis leaders, made King an easy and highly publicized target.

Now the staff, with Ralph Abernathy having succeeded King, had to deal with the horrible reality of the death of their charismatic leader. King had often discussed with his closest staff the possibility that he would be killed, but he had instructed them that they must carry on, "lest the enemies of progress believe they can stop the movement for social change by killing the leaders." So, after the funeral they dove into preparations for what was called Resurrection City in Washington. Resurrection City, a temporary area of housing built on the Washington Mall in the summer of 1968, was intended for the army of demonstrators who SCLC hoped would besiege official Washington that summer, the culmination of the Poor People's Campaign. Unfortunately, the logistics of organizing the various groups traveling to Washington in addition to managing problems involved with the hastily erected tent city were simply overwhelming. The SCLC staff was dismayed to discover that they not only had to organize demonstrations at various governmental departments, they were also forced to administer what, in effect, was a small city—provide services, keep order, and so forth—tasks for which they had no prior experience. Criticism from Congress and the press was unrelenting. To make matters worse, Washington was inundated with torrential rainstorms during the summer of 1968. Resurrection City was transformed into a sea of mud, "Quagmire City"—and all the summer's optimistic plans ended up metaphorically and literally stuck in the mud, spinning wheels but going nowhere. Finally, the government moved in and bulldozed Resurrection City, and everyone went home.

In the ensuing months the SCLC staff seemed to be stymied by inertia. Some were unhappy with Abernathy's leadership and departed, never to return. The organization seemed to be in disarray. When the Charleston situation appeared on the horizon, however, and when the friendly Local 1199 invited them into a partnership on the day the strike began, SCLC jumped at the opportunity. It was a chance for a much-needed success, and a way of reviving the Poor People's Campaign. Learning from their horrible experience in Memphis, they would be coming in early as part of the strike-organizing team, not as "visitors." They would participate in the negotiations for a settlement. Furthermore, they would organize and hold nightly meetings in supportive churches, the tried-and-true method of winning support in previous campaigns. Finally, they would rally their national constituency and hopefully, in the end, prove that they were still a viable organization that could change with the times.

From the standpoint of Local 1199, Charleston was a special opportunity also, but with clear drawbacks. If they had had their choice of a southern town in which to organize, it would hardly have been one in the state of South Carolina, which was so rigidly antilabor. But win or lose, Charleston was a good town to learn in, and their campaign there might be seen by other unions as an opening that would eventually expand to the crucial textile industry.

For the hospital workers themselves, the objectives were much more limited. They wanted the minimum wage raised to $1.60 per hour, a raise of $0.25 per hour. They desired the establishment of an adequate grievance procedure. They requested that job assignments be on a nonracial basis. Finally, they hoped for union recognition, with a dues-checkoff system as part of their salaries. And of course they demanded that the twelve fired workers be reinstated.

The Medical School Hospital's first move was to hire a consultant, who launched a campaign caricaturing Local 1199 as a group of crass northern opportunists come south to exploit the naive hospital workers. This strategy boomeranged, stiffening the resolve of the strikers. Meanwhile, a coordinating committee was established by the allied organizations to manage the strike. Henry Nicholas represented Local 1199, Andrew Young represented SCLC, Bill Saunders represented the supportive Charleston community, and Isaiah Bennett the hospital workers. None of the workers themselves was on the committee, which, as it turned out, was a crucial mistake.

The coordinating committee immediately instituted the picketing of the two hospitals, marches downtown, nightly meetings at important churches like the Morris Brown AME, Morris Street Baptist, Emanuel African Methodist Episcopal, Plymouth Congregational, and Fourth Baptist, Charleston's most historic black churches. Meanwhile, they publicized the strike nationally to win support among their longtime civil rights constituency. Charleston was thrown into turmoil, and for the next three months it experienced a siege of protests and unrest. It was as if a massive storm had blown in from the sea, whereas the hospital administrators were only prepared for a hard rain. Governor McNair (who had ordered the state police into Orangeburg in 1968) called out the National Guard to assist the police. He instituted a 9:00 P.M. curfew. During the entire spring of 1969, however, the hospital administration would not talk with the union or the negotiating committee representatives.

As Easter approached, the coordinating committee called for a boycott of Charleston's stores, excepting those selling food and medicines. It was the same type of boycott that had worked so well in Birmingham in 1963 when it transformed the downtown business sector into an Easter season ghost town, except for picketers and the police. Tourists avoided Charleston: Charleston businesses lost an estimated $15 million during the spring of 1969. Heavy picketing of downtown stores kept away white shoppers as well as blacks. Picketing was expanded to include popular tourist spots, the homes of hospital officials (including the president of the Medical Hospital), and the homes of prominent Charleston politicians. More than nine hundred demonstrators were arrested, flooding the jails. Several prominent whites, including Catholic priests, particularly Father William Joyce of St. Patrick's Parish, joined the demonstrations and marches. The threat of violence was ever present, and there were violent incidents, though fortunately no deaths. A dramatic Mother's Day March was led by Coretta King, with United Auto Workers leader Walter Reuther and other dignitaries of the broad civil rights and supportive labor constituencies marching beside her. Reuther donated twenty-five thousand dollars to the strike coffers.

Still, Dr. McCord refused to meet with the workers or their representatives. When he was asked by the press why he didn't begin negotiations, he responded, "I'm not about to turn a twenty-five-million-dollar complex over to a bunch of people who don't have a grammar school education."

In late May and early June, the coordinating committee took additional steps. Support was solicited from sympathetic unions that could impact the situation in South Carolina. Mary Moultrie was sent on a national speaking tour to provide information on the conditions that had led to the strike. Ralph Abernathy, speaking in New York, mentioned that the committee was considering asking the state textile mill workers to walk out as a show of support for the hospital workers. A few days later, the International Longshoremen's Association, which was strong in Charleston, announced it was considering shutting down the port of Charleston, the fourth largest port on the East Coast. The committee decided to defy the curfew by instituting night marches. As a result, many demonstrators, including some of the leaders, were jailed.

And then it was discovered that the Medical School Hospital was in violation of thirty-seven HEW civil rights guidelines, and had been since September 1968. In fact, Dr. McCord was under order to submit an affirmative action program, or the hospital would risk losing $12 million in federal funds.

With these increased pressures on the hospital, and with the situation now worrying President Nixon and South Carolina congressmen, Dr. McCord finally agreed to begin behind-the-scenes negotiations with Andrew Young. Bill Saunders was also involved in separate negotiations. Finally, on June 27, amid a mood of triumph and relief for the hospital workers and their representatives, a settlement with the Medical School Hospital was announced. It was agreed that the minimum wage for nurses' assistants would be raised from $1.35 to $1.60 per hour. A grievance procedure to handle worker complaints was to be established. All of the striking employees, including Mary Moultrie and those who were fired with her, were to be rehired. And finally, a credit union would be established at the hospital to collect union dues.

Actual recognition of Local 1199 by the hospital was *not* part of the settlement, however. The issue of recognition of Local 1199 was left unresolved, as the hospital continued to insist that they could not, as a state institution, agree to unionization. Omission of union recognition, over time, proved to be a telling point because the workers had no real protection, though in the euphoric atmosphere following the agreement both Local 1199 and SCLC implied the dues-checkoff system constituted a victory.

Meanwhile, there was still the issue of the strike at the County Hospital, which had seventy striking workers. When the County Hospital administration balked at an agreement, the coordinating committee decided to resume picketing. Finally, the County Hospital also came to the table, establishing a minimum wage of $1.70 per hour, and agreeing to reinstate all of their striking workers. However, they also refused to recognize Local 1199.

After 113 days, the hospital workers strike was finally over. The *Charleston Post* editorialized on July 21: "Important lessons have been learned this summer. The most important is that of the growing power of elements of the community who have hitherto been relatively voiceless."

For SCLC, the campaign was considered a success, and they received considerable national acclaim for their efforts. As it turned out, however, the promising civil rights-labor union collaboration that seemed to be a harbinger of the future was, instead, the *last* campaign of this type in the South, and also the last major campaign undertaken by SCLC. It was not so much that the organizations changed; the times changed. The 1970s and '80s marked a turn away from large-scale, mass-participation efforts to address economic inequities. Even labor unions found it difficult to dramatize their grievances.

Having failed to achieve recognition, Local 1199 pulled out its national staff. Even though Mary Moultrie and her most active compatriots kept open a union office for a while, working on their own time, the office was finally closed and its efforts to maintain an unrecognized union slowly petered out. SCLC left veteran organizer Jim Orange in Charleston to work on poststrike issues, but after a while he too moved on to other concerns.

Now, I wanted to seek out some of the key persons involved in the strike who were still in Charleston, to find out how they remember those spring and summer days of 1969, and what they think was gained, or not gained. "Mary Moultrie, who led the walkout, is still around," Myrtle informed me. "She works for the city as director of a community center." I called around for her number and reached Ms. Moultrie at the East Side Community Center. We arranged for me to meet her during her lunch break the next day.

⌒

The East Side Community Center is situated in a small black neighborhood not far from the commercial docks. The center is housed in a recreation/meeting-hall-type building, no fancy decor. Walls of simple painted brick, gauche colors. We talked in a room on the second floor; there was a prominent sign on the wall: SAY NO TO DRUGS.

Ms. Moultrie was heavyset, dark skinned, well spoken, but careful of statement. She appeared to be in her late forties or early fifties. Though she was obviously intelligent and articulate, I detected none of the polish of higher education. She did not appear to be the type of person who indulged in humor or frivolity. She knew I wanted to discuss the strike, but her look told me, "I'm tired of discussing the strike." I decided instead to begin by asking her about her family and upbringing.

Ms. Moultrie was born in Charleston, but her family is from Wadmalaw Island, one of the large barrier islands south of Charleston. She attended Charleston public schools, graduating from Burke High School in 1960. She left Charleston to attend Morgan State College in Baltimore. After a year of college she emigrated to New York City.

I was quite surprised to hear Ms. Moultrie mention that while a student at Burke she worked for Esau Jenkins, whom I had always associated with Johns Island, not Charleston. It seems that Jenkins lived on Johns Island, but he owned a restaurant in Charleston (the teenage Mary Moultrie worked as a waitress) "at the foot of Spring Street." The city confiscated his property when the new eastbound Ashley River bridge was built in 1960, she explained.

"Mr. Jenkins took me in almost as a family member," she added.

Esau Jenkins was the most important black leader to emerge from the barrier islands in the postwar period. He cast a powerful, long shadow on the entire Charleston area until his death in 1972. But in none of my research on the hospital workers, strike had I heard of Jenkins's influence on Mary Moultrie. She explained that Jenkins frequently dragged her, along with other young folk including his own children, to civil rights meetings in the early 1960s. Sometimes she delivered memorized speeches, remembering the title of one as "The South Awake at Midnight."

It was Jenkins who encouraged Ms. Moultrie to attend college, "though my family couldn't really afford it." She chose Morgan State in Baltimore because she had an aunt and cousins who lived in the Baltimore area. She lived with them while attending college. When I inquired further about her family in the Baltimore area (why Baltimore, I wondered), she said several members of her family had migrated from Wadmalaw to the Delaware-Maryland area. "There was seasonal farm work at a town called Delmar, Delaware." When I searched for Delmar on the map later, I discovered if you followed U.S. 17, which runs through Charleston, right up the Atlantic coast until it becomes U.S. 13 at Wilmington, North Carolina, then farther northward through Norfolk, across the Chesapeake Bay Bridge and on up the Maryland peninsula, you will arrive at the town of Delmar, situated on the Delaware-Maryland border. Recruiters from Delmar ventured down to Charleston and Wadmalaw Island every year in search of farm workers, Ms. Moultrie explained. "My family became regulars with them because there wasn't any work on the island." Eventually, some members of the family decided to settle in Delaware. Some of that group eventually moved to Baltimore.

Ms. Moultrie also had relatives in New York City as a result of a further migration up the East Coast. She was able to find work at Goldwater Memorial Hospital on Welfare Island. There she entered a training program for nurses. She remained in New York until 1968, residing near the Polo Grounds in Harlem. In New York, she said, she was not active in any sort of civil rights work, but her experience was extremely valuable: "It was my first real job. I had my first interracial contacts, and I met several fellow workers from the West Indies."

Goldwater Memorial had been unionized by the Teamsters. Ms. Moultrie joined their Local 237, and her last year there she served as a shop steward for the local. She was not that active in union activities, she said, but the very fact that she knew unions existed and how they worked proved to be of great value a year later.

While she was living in New York, Mary Moultrie frequently returned to Charleston to visit her family. In early 1968 her family needed her at home, so she moved back to live with them. She immediately sought hospital work in Charleston, but the best job she could find was as a nurse's assistant at the Medical School Hospital, "making a lot less than I was earning in New York.

"From the moment I began work, there was unrest all around me. Low-level employees were being fired by nurses right and left. I called Bill Saunders, who was a good friend; he's from Johns Island, and we shared the Esau Jenkins tie-in. When I told him what was happening, his response was 'You need to do something.' And we did do something. But there were problems. For one, Saunders was thinking of the workers organizing an association, not a union. This caused problems with people like Isaiah Bennett, who believed in unions. And then when the union invited in SCLC, the established Charleston NAACP leadership went bananas. They were reluctant to support us at first. Really, they thought our issues could have been settled without a strike."

I asked if she thought the local NAACP leadership had resented her leadership.

"Well, they didn't know me, so that was a problem with them. I had a problem with the union leadership, too. One Local 1199 official told me when we were deep into the strike, 'Listen, you're not leading anything. You're going to follow orders.' Some of the NAACP people visited the union hall every night. 'Why you bringing in all these people?' they would say about the SCLC leaders. 'Who asked for them to come in?' The news media continually attacked SCLC as 'outside agitators.'"

I pointed out that this was an almost clichéd response by the media, and asked her if it had really come as a surprise.

"We did not anticipate what would happen. We were just at the point where we knew we had to do something, especially after the twelve of us were fired."

I asked Ms. Moultrie if she was satisfied with the terms of the settlement. "Some people say the strike was settled too easily."

"I agree," she responded carefully. "But I don't like to lay blame. I'm appreciative of Local 1199 and SCLC. They put a lot of time and money into Charleston. But it really disappointed me that I wasn't here when they settled. I was at a meeting in New York. I wasn't consulted. I thought we, as the striking workers, should have been involved in the settlement. They called me in New York and told me the strike was settled. I was so hurt and upset, but I didn't complain about it. Later, I came to believe that Local 1199 knew we weren't going to get recognition. When they left, I felt abandoned. I just felt bad."

What was it like when she returned to her job after the strike? "It was a struggle. I didn't know how they would accept me. It was really, really hard. I was placed in a psychiatric unit working with nonstrikers. I was ostracized by blacks and whites. I suppose I was considered dangerous. Finally, some of the white nurses became curious. They encouraged me to join them when we ate because I was eating alone. We didn't really become friends, but they were concerned about how I was feeling.

"I remained at the Medical School Hospital another five and a half years. A lot of pressure was put on me, writing me up and so forth. I began taking classes at the College of Charleston, and if I was late five minutes to work I was written up. There was no support from my superiors. They kept the heat on until they got me out of there."

"You just decided you'd had enough?"

"Yes."

"And the other strike leaders?"

"We were picked off one by one. We never got a union. Now I hear people who work at the Medical Hospital complaining. There's a lot of fear of speaking out. They still call me sometimes, the workers do, in the hope I can help, but I'm no longer connected." Within a year after the settlement, Ms. Moultrie said, it was clear the hospital was not going to agree to the credit union checkoff system. As for the grievance procedure, she explained, the hospital undermined it by limiting the number of times the same person (a union representative) could serve as a grievant's representative.

I was impressed by Mary Moultrie's honesty, humility, and quiet strength. She had been groomed early for a leadership role by Esau Jenkins, but neither she nor Jenkins could have dreamed in what way her preparation would manifest itself. Ms. Moultrie brought to the strike her New York experience of working in hospitals, an exposure to the world of unions, and a sense of proper grievances. Clearly, her experiences outside of Charleston were an essential ingredient in her determination to take a stand.

Isaiah Bennett asked me to meet him at his home on Race Street, deep in the neck of the peninsula. His home is a worker's house, modest but comfortable. Now in his sixties, Bennett is short, slightly stocky, and well spoken. Despite his age, Bennett conveys the air of a youthful working-class activist. He seems perfectly comfortable with his role as a longtime blue-collar union man.

He told me he was raised mostly in Charleston, and had been a factory worker since his youth. He had attended South Carolina State in Orangeburg for a year, then was drafted into the military during World War II; upon release he worked for the American Tobacco Company, a cigar manufacturer. Early on, he became active in the Food, Tobacco, and Allied Workers Union (as it was called in 1969), which at that time was segregated. Its first struggles were against segregation in the workplace. "We had separate rest rooms and water fountains, separate doors for Colored. Separate cafeterias. We complained and complained, but we didn't completely rid ourselves of that until 1963." I asked if he had always been in the forefront of such activities. "It was my father," he explained. "He worked for the Coast Guard station virtually his entire life. He lived until he was ninety-three. He always said, 'The only solution for bettering your condition is to organize.' "

"What made the hospital strike take off?" I asked.

"The firing of the twelve workers. And McCord's duplicity [in refusing to meet with Ms. Moultrie and her group two days earlier]. We laid the complaint of the workers on the black community, and they came through. We were looking for help from wherever. Television helped us. Every night when we held meetings in various churches, there was television coverage, which served to spread the word. In that way, the media helped us.

"We were trying to get the message across that things were not well in the city of Charleston." He described the marches. "We marched down King Street [the main Charleston commercial street], right down the middle of the street. When we got downtown, we stopped and held a prayer meeting. We knew we were blocking traffic, and we didn't worry about it."

"Wasn't there a problem getting march permits to do that?"

"We ignored march permits. They weren't going to give us march permits anyway, so why bother? They arrested us. There was a lot of pushing and shoving with the police. When the governor called out the National Guard, they brought out tanks."

"Tanks?"

"Tanks. This place was like a war zone."

I asked if other unions in the city had supported the hospital workers in their strike.

"A majority of the union organizers in Charleston are white. They gave us a little support, but not much. We got a lot of support from the longshoremen, which in Charleston is basically a black union. We received support from the textile workers."

"What was going on with the NAACP people?"

"This was strong NAACP country, led by Delpert Woods and J. Arthur Brown. But 1199 was aligned with SCLC. I never saw why they couldn't work together. But money was in it, fund-raising. In the end, the SCLC and the hospital union forgot the workers' cause. But by that time, I had become a small voice. SCLC was in trouble and Charleston helped them out. Local 1199 didn't succeed here, but they organized workers in other towns in the South later. Charleston was their testing ground."

"Well then, what came out of it?"

"Afterward, the workers still had problems, but not quite as blatant. That's my sense of it. At the time, it was very, very exciting. We got most of the people back to work. We got a wage increase. And a little more respect. And things weren't based so much on race. Now, seniority means more in terms of job security."

"That doesn't sound so bad."

"No. But the workers felt they were betrayed because they settled for too little. There was resentment against Local 1199 in particular."

Pondering Bennett's last comment, I asked if expectations among the workers had been too high.

"They didn't expect too much," Bennett answered. "They expected more than what they got in the Memorandum of Agreement." I mentioned that Mary Moultrie had expressed resentment that the agreement was announced while she was in New York. "Well, I can understand that," he replied. "You see, the workers started it and the workers should have finished their own strike. None of the nurses' assistants themselves were part of the final negotiations."

It seemed as if there was quite a bit of lingering discontent over the settlement. Several people suggested I speak to Naomi White, one of the strikers who had returned to the Medical School Hospital to finish her career there. I had a hard time reaching her on the telephone, but finally was able to speak to her. She responded with a friendly "Come right over."

Ms. White ushered me through the rooms of her well-kept home to her kitchen, where we talked. The mother of six children, she had retired from the Medical School Hospital in 1985, having worked there twenty-four years. Light skinned, soft-spoken, but to the point, once Ms. White got rolling with her musical Gullah accent she made her points in perfectly inflected tonal pitches. She did not appear to be the type of person you could take lightly once she became determined, or had set her mind on a course. Ms. White explained with pride that the area where she lived was one of the oldest black areas in Charleston. It was near the community center where Mary Moultrie works. She called it "the East Side."

"Basically," she recalled, "we were all paid poorly at the Medical School Hospital, whites and blacks. But it came as a shock to us when we discovered by accident that white nurses' assistants were paid more. We did the same work, and I would say the blacks did more. The whites had been told not to divulge their salary. But one day when a white assistant threw her pay stub in the trash, I retrieved it and compared salaries. She was making almost twice what we were! When we went to the supervisor to inquire about the difference, she demanded to know how we got our information. So this really started the rumbling of discontent."

"Once the complaints began, was there any support from white nurses and aides?"

"At first, yes. Among a few. But then it became clear their jobs were in jeopardy if they supported us. So they didn't join us in the walkout. Some white medical students wanted to support us, but we told them there was no use for them to endanger their careers. Some of the black licensed practical nurses did join the strike. Some other licensed nurses wanted to join us but were prohibited from doing so by their spouses."

As Ms. White was speaking, I realized I had left several pieces of recording equipment on the backseat of my car. I decided I had better check it, as several young men were conversing near where I had parked. But everything was in order, and when I returned to the kitchen, Ms. White said, "They're not going to bother your car. They know better." This very comment reminded me of some other mythical time in American cities, as did the wording of her reassurance. Having lived in New York and Harlem, it was a natural reflex to worry about anything showing on the rear seat, particularly if there were males standing around whom I didn't know. I felt sheepish about checking, but I had too many friends who had suffered automobile break-ins. I had asked Mary Moultrie about the extent of the drug problem in Charleston, which is always associated with petty crime in my mind. "It's here," she assured me, "but maybe not as bad as in some other places. Not as bad as Columbia."

Ms. White had not been involved in the extensive prestrike meetings and planning. "A week or so before the walkout, a coworker who was involved had whispered to me, 'You know, we might have to strike.' She wanted to know was I 'with' them. Since I wasn't part of the planning group, they didn't expect me to participate. All they were asking was that I not cross the picket line if there was a strike."

"But you walked out with the original group, didn't you?"

"Yes, I did. In fact, I was not only 'with' them, I was the first worker to go to jail! Once we got organized after the events of March twentieth, it was agreed that everyone would picket their particular shift. I picketed in that hot sun in the afternoons for a week. Now, the real action came when shifts changed. At shift-change time, we tried to discourage workers who didn't go on strike from going in; a few weeks later we were trying to discourage scabs and there were plenty of them. Work was so hard to get. A black lady who worked in housekeeping—this lady was making ninety cents an hour—hired a white private detective to help her get through the picket line. She didn't hire him, the hospital was helping scabs every way they could, because once the strike began, the hospital was losing out. Families were moving their sick relations to other hospitals.

"Anyway, I told this woman's detective he couldn't cross in front of *me*. If he could get her in there otherwise, fine with me. That's when he flipped his badge and told me he was hired to see that she got in. I said, '*Well*. She's *not* comin' in here by me.' And so he says, 'I don't want to hurt you or nothin', so just move and let us come by.' I said, 'No,' and he insisted on taking her by the arm and *shovin'* her by me. She had some chains around her neck and I grabbed her by the chains and jerked her back and that started a free-for-all. What provoked me was, as I told her, 'Here we're out here fighting for better wages; you shouldn't be going in there for ninety cents an hour; then you got the *audacity* to hire an escort to see that you get in there!' I say, 'Not *today!*' and when I grabbed her, that's when the detective went to grab me and some of the guys supporting us grabbed him. Anyway, we had a *time* out there. Next thing I knew, I was in the paddy wagon going to jail. They arrested about six of us. We were the first to be arrested. Isaiah Bennett came and got me out."

"Was this kind of physical confrontation common?"

"Yes. That's the way it was. I went to jail several times, never having been in jail before in my life, even to visit. Once I was arrested on King Street when a policeman was holding one of our strikers. The policeman told me to leave, but I told him, 'Well, you *not* gonna arrest her by herself. So if you want to take her, take me too.' We had a policy of not letting our people go to jail by themselves, because you never know what might happen. So he say, 'I'm not gon' take you 'cause I don't have no reason to take you.' So I *slapped* his face and gave him a reason. He told me, '*Now*, you going.' We were in jail fourteen days before the union could bail us out.

"There were a lot of fights like that, and I was in the middle of them. After the strike was over, one of the policemen I had a fight with during the strike came in on my floor as an eye patient. I recognized him. He told another nurse, 'There's something about that red-haired nurse, I know her from somewhere.' I had to patch up his eye. He said, 'I'm trying to remember where I know you from.' I said, 'You know me from the strike because I and you fought the Battle of Jericho out there on the hospital steps.' He said, 'That's right. Oh, my God.' And he said, 'Nurse, please be nice. Don't hurt me.' He was at my mercy then, but I was professional."

"Was there anything in particular about the strike that made it successful or not successful?" I asked.

"For one thing, it's not usually mentioned that most of the low-level hospital workers were from the barrier islands, particularly Johns Island. It was islanders, not so much native Charlestonians, who were the backbone of the strike." I remembered that both Mary Moultrie and Bill Saunders had strong island ties.

"But then, I have to also say most of the scabs were islanders. Some people were so poor they would do anything to get work; even take our jobs. The only thing we could do about that was fight back. I complained that we were letting too many scabs get by our lines. So we had to night-ride late at night, catching scabs on their way to work the midnight shift. The hospital tried to cross us up by changing schedules, but we had friends on the inside who tipped us off. Some of the scabs went to work with *paper bags* over their heads. Once we beat up some scabs on a hospital bus. I'm telling you what really happened. They would meet at a certain bar; the hospital would send a bus to pick them up and drive them past us and into work. One woman's house was fire-bombed to keep her out; I don't know who did it. Another woman was so frightened she never left the hospital, even when she was off. Her mother used to come to the hospital to get her check so they could spend the money. That's what we had to do. I knew if we didn't stop people from taking our jobs, we'd be out there picketing *forever*. There would never be a settlement."

I asked about conflict between the strike leaders and the old-line NAACP leadership, which resented, it was said, the entrance of SCLC and Local 1199 into the strike effort. "Maybe. But here, in Charleston, as long as it's local people trying to do something, you won't get lasting support. But if it's national people, you won't even have standing room when you call a meeting. When SCLC came into it, we started pulling people to the churches. People came to hear speakers like Ralph Abernathy and Andy Young. Without SCLC and the union we couldn't have made it. You see, for us this was a first-time venture. Walking out is one thing, but how you survive afterward is something else. We needed people with experience in strikes. But then, there's no doubt we helped SCLC and Local 1199 in turn. A lot."

I mentioned that Mary Moultrie and Isaiah Bennett didn't think the settlement was so favorable, particularly since union recognition was not achieved. "I was told," Ms. White responded, "that had we held out another week we would have gotten everything we wanted. But it came down to negotiating. Ms. Moultrie should have been at the table. But they *sent* her out of town. She said she wouldn't have never gone for the terms. And it should have been put to a vote by the strikers."

"It wasn't?"

"Local 1199 and Abernathy settled the strike. But none of us were there. We wanted recognition of the union as our representation. They said they couldn't do that. Not like we wanted it. Instead, we created a credit union to collect union dues, but without actual recognition the effort just ran out of gas."

"So, did conditions improve when you returned to work?"

"In some ways. It got better for a while. When we returned to work, we were not placed in our former units. It was very difficult for those of us who were deeply involved in the strike to keep in touch with each other while we were on the job. Most of the strike leaders became discouraged and either left or were forced out. The grievance procedure was set up in such a way it didn't work for us, it was for the administration. So it's pretty much back to where it was. I don't know what's wrong with these younger people, because they're so intimidated. Terminations are frequent. People are too afraid to speak up for their rights." This reminded me that Bennett had commented, "A strike like that could never happen now. That was a different time." I understood him to mean that the 1960s were a time when activism was more accepted, when national organizations were ready and willing to support social protests and causes they thought worthy even when those causes were at first extremely unpopular, like opposition to the Vietnam War. At that time unions were also organizing far more aggressively than they are now.

"Are there black supervisors?"

"There was one. But she gave up the position. She had such a hard time of it." As I was leaving, I complimented Ms. White on the sharpness of her memories. "Up until this day, no one forgets that '69 strike." She smiled. "It's like Hurricane Hugo [which occurred in 1989]. Charleston will never forget it."

Fortunately, I was able to reach Jack McCray, the reporter whom I had interviewed on my way to Orangeburg for his eyewitness accounts of the Orangeburg shootings. McCray was still in college when the hospital strike occurred, but I wanted to hear what he had heard about the strike through the years. Since I sensed that McCray was not trying to impress me or anyone else, I went to him for a "read" on Charleston events and key individuals. It was beside the point, but it didn't hurt McCray in my eyes that he hosted a first-class radio jazz program on Sunday afternoons, maybe the only decent jazz radio show in the state of South Carolina.

We talked in a chain steak house restaurant filled to the hilt with uniformed students from The Citadel. It seemed to be their night out on the town. "The general impression of the strike settlement among blacks," offered McCray after we settled down, "is that it was a sellout. But I don't really know because I wasn't in a position to know. But that's the way a lot of people feel. In fact, growing up in Charleston, there is a long tradition of 'selling out.' It's just in the air. Blacks feel they can't take a strong position on anything without some other blacks undercutting it."

This evaluation rather bothered me, at least as far as the strike was concerned. I wondered, once again, if expectations had not been unrealistically high? To confront a strong established state institution like the Medical School Hospital was an achievement in itself. Winning unionization in a state that was known to hate unions would have been very difficult in 1969. I had discussed with Andrew Young the often heard criticism that SCLC sometimes too easily reached settlements that were not all that favorable. "The problem, Tom," he responded, with a degree of agitation at me for bringing up the question, "is that at some point *you must settle*. You can't continue a high-intensity campaign involving large numbers of people forever, no matter how compelling the issue. People get tired, they have to return to work, must care for their families; also, if a campaign drags on too long, everyone loses sight of the issues. And you can't expect people to remain in jail forever. Encouraging people to be jailed without knowing when or how you will bail them out is irresponsible."

And then, too, Young had argued, local leaders sometimes fall in love with the excitement of the campaign, the daily attention from media, being at the center of events. But dramatic speeches can't last forever. Campaigns have natural peaks and valleys. You have to assess what you have gained against your capacity to effectively continue, and make a judgment on what you gain through settlement. From settlement on, you continue to struggle toward your objective on other levels.

I repeated this argument to McCray. He simply responded, "I'm just telling you what people say, how they feel."

Part of the problem with "how people feel" about what happened during the strike has to do, I was coming to realize, with how Charlestonian blacks perceive the possibilities of racial progress in Charleston. When I had a chance to sit down and talk at length with Myrtle Glascoe, I was interested to hear her impressions of Charleston with respect to this question of attitude.

Raised in Arkansas and Washington, D.C., Myrtle, now in her mid-fifties, intense, inclined toward "earth colors" rather than conservative dress, was to me a scholar who maintained a commitment to the "folk" who were the foot soldiers of the civil rights movement. She took her time responding to my questions, mulling them over, letting them sink in, measuring me as she responded.

"When I first came here, they told me this place was like New Orleans. But there's no energy here," she began. "At least I haven't found it. I literally drove up and down the street looking for blacks on the corner; you can count those places on one hand. New Orleans breathes energy, particularly when it comes to music. There's no night life here, nothing like that." I asked her if she thought there had been any racial progress. I was thinking there must be some legacies from the hospital strike besides memories of an effort that didn't quite result in the tangible gains people had hoped for.

"Well, I suppose all that has to do with Charleston itself," she replied.

"When I arrived in the mid-eighties, my sense of Charleston was that it was about to enter into the sixties. People were talking about doing things I remember hearing people talk about in D.C. decades ago. There was an excitement over black appointments, 'the first' this and that, but they weren't in tune with the wider picture of how much influence those 'firsts' would or would not have.

"You see, Charleston is very tied into the good ole boy system. Among blacks, you still have active divisions that developed during the antebellum period—over connections—black families and their relationships with certain white families. There's a lot of importance placed on which white folks the black folks worked for or are connected to by blood—some black Charlestonians make strong distinctions between themselves on one hand, and the blacks who live on Johns, James, and Wadmalaw islands, on the other. They consider the island people deprived and backward. The blacks on the islands were 'field niggers' with no access to 'culture.' They're dark skinned, they're ignorant, and so forth. There's a church in Charleston where it was said if you were darker than a brown paper bag you could not gain entry. There are cemeteries set aside for certain black people. One of the measures of how well you've made it in life is which cemetery you're buried in." Growing up in New Orleans, I had been aware of similar stories about the Creoles of color, but I was hoping Charleston had moved past that kind of intraracial color prejudice by the 1990s, in the same way we had tried so hard to do in New Orleans.

"Have you ever heard of the Brown Fellowship Society?" Myrtle asked after a pause. I had heard of the Brown Fellowship Society, but I wasn't clear about what it was. "They began as a self-help society of free blacks before Emancipation, but as they grew in the late nineteenth and twentieth centuries, they became known for excluding darker-skinned blacks, no matter how accomplished, and limiting membership to certain families."

"But the Brown Society is a relic of the past, isn't it?" I asked.

"Technically. But I'm still dealing with it. You see, Avery was considered a school for light-skinned blacks only—if you were darker and wanted to go to college, you went to State, Claflin, or Benedict in Columbia. Trying to make the research center available to the entire community, I still have to deal with some of those insular attitudes, and I won't play the 'society' game. And then, too, I am an 'outsider' and I guess I'll always be considered an outsider. I feel most at home with people who were involved in the struggle, I don't care who they are."

Because Myrtle was not from Charleston, I thought I might get another angle on the social dynamics of the community from Millicent Brown, the daughter of the late J. Arthur Brown, the NAACP president at the time of the strike. Conveniently, Ms. Brown also worked for the Avery Institute. J. Arthur Brown was well-known for his NAACP leadership in Charleston; Ms. Brown was currently writing her Ph.D. dissertation on her father's life and career. To me, she appeared to be both free of, and maybe not so free from, a background of relative privilege. She began by telling me the story of how it felt to be a member of the first group of eleven children who by court order integrated the formerly all-white Charleston High School in 1970.

"It wasn't exactly a role I relished," she remembered, as we talked over drinks at a restaurant near the City Market. "It's never fun being the first, particularly when you're a child, but I had no choice. If my father wasn't willing to offer up his own children for the cause, how could he ask anyone else to volunteer their children?"

"What drew your father to NAACP work?" I inquired.

"Frankly," she replied, "he could afford to take on causes that would have been difficult for others because he didn't have to work." Ms. Brown explained that her grandfather was a building contractor who emigrated from James Island to Charleston in the early part of the century. The elder Mr. Brown was very successful, "despite the fact he had only a third-grade education. He built several houses in Charleston. When he died, he left Dad a home of his own plus several other revenue properties in Charleston and on James Island. These properties were poorly managed," she revealed. "Had Dad built upon what his father left him, he would have been quite wealthy. Meanwhile, his financial security gave him the independence to pursue civil rights, file suits, and make our house at Two-seventy Ashley Avenue a constant meeting place for NAACP leaders while he somehow paid for whatever had to be paid for. He didn't have to worry about being fired the next day." I asked Millicent if the old house on Ashley Avenue still existed.

"Nope. Our house, like many others, was torn down to build the new Ashley River bridge. I do cherish memories of [NAACP Legal Defense Fund director] Thurgood Marshall staying with us whenever he came to Charleston to argue our teacher, voting, and school case appeals before the federal courts. They had a lot of meetings in our basement. It was a memorable time."

"Why did the NAACP group oppose the hospital workers' strike, at least at first?" I asked. "Or rather, why did they oppose SCLC's participation in the hospital strike?"

"By then I had left Charleston for school. But I know there was a resentment of SCLC on the part of my father and his group. This was an NAACP town, and they were the NAACP. The hospital strike introduced an entirely *new* cast of characters—Saunders, who had not been active before; Mary Moultrie, who no one had heard of; plus SCLC and the union leaders—the old leadership had a hard time dealing with it. The very thought of the strikers bringing in Abernathy and Coretta King was unacceptable. Eventually, though, Dad realized he had to join in like everyone else. And so did most of his group. They couldn't just stand on the side and complain."

To obtain still another angle on the psychology of the Charleston black community, Jack McCray suggested that I interview Rev. James Blake, formerly one of Charleston's most prominent African Methodist Episcopal ministers, though Blake was not in Charleston during the 1969 strike. A graduate of Boston University Divinity School, Blake is now pastor of a church in nearby Moncks Corner, South Carolina, about a half-hour drive northward from Charleston on U.S. 52, and I arranged to meet him there.

Dark skinned, a smooth, stylish speaker, and in his late forties, Blake, as he related his story, had had quite a career as a youthful activist. It came naturally, because he was raised, he said, in an "NAACP family." He was president of the NAACP Youth Council in 1963 when, during that summer, the group decided to launch demonstrations against downtown merchants who were still segregating. They decided to take this action, however, without informing the adult NAACP leadership. That summer Blake was home from Morehouse College, where he was a sophomore. Most of his fellow Youth Council members were Burke High School students.

When the adult NAACP leaders—the previously mentioned J. Arthur Brown, the Reverend DeQuincy Newman, and Herbert Fielding—heard their own youth were launching demonstrations without their permission, they were furious. So were state NAACP officials, for they had already decided there would be no demonstrations in South Carolina during the summer of 1963.

The eager Charleston merchants jumped at the chance to exploit this embarrassing split by offering an agreement to the adult leaders that would bring demonstrations to an immediate halt, but Blake and his teenagers rejected the agreement, defying their elders. Then, relishing the moment twenty-eight years earlier, Blake told the story of how his group called a mass meeting to test their strength, winning a vote of confidence to continue picketing. Eventually, Roy Wilkins, the national NAACP executive director in New York, was called to settle the dispute. Wilkins, usually the most conservative of civil rights leaders, sided with the Youth Council.

"What he liked so much," said Blake, "was that ours was a total NAACP effort. You see, I promised to keep other organizations out at a time when SNCC and SCLC were running away with the activist Movement in the South and leaving the NAACP in the lurch.

"Every night that summer until mid-August, we marched and picketed. But our efforts never made national news because the news was suppressed. The *Charleston News and Courier* pretended nothing out of the ordinary was going on, and they didn't carry stories about our efforts. Maybe they thought if they didn't report it, it didn't exist. Finally, in August we reached a settlement: King Street businessmen agreed to offer employment opportunities and courtesies to blacks, and equal pay for equal jobs, one of our key demands. Then, in a mood of triumph, we all caught the train to ride to the historic March on Washington."

It didn't take long for Wilkins to bring Blake to New York to join the national staff as a field director after his schooling at Morehouse and divinity school. Blake returned to Charleston in 1972, working for the state's Commission for Farm Workers until 1980. That year he became pastor of Charleston's prestigious Morris Brown AME Church, which he served until he moved to Moncks Corner's Greater Zion AME in the late 1980s.

Blake does not feel hopeful about the potential for social and racial change in Charleston. The lack of follow-up gains from the hospital strike is only one part of a depressing larger picture, he feels. "I just don't see the leadership," he bemoaned, leaning back in his chair. "What we do in Charleston is either castrate or annihilate black leadership. There's a lot of infighting, in addition to the white opposition. There's a fear of rocking the boat. Other potential leaders are bought off. Many of us who have been in the heat of the battle say, 'I'm not going to get out there and get cut down anymore,' though that's a hard thing to say."

As for young people, "we're not seeing a cadre of leaders coming up, as I and my friends did. Don't forget, it's the demands of the younger generation that keep the drive for social change alive. If they don't do it, who will? But the younger generation is not interested in social movements or group causes. Also, it hurts Charleston that it has no black college; colleges discuss ideas and create a small intelligentsia. A college would provide a way to attract promising youth from other towns, and maybe hold some of our own talent here. Right now our brightest kids can't wait to leave Charleston for greener pastures."

"And the churches?" I asked. "They don't impact social conditions?"

"Of course they say they do, but not really. They're dealing mostly with internal stuff; they don't have the time for larger societal concerns outside church business. This wouldn't happen in Atlanta, for instance, where leadership has always stemmed from the black Protestant churches."

Seeking still another voice, I thought it wouldn't hurt to hear what Miriam DeCosta-Willis of Memphis had to say about Charleston. An esteemed literary scholar now teaching at LeMoyne-Owen College, Mrs. Willis just happened to be visiting family members in Charleston while I was there. She is the daughter of Frank DeCosta, who was considered a member of the Charleston black elite; he was a principal of Avery Institute during the 1930s. Mr. DeCosta left soon after his Avery stint, however, to work at other schools including State in Orangeburg, so his daughter's coming-of-age experiences were quite varied. Charleston, however, was the site of her girlhood years.

We talked in the comfortable home of her aunt in the largest intact black neighborhood, which exists on both sides of the King Street spine. Ms. Willis, now approaching sixty, I guessed, appeared to me to be more reserved than she probably is. She in no way uses her education as a superficial barrier between herself and others, as do some blacks of academic achievement and status.

"I have many ambivalent feelings about Charleston," she began. "I love it, but there's so much division here; class stratification based on family, lineage, color, hair, along with tremendous disparities between the black haves and have-nots. It's like New Orleans and the Caribbean. The Brown Society worked to extend stratification.

"At the same time," she continued, "the Low Country culture surrounding Charleston is very rich in African retention. Windows were painted blue to keep away evil spirits. Steps were wiped down with urine to protect against evil spirits.

Dresses were long. There was the Gullah island dialect, and so forth. Zora Neale Hurston [the famous black anthropologist and novelist of the 1930s and '40s] lived with our family for two weeks while she was studying roots, voodoo, and black folklore in this area. And there's a remarkable folk strength in the barrier islands all the way down to Savannah. The question is, why has this folk strength not been converted into political and economic strengths? As for Charleston itself," she sighed, "I see it as isolated and racially paranoid. For instance, there was an oak tree on Ashley Avenue where it was said slaves were hanged because other blacks betrayed them. I was raised hearing that there was no point in resisting injustice, or trying to change the racial status quo because resistance would be violently stamped out, and *because you could not trust your own people.* Not around here."

That must have created an inordinate amount of fear, even if nothing was being done, I commented. "Yes. Fear here has prevented more radical actions. Fear of what would happen to you. Fear of betrayal. I grew up hearing stories about people who could not return to Charleston because their families had been traitors."

The conversation had made Mrs. Willis somewhat pensive, wistful. "Charleston is not a place you return to," she said. "There is nothing to return here for if you're black. I feel very claustrophobic when I return here to visit my family."

Echoing Blake, but from a vastly different perspective, Miriam DeCosta-Willis was also critical of the Charleston churches. "There's no social action coming from the Charleston churches. In Memphis, for instance, the leaders of even the fundamentalist churches provided dynamic leadership. I think Charleston is a dying community. It's in the backwaters of the Low Country."

I was detecting an air of underlying despair in the comments of Miriam DeCosta-Willis and other Charleston blacks I interviewed about the strike, and about the potential for racial progress in Charleston generally. A feeling of helplessness is not an unknown aspect of black American culture, of course, or among any people anywhere who have been suffering from a condition of subjugation for a long time. But the remarks about Charleston went deeper, referring to fissures within the black community and a community disunity that was singularly pervasive. If the strike didn't bring lasting results, that was to be expected, I seemed to be hearing. It was only a historical anomaly.

I believed the roots of these attitudes had to lie in Charleston's peculiar racial past, and in its slave history. In fact, we don't have to go far; we can examine the disturbing story of the Denmark Vesey Conspiracy of 1822, which cast a long shadow over Charleston's racial psychology, for clues.

Charleston was not just a place where slavery thrived. The early town served as the most important slave port and slave market along the Atlantic coast. African slaves were first imported in 1671 when Charles Town and the Carolina colony were only a year old. As related in *Charleston! Charleston!* by Walter J. Fraser, Jr., the early introduction of rice farming created a need for very large numbers of slaves, because rice farming required intensive manpower. The armies of slave labor in the Carolina Low Country, however, set in motion a dilemma that continually plagued Charleston and South Carolina: The planters needed slaves to work their fields but they feared large numbers of imported Africans because of the inherent potential for rebellion, a fear always uppermost in their minds. Rumors of slave revolts dominate early Charleston and South Carolina history. Slave runaways were a problem, though runaways were faced with the reality that South Carolina was too far south to make escape northward across the Mason-Dixon Line a probability.

In 1739 an aborted slave revolt did occur in Charleston, the Stono Rebellion, notable not because it succeeded but because it was the earliest major slave rebellion in the American South. The Stono Rebellion began on a plantation south of Charleston at the Stono River on James Island. A group of slaves killed about a dozen whites and began marching southward to Georgia, headed, one supposes, for St. Augustine, the Spanish North American capital, where possibly the longtime enemies of the English would provide them assistance and sanctuary. But it wasn't long before the march flagged, then disintegrated into drunkenness and disorder. The blacks were overtaken and confronted by a hastily organized militia at what is today the town of Jacksonborough. Many were killed on the spot; a few escaped into the surrounding woods. In a fever of revenge and excitement, blacks thought to have participated were hunted down like animals and shot. Slaves, and even a few Native Americans who assisted the militia in identifying insurrectionary suspects, were well rewarded.

Despite continual oppression, some Charleston slaves began to exercise limited independence. The Charleston market was almost the sole province of slaves, who sold produce for their masters. Fishing was a slave specialty. Most blacksmiths were black, as were many carpenters.

Several of these relatively independent black people passed into freedom, either via manumission by their owners, or by earning enough through their endeavors to purchase their freedom. Slowly, a class of free Charleston blacks began to emerge, which by the time of Emancipation was second in number only to the free blacks in New Orleans.

Thus the stage was set for the Vesey Conspiracy of 1822. All of the historical documents relating the conspiracy are derived from the court records and government documents, which present quite a problem with respect to the objectivity of the sources.

Denmark Vesey emerges from hazy origins; we do not know his childhood name. In 1781 as a boy of fourteen he, along with several other slaves, was purchased by Captain Joseph Vesey on the island of St. Thomas to be sold in Santo Domingo. St. Thomas was a Danish colony, which is probably how the young Vesey came to be called Denmark. After a year, the purchaser in Santo Domingo returned Denmark to Captain Vesey as physically unfit because he was given, they said, to epileptic fits. Captain Vesey thereupon made the boy his personal servant. Captain Vesey frequently plied the Caribbean, operating as a slaver between the West African coast and the Caribbean. Through these journeys, young Denmark acquired an extraordinary firsthand knowledge of the islands, the middle passage, perhaps something of Africa, and certainly an awareness of the brutal conditions under which slaves were transported to the New World. In 1783, Captain Vesey decided to purchase property in Charleston and settle there. Denmark, who learned to read and write, resided in Charleston with him, hiring himself out as a carpenter and moving about with considerable freedom despite his slave status. Then, quite remarkably, in 1800, at the age of thirty-three, Denmark won $1,500 in the Charleston lottery, and with $600 of that money purchased his freedom. This, of course, did not mean he could exercise all the rights of a white man—far from it. Free blacks in Charleston could hold property but not vote, could testify against one another but not against whites, were excluded from juries and the militia, and were subject to abduction and resale into slavery. (Many of these conditions applied in the North also; at the time of Emancipation, blacks could vote in only six nonslave states.)

During the next two decades, Denmark Vesey went into business for himself as a carpenter. Apparently very skilled and industrious, he became relatively prosperous, eventually purchasing his own home on Bull Street. As a free black Vesey joined a group of about one thousand others during the early nineteenth century. This group of free blacks organized two significant societies to further their interests: the Brown Fellowship Society, comprised of mostly light-skinned free blacks with a policy of excluding those who were dark skinned, and the Society of Free Blacks, an alternative group that any free black could join, of which Vesey may have been a member.

Vesey's most critical and crucial association was as a member of the African Church of Charleston, organized in 1817 as a Methodist spin-off from white churches, which seated blacks in separate areas, usually the balcony, or which held separate services for blacks. Vesey belonged to a section of the African Church that met not far from where its successor, Emanuel African Methodist Episcopal Church on Calhoun Street, is situated today. The leader of this breakaway religious group, which had several sections, was Morris Brown, a light-skinned, mulatto self-made preacher whom everyone remembers as gifted with uncommon intelligence.

The formation of the African church alarmed the white authorities, who quickly closed it down, arrested its leaders under the Negro Act, and sentenced them to be whipped. Nevertheless, the church, *which included both slaves and free blacks,* continued to meet. It was among them that Vesey first began to proselytize against the legitimacy of slavery, basing his arguments on biblical principles, employing his knowledge of the cataclysmic Haitian revolution that began in 1791 and ended with the establishment of the republic in 1804, and citing pamphlets and speeches against slavery that he, among very few blacks in Charleston, had knowledge of, despite the vigilant efforts of the authorities to ban such incendiary materials. (A black seaman who brought in antislavery material in 1809 was deported and banned from Charleston forever.)

All of the blacks who later testified against Vesey attested to his unusual powers of persuasion and his apocalyptic vision. Very soon after the banning of the African Church, Vesey, according to the trial testimony, began to plan a major insurrection designed to do no less than capture the city of Charleston. The insurrectionists would tender no mercy to whites, or to blacks who did not join them. In planning the insurrection, Vesey took into confidence only certain members of the church, and a few free artisans and relatively independent slaves who were allowed to contract themselves out to work for pay—these became his chief lieutenants. The lieutenants were assigned to recruit supporters in Charleston and the neighboring countryside, including the plantations on James and Johns islands. Two of Vesey's key lieutenants were the personal slaves of the governor. Vesey's lieutenant on Johns and James islands was Gullah Jack, well known as an African priest and reputed to possess extraordinary powers.

During Christmastime, 1821, the group began to acquire weapons. A target date of July 14, 1822, was set for the uprising, a time when many of the most prominent whites would be out of town on summer excursions. July 14 was also a Sunday, a day when numbers of slaves from the islands were usually visiting Charleston. Apparently, Vesey hoped that once the uprising was successful and the blacks had taken control of the city and port, an army from the newly independent state of Haiti would arrive to aid them, or if need be, they might effect an escape to Haiti. Vesey attempted to send two letters to Haitian President Boyer notifying him of their intentions and requesting assistance, though it is uncertain whether this communication was actually received. In all his preparations, Vesey warned of the necessity of keeping his plans secret from those Charleston mulattos whom he considered too close to the ruling whites.

It was the inadvertent violation of this last safeguard that finally set in motion the exposure of the plot. In May, on a Sunday, one of the insiders casually asked a mulatto acquaintance, as they stood on the Battery looking out upon the bay, if he knew something momentous was to happen soon; blacks were going to rise up and take Charleston. The acquaintance, surprised at the news, immediately went home and informed his master. As a consequence, the person who let slip the initial information was quickly apprehended by the authorities. Under torture or threat of torture he revealed the broad outlines of the plot and the names of Vesey's key lieutenants.

Astounded by what they were hearing, the authorities followed up those leads, and with information provided by a free blacksmith, a member of Vesey's African

Church who was not involved, they quickly ascertained that the plot was real, extensive, and centered around certain members of the church. As it became obvious an investigation was under way, Vesey decided to move his target date up to June 16, but by then the authorities were thoroughly alerted and on guard. An attempt at an action was called off. Within a few days, a court of seven whites was established to hear testimony. Finally, Denmark Vesey's name was mentioned as the leader by the slave whose indiscretion had led to the unraveling of the conspiracy, and after a futile attempt to hide, Vesey was apprehended.

Under all sorts of threats, tongues loosened in the Charleston prison. Vesey and five of his lieutenants were brought before the court, tried, quickly convicted, and sentenced to hang. According to *Denmark Vesey's Revolt* by John Lofton (p. 161), upon sentencing, Vesey was the recipient of a stern lecture by the presiding judge—a lecture designed not just for Denmark Vesey:

*A moment's reflection must have convinced you that the ruin of your race, would have been the probable result and that years would have rolled away, before they could have recovered that confidence, which they once enjoyed in this community. The only reparation in your power, is a full disclosure of the truth. In addition to treason, you have committed the grossest impiety, in attempting to pervert the sacred words of God into sanction for crimes of the blackest hue.*

Vesey never "disclosed," or named, anyone else; nor did the five others convicted with him. Peter Poyas, Vesey's chief lieutenant, is remembered for admonishing a whimpering companion, "Do not open your lips! Die silent, as you shall see me do."

On July 2, the six convicted men were taken to a spot in a field that would now be located, according to maps, about where Nassau Street meets the Cooper River twin bridges. Before a large crowd they were hanged, left to swing for a few hours, and their bodies removed and buried in unknown graves, so that there would be no proper rites, martyr's funeral marches, or grave sites that might later become shrines.

These first hangings loosened more tongues, as the promise of pardons was

dangled before those arrested. Gullah Jack and a fellow island slave were apprehended. Within a few days they were tried, pronounced guilty, and hanged on what
is now Calhoun Street, near King Street. These hangings in turn caused even more
conspirators to be named, with rumors that up to nine thousand slaves were involved
in the plot. More summary trials resulted, with death sentences almost flippantly
pronounced. On July 26, Charleston was treated to a spectacular public hanging of
*twenty-two men* strung up on a specially constructed gallows at The Lines (a militarily
protected boundary), now Calhoun Street. The entire city turned out for the occasion. There was so much excitement at the scene that a small slave boy was trampled
to death by horses during the executions.

All together, when the trials were completed, thirty-five blacks were hanged,
thirty-one were to be banished, twenty-seven were acquitted, and thirty-eight were
released after questioning for lack of evidence. Four white men were also apprehended, tried, and convicted for "inciting slaves to insurrection." One, a German
peddler, had been overheard telling several blacks that those executed were innocent
and had been murdered, and that the remaining prisoners should be rescued. All
four whites received prison sentences of up to a year, and monetary fines.

Pointedly, those who testified against Vesey and the other conspirators, who
named names and revealed crucial plot details—particularly Monday Gel, one of
Vesey's key lieutenants—received pardons "upon condition that they be sent out
of the limits of the United States, into which they are not to return under penalty
of death." There is no information about where they were banished to, or whether
this part of the sentence was carried out. The court took pains to point out that
"we regard it to be politic that the Negroes should know even their principal ad-
visors and ringleaders cannot be confided in, and that under the temptation of ex-
emption from capital punishment they will betray the common cause."

Slaves who fully cooperated with the authorities and who, it was believed, were
not involved in the plot, were ordered freed and were deeded an annual reward for
life. Two free black men who cooperated were also rewarded. One of the slaves
freed for exposing Vesey and company eventually became a slaveowner himself.
Morris Brown, who was not involved in the conspiracy, and who was in Philadelphia
at the time of the arrests, was banished from Charleston forever, and his African
Church demolished.

The system of punishment and rewards utilized by the Vesey Conspiracy court was designed to instill a fear that any action against the stated order was doomed to failure. And the memory of the Vesey Conspiracy in Charleston, such as it is remembered by blacks, is richly allusive—it was an antislavery rebellion that consisted of conspiracy, talk, confession, and finally, betrayal. "As a small child, I had not heard of Denmark Vesey," Miriam DeCosta-Willis had remarked. "Now that I well know the story, Vesey becomes a lesson. For everything."

The Vesey sentences were quickly followed up by additional repressive measures. First, a prohibition was placed on teaching slaves to read and write. These laws were tightened again after the Nat Turner Slave Rebellion of 1831 in Southampton, Virginia, during which fifty-five whites were killed before the participants were rounded up and executed.

Second, in 1823 a more organized police force was created to keep the movement of blacks under control and to enforce curfews.

Third, Charleston acquired a larger and more secure arsenal. A state appropriation was made to construct the Citadel Fort in the years immediately following the Vesey executions. The Citadel and an increased police presence helped impose a heavy aura of militarization over Charleston.

Fourth, a tax of fifty dollars per year was levied on free black males aged fifteen to fifty who had not resided in the state for at least five years, a provision designed to make South Carolina an undesirable destination for free people of color.

Finally, the Negro Seaman Act of 1822 declared that black seamen who entered the port must be locked up until their ship departed. In addition, captains were required to pay the cost of such jailing, or the seamen could be sold into slavery. This law was bitterly protested by the English, who regularly tended at the port of Charleston with black seamen. The Negro Seaman Act so blatantly contravened the commerce clause of the U.S. Constitution it was declared unconstitutional in 1823, to the bristling resentment of Charleston and South Carolina.

The Vesey Conspiracy and the harsh measures against blacks enacted in its wake can also be seen as a major propelling force in South Carolina's headlong drive toward a national confrontation with the northeastern states over the issue of slavery and states' rights. Reduced to its lowest common denominator, states' rights meant the right to own and sell slaves. Secession in 1860 followed naturally, and after it the taking of Fort Sumter in the bay, the opening battle of the Civil War.

After the Civil War, freedmen from the Low Country were prominent in South Carolina Reconstruction legislatures, to the chagrin of former Confederates. Then, with the overthrowing of Reconstruction in the 1880s, blacks were thrown out of the legislatures and systematically disenfranchised, not to mention the further pro-scriptions sternly imposed via a maze of segregation laws by extremely white-supremacist politicians like Pitchfork Ben Tillman. In Charleston, except for a few independent craftsmen, blacks were relegated to menial work for white families. Black women worked mostly as maids and cooks. This early-twentieth-century period is more than aptly captured in the autobiographies of two extraordinary black Charleston women, Septima Clark in her *Echo in My Soul* and Mamie Fields in her *Lemon Swamp and Other Places*.

Toward the middle of the twentieth century, Charleston blacks instituted several legal actions in the federal courts designed to reverse disenfranchisement by challenging primaries in which only whites could vote, which were ruled unconstitutional. In addition, they targeted the practice of paying black public school teachers less than their white counterparts, a case they also won. These federal suits, which significantly expanded the rights of black citizens in South Carolina, were decided by trailblazing Charleston district judge J. Waites Waring of the Charleston elite, to the hysterical consternation of white Charleston.

Today the Vesey Conspiracy and its repressive aftermath may be consciously forgotten in Charleston, and for understandable reasons. To whites, the conspiracy represented the realization of their worst fears, the total negation of the image of a happy, subjugated people. Vesey was a free craftsman in a relatively favorable position who aligned himself with slaves in defiance of the segmentation of the black population that always worked to the advantage of the ruling whites. Also, the fact that the conspiracy, though probably not as enormous as it was reported to be in the trial, clearly implicated the most trusted personal slaves of the governor destroyed all the illusions of security white Charlestonians may have enjoyed.

For blacks, the Vesey Conspiracy can be interpreted as a heroic failed strike for freedom, but the mass hangings and the draconian policies that followed reverberate with particular horror down through the years. The fact that the discovery of the plot was set in motion by a loyal slave and a group of free blacks—who were rewarded as a consequence—is hardly a pleasant memory. Somewhere in here, it seemed to me, lay the origin of a statement I so often heard: "The problem with black folks in Charleston is they're too identified with white families their families worked for."

This historical background casts a rather different light on the entrance of Local 1199 and SCLC into the hospital workers' strike. It makes one think Charlestonians themselves probably would have never been able to sustain a protest without the outside help they received. I think Naomi White, in her interview, said as much.

～

There was nothing on the surface of the Charleston I was visiting in 1991 that suggested such a troubled racial past. Charleston did, however, remind me of New Orleans in that tourism is its major growth industry.

I decided to take a few days to explore this aspect of Charleston a little more carefully. For part of my touring, as I became a tourist myself, I was fortunate to have Jack McCray join me.

Driving along Calhoun Street toward the wharf, we first went looking for the Medical School Hospital. It has been extensively remodeled since 1969, McCray informed me, and now it sits one block off Calhoun at Barre and Mill streets among a complex of modern medical buildings, all of which are extremely uninteresting. I didn't see any point in going inside to look around.

We followed Calhoun down to the intersection of King Street, the major spine that runs from the north end of the peninsula (North Charleston) to the Battery at the tip of the south end. King and Calhoun is a key intersection, though King is not at all a broad street. At the intersection there is a city square, Marion Square, with a statue of John Calhoun looking southward. Calhoun was the pre-Civil War legislator famous for his passionate defense of states' rights and slavery. Behind the park are old structures, the first Citadel buildings. The former fort, now a military college, has moved to another location north of Calhoun Street.

King Street to the left, away from downtown, is primarily a street of businesses that cater to blacks. The street sort of runs through the center of the largest black neighborhood. To the right, King Street is still the major downtown shopping street, and it continues to do a brisk business though greater Charleston is encircled by shopping malls as is every other major southern city. I found good clothing stores along King, one or two bookstores, a stationery store, furniture stores, shoe stores, and so forth. This is the street that was tied up with picketing in 1963 by James Blake and his youth group. It was also the site, along with Calhoun, of major SCLC marches during the 1969 strike. Before the 1960s, blacks didn't work as salespeople along "white" King Street, and most stores did not allow black customers. Blacks were expected to shop along "black" King Street. Now the stores are happy to have whatever customers they can coax off the street, and stores popular with young blacks have clerks of color. This is particularly true of "new" businesses like Block-buster.

A block below King Street toward the wharf runs Meeting Street. A few blocks farther is East Bay Street, both long streets that parallel King, and which, to the south, lead into the major tourist area and the City Market. When we reached the intersection of Calhoun and East Bay, McCray had me pull over. He pointed out a small area that he called the Borough, which was once a black area, the neighborhood where he said he was born and raised. Now it's remodeled into expensive renovated housing, shops, and restaurants. The new Municipal Auditorium occupies part of this area; so does a small shopping mall on East Bay, and a snazzy informal restau-rant/coffee shop I learned to like.

Southward, toward the Battery, it is only a few blocks to the market, which runs three or four short blocks between Meeting Street and East Bay. This historic market, once the site of vegetable and fish markets run by blacks ("My parents moved to Charleston to sell vegetables here," McCray said), now consists of rented shops and stalls selling all kinds of stuff, from jewelry to leather to pottery to ceramics, depending on who rents a stall.

At the far end of the market, black women weave and sell their beautiful baskets, made from dried bulrush, sweet grass, and bonded with fresh palmetto. The basket makers are not Charlestonians, however; the basket-weaving tradition comes from Mount Pleasant, a small town north of Charleston. These baskets, which come in about ten shapes, have been recently traced to the Mende people of Sierra Leone in West Africa.

Clothing stores, knickknacks, and restaurants line both sides of the Market. Walking in the direction of Broad Street, we come upon the oldest historical structures: the oldest theater, old churches, the old courthouse, along with bookstores and specialty shops, one or two music clubs, expensive legal offices—very similar to the French Quarter of New Orleans.

Across Broad Street is the most prestigious housing area, called South of Broad. These houses are big, raised frame structures, set along narrow streets that are almost alleyways. It was in one of these actual alleyways near the wharf, McCray informed me, that the Catfish Row of DuBose Heyward's novel *Porgy* was set, for there were once black people living in the area along the wharf. Finally, we arrived at the Battery, an attractive sea wall with a walkway, which you can slowly drive along for a good mile or so looking out at the bay, which is the confluence of the Cooper and Ashley rivers.

To me, the Battery is the most attractive spot in Charleston because it is actually used by natives, a bridge between old Charleston and new Charleston. On weekends young people, black and white, drive and park along the Battery in droves, and stride along the walkway day and night. This is the same Battery where the conversation took place that led to the revealing of the Vesey plot in 1822. I didn't see any racial trouble, either. The Battery sort of reminds me of the drive along Lake Pontchartrain in New Orleans, used extensively by both races, but in separate groups. One afternoon I observed a young black couple fishing. In such an urban setting, I thought that was a very relaxed, and southern, touch.

During the weeks I was in Charleston, I noticed, however, something strange about the Charleston downtown and tourist area in comparing it with the New Orleans French Quarter. There was a politeness and orderliness that was certainly lacking in New Orleans. For one thing, while I was there, I observed no indigenous cultural activity that Charlestonians attended or partook of, except for congregating along the Battery. Compared with the French Quarter of New Orleans, downtown Charleston was too sane. It lacked the eccentrics, the crazies who stroll the streets of the French Quarter feeling perfectly normal. I found myself searching for their Charleston cohorts in vain. Where was the "duck woman," the redhead who walks around the French Quarter with her duck trailing by a string, as if that were the most natural thing in the world? And where was the white "Marie Leveau" (the voodoo priestess), who wanders around in a different costume every day, her favorite lately being a long eighteenth-century black dress, her contorted face usually staring out from under a motorcycle helmet? "Marie Leveau" speaks to no one and if you speak to her, she screams at you in tongues. And where are the dashing "queens" who contest the grandest gowns and the most exciting dresses during the carnival season, or any season, or any excuse for a season? And how about the hippies, descending upon New Orleans from every hick town in the country, assured that they will be right at home among kindred free spirits? Or the man who wanders the streets stuttering languages no one can understand, as if giving profound speeches at a UFO convention which we mortals simply cannot comprehend? Or the thin black man who has wandered the streets for years in an intense rush, always carrying bags, but never seeming to reach a destination? Or the street musicians of all types? Or the self-proclaimed clowns in painted whiteface supposing, I imagine, that outlandish makeup is perfectly normal in the home of perpetual carnival? Where *was* the duck woman of Charleston? It's not that Charleston doesn't have its eccentrics, I am sure, but I wondered if maybe the outstanding specimens had all left for New Orleans, or New York, where they no doubt feel more secure.

A few days later, I was able to arrange for McCray's help again in guiding me through the black areas of Charleston, located primarily on the north side of Calhoun Street.

We stopped first at the impressive Emanuel AME Church on Calhoun Street near Meeting Street. Emanuel is the successor church to Morris Brown's original African Church founded in 1817, to which Denmark Vesey belonged. The church was closed several times by the city and by state law in 1834. It reopened after the

Civil War, and the present beautifully maintained, cream-colored structure with its prominent steeple was constructed in 1891. "This church," McCray reminded me, "belonged to the Borough, where I was born." Because it is so well known, Emanuel Church had been one of the most important meeting sites during the strike.

"While we're at it, remember that the neighborhood near Avery Institute on Bull Street was an old black neighborhood," McCray added. I had seen a tiny housing project in the area when I went to visit state senator Herbert Fielding at his funeral home on Logan Street. Fielding cited the intersection of Tradd and Logan as the center of the former black community.

From Emanuel, we drove northward so that McCray could show me the site of the former Robert Gould Shaw School on Mary Street. This was the first school for blacks after the Civil War, named for the Massachusetts Union officer who was killed while leading black troops in an assault on the Confederate Fort Wagner at Morris Island, one of Charleston's barrier islands.

Then we drove over to King Street, that is, "black King," the hub of the former black business district. Now this area is in decline, but not completely; not as completely as Greensboro's old black business areas. Small stores of various types still exist, along with the usual barbershops, including clothing stores that feature styles favored by blacks, cosmetics, and beauty supplies. "Black King" was the prime avenue of marches during the strike, since it runs right through the middle of the primarily black community all the way to the beginnings of North Charleston. The major black community landmarks are the dominant churches. Most noteworthy, at the intersection of King and Morris is Morris Brown AME, a magnificent church, recently renovated with handsome woodwork. Further down Morris Street is Morris Street Baptist Church; both edifices hosted nightly community meetings during the strike.

While in the area, we stopped to eat at a small black restaurant; I tried the red rice. Not bad, though New Orleanians are notoriously chauvinistic when it comes to food. There didn't seem to be many small restaurants of this type. Apparently, Charleston is not an "eating out" town.

We drove to the wharf area along East Bay Street, which contained mostly warehouses, small factories, the railroad yard, and a large black housing project situated between East Bay and Meeting Street. Blacks work in these shipping-related industries, and in the factories of North Charleston, or in service jobs supporting the tourist industry. Farther up East Bay, and parallel to the railroad, are located Charleston's several cemeteries. Whites and blacks are interred in separate burial grounds.

From King Street facing away from the docks is some of the nicest housing in Charleston, occupied by whites and blacks, but mostly blacks. McCray, Myrtle Glascoe, and Isaiah Bennett live in this area. Burke High School, Hampton City Park, the baseball stadium for Charleston's minor league team, and the Citadel military academy are also in the neighborhood. For those who really like Charleston, I could well understand their attraction to an unpretentious neighborhood of this type, with adequate spacing between the homes, many with unique side porches (I haven't seen that design anywhere else in the South). There is a feeling of a small country town and, at the same time, of an urban city. Not too urban, for there is no "street life"; Myrtle Glascoe was certainly correct about that. Not as there is in New Orleans, where people parade up and down the street to music, or just hang out, sitting on their stoops yelling at each other.

As we drove around, I noticed that the continuity on the north side was uncomfortably disrupted by the heavily traveled U.S. 17 expressway, which splits the peninsula between the Ashley River bridge to the south, and the Cooper River bridge to the north. The U.S. 17 traffic is a virtual thruway around 5:00 P.M. Interstate 26, which originates in Charleston, begins in the middle of the U.S. 17 expressway, then runs up to North Charleston, and on and on to its termination point of Asheville, North Carolina. Of course, none of this disturbs downtown or tourist districts, which are far enough away from the traffic to hardly know it exists.

North Charleston is primarily industrial, anchored by the huge naval base and hospital; then by shopping malls, auto dealerships, chain restaurants, and motels; it is very similar to the High Point Road area in Greensboro, only a little bit more grand. Driving on I-26 at a certain point between Charleston and North Charleston, there is an awful smell; "probably from some factory," McCray laughed. "We smell it, too." At a Grandy's restaurant in North Charleston, I did discover the best-tasting iced tea in the Western world.

Now I was ready to explore the barrier islands. First, and most important, I wanted to interview Bill Saunders, one of the key negotiators who had helped settle the strike. I was to meet him at the office of his radio station on Wapoo Island. I drove out U.S. 17 south to Wapoo Road, crossed a short bridge, and easily found the station, which was located in an old house fronting a small creek. It was beginning to rain.

Now in his fifties, his hair graying, the somber Saunders worked out of a low-key wood-paneled office. It was late in the afternoon and only one or two people were in the office. They seemed to relate to Saunders without excessive or artificial deference.

Saunders had an air of confidence about him, a demeanor that suggested he had "made it" in American society, and in a lot of ways he had. ("I always carry three sets of clothes," he said, "my street clothes, my working clothes, and my Chamber of Commerce suit and tie.") He spoke in an eloquent, musical Gullah accent, which reminded me of the West Indian accents I heard when I lived in New York.

Before we began the interview, I let Saunders read an introductory statement I had written on Charleston, saying, in effect, that as far as civil rights was concerned, nothing had ever happened in Charleston other than the hospital strike of 1969. Saunders let me know right off that he was unhappy with that assessment.

"First of all," he began, "you can't speak about Charleston, or the hospital strike without including the islands. If you include the islands, a great deal that was important in the civil rights movement happened in Charleston. We're talking about five islands: James, Johns, Wadmalaw, Edisto, and Younges. Wadmalaw is seventy-five percent black. Johns just lost its black majority. James lost its black majority a good while ago."

I replied that I thought Charleston was Charleston and the islands were the islands.

"Well, we're part of Charleston County," he replied. "Really, you can't consider Charleston, particularly black Charleston, without the islands. Particularly Johns Island, where I'm from."

I asked Saunders to draw distinctions for me between islanders and Charleston blacks. "We [islanders] are different in our orientation toward each other as people, for one thing. Our respect for leadership, and our religious beliefs give us, and me, an anchor they [Charleston blacks] don't have. They laugh at our language because of our Gullah; they say we can't speak English, but our culture *unifies* us.

"There have been blacks on the islands who were well-off, but they were considered the same as those who had nothing. In Charleston those kinds of economic differences would create all kinds of class barriers. We have respect for our elders, *even when we know they are wrong.* This kind of thing holds us together. On Johns Island there's a huge oak tree, the Angel Oak. It's been there as long as anyone can remember. Stood through many a storm. The Angel Oak is our symbol of survival. Grandmother used to say, 'Anything that can bend will not break when the storm comes. When a storm comes, the oak bends and swings. The pine tree pops.' When the sun comes out again after the storm, the Angel Oak is still there, standing majestic, no matter how many limbs were taken by the storm."

I was interested to know the source of the island's and Saunders's own political activism, which eventually had led him into the very center of the strike.

"It has to do with Esau Jenkins," he replied. Jenkins's name certainly struck a bell. "Esau Jenkins was the catalyst behind progressive changes on Johns Island." Bill Saunders had entered manhood as a protégé and devotee of Esau Jenkins. Members of the same church, Wesley United Methodist, Saunders was one of several island kids that Esau bussed to Burke High School in Charleston in the early 1950s, for there was no high school on the island. After two years of high school, Saunders joined the Army. He was only sixteen, though he passed for seventeen. Discharged two years later, he returned to Burke to complete high school in 1956. "I didn't know we islanders were 'different' until I attended Burke. Charleston kids laughed at the way we talked and dressed. In the Army, some of the guys would tease me just to make me angry. When I'm angry, my speech becomes heavy with accent, and I slur my words. When you hear an islander slurring his or her words, get out of the way," he joked, unsmilingly.

"What were your expectations as you grew up on Johns Island?" I asked. "Were you eager to leave?"

"I was. Most of us were. But I suppose being in the Army taught me I could do what I wanted to here if I worked at it. When Esau ran for the school board in 1956, you couldn't imagine how exciting that was. People were amazed to see his name on the ballot. That kind of political activity was needed. In my school there was no electricity. If the weather was like it is today [cloudy and rainy], we wouldn't be able to have school. Too dark."

Saunders was a key member of Esau Jenkins's Progressive Club; despite his youth, he managed the club store. "However," he said, "in the late sixties, I began to move away from Esau and the nonviolent movement. By then I was in my mid-twenties, married with *five* kids, and working in a mattress factory in Charleston." Saunders was fascinated with the speeches of Malcolm X, and was a supporter of the Black Muslim leader, and gravitated toward the positions of the former SNCC chairman, Stokely Carmichael, who preached black power. "Stokely and Cleve Sellers spent time on Johns Island resting and talking with us." At that time, Saunders also edited a militant newspaper, *The Low Country Newsletter*. He let me see an issue. One article lambasted and caricatured Charleston NAACP leader Herbert Fielding as a hopeless moderate. "As for Esau, he wasn't with us. He really believed in nonviolence to the core, and the language of black power was too strident for him. However, three of his children were in *my* group. My relationship with Esau was getting to be"—here he slipped into heavy Gullah for emphasis—"*baaad.*

"Finally, I decided I had to seek Esau out. We had to talk. He agreed and one night we just had it out. He accused me of being too militant. I told him, and I remember that night till this day, that his problem with *me* being militant was not one I could understand because I was not *ever* as militant as he was, to have done the things for people he did when he was virtually alone out there. After that night, we came to a kind of understanding." Together, Jenkins and Saunders, along with the Reverend Michael Goodwin of Wesley Church and other key islanders, estab-lished an innovative, badly needed island health program, all the more crucial because it attempted to address the needs of seasonal migrant farm workers who Saunders said are now coming to the islands regularly to work the larger farms. This project, called Rural Missions, grew into the Sea Islands Comprehensive Health Center Project and Nursing Home, which opened in the early 1970s; it is quite an extensive facility, unmatched on any of the South Carolina or Georgia barrier islands.

"Esau's genius was the ability to formulate proper questions," Saunders reflected, "though he looked and sounded 'country.' He had little formal education. He did have a vision in his efforts to bring in outside help to improve conditions on Johns Island."

"So, how did you get involved in the hospital workers' strike?" I finally asked Saunders.

"I was working in the mattress factory then, but I knew a lot of people involved with the strike. I knew Mary Moultrie through Esau Jenkins. When the first nurses were fired, I was one of the ones she asked to help. I contacted Reginald Bennett, senior, who was serving on the Civil Rights Committee of the federal agency he worked for. He was able to get the first nurses reinstated. From then on, I was part of the meetings at the union hall where we were hearing the complaints of hospital personnel."

"Did you ever believe, once the walkout happened, that the strike would hold?"

"Well, there was a difference of opinion. Isaiah Bennett and some others didn't feel they could win against those big, powerful hospitals. They would have preferred to challenge a smaller hospital first. They were primarily interested in *unionizing* hospital workers as a building block for labor in this state, and in the South. I was more interested in going after the state's minimum wage scale of a dollar-thirty per hour, since the medical school was a state institution. If they were forced to raise the scale at the hospital, the minimum would also have to be raised in *all* state jobs. Management knew that, and that's why they fought us so hard."

"Wasn't the inability to win union recognition a kind of failure?" I asked gingerly. "How could the workers protect themselves after the strike without a union?"

"I wasn't *interested* in union recognition," Saunders replied. "I wanted to see a hospital workers association formed which would cover a wide range of categories of workers. The physicians have an association which everyone recognizes. Why couldn't the nurses, nurses' assistants, and other help have a beneficial association? But it was 'union, union, union.'"

"How about white nurses and nonskilled workers?" I asked. "How much support did you get from them?"

"There were several whites who wanted to join us, but we treated them poorly, I have to admit. We made the mistake of believing all the whites were doing okay. Later, after it was all over, we realized they had the privileges of being white but they weren't making any money, either. I had to change some of my ideas. The whites who openly came into our meetings were fired once the administration discovered they did. Really, to be honest, we didn't know how to effectively bring whites into the strike effort. And we didn't trust them."

As did others, Saunders cited the lack of enthusiasm emanating from the traditional black leadership class in Charleston as a problem. "The entire black leadership was opposed to the strike," he said. "Early on, they told the mayor, since *they* weren't involved, the strike *couldn't* last. So we had to sustain ourselves with rank-and-file people, and there was quite a bit of roughness involved. But it was the only way we could protect our people, especially when they were in jail. Toward the end, when the black leadership realized we were going to have a victory anyway, they came around. Until then, we felt like the powers that be were sending in certain people to try to take us over."

"Certain people?"

"Herbert Fielding [a state senator and one of Charleston's most prominent funeral home owners] was one. Now"—Saunders smiled—"Fielding and I get along quite well."

"Twenty-two years later."

"Yes. But time and perspective change people." He paused for a while. It was beginning to storm outside. "The city government sent Herbert to take control of the strike, tell us what to do. The Fielding brothers were one of the most prominent funeral home families in Charleston. I didn't know them then, but I knew *about* them. When I was a boy, their father used to send Christmas presents to our church. Those were the only Christmas presents I got as a child."

"People I talked to," I ventured, "feel the condition of the hospital workers is bad *now*. Was there a way to offer more protection for them through the settlement?"

"Listen," Saunders responded sharply. "Anyone who *isn't willing to stand up* if the grievance mechanism is in place, I can't defend. Before the strike there weren't even any job descriptions. Now folks are saying, somebody needs to *save us*. Martin Luther King. Jesus. Anybody. Well, *there're no saviors out there*. We've got a plantation mentality. . . . During the sixties and seventies, we have somehow given black people the notion *they don't have to do anything for themselves*. They don't have to be *responsible* for anything. We were trying to *empower* people. But folk don't want that. They want us to come over and beat up on somebody. Or do something for them they are quite capable of doing for themselves. It *depresses* me."

It was beginning to depress me, too, and Saunders was slipping into heavy Gullah. The time to end the interview had arrived. I shut off my tape recorder and packed up my notebooks. As I was leaving, he said, "I'll expect you to visit our church on Sunday." Well, I certainly wanted to visit Wesley United Methodist on Johns Island, which was also Esau Jenkins's church.

"I'll be there," I promised. "Maybe we can talk some more."

First, however, I wanted to do a little research on Esau Jenkins. I had first heard the name Esau Jenkins in 1973 on a flying trip to Charleston with Andrew Young. Young, who had just been elected to Congress from Atlanta, was to speak at the dedication of a new health facility on Johns Island named for Mr. Jenkins, who had died in 1972 as a result of injuries suffered in an automobile accident.

Born on Johns Island in 1910, Esau Jenkins had devoted his life to forging a road through forest, underbrush, and swamp to construct connections between the isolated and dormant barrier islands and the mainland society of Charleston. The five Charleston-area Sea Islands, Johns being the largest, had been since colonization the home of extremely profitable rice and cotton plantations. During the Civil War, when several plantation owners abandoned their lands to seek safety on the mainland, their properties were confiscated by the federal government and partitioned off by the Freedmen's Bureau, in portions no larger than forty acres, to former slaves. Thus, Sea Island blacks became small landowners or wage workers on the reconstituted plantations. Generally, these blacks, even when they were landowners, were very poor, and they had a hard time holding on to their land. The islands were isolated and could only be reached by primitive railroad and boat—the journey between Charleston and Johns Island, for instance, required the better part of a day during the early years of the twentieth century. Schools for blacks were virtually nonexistent, and the situation was not much better for the minority of whites. The whites who remained after Reconstruction still pretty much controlled the islands. Under Redemption, blacks did not vote or even think about voting for fear of reprisals, as was universally true in South Carolina.

Young Esau attended grammar school only through the fourth grade—and this only part-time, for black children did not attend school when they were needed in the fields. His mother died when he was nine. He recalled, in *Ain't You Got a Right to the Tree of Life?*, recorded and edited by Guy and Candie Carawan (p. 142):

> *We had around 50 children and one teacher with a one door school. And besides that they painted it black, that we could be identified as to who goes to the school. It discouraged me when I got some pride. I left school and went to Charleston and started working on a boat. But I still was serious about getting an education. . . .*
>
> *Then I got married some years later [at seventeen] and found out that I have a great responsibility, and I know that my education is limited. So I decided that I would work and go to school at the same time.*

Thus began Esau's lifetime passion for education, rooted in a self-education that was designed to overcome the limitations of his formal public schooling. He undertook night school classes in Charleston, despite the immense difficulties of travel between Johns Island and the city. He acquired the habit of ordering books and journals by mail, and developed an avid interest in what was then called Negro history, and anything else he could think of that could expand his consciousness and self-knowledge, recalled Ethel Grimball, Esau Jenkins's daughter, whom I met at the Comprehensive Health Center where she worked. She remembered that family discussions centered around what he was currently reading. "Every Sunday morning before church we had family meetings during which we discussed books, religion, behavior—anything anyone wanted to bring up. As children we were assigned passages of the Bible to read aloud and interpret."

Jenkins's photos reveal a pudgy man with a receding hairline, dressed unstylishly in a conservative suit and tie. Like other islanders, he was dark skinned. He did not let Charleston's color prejudices deter him. "He always taught us you are no better or worse than anyone else," remembered Ms. Grimball, intensely. "He would say, 'Pigmentation is the least important quality in determining who you are.'"

Esau began farming for himself in 1930, at the age of twenty. He grew cotton for five years, then gave that up as unprofitable and raised vegetables, purchasing a truck for the long journey to the Charleston market. Many of the Charleston market merchants, he discovered, were Greek. "They buy all kinds of vegetables. So I thought the best thing for me to do then," he recalled, "is to try to learn the Greeks' language.... So I went and took Greek ... and I was able to understand the Greek language in everyday speaking in business and that helped me to go on."

During the postwar period, as bridges were constructed between the islands and Charleston, Esau, ever enterprising in developing his businesses, opened a motel and café for blacks on Spring Street. It was during this period that the young Mary Moultrie worked for Jenkins and his wife at the Spring Street café. Meanwhile, conditions remained the same on the islands. Poverty and poor health conditions were the norm. Educational standards remained abysmally poor.

In 1945, Esau Jenkins purchased a bus for the purpose of transporting island teenagers, including the eldest of his own eight children, to Burke High School in Charleston. At the same time, he began agitating for the building of a high school on the island. Herbert Fielding told me, "Esau drove them so crazy demanding this and that for the Johns Island kids at Burke and making the state reimburse him for their transportation to Charleston, that the county school board finally built a black high school on the island," which became Haut Gap School. Despite that achievement, adults on the island felt, according to Ethel Grimball, that the new school was inadequate, and poorly kept up, so they continually pressured for improvements.

In 1948, Jenkins expanded his bus service in order to transport islanders to and from work in Charleston. At the same time, he was interested in increasing the number of registered voters on Johns Island. In a moment of inspiration, he hit on the idea of tutoring his passengers on sections of the United States Constitution they would most likely be required to know to pass a voter registration test. He somehow did this while running his bus between Charleston and the island, though that's rather difficult to envision. It was Jenkins's habit, when asked what spurred his interest in voting and community political activization, to tell the story of How a Black Man Was Killed for Running Over a White Man's Dog.

"In 1938 two black men were riding in a truck on Johns Island. A dog ran out of a gate. The driver tried to avoid it, but he couldn't; he hit the dog and killed it.

The dog's owner, who was white, ... jumped in his own car, and he carried a shotgun and ran this man down." He confronted the black man and killed him. Nothing was ever done to bring the killer to justice. Jenkins realized that absurd incidents of violence against blacks would continue unless they sought to protect themselves through political strength. Toward this end, he organized the Progressive Club. The Progressive Club thus became the first modern black civic-political organization on the South Carolina Sea Islands.

At this juncture Esau Jenkins's story broadens to touch base with the life of Septima Clark. Mrs. Clark had known Esau since he was fourteen, when he first ventured to Charleston as a boy to work on a boat. She assisted him in his efforts to enter night school; in fact, in her autobiography, *Echo in My Soul*, she says she taught Esau to read.

During the summer of 1954, Mrs. Clark attended a workshop at Highlander Folk School. Founded in 1932 by Myles Horton and Don West, Highlander by 1954 had become one of the most innovative retreat centers in the South. Horton, who had come to be the person most identified with Highlander, actively encouraged interracial gatherings as a necessary step toward the advent of racial justice in the South. Located about fifty miles north of Chattanooga on a two-hundred-acre farm near Monteagle, Tennessee, Highlander maintained a small full-time staff that conducted adult education workshops and sought to establish "citizenship schools." Highlander's main value was its relaxed setting away from the glare of public scrutiny, where blacks and whites could beneficially exchange experiences and ideas. Few other such institutions existed on an ongoing basis in the South during the thirties, forties, and fifties.

Septima Clark had followed Esau's progress and knew of his interest in bettering the conditions of islanders. She convinced him to attend a Highlander workshop, and he did in 1954 and 1955. One particular session was on the United Nations. During the course of discussion, Esau recalls (p. 150):

> *They asked each person to give the immediate problem in his locality. My immediate problem was adult education, because so many people couldn't read or write ... I would have been in the same condition if I didn't go back to school. So I asked the Highlander School officials if it were possible to help us set up night schools for these people to help them become better citizens. Myles said if I could find a place, could find a teacher, he could take care of the expenses.*

When in 1955 Septima Clark, at the age of fifty-six, was fired from the Charleston public schools because of her NAACP activities, Myles Horton lost no time in inviting her to become director of workshops at Highlander. She moved there in June 1956. Esau also began frequently traveling to Highlander, taking groups of people with him, building a strong relationship between Highlander and Charleston and Johns Island. The establishment of a citizenship school on Johns Island became a priority.

To house the school, the Progressive Club purchased a one-story building on the island. In the front they set up a store; two rooms in the rear were planned for the citizenship classes. It was hoped that Septima Clark could do the teaching, but she was fully occupied with her Highlander duties. So Myles asked Mrs. Clark's cousin, Bernice Robinson, a beautician and seamstress, to do the teaching.

Septima Clark had died in 1987 at the age of eighty-nine, but Bernice Robinson still lives in Charleston, and I arranged to visit her to get her part of the citizenship school story. A native Charlestonian and a graduate of Burke High School in 1930, Ms. Robinson emigrated to New York in 1936 in the wake of a marriage that didn't work out. "The only decent work here was teaching and nursing," she remembers. "Other than that it was domestic work." In New York, she became a seamstress in the garment district. At night she studied cosmetology, which led to a job in a Harlem beauty shop. In 1941 she joined the U.S. Signal Corps (military communications) in Philadelphia, but she didn't like Philadelphia. In 1942 she returned to New York to work for the Internal Revenue Service. Because her schedule was constantly changing, she transferred to the Veterans Administration in 1943, where she labored until 1947. That year Ms. Robinson returned to Charleston with her daughter to care for her ailing parents. "I expected to return to New York the minute they got better, but I soon realized the situation at home was one I couldn't so easily leave.

"It was difficult to readjust to life in Charleston," she remembers, "and there was still no work. It wasn't very different from when I left in 1936. And I found it very painful to accommodate myself again to segregation.

"There was no organized movement for racial progress here. The only thing happening was Judge Waring's decision that blacks could vote in the primary, though that was very, very important." Her first job in Charleston was with a black uphol-stery company, where she made fifteen dollars per week. Soon after, she opened her own beautician business.

Once Ms. Robinson realized she would be in Charleston for an indeterminate period, she joined the NAACP and became deeply involved, serving as secretary during J. Arthur Brown's presidency. With a new consciousness of the value of the ballot, no doubt encouraged by Judge Waring's decision, the Charleston NAACP was able to quickly increase membership from 300 to 1,200. "I recruited right through my beauty shop," she laughed. "My clients *had* to join. If they were afraid, I told them their membership cards could be mailed to me at my business, and no one would ever know the difference. In fact, they didn't have to be mailed at all, since I was the secretary." During this period Ms. Robinson met Esau Jenkins, who was in the process of forming an island-city civic and political alliance with J. Arthur Brown, called the Citizens Committee of Charleston County. She remembers Esau as "a very innovative person." Ms. Robinson also was familiar with Highlander, for it was she who drove Septima Clark back and forth from Highlander to Charleston; Mrs. Clark did not drive.

"In 1956 we were making the trip to Highlander just about every week—four hundred fifty miles. I would stop in Augusta for gas because there was a station there where we could use the bathroom, and there was one station we could use in Atlanta. Once we reached Tennessee, I flew around those mountains," she remem-bered, relishing the good ole days.

Ms. Robinson attended the United Nations workshop where Esau Jenkins brought up the need for a citizenship program on Johns Island. "Esau told the story of one of the islanders he was coaching. She had memorized the section of the Constitution she was supposed to read for the registration test, though she couldn't read. What she did was stare at the page as if she was reading, and recite the section from memory. She fooled the registrar and we had a good laugh, but Esau said memorization wasn't good enough, people needed to actually learn to read.

"When they first asked me to do the teaching, I said, 'No, I'm no teacher. I'll do anything else to help.' But Myles Horton said, 'We don't need a schoolteacher type; we need someone who can deal with adults as adults.' So I said, 'I'll try it.'"

With Esau's help ("Ordinarily you couldn't come from Charleston to the island and be accepted unless someone knew you"), she did remarkably well. The citizenship program utilized her considerable abilities and extremely varied occupational experiences in a way she could never have anticipated. "I decided *not* to use elementary school material. The elementary school textbooks were demeaning to adults. The islanders wanted to learn practical things, like how to write letters to relatives who had moved away. And they needed to be able to read letters. We had to work quickly and in a very limited time period—we only held classes in December, January, and February, when people didn't work in the fields."

The first class in 1957 had fourteen people in it. Some of the women brought their teenage girls, because they couldn't leave them at home alone. As the school developed, Myles Horton became more and more wrapped up in Johns Island. So did folk singer Guy Carawan of the Highlander staff, and his wife, Candie; they moved to the island during 1961–1963. It was on Johns Island that Carawan heard a version of "We Shall Overcome" sung by the islanders in their distinctive a cappella shout style as "I Shall Overcome." (An early version of the "Overcome" hymn had been used by striking food and tobacco workers in Charleston in 1945 as "We Will Organize.") Carawan, who frequently played at Movement events in the early days, helped popularize "We Shall Overcome"; it didn't take long before it was adopted as the anthem of the civil rights movement. It is probably on the island that he also heard the hymn "Keep Your Eyes on the Prize," another Movement classic. Fascinated by the religious singing on Johns Island, Carawan arranged for the Morning Star Hall Singers to travel to folk festivals around the country, and recorded and helped authenticate their music.

By 1960, Highlander's profile had been significantly heightened, and as far as the segregationist South was concerned, heightened too much. The state of Tennessee had been trying to find an excuse to close Highlander since it opened, and now, with interracial activity and voter registration increasing, Highlander was branded "Communist." Suddenly, highway billboards throughout the South were depicting huge blown-up photographs of Martin Luther King, Jr., in attendance at a Highlander session, captioned "Martin Luther King at Communist Training School."

In July 1959, while a citizenship workshop was in session, a local prosecutor and eighteen deputies raided the school, searching, they said, for alcoholic beverages, which the school did not have a license to sell. Myles Horton was in Europe at the time; Septima Clark was in charge. The officers searched the entire school grounds and buildings until they found a jug in one of the houses, filled it with moonshine liquor, padlocked the school, then arrested Mrs. Clark and took her off to jail. Despite the seriousness of the situation, when the news got out that Septima Clark had been arrested on a charge associated with homemade liquor, the Tennessee officials became the subject of widespread ridicule within civil rights circles, for everyone who had attended a Highlander session well knew Septima Clark did not drink at all, and didn't look favorably upon those who did in her presence. Nevertheless, the objective of curtailing Highlander's activities had been temporarily achieved, and though Highlander fought the charges in court, its charter was revoked on February 16, 1960.

It is at this point, in 1960, that Andrew Young, a twenty-eight-year-old Congregational minister working as an executive for the National Council of Churches in New York, enters the story. Young, my childhood friend from New Orleans, decided he wanted to become more directly involved in the southern civil rights movement than was possible while living and working in New York. A graduate of Howard University and the Hartford Seminary, he was one of the Council of Churches' most promising youth executives, but he and his wife, Jean, an Alabamian, were ready to return South.

Young had recently met Myles Horton and they talked about Young's interests. Horton proposed that Young move to Highlander in 1960 to establish an expanded, Southwide citizenship program based on the existing model. Septima Clark had suffered a heart attack in 1957 (two years before her arrest), and could not take on increased responsibilities. Bernice Robinson had her hands full working with the Johns Island citizenship school while trying to sustain her beautician business. So Horton looked forward to Young's arrival.

Then, when charges were brought against Highlander, and the school lost its appeal in Tennessee courts, Horton asked Martin Luther King, Jr., if his Southern Christian Leadership Conference could sponsor the citizenship program. King agreed, and the citizenship program was shifted from Highlander to SCLC. (The Field Foundation, which supported the program at Highlander, continued its funding through the United Church of Christ Board of Homeland Missions.)

Andrew Young's very first church as a young Congregational minister had been in the southern Georgia town of Thomasville. During his two years in Thomasville, Young had several times visited the Dorchester Center for youth conferences. The Dorchester Center was once a Congregational Church school located in Liberty County, Georgia, on U.S. 84, about forty miles south of Savannah between the hamlets of Midway and McIntosh. Though Dorchester was no longer a school, it still maintained its campus with dormitory and a classroom building. Young convinced the United Church of Christ Board to use the Dorchester site for the citizenship school seminars, to be held one week each month. Dr. Wesley Hotchkiss of the United Church Board was instrumental in winning approval for this plan. The citizenship school under SCLC's tutelage would be modeled on the Johns Island program. That summer of 1961, Young, Septima Clark, and Dorothy Cotton of the SCLC staff undertook a month-long whirlwind driving tour through the Deep South to recruit the initial participants.

Over the next few years, almost all of the new southern civil rights volunteers attended the Dorchester sessions, with the intent that they would in turn organize voting education programs in their own communities. The citizenship program, along with the voting education program operated by the Southern Regional Council in Atlanta, thus became a crucial training ground for black voter registration in the South during the 1960s.

Within a year or so after his move to Atlanta, Young became deeply involved in SCLC administration. His citizenship school duties were assumed by Dorothy Cotton, with Septima Clark and Bernice Robinson continuing as teaching and program mainstays. As I became aware of this complicated history of personal and professional relationships, I understood better why the SCLC had felt so secure entering the Charleston strike in 1969, despite protestations by the NAACP that Charleston was an "NAACP town."

In 1972, on a return drive from Highlander, Esau Jenkins was seriously injured in an automobile accident, and was hospitalized in Charleston. A week later, he died from complications resulting from his injuries.

Esau Jenkins, because of his determination to break out of the limitations of his Johns Island upbringing, had quietly changed the course of island history. And by extension, through the model of the citizenship school as preparation for voting, he and Bernice Robinson and Septima Clark and Highlander Folk School had helped change the South.

I never forgot that Jenkins, and those he inspired, were ordinary people who did extraordinary things in an extraordinary time in our history. Really, they represent the soul of the southern movement, the spirit that made change possible.

As for the importance of the islanders, particularly Johns Islanders, I had to admit that Bill Saunders had a point. They helped make black Charleston different; they were protagonists because their conditions were so poor they could not afford to stand still. Islanders were the leaders in the strike walkout, everyone agreed. Mary Moultrie is of island heritage. It was not for nothing that she was a protégée of Esau Jenkins.

I drove over to Johns Island the next Sunday morning. Following the main road through the island, I turned off on the wrong road and got lost. Finally, I found the correct turn and located the church. I was a little late; church had already begun. Wesley wasn't a very large church, a capacity of about two hundred, I guessed, but it was full. Saunders, as a deacon, was sitting in the pulpit, and as I entered from the rear he motioned me to the front row, where there was sitting room. In a congregation of that sort, where everyone has known everyone else for next to forever, I certainly was noticed. I took notice of the young minister, the choir of elders, and the wall behind the pulpit, where there hung a painting of a black Jesus.

My nervousness was quickly subdued by the communal singing of the congregation—it was marvelous. There was a feeling of exultation conveyed by the organ-accompanied singing, punctuated by hand clapping; then, as if on signal, the congregation doubled the rhythm. "Stand by Me" was enthralling, as was "Something's Got a Hold on Me."

It was not so much the singing of the choir, but of the congregation, that impressed me, and here it was the elders who led the way. During one song an elderly woman marched into the aisle behind me and grabbed the lead, holding steadfast in the middle of the circle the congregation had now become, as everyone responded to her shout. An elder prayed in Gullah; a teenager read the "Announcements"—not without some difficulty—but I recognized that his participation was a symbol of the responsibility that must begin at youth. The minister delivered a sermon, somewhat formally. Afterward, Bill Jenkins, Esau's son, a retired Air Force major and now director of the Sea Island Health Center, came forward to speak to the congregation about the need to aid a local black political official who was having difficulties.

Finally, at the end of the service, everyone held hands and sang "God Be with You Till We Meet Again." I sensed that no matter where you might be, or what happened to you, someone there cared, and you could count on them.

"These people are hard-pressed people," Esau Jenkins had observed in *Ain't You Got a Right to the Tree of Life?* (p. 67),

*and they are optimistic enough to believe that there are better days coming. When they get into these religious shouts, they feel so happy until that's all they can do but shout. The motions go into the hands and into the feet and they start clapping, and you can't see them sitting—not when they start clapping, brother—people 60 years and 70 years old clap and shout and jump all over the floor without falling down.*

*These people are trying to satisfy themselves, satisfy their soul. It's the only place they can be happy because life is so hard and sometimes there are any number of persons who do not know where the next meal is coming from. They can't talk back if they go on the farm, regardless of how mean they were treated. Sometimes the task they had was overburdening. Sometimes somebody watching them that they didn't even have a chance to stoop. They sometimes sad, but they're trying to get rid of it. If you could come and see them how they look when they singing and shouting, you can see they singing for a better day. And that's the thing that make them keep on shouting.*

After the service, I thanked Saunders for inviting me.

"Hold on," he said. "We're gonna take a tour of the island."

⁓

When I told Saunders I wanted to see the sites of the citizenship school and Progressive Club, he replied, "Listen, please let me do this my way. I have a whole tour I'm going to give you. And let me drive."

We headed first for James Island. James Island, as Saunders had mentioned, lost its black majority long ago, and has now become so developed he said people call it "the city part of the country." James Island appeared to be a new, suburban Charleston for whites, the traffic to and from the mainland always heavy. Saunders pointed out the spacious municipal golf course that J. Arthur Brown sued to be able to play on during the early 1960s. We saw some of the James Island black lodges; most of them, he mentioned, grew out of burial societies, as did similar societies in New Orleans.

We visited the cemetery and the grave site of the crippled black man upon whom the character of Porgy in DuBose Heyward's novel *Porgy* is based; Saunders and a group of islanders had affixed a dignified marker. (None of the blacks I met in Charleston cared much for *Porgy and Bess*; they considered it racist caricature.)

I asked Saunders how people related to each other on the various islands. "The dialect on James Island is different from the dialect on Johns Island, which is different from the dialect on Wadmalaw Island. 'We've [Johns Islanders] been persecuted for our language, I can tell you that." This complaint was uttered so repeatedly by Johns Islanders I began to wonder about the source of the prejudice. Maybe James Island was more "mainstream Charleston" than the more isolated Johns Island. Maybe it had to do with the stigma of being considered "country," or unsophisticated. Even Septima Clark and Mamie Fields, those early island teachers, couldn't resist portraying Johns Island in their autobiographies as a bastion of superstition, ignorance, and unintelligible language, which they, as teachers, were determined to root out with the education they bravely imported from the mainland.

We drove on to Folly Beach at the Atlantic Ocean, all developed—restaurants, hotels, condos—all white. "Why?" I asked. "Beach property didn't mean much to blacks. In the old days everyone had access to the beach. Then the people woke up one morning and discovered the beach was fenced off from them. And that was that." I remembered it was the same along the beaches of West Africa; "development" was a sure sign of European enclaves—hotels, homes, villas.

We passed the Secessionville area; here black soldiers from Massachusetts and South Carolina first fought and many died as part of the long siege of Charleston during the Civil War. "Wherever you see trees in the middle of a farm, that was probably a black graveyard," Saunders noted as we headed toward Johns Island. "I grew up believing that the oaks moved at night, smashed into cars, then returned to their original spot."

"Are there many police out here?"

"There's more now that there's more whites living on James Island." The small clusters of black communities resembled African villages. "These people living close together like this are usually related," Saunders noted. He indicated houses built by the father of J. Arthur Brown. "They were a light-skinned James Island family."

We crossed the Stono River to return to the more sparsely populated and less developed Johns Island. "Johns is the second largest barrier island in the United States, but underpopulated. Only ten thousand people." As we neared the Johns Island airport, which looks as if it services only the private planes of the wealthy, Saunders confided that the airport had bad memories for him. "When I was a kid during World War Two, they brought in German prisoners to help build this airport. The German prisoners were treated a whole lot better than the blacks who lived out here." As he drove farther, he pointed to a crossroad. "This is where I grew up. Now those are all migrant workers back there, living in those huts."

I wasn't sure where I was anymore; the island was just fields and roads. Pretty soon we came to the site of Morning Star Hall, the main traditional hall in the old days, now a church, though Saunders said it was still used occasionally for lodge meetings. I asked how long blacks had owned property on Johns Island. "Some of it is one hundred years old," he said. Or even longer, I thought, if the property was acquired during Reconstruction and passed down. As we drove, we could see the damage caused by Hurricane Hugo in 1989—so many trees down. Pretty soon we came across the original site of the citizenship school and the Progressive Club and store. The structure seemed too small and modest to be the setting for all that took place there. But then, there weren't any impressive sites on Johns Island owned by blacks.

I observed plenty of children as we passed clusters of houses. "At one time on this island if a woman couldn't have a baby, she was outcast. People got into heavy roots in an effort to cure childlessness."

"Roots?"

"Yes. When I was a child, every medicine we used came out of the woods. My grandmother knew root medicine."

Saunders pointed out the properties owned by whites. "So many of the white folk that we knew around here have gone broke," he remembered, but didn't explain. We passed lodge halls, old picnic grounds, famous nightclubs where people congregated on holidays, meeting halls. I told him how much I had enjoyed the singing in Wesley Church. "We call it a 'shout style.' Not many churches do that kind of singing anymore." Was the blues popular on the island as a secular music, I wondered? "Besides church, there isn't that much live music out here. But a blues musician would do very well."

A few days earlier, while walking in the Charleston market, I had come across a poster advertising the annual concert of the Society for the Preservation of Spirituals. Good, I thought, blacks are trying to preserve their music; though the term "spirituals" is so dated it was suspect; what used to be called "spirituals" are usually now called "gospel." Then, when I looked at the photo of the preservation group, I was surprised to see they were all white, dressed in tuxedos, as if prepared for a society affair. It was unbelievable. "Saunders," I asked, "what's the Society for the Preservation of Spirituals?"

"That's something high-society whites have been doing for years. They pass it on to their children. There's a guy in one of the clubs I belong to who almost breaks down in tears whenever he talks about it: 'My grandfather passed it on to my father and he on to me.'"

"You've got to be kidding."

"No, I'm not."

"Well, can they sing?"

"Who knows? Far as I know, no blacks attend the Society concerts."

I knew the capacity for racial masking was taken to extremes in Charleston, with plenty of fascinating racial reversals, but here in this one it seemed to me the white folks were saying, "If blacks won't keep up their reassuring music themselves, we'll just do it for them."

⌒

Reflecting on masking as we passed Kano Street, then Ghana Street, I asked Saunders what he thought about the color consciousness of Charleston.

"At one point it existed at a very high level. Light-skinned blacks were basically the sons and daughters of masters—they're the ones who developed trades, etiquette, and so forth. This was intentional. Now it's mostly a social thing, and doesn't bother me, as long as they don't mess with us. In fact, some of the children of that group want to revive the Brown Fellowship Society, arguing it never had to do with exclusivity. Of course, that's what the whites say about their social organizations. It's a kind of cleaned-up history."

As we headed to Saunders's home, we discussed the NAACP. I said it seemed an outdated organization in the 1990s. "Yes," Saunders agreed. "But we need organizations. We really need an underground organization."

I asked him what he meant by that.

"Not pinpointed toward any one issue. Not one that complains about situations to the press. It's always better if you don't go to the press," he added. I found this thought a bit curious, because the whole logic of the hospital strike, along with other civil rights actions in the South, had been to publicize conditions of powerlessness and injustice in the hope of evoking favorable public opinion. But then I remembered that on Johns Island most of the strength had come from lodges—the Progressive Club was a form of lodge. "And we have to remember," Saunders added, "everything is more complex now. Almost any issue you bring up, blacks are on both sides. Race is always a factor, but not so simply, as was the case in the sixties and before."

I well knew what he meant. As more blacks have entered the mainstream of American society, they have come to the point where they, too, have an investment in the status quo. Excessive economic change would endanger their positions. In politics, they are expected to represent the interests of whites in their districts or municipalities, not just of blacks, or those on the underside of society. Simplistic calls to racial unity in these more racially complex political and economic times would not work as they did when African Americans suffered total exclusion.

I asked Saunders if there was any legacy of the strike that still has meaning for him now. "Yes," he answered. "The strike changed South Carolina by bringing it under federal minimum wage laws. Secondly, it demonstrated we have the power to disrupt the economic system. White leadership began to realize that a conflict of that type set race relations back, and peaceful race relations are important to the white community. Now the struggle is to be able to be recognized at the conference table. To be a part of the system. To be able to negotiate."

When to disrupt, when to negotiate—it all seemed to circle back to the debate we began with. That particular dilemma had a way of ringing with special resonance within Saunders's psyche, and not just recently. Anyway, as he said, things are not so simple anymore, not that they ever are for those who choose to act on their beliefs.

I bid Saunders good-bye, thanking him for the time he had given me, and was soon on the road back to Charleston. It was with a sense of glorious delight that, in the course of leaving the island, I had to cross the perfectly named Esau Jenkins Bridge.

<br>

I felt it was time to leave Charleston, but before I did I was interested in speaking to some younger people to see how they perceived their future and whether they would choose to settle in Charleston. I decided to call two young women at the tiny black weekly, *The Coastal Times*. They obliged me, and I met them at noon in their offices on East Bay Street. Mignon Clyburn is the editor; Arleen Reid is the sole reporter. Both were attractive and articulate young women whom I guessed to be about thirty, if not younger. Clyburn is a Charlestonian who attended the University of South Carolina, returning in the late 1980s to manage the paper, which, she told me, is owned by her father, Jim Clyburn, one of the most respected black political officials in the state. Reid attended South Carolina State in Orangeburg. Both said they liked Charleston, its history, its laid-back atmosphere. "Columbia is more cosmetic, but lacks character," offered Clyburn. Reid called Columbia "a gray city. A place to take care of business. Charleston is a place to live." I asked them what they would do to improve conditions in Charleston if $10 million suddenly fell into their hands, legally. Reid said she would try to strengthen black businesses, develop a black bank. Clyburn agreed. "I admire the Jews. They support each other financially." They decried the debilitating effect of drugs on the city, though Reid quickly added, "We're not in a league with Miami when it comes to drugs."

As the three of us were leisurely speculating, a young man arrived to join Reid and Clyburn for lunch; he brought his own sandwich. He introduced himself as Mike Vanderhorst. Vanderhorst, who looks to be about thirty also, had recently moved to Charleston from Washington, D.C., to open a mailing and duplicating business, the only black person I have ever known in that business. He attended North Carolina Central in Durham, and was commissioned an ensign in the Navy.

Upon discharge, he worked on a military-related job in Washington. His new business is located in the East Bay Street Mall across the street from the restaurant I frequented. I was eager to find out more about him, and why he decided to move south to Charleston.

We met a day later during his lunch break.

"Why Charleston?" I should have known that Vanderhorst is a Charleston Dutch name; his family is from here—but his parents are military people ("I grew up all over; I'm a military brat"). Vanderhorst sparkled with a kind of bright-kid intelligence, displaying no stereotypical southern characteristics; he had a sort of I-can-make-it young, business-minded dedication to the success ethic. There was no black or southern trace in his speech. When I visited his business, his trade consisted of white tourists mailing packages back to their hometowns.

"We always came back to Charleston to see my grandmother," he explained. "I liked it. In fact, returning here was a part of my marriage; I met my future wife at a party in D.C., but I *proposed* to her here on Vanderhorst Street, at the wharf. She works as a schoolteacher. We know we have a long way to go, but we're going to make this business work."

I wanted to know more.

"I came to believe my generation of blacks had been basically lied to," he explained with an intense, nervous energy. "Associate, assimilate, rise up the corporate chain! I believed all that. But how far can we go up the chain? Any brother who did achieve advancement in a corporate structure found his power was still limited. I said to myself, 'If we could ever pool our efforts...' But I knew for me to do what I wanted, I would have to strike out on my own. I sold my house in D.C., got married, moved down here, and opened this store all during the past year. It was a lot of stress, but it was the right thing to do." I found that rather startling; Charleston was known for having its young black talent run away, not as an attraction for young people from the North.

And now, a year later? What did he conclude about Charleston?

"I see a lot of holdovers here from what we call a slave mentality. In the old days if you were a servant of the patrician class, you had more status than the other servants." I had heard that before. "But they were still servants. Some blacks still think they have name status. Despite that, I like Charleston. There's something different about the way it feels. Hey, maybe we're the first wave of a group of blacks that will reject the big cities in the North and come home to the South."

"Home?"

"Yes, home. It feels like I'm home."

While I was in Vanderhorst's shop, a young man who seemed about twenty walked in. He was light skinned, and had come in to run off an elaborately designed flyer advertising a reggae bash he and his brother were planning at a black club on the weekend. He had that southern look, but with his Rastafarian dreadlocks and his correct, yet hip, speech. I couldn't figure out what I was looking at. Reggae in staid, laid-back Charleston? It sounded like a contradiction.

He introduced himself as Azikiwe Chandler, a student in architecture at Notre Dame. In the fall he was slated to begin a year in Rome under a special scholarship. ("That boy," Myrtle Glascoe said when I related the story of meeting Chandler, "is brilliant.") I arranged to meet him at the restaurant on East Bay, where he told me his story. Chandler was born in New York, moving to Charleston at age ten with his parents. His father had been a devout member of The East, a Brooklyn black cultural nationalist organization, and Chandler and his slightly younger brother had been since childhood schooled in African-American liberation schools. "We were taught sciences at a very early age," he explained. Entering the public school system in Charleston, Chandler quickly established himself as a top student. "When I entered the public schools, I was way ahead of the rest of the class," he remembered. "At first, we lived in North Charleston, so we went to primarily white schools. My brother Cheo was always in trouble, being sent home. I was always coming home with migraine headaches. When we moved down to the peninsula, my brother came under discipline and my headaches disappeared." His father introduced reggae music to Charleston on his radio program, and unprecedentedly for Charleston, he established a soccer league (his mother started a girls' league) in the black community, recruiting players from the projects.

I asked Chandler what reggae and dreads symbolized to him. "In the Caribbean, reggae means an African consciousness; they're speaking about Africa," he answered. "Reggae is associated with the Caribbean, but I feel the spirit of the music extends to anyone who wants to see injustice eradicated. It's more than music. The singers are prophets." Chandler said he was raised listening to Bob Marley, playing soccer, thinking of himself as a prideful African American and making A's. "We never celebrated Christmas. We celebrated Kwanza. When we brought those ideas here, we were highly ostracized. I wore dreads at ten, but my brother and I wore caps to school to protect ourselves from abuse. We told the principal our religion required us to wear caps and *he believed it!* Even so, other kids would pull off our caps and laugh. We were outsiders. But it made me stronger.

"It's real disappointing to me," he elaborated on Charleston, "that so many people here are caught up in the servant-master mentality. We're just *too* used to working in the kitchen. This place is like *Gone with the Wind.* I'd like to come back here when I finish school and change all of that. And encourage more kids to go to college. It hurts that we don't have a black college here—the thinking here is vocational school. At first I thought I would never want to return to Charleston to live. Now I think I do—I want to start my own school of Afrocentric education. It's needed here. And, after all, this is home."

⌒

I felt a sense of positive future in these young people. I felt if this new generation of young blacks, those gifted with the benefit of a first-class education, return to the South to live and work, they will possess a sense of *owning* part of the southern experience, though they might not own land. In fact, southern towns that have been home for generations of black families are the only places in America that blacks can claim as their own. They have worked the land, built houses and businesses, performed crucial roles in the commercial success of southern towns, whether they owned properties or not. They are the spiritual heirs of the South and whatever riches the land holds. I felt a little better about the possibility that an educated and history-conscious younger generation of black southerners will be aggressive in reclaiming what their ancestors were denied. And they will have to be aggressive.

⌒

One final person who was in a good position to assess the city, its assets and faults, was Steve Hoffious, who works for the South Carolina Historical Society and serves as editor of the *South Carolina Historical Magazine*. I met Hoffious at his office on the third floor of an old building in the downtown Historical District. A native of Michigan in his late thirties, a veteran of the Southern Regional Council in Atlanta (long a bulwark of liberal rights and advocacy), and a former staff member of *Southern Exposure* magazine in Chapel Hill, North Carolina, Hoffious was about as distant from the old-boy Charleston elite as one could be while still working for them. "The thing that amazes me," he noted, softly, "is the extent to which white society leaders here believe their own myths of 'society,' and the extent to which those who are not part of that believe they're excluded from something important. Living in the past is taken so seriously. The whole thing is about heredity, not money. Thus, anyone who's not born into the set is excluded—whites and of course, blacks. There are no blacks on the Historical Society board."

"So," I asked, "what do these establishment whites think of the hospital workers' strike?"

"They're embarrassed by it. They seem to feel they should have been able to prevent such a traumatic mess. But they realize things had to change a little. Basically, they don't talk about it.

"I did one issue of the *Historical Magazine* with three articles devoted to racism, and I received a lot of complaints about that." As for the strike itself, Hoffious, who wrote the best short account of it and its aftermath for *Working Lives*, concluded, "it was a short-time victory and a long-time defeat. Less than a year after the strike was over, there was nothing." Nothing, I suppose, other than the heady memory of the effort to create meaningful change in a place "living in the past." "But," said Hoffious, "the workers should have known that the strike settlement was only the *beginning* of their struggle, not the end."

And that was enough of Charleston. I liked it. I felt mystified by it; I learned more than I ever expected I would, and tomorrow morning, in June 1991, I will be plunging southward deeper into the Black Belt where the racial conflict of the 1960s was more highly pitched and where the percentage of black population made substantial alteration in the racial balance of power more portentous than at any time in American history since the Civil War.

# ST. AUGUSTINE

~

*In the spring of 1964 blacks in St. Augustine, Florida, attempted to launch protests against the elaborate segregation in public places and tourist businesses. Such protests were considered unthinkable in north Florida, which had never before experienced any sort of direct-action protest by blacks against racial injustice.*

*The Southern Christian Leadership Conference decided to enter the campaign to help the beleaguered St. Augustine blacks. They knew that demonstrations in "America's oldest city" would win media attention all over the world. SCLC and the St. Augustine activists also knew that exposing to the nation the extent of the town's racial barriers at a time when the city was preparing to celebrate its four hundredth anniversary would act as a catalyst for the passage of a new, far more comprehensive civil rights law, a major objective of the campaign.*

*Now, St. Augustine is considered a footnote to the larger and more well-known civil rights battles fought in Montgomery, Birmingham, and Selma. How do blacks in St. Augustine remember their time of troubles? And what is "America's oldest city" like today?*

For some time I had wanted to visit St. Augustine, Florida. Like Charleston, St. Augustine is a tourist town, only much smaller, and with a Spanish rather than English colonial history. That would have meant nothing to me except for St. Augustine's brief but noteworthy role in the march to winning the 1964 Civil Rights Act. And the fact that there was so much bitterness and violence in this little town along the north Florida coast.

I departed Charleston in late June, driving southward through a driving rainstorm on U.S. 17. An hour later, by the time 17 had merged with I-95 and its truck traffic headed south for Miami, it was raining harder, so I pulled over to the side and let the trucks rumble by.

I realized that my route down the Atlantic coast would take me very near the location of the old Dorchester school where the SCLC citizenship education program, based on the Johns Island and Highlander models, was located. I had read and heard so much about the place, because so many southern civil rights veterans had participated in the Dorchester week-long citizenship and voting classes; I decided to make a slight detour to see if I could locate the site thirty miles south of Savannah. I exited I-95 to return to U.S. 17, which was running parallel to it, and arrived at the village of Midway near the intersection of U.S. 84. I found that the town of Dorchester, in Liberty County, was located on my map on U.S. 84 between Midway and I-95. But I could not find the school grounds. I thought I was where the town of Dorchester was supposed to be, but there was no trace of the school, even though Bernice Robinson had assured me it was still there. I was in a very isolated area. (No more than three automobiles had passed me on U.S. 84 during the last half hour.) Finally, I decided I had to ask for directions, so I stopped at one of those newfangled combination fast food/service stations just off the interstate.

"Oh yes, Dorchester exists," the black woman clerk assured me, "It's back that-away a few miles." She pointed in the direction on U.S. 84 I had just come from.

"The Dorchester Center is not in Dorchester?" I asked incredulously. "I thought this was Dorchester."

"Well, not quite. All this once was, used to be Dorchester." In fact, the entire area was saturated with "used to be's." State highway signs in nearby Midway indicated towns, particularly Old Sunbury, "a former leading port and educational center" east of the interstate, that were no more. I realized I was traveling through an area of former colonial Georgia towns that were now basically memories.

So I decided to continue westward on U.S. 84 past Midway, and soon I came upon a wooden Congregational church and dormitory; beside it, a well-kept grounds complete with a baseball field. There were a few black people sitting on the dormitory steps, including an elderly man who turned out to be the caretaker. I walked around the grounds and peeked into the dormitory. Outside, carloads of young men were arriving to prepare for a Saturday-afternoon game.

Dorchester Center is now adorned with a state historical sign stating that formal education for the large number of blacks freed from coastal plantations began in Liberty County at this site during Reconstruction under the Freedmen's Bureau. The first school was called Homestead. Support for Homestead was assumed by the American Missionary Association of the Congregational Church in 1870, beginning a long, beneficial relationship to which the present small, well-preserved Midway Congregational Church is eloquent testimony. In 1874 the Congregational Church renamed the school Dorchester Academy. In 1890, Dorchester Academy added boarding facilities, as it was a countywide school, and increased its attendance to about three hundred students. It was probably the only high school for blacks in the entire Georgia coastal area. In 1940 the academic program was closed down, probably because of the establishment of a public high school in the area. The former boys' dormitory was expanded into a community center, the center Andy Young visited in the late 1950s when he was pastor of his first church in Thomasville, and which in 1961 became the site for the citizenship school.

It was growing late in the slowly fading afternoon, and I hoped to make Jacksonville that night, if not St. Augustine, so I resumed my journey southward on U.S. 17 through Riceboro. Then southward along the unbelievably isolated U.S. 17, closely paralleling I-95, which no doubt drew all the traffic, passing "the Smallest Church in America" (about the size of an ordinary bathroom), and historical signs documenting abandoned colonial sites and coastal ports. Down through the tiny port of Darien, burned during the Civil War by Union troops. Huge pines now cast long shadows over the road; a sign indicated New Hope Plantation. New hope for whom, I wondered. Then on down to the coastal town of Brunswick. Brunswick looked the part of a small port; it had been a fishing and shrimping center of some importance. It was also the gateway to expensive resort coastal islands, like St. Simons. It was home to industries like seafood-processing plants and lumber-product factories. As I detoured through Brunswick, I was amazed at the extent to which the town had maintained a large, intact black community, which though in no sense prosperous, as far as I could see, still retained its character—there must have been steady employment in Brunswick, even for blacks. There were signs of a Saturday night life; so many people out on the streets.

By the time I departed southward from Brunswick, darkness had descended. U.S. 17 once again merged with I-95 for the duration of the eighty-mile drive to Jacksonville, Florida. When I arrived in the Jacksonville area, I decided to find a motel there, instead of traveling on to St. Augustine. I was finally able to find a room on one of the exterior superhighways. Motels seem to be very busy on Saturday night in Jacksonville, possibly due to the large number of servicemen in the area.

On Sunday, I drove through downtown Jacksonville. What had happened to what appeared to have once been a vibrant black community? I saw blocks of boarded-up houses and deserted businesses. Davis Street, the former main downtown black street, appeared to have undergone a mass exodus with only a few stragglers remaining because they had nowhere else to go. Jacksonville was not my destination, however; St. Augustine was, and early in the afternoon I took the quick forty-mile drive down I-95 to the cutoff that led into town.

⁓

The St. Augustine exit fed a seven-mile drive that led into U.S. 1 and San Marcos Avenue, which leads to the Plaza, the center of the historic area. Here the selling of the past was taken to an extreme that would make Charleston blush. I was beginning to ask myself, did I need to come to this place? Souvenir shops, T-shirt outlets, hotels and motels, quick-stop stores, a few trendy shops, and the stone Castillo de San Marcos National Monument, the old Spanish fort first built in 1672. Finally, following down the San Marcos Avenue, we come to the Plaza, which is a rectangular park facing the Mantanzas River, which separates the town from its barrier Mantanzas Island. At the Plaza was St. Augustine's old slave market (marked by a historical sign), the only historical site referring to the town's black citizens. That site was the destination of determined marches against rigid racial segregation in 1964 and the gathering place of hate-filled crowds that abused and vilified the marchers. The memory of those events provides a harsh and ugly underside to St. Augustine's smiling tourist-greeting image.

From the square back into town along King Street, I drove past the city complex of office buildings, Flagler College, the Trinity Episcopal Church, the Cathedral Basilica, and several surrounding streets with small shops and restaurants. The city buildings, Flagler College, the Lightner Museum, and the Castillo were particularly striking because of their native coquina shellstone exteriors, which made them look like medieval castles.

On the ocean side of the Plaza, steady traffic across the Mantanzas River bridge led to the sparkling, well-maintained public beaches on Mantanzas Island. Historically, these beaches were off limits to blacks, except for a small stretch called Butler Beach. Butler Beach was also the site of a small neighborhood of houses and black businesses, none of which exist now. When interracial teams decided to deliberately violate the whites-only beach policy as part of the 1964 demonstrations, they were attacked and almost drowned by vigilante whites who waded in to attack them.

Almost all of the tourists I saw were white; most seemed to be family vacationers. The only blacks I saw on the Plaza, other than those working, were a group that appeared, from their accents, to be from the West Indies. I got the feeling that many St. Augustine tourists stop off for a quick tour and meal en route to southern Florida and the Miami-area beaches. I located a motel run by an Indian family on San Marcos Avenue and settled in. I seemed to be the only black staying there, though I had no problems whatsoever.

Exploring the town over the next few days, I didn't have much trouble locating St. Augustine's main black community, called Lincolnville. It is, in fact, within walking distance of the Plaza. St. Augustine's black community is south of King Street, not far from the Plaza. It's an old community, known originally as Lincolnshire. Another disappointment, though not as disappointing as Jacksonville's battered black community. Lincolnville is bounded by Riberia Street, Bridge Street, Washington Street, and Park Street. St. Paul's, St. Benedict the Moor, and First Baptist were Lincolnville churches of substance that stood out in the neighborhood.

An additional area of black housing exists across the San Sebastian River. That area sits on both sides of King Street, which originates downtown and runs westward into the countryside. Driving out King for a couple of miles, I came across the mini-ghost town that once was Florida Memorial College, a black Baptist school that departed St. Augustine for Miami during the late 1960s. The West King area had the look of a rural village, and in fact, I learned later it is legally and politically under the jurisdiction of St. John's County, rather than the town of St. Augustine.

I was simply amazed at the number of gun shops and gun clubs in this small town. There was an evident love of weapons, and, I suppose, by extension, of violence which mystified me. During my drive down from Jacksonville, I listened to a radio talk show. The sugary-sweet-voiced hostess was waxing ecstatic over the Persian Gulf war victory parade in New York just held over the weekend. A male caller quipped,

"While we're at it, I think the idea of having a military ship go from port city to port city in *America* would be wonderful. They could lob a few shells into the high-crime areas." "Mercy, mercy, mercy," the hostess shrieked.

~

St. Augustine's early history as a Spanish colonial outpost in North America was replete with violence and warfare. Settled in 1565, the Spanish hoped the settlement would serve as a counterbalance to the early English Atlantic coastal outposts up the coast at Savannah and Charleston. The Seloy Indians, whose village was located near St. Augustine, were quickly brought under control and are now a vanished people.

Raided by Sir Francis Drake in 1568, sacked by English pirates in 1668, raided by English soldiers from Savannah in 1702 and 1740, the fort, along with the entire Florida Territory, was lost by treaty to the British in 1783. In 1803 the Florida Territory became Spanish again. But with Americans expanding westward and south-ward relentlessly, Spain was forced to cede Florida to the United States in 1819. Central Florida was defended by determined Seminole Indians with the assistance of runaway slaves. The Seminoles fought fierce guerrilla battles against the U.S. military until they were forced to give up their lands in the 1850s, thus somewhat delaying Florida's development until the latter half of the nineteenth century when white settlers flocked into central and south Florida.

As for St. Augustine, it remained a minor fishing village for most of the century, in stark contrast to Charleston and Savannah, which became major seaports. Then, unexpectedly, in the 1880s St. Augustine's fortunes took a surprising turn for the better. Henry Flagler, a wealthy partner of John D. Rockefeller in the Standard Oil Company of New Jersey, fell in love with St. Augustine while visiting the Florida coast. In 1881, Flagler moved there, and quickly began to explore his vision of the port as a major tourist and retreat center. He invested millions in a spectacular building campaign: new hotels, striking churches, and a railroad line running from Jacksonville to Miami in order to facilitate the east Florida coast as a resort corridor. St. Augustine's present shellstone structures, except for the old fort, were built by

Flagler and those of his northern set. His group also soon established themselves as the dominant economic and social class in their adopted town, according to David R. Colburn in his excellent analytical study, *Racial Change and Community Crisis: St. Augustine, Florida, 1877–1980.*

St. Augustine's new tourist economy did not substantially change the preponderantly dependent status of the town's black freedmen, however, who constituted about a quarter of the population. St. Augustine, like Charleston, had been a slave market town; it always had a black presence, though blacks were never major players in St. Augustine's political and economic life (except briefly during Reconstruction).

During the early twentieth century some blacks established themselves as independent fishermen, and others improved their economic and social status by becoming schoolteachers in the new (segregated) public school systems. Still others were able to obtain solid jobs in the postal service, jobs protected by the federal government. There were also a few relatively economically independent blacks who taught or were on the staff of tiny Florida Memorial College, a Baptist school that moved to St. Augustine from Jacksonville in 1921.

This was pretty much the racial situation in St. Augustine when, in 1963, the first extremely unwelcome civil rights demonstrations occurred.

To provide some background, the local NAACP chapter, which had not done much of anything to protest segregation, decided in 1963 to take exception to St. Augustine's anticipated four-hundred-year anniversary in 1964–1965, for which the city was applying for federal funds. An estimated 85 percent of the town's income was derived from tourism. The NAACP began by requesting that city officials remove or initiate the removal of segregation signs in public facilities and businesses. The NAACP also requested that the city establish a biracial commission to deal with complaints from the black community. According to David Colburn, these requests were dismissed by city officials. After the failure of these initial efforts, the NAACP began to consider far more aggressive tactics.

The key protagonist in this story, according to almost all accounts, was Dr. Robert Hayling, the town's lone black dentist. Hayling was the adult adviser to the NAACP Youth Council. A native of Tallahassee, Hayling's father taught at Florida A&M, one of the South's best-known black state colleges. A graduate of A&M and an Air Force veteran, Hayling, after earning his dental degree from Meharry Medical College in Nashville, had moved to St. Augustine in 1960 to take over the practice of an older black dentist.

Hayling was considered brilliant, one of a new class of black southern professionals who were fed up with second-class treatment, and who like George Simkins of Greensboro and a few others assumed leadership roles in the NAACP in the late 1950s and early '60s. Many of these professionals identified strongly with the younger generation and their styles of direct protest against segregation. The older leadership preferred persuasion and legal action. Hayling was soon to push the St. Augustine NAACP in the direction of a much more aggressive stance.

After the first overtures were resisted, the NAACP requested a permit to hold a protest march in the downtown area, which was denied. Then in March 1963, the St. Augustine NAACP chapter wrote to Vice President Lyndon Johnson, asking him to cancel a scheduled visit to St. Augustine to dedicate a historical monument. Segregation in the city was cited as the reason Johnson should stay away. A flurry of communications followed. Johnson did attend the dedication after the city agreed to add a few blacks to the official committee, though NAACP members were excluded.

In May, the NAACP addressed a letter to President John F. Kennedy asking him to withhold federal funding of St. Augustine's upcoming quadricentennial. The note to the President was written after a further unproductive meeting between NAACP members and city officials during which the NAACP again requested the city to initiate desegregation, hire more blacks for skilled city positions, poll workers, and as policemen. The NAACP followed up its letter to the President with a missive to the city threatening serious demonstrations that would make St. Augustine "another Birmingham." Birmingham was then much in the news as a result of the dramatic SCLC campaign, and the jailing of Martin Luther King, Jr., and other civil rights notables.

Once this correspondence became public knowledge, Dr. Hayling received several telephone threats. On June 19, Hayling warned in an interview with the *St. Augustine Record* that he and other NAACP leaders were armed. He was quoted as saying, "We will shoot first and answer questions later. We are not going to die like Medgar Evers," the Mississippi NAACP leader who had been assassinated in Jackson, Mississippi, earlier that month. As a result of Hayling's statements, the city's white leaders became angered, and ruled out any further attempt to discuss demands. Up to this point, no marches downtown or sustained sit-in efforts had occurred.

On June 25, a small group of high school and Florida Memorial students under the aegis of the NAACP Youth Council began picketing Woolworth's on the Plaza. On July 16, sixteen youths were arrested at a sit-in at a local pharmacy lunch counter. When their cases were tried, the judge attempted to pressure their parents into prohibiting their children from demonstrating. Four refused to do so. The judge thereupon sent four of the arrested children to *reform school.* The jobs of blacks whose children were members of the Youth Council were threatened.

These initial efforts during the summer of 1963 split the St. Augustine NAACP. Some of the more conservative or fearful members opposed the efforts of Hayling and the Reverend Goldie Eubanks, who was also a Youth Council adviser, calling them "troublemakers" who didn't understand St. Augustine. Despite the fledgling demonstrations of the summer of 1963, there was hardly a decline in tourism. There was, however, an increasing air of lawlessness and violence; white youth took to "night-riding" through Lincolnville, firing shots into black homes. During the course of one of these attacks, a white youth was shot and killed, the Reverend Mr. Eubanks was arrested, and the situation became explosive. After the summer of 1963, the Youth Council operated pretty much on its own. Finally, the NAACP members who favored an aggressive stance and the Youth Council in entirety were run out of the chapter. Executive director Roy Wilkins, who was called in to mediate, demanded the resignations of Hayling and Eubanks. In the wake of these actions, Hayling, Eubanks, and Henry Twine, a key NAACP member, postal worker, and community leader, decided to seek out Dr. Martin Luther King, Jr., and his SCLC, to request their support in St. Augustine.

Toward this end they drove to Orlando, Florida, in March 1964, where SCLC was holding a meeting, to introduce the idea. They weren't able to speak to Martin Luther King, but they told their story to the Reverend C. T. Vivian, a key SCLC leader, who suggested to King that an SCLC campaign in St. Augustine might be a step toward establishing an SCLC beachhead in Florida, which was the purpose of the Orlando meeting. During the next few weeks of the spring of 1964, an extensive debate took place among the SCLC leaders in Atlanta over the wisdom of entering

St. Augustine. An immediate rationale for doing so, they agreed, was the publicity the effort would generate toward compelling Congress to pass a new, comprehensive civil rights act. All civil rights organizations were then lobbying for a federal law that would completely outlaw segregation in public facilities, overriding once and for all the multiplicity of local and state segregation laws. From the reports they received from the St. Augustine contingent, they were sure that attempts to deseg-regate would be met with such strong resistance that the need for a sweeping law would be made painfully clear.

SCLC dispatched key organizer Hosea Williams and program director John Gibson to St. Augustine to assess the situation; both decided in favor of a campaign. In Atlanta, according to Andrew Young, the SCLC staff did feel, because of the potential for violence, that Dr. King should not take part in the planned demon-strations. Once SCLC decided to come in, the St. Augustine activists who had been kicked out of the NAACP became SCLC organizers pledged to adhere to a policy of nonviolence. Meanwhile, the Easter holidays, a key tourist period, were targeted for the advent of demonstrations.

SCLC began its St. Augustine campaign by inviting northeastern college students bound for their traditional Florida spring vacations to join them in St. Augustine, not as tourists, but as picketers. This strategy was part of a widespread SCLC appeal to all tourists to boycott St. Augustine until it was desegregated. A master stroke of the campaign was the decision of Mrs. Malcolm Peabody, the seventy-two-year-old wife of an Episcopal bishop and the mother of the governor of Massachusetts, to join the St. Augustine demonstrations, along with some of her friends.

Mrs. Peabody, Hayling, and several other prestigious visitors were arrested in April 1964 while attempting to be served at the upscale Ponce de Leon Motor Lodge restaurant. These arrests unleased the hoped-for national publicity, and little-known St. Augustine suddenly became the focus of worldwide unwelcome attention for its racial policies, just at the time when it was hoping for favorable acclaim as "America's oldest city" celebrating its four hundredth anniversary.

The mayor and city officials were outraged. The Peabody arrests did succeed in keeping away tourists, because marches, picketing, and arrests signified "trouble." Even those who could care less about civil rights preferred to avoid a vacation spot where they might encounter strife and unrest.

Desegregation tests of motels and popular tourist sites were launched by interracial teams; the "testers" were quickly arrested. Those arrests also received national media exposure. Even so, there was still no sign from the city administration that it was willing to negotiate, or take the lead in initiating desegregation. In May, with Hosea Williams firmly in charge and the St. Augustine effort invigorated by SCLC's presence, nightly marches to the "slave market" were begun. Night marches were dangerous, but most black adults had to work during the days, except for Sundays. Either they marched at night or not at all.

~

The night marches to the Plaza in St. Augustine turned out to be some of the most lonely marches or demonstrations in the entire history of the southern movement. The groups were met with increasingly large and hostile crowds of white rowdies who flocked to St. Augustine from surrounding towns in north Florida, and as far away as Georgia. As the demonstrators walked in twos from Lincolnville to the Plaza, the usually not more than two dozen volunteers were greeted with insults, and sometimes stones and bottles, once they entered the Plaza. It didn't help that the sheriff, L. O. Davis, did little or nothing to restrain this screaming, harassing mob. It was all Williams and the SCLC monitors could do to maintain discipline, which called for the marchers not to respond to abuse, and to continue moving forward to the front of the Plaza. Then they had to return through the same gauntlet to Lincolnville.

Communicating by two-way radio, white vigilantes drawn to St. Augustine converged at the Plaza every evening creating their own racist theater. There were speeches by the likes of J. B. Stoner, who had come down from Georgia to hurl insults; the Reverend Connie Lynch, who came from California; and Holstead "Hoss" Manucy, head of the St. Augustine Ancient City Hunting Club, which was a front for the Klan. The mayor and city administration took no action to try to bring this situation under control.

Two weeks or so into the campaign, SCLC vice president Andrew Young joined Hosea Williams in St. Augustine. Very soon after he arrived, Young was attacked by a white youth who punched him from behind, then kicked him while he was rolling on the ground. This beating was captured on national television news. Andy joked later when he told me about that night, "I was one of those who voted against a St. Augustine campaign at our Atlanta staff meeting because I thought it was a sideshow we didn't need. But after that beating, I became the number one advocate for staying right there in St. Augustine until we won something."

Meanwhile, Dr. King, observing events from Atlanta, was eager to join the campaign. He overruled his staff and flew to St. Augustine determined to become involved and go to jail if necessary. He told his staff, according to Young, that he felt it only proper, as a leader, that he be subject to the same risks as any other participant. This position was characteristic of King's strength of commitment over the years, but many of those closest to him thought such physical and moral courage was not necessary, given the explosive situation in St. Augustine.

When King did arrive in town, elaborate care was taken by St. Augustine leaders to conceal where he would sleep, a well-advised precaution because the cottage originally chosen for him at Butler Beach, the small black section on Mantanzas Island, was shot into, then burned to the ground, once it was rumored King might be staying there.

With the advent of June, and with Congress debating the civil rights bill, SCLC, with King on hand, accelerated the testing of St. Augustine motels and tourist sites. When Dr. King and a group of SCLC officials were arrested at the Monson Motor Hotel, there was heavy media coverage. King was jailed in Jacksonville, though he was soon bailed out. A few days later, at the same motel, an integrated test group jumped fully clothed into the swimming pool. The whites in the pool scampered out, as if they were in danger of becoming contaminated. The owner then poured in bottles of acidic cleaning fluid. When that failed to drive out the demonstrators, a policeman, also fully clothed, plunged into the pool to drag them out and place them under drenched arrest.

Meanwhile, the night marches, which were devoid of such almost comic touches, continued. King, Ralph Abernathy, Young, and Hosea Williams were frequent speakers at the key churches that were the starting point of the marches. The SCLC staff, however, pleaded with King not to lead a night march, fearing for his life. This time King acceded to their wishes.

Young told me how the group departed from the churches singing hymns to bolster their courage. "For one of the few times in my life I was afraid," he admitted, "and it didn't help that at first the marches consisted of mostly elderly women." Most of the early marchers were elderly churchgoing women because they had nothing to lose and a few volunteers from out of town, who were housed in the homes of the Lincolnville residents who were sympathetic to the effort.

It was almost impossible to get working black adults to join the demonstrations because of the constant fear they would lose their jobs. Most of the work for blacks was marginal service employment in the tourist industry, totally under the control of the very whites the protests were being waged against. "It took quite a while," Young said, "to get high school students to march with us, and to get them to adhere to our march principles. But teenagers *were* less afraid, and once we got them to act as marshals, forming an outer protective corridor, we were able to convince the St. Augustine authorities that no matter how intense the intimidation, we were going to keep coming until they were willing to talk about beginning the process of desegregation." Instead, the city went to court to try to stop the marches.

The St. Augustine city and lower-court injunctions against skirmishes continued throughout the month of June 1964—on the streets the demonstrations finally ended up before the federal district court of Judge Brian Simpson of the middle district of Florida. Judge Simpson was one of the southern federal judges who had established successful careers during the days of entrenched segregation, but who ended up caught between sharply contending forces during the civil rights years. Those judges were forced to choose between their sense of justice and their willingness to uphold the Constitution and Supreme Court precedents, and their old political and personal friends, who were often defending segregation.

Caught in this painful dilemma, there were a few judges who very slowly moved away from their segregationist stances to become strong defenders of civil rights. Simpson belongs to this latter group, even though the St. Augustine city officials, state officials, and the governor (an old friend of Simpson) expected "their" judge to support their attempts to close down the night marches. Simpson refused to go along with them, despite the considerable personal abuse he was subjected to, and in the end he defied the sheriff and his posse and pushed the governor toward a position of mediation. In a series of rulings, Judge Simpson found that the sheriff had actually deputized vigilantes. He ordered the sheriff to cease this practice, and ruled that marches could continue under more protected conditions.

In June the real focus of civil rights attention, however, shifted to Washington, where Congress was debating, and finally passed, the Civil Rights Act of 1964. Then, on July 2, President Lyndon Johnson signed the bill into law, surrounded by key congressmen and civil rights leaders including Dr. King. The new Civil Rights Act suddenly made the marches, speeches, and arrests in St. Augustine moot, except for the matter of implementation. The town merchants were not that unhappy; they had had enough. Their businesses were suffering from an estimated 50 percent drop-off. They also realized, or most of them realized, they had no choice but to comply with the Civil Rights Act—a new day, like it or not, had arrived. Slowly, one by one, they opened their doors to blacks, realizing of course, that once the "testing" was over, very few blacks would want to patronize their businesses, anyway.

Within days SCLC withdrew its staff; the volunteers also departed. St. Augustine quickly receded from the national consciousness as a focal point of civil rights activity, and was, except for those who lived there, pretty much forgotten.

⌒

Now, twenty-seven years later, I was wrestling with the question of what St. Augustine's struggle meant. The first person I sought out was Henry Twine, one of the local leaders who had invited SCLC to come to St. Augustine in 1963. We met at the motel where I was staying. "My wife was arrested in this very motel restaurant," he noted, as he told me something of his background.

Mr. Twine's family was an old one in St. Augustine—he traced his ancestry back to Antoine Proctor on his mother's side. Proctor—considered one of the founders of Tallahassee—was a guide for American troops in fighting Native Americans (American armies, particularly Andrew Jackson, used black and native guides quite extensively). According to Twine, he also owned property in St. Augustine. Proctor's grandsons became state legislators during Reconstruction. Now Twine himself, in the almost thirty years since the marches to the Plaza, has been a member of the City Commission for the past ten years. At the time I interviewed him he was vice mayor. Graying, in his late sixties, rather lean and serious, Twine was, to me, representative of the many intelligent and rather conservative black postal workers I had known growing up in the South. (Postal work was considered "good work" because it was federal work that maintained high standards of performance and was open to blacks who could pass the necessary examinations.)

Twine told me St. Augustine had always offered opportunities for aggressive and enterprising blacks and surprised me by adding, "It's just that there aren't many aggressive and enterprising blacks." Based on the extreme white reaction during the 1960s, and the historically depressed economic condition of St. Augustine blacks, I could understand why aggressive people were hard to come by. Individual initiative was not encouraged or rewarded—dependency and conservatism were much more to the liking of white St. Augustine. I thought Mr. Twine might be bending over backward to say a good word for his town. I remembered that he was one of the group that decided the racial situation in St. Augustine was so ominous they sought out King. King and SCLC didn't initiate the process that brought them to "the Ancient City."

"What about the Klan and violence?" I inquired.

"You have to realize," he responded, "that what happened here in 1963 wasn't representative of St. Augustine. Wherever King went he attracted racists. He brought the worst out of them. The Klan mob was mostly from Jacksonville. They came from everywhere—this was the battleground in 1964. This was a last stand for them."

"A 'last stand'?" I asked.

"I can't tell you why," he insisted. "St. Augustine has always been an integrated community. Blacks still own property all over St. Augustine."

I mentioned that I hardly saw any blacks working downtown, or living in areas other than Lincolntown on West King. Since blacks were only 25 percent of the town's population, they would obviously be less visible than in heavy Black Belt towns, but still, I was seeing hardly any. Twine assured me that jobs were available for blacks, if they wanted them. "I served as head of the NAACP for ten years. People come to me asking, 'Mr. Twine, why don't you'all do this or that . . .' and

I answer 'Why don't you try to help yourself?' I worked at the post office for thirty years, but so often blacks wouldn't come take the exam. We have black tellers in both banks. Our superintendent of county schools is black."

I asked him why he thought there was a lack of initiative coming from the black community in St. Augustine.

"Lack of motivation," he responded. "Let's face it, blacks need a lot of motivation. For instance, when we asked King to come here, not all blacks supported him. There was resistance to him coming here in the first place. They said we ought not to be 'doing that.' Just accept the status quo. We were upsetting the racial harmony."

This was the NAACP adult establishment, I surmised. Twine didn't want to name names.

What about now? I wondered. Was there a citywide black political organization, for instance?

"No more than the NAACP. Everything like that revolves around the NAACP. But you can't get people to come to NAACP meetings."

I wondered how black St. Augustinians felt about SCLC, King's group, since so many of them left the NAACP to join the SCLC. But then, I asked Twine, hadn't SCLC kind of dropped St. Augustine?

"I hate to say it," he admitted, "but it's true. We had always been NAACP people. I was one of those who asked SCLC to come in, but now we've gone back to the NAACP. Not that we didn't take care of King when he was here. It was exciting, I can tell you that. But it was a dangerous time.

"What upsets me now is we don't have people available to take advantage of the new opportunities. Too many of our people think, 'I'm black, give me a job.'" This sounded like Bill Saunders in Charleston. "There's a good county technical training school here, but we have to almost force people to go."

"So what happens? Young people leave St. Augustine?"

"Yes. And stay away until they retire."

I asked Mr. Twine if he would drive around town with me and show me places he considered interesting. I especially wanted to tour Lincolnville with him.

We drove to the Florida State School for the Deaf and Blind, "one of the best schools for deaf and blind in the United States. My mother worked for the black section of the school; she earned forty-five dollars a week." We drove out U.S. 1 to the site of the former Fort Mose on Robinson Creek. We stopped and read the historical sign as traffic whizzed past. According to this marker, the site was originally "a Spanish mission for Indians left homeless during Queen Anne's War." Probably a military alliance against the English. "Since 1688 Negro slaves had found refuge in St. Augustine," the sign added. Slave runaways were kept here by the Spanish in 1738; their village was named Gracia Real at Mose. The English pretty much destroyed the site in 1740 during their failed effort to take St. Augustine. Now, Twine informed me, there are archaeological digs, as there seem to be at several other St. Augustine sites, in an effort to discover more about the early Spanish colony.

Twine was proud of the Fort Mose site and his advocacy within state political and historical circles necessary to preserve it, and I appreciated his interest. Upon our return drive, he continued to reminisce about St. Augustine in the vein of "what used to be." "A black entrepreneur, Frank Butler, developed a beach site at the ocean which was eventually called Butler's Beach for blacks." I had read about Butler Beach. "Butler also built homes along the shore, but he is long gone. So are the homes. Of course, blacks go to any beach they want now."

Then we drove over to Lincolnville. Twine lives in the neighborhood and he knew where the important community sites were, or rather, used to be. Though Washington Street was once an important street of businesses and meeting places, those sections of the street were now a boarded-up ghost town, a phenomenon I was encountering in virtually every town I visited. The neighborhood itself still retained good inexpensive housing, and the churches were still there, but a community vibrancy was sorely missing. That was all the more evident when compared with the recently discovered and restored Lincolnville photographs taken by Richard Aloysius Twine, Henry Twine's distant relative, between 1922 and 1927. Restored by the St. Augustine Historical Society, the group of sixty-six pictures was being exhibited in the Jacksonville Public Library. These handsome photographs depicted Emancipation Day celebrations, schools and churches, portraits of individuals, businesses, pool halls, cafés, grocery stores, barbershops, the officers of the Roman Catholic Order of the Knights of St. John in regalia—what the community used to be. Now, in 1991, we were driving through a community limited to housing and churches, with young men idling on street corners looking suspiciously like they're involved in drug activity. "Yes," Mr. Twine agreed. "We have a big drug problem here."

As I was returning Mr. Twine to his automobile, I asked if he would help me locate Dr. Robert Hayling, the dentist who had godfathered the first demonstrations. I also wanted to interview the Reverend Goldie Eubanks, Hayling's fellow NAACP activist. Both, Twine informed me, had left St. Augustine soon after the 1964 demonstrations ended.

"Hayling moved to south Florida a long time ago," he said. "He took a licking here because he didn't have the support of the ministers, the leading people—he's very bitter."

I asked if he ever returns to St. Augustine, and if there was some way I could contact him.

"Sometimes he'll drive through," Twine replied laconically. "He comes by the house when he does. He still has a few friends here. But I don't have a telephone number or an address for him."

"And what about Eubanks?"

"I would suggest you call his nephew, Gerald Eubanks, who works in the school system," Twine said. "Or Cherry Eubanks McDougal. But Goldie is long gone." Mrs. Lucille Plummer, who was the SCLC secretary in St. Augustine, had also departed. In fact, an exodus seemed to have occurred among most of the activist leaders; either they had given up or they were forced out. Hayling and his family had continued to receive threats after 1964, Twine said. Many of the whites in town blamed him for initiating St. Augustine's civil rights troubles. And he hardly could have forgotten that in September 1963, he and three of his youth workers were abducted and almost lynched by a white mob just south of St. Augustine.

Hayling was the only black dentist in town; he had not been replaced. Nor had Lincolnville been promising enough to attract a black physician or attorney. St. Augustinians who preferred black doctors, dentists, or lawyers had to go to Jacksonville to find them.

Even Florida Memorial, whose president during the 1960s, Dr. Royal Puryear, barred his students from participating in demonstrations after the initial sit-ins, and who bent over backward to work with whites in town, gave up and moved to Miami in 1968. The move was brought about by difficulties in finding decent jobs for Memorial graduates, according to author David Colburn. The consequent loss in terms of community income, education, and cultural activity, not to mention the inevitable energy that emanates from youth seeking to better their condition, was substantial, to say the least. With the St. Augustine income so firmly based on tourism, and if blacks can obtain only menial jobs in that industry, one can see why the college backers thought it a waste of time to have their students go through a four-year course only to end up washing dishes in a restaurant. Since 1964, a few blacks were hired by the city, but those jobs were few and far between, as were teaching posts in public schools. In 1972, St. Augustine's Fairchild-Hiller aircraft plant, which did hire a few blacks because of federal equal opportunity provisions, closed down. Lincolnville's depressed look did not come by accident.

~

In an effort to further explore Lincolnville and its present condition, I called the Reverend Fred Richardson, the pastor of St. Paul's AME Church. St. Paul's is one of the community's most prestigious churches, and a site where the nightly meetings and canvassing for marches to the Plaza took place. Mr. Twine had suggested I speak with Richardson.

Located on the former Central Avenue, now renamed to honor Dr. King, St. Paul's is indeed a landmark, though not as imposing an edifice as the great black AME churches in Charleston. The Reverend Mr. Richardson, a small polite man in his forties, spoke in carefully modulated tones, as do many black ministers. He ushered me into his office in the church basement meeting room. A native of Jacksonville, Mr. Richardson has lived in St. Augustine since 1984. "When this church hired me, I was asked, 'Do you plan to live here?' Well, I am here. I suppose I play the role of the 'community pastor.' I've become a racial go-between, though I didn't ask for that." I suppose he meant that his appointment to the ministerial chair at St. Paul's—recognized by whites as well as blacks as an important church—automatically cast him into the role of racial diplomat and spokesperson, whether he relished the role or not.

I asked Mr. Richardson about his impressions of Lincolnville.

"At one time . . ." he began; then he listed the various businesses in Lincolnville which are now no more—restaurants, clubs, barbershops, funeral homes, and so forth. "When Florida Memorial left, that hurt. Their faculty represented a certain kind of community strength, though they were certainly not activists. As for the will to change things, among those blacks who have something there's now the attitude 'I don't want to lose what I have. Dr. King is gone.' That sort of thing. And don't forget, most St. Augustine blacks *weren't* supportive of the Movement. It was just a few people, mostly youth.

"The lack of energy here exists not just with older folk: Youth who need jobs feel so defeated they don't even apply. Hotels and restaurants call me looking for people." Richardson's assessments were essentially the same as Twine's, and equally depressing. If apathy is an infectious disease in St. Augustine, affecting young and old alike, what was its root cause? I asked Richardson.

"As far as I can see," Richardson answered, and it was obvious he had given the question considerable thought, "apathy and a lack of hope come from break-downs in our families. We have a tremendous number of single-parent families in Lincolnville. Young people have children before they can support themselves. Problems are multiplied by generations of family problems.

"Add to that the problem of illegal drugs. Whoever introduced crack-cocaine into this community was able to sell it as the panacea for all problems. Instead, it *created* problems we haven't been able to cope with, taking a toll on our younger people, creating fear in our older population. Burglar bars are going up all over the place. Elders are being robbed in this community. There's just a total lack of respect that we have never before seen."

I asked Richardson about the plethora of area gun clubs and gun shops in St. Augustine, which I saw as aligned with racist vigilante groups. Maybe the frightening hostility from whites in 1964 was not merely a coming-in-from-outside phenomenon.

"Guns," he replied thoughtfully, "are a continuation of southern thinking. There's this theory that guns provide a protection needed . . . needed"—he paused as he searched for a word—"against the *other*."

"The other?"

"Yes. Whoever. Whatever. But alien to 'us.' That kind of thinking is alive and well around here." He paused again. "Listen," he continued after a moment of reflection, "there's still a lot of people in this community who abide by the beliefs of the Ku Klux Klan, though few of them would participate in the rituals. Things *have* changed a little bit. A few years ago some Klan members—they were from Flagler County, I believe—were handing out leaflets down at the Plaza. I heard about it and went there to argue with them. The white onlookers were encouraging me, particularly Flagler College students; everyone was white, except for me. The police were protecting the Klansmen, keeping the tourists away from them. The tourists were screaming at them to leave and go back where they came from. So that kind of blatant thing is suppressed and there's changes, but if you dig deep enough..." He trailed off without finishing the thought. "Blacks and whites have related to each other since the founding of St. Augustine, but there has always been that thing where you know your role and I know mine. Blacks have learned how far to go. This was the problem so many people, white and black, had with Hayling: He wanted to go too far too quick. A kind of safe thinking has been passed down from generation to generation. More ambitious blacks leave for elsewhere. They prosper elsewhere, but not here."

I, too, could imagine myself plotting to leave for "elsewhere" if I had been born and raised in St. Augustine. The effect of the town's long history, its aged edifices, and the lack of blacks who played any meaningful role in the process by which the town thrived was one I had rarely experienced in any place in the South outside of Mississippi. It made one feel that change could never come—at least not without a fundamental overhauling of the entire place and its reason for being.

The drug problem was so often mentioned I arranged to talk with James Allen, a young black man, about thirty, who works as a counselor to parents and community groups in a drug prevention program housed in a cinder-block structure I had seen on West King Street. Gerald Eubanks, the nephew of Goldie Eubanks and the president of the NAACP Youth Council back in 1964, had suggested I speak with Allen after he explained that I wasn't going to be able to interview Eubanks. In fact, Gerald, though very helpful, asked that I not use his detailed remarks. At the program office on West King, between telephone calls Allen told me the program is state funded; minority youth are the target group. The subject turned to problems in Lincolnville.

"I grew up in Lincolnville," Allen informed me. "Now there're a lot of absentee landlords who don't want to live there. There are a lot of irresponsible teenagers who are renting in the area—these are young families with plenty of problems. The St. Augustine black community is fragmented by class and background. There's not a desire anymore to help others. Drugs around here are a big problem because this is a coastal area. Some say the volume of drugs imported in this area is as large as south Florida.

"We have an exceptional problem because our youth are the sellers. Then the sellers become users. As far as jobs are concerned, when there are jobs, it's the same as always: Blacks are the last hired, the first fired." A statement Mr. Twine made earlier continued to nag at me.

"You know," Mr. Twine lamented, "in exchange for individual freedom to live 'anywhere,' we sacrificed the strength of our black neighborhoods." The way Twine phrased it, the process was a little clearer: We were not "allowed" into the white economic and political world as a consequence of the civil rights movement, admitted merely as beneficiaries and bringing nothing into the bargain—but rather, we "exchanged" the institutions, lifestyles, and social relationships we had developed since Emancipation, defined as inferior though they may not have been, for something else we thought *must* be better since we were always denied it. Maybe we thought this would not affect the old black communities, but it did. Now, thirty years later, blacks are beginning to evaluate the overall effects of that exchange. Today, few blacks of any means choose to live or maintain properties in the old black communities of the South, for under segregation these neighborhoods were viewed as imposed upon blacks, and viable as they may have been, they were resented. The ability to move out became proof of economic means. Once the black middle class moved elsewhere, the old communities began to collapse because of a lack of financial and professional support for community institutions and businesses. And because the black middle class was smaller than the number of those who fall below the poverty line and those who suffer from fractured families, the removal of key support has become all the more disastrous for black neighborhoods. Of course, this was not the only reason for the decline of Lincolnville.

During the past few days I had been trying to reach Dr. Hayling by telephone. I found a number I thought might be his from long-distance information. I took a chance and called the number, but reached an answering machine. I left a message explaining who I was, that I was interested in talking to Dr. Hayling about St. Augustine, and that I would be willing to drive down to south Florida to meet him if necessary.

After a few days he called me at the motel and we had a long conversation, mostly about mutual friends, but he steadfastly refused to be interviewed on St. Augustine, and asked me not to drive down to south Florida to meet him. I felt he enjoyed talking about St. Augustine, but I sensed that his pleasure was tinged with a fear associated with his horrific experiences in the town. He had been so harassed there, it was as if he felt someone in St. Augustine might still do something to him, and though I didn't think that was a realistic fear, I had never had my home shot into, or received numerous calls threatening my life.

Dr. Hayling spoke intelligently and I sensed he must have been quite an iconoclast in this bastion of conformity. I was sorry I was not able to break through Hayling's protective shell, but I could well understand his reluctance, his air of suspicion. Someday, though, I hope he will tell his story.

A few days later I decided to take a drive down the Florida coast to Daytona Beach on U.S. I, a distance of about sixty miles, to see Bethune-Cookman College. I had visited Daytona and Bethune-Cookman as a teenager to play in the annual tournament of the American Tennis Association, the black tennis association, which was held at the college. (I had had plenty of time to look around, because I lost in the first round of the junior division.)

That trip was a pleasant memory. Daytona was a small, viable black community and Bethune-Cookman an important private black college. The guiding spirit of the college was its president, Mary McLeod Bethune, one of the great women of the pre-civil-rights period, a friend and counsel to Eleanor Roosevelt. Mrs. Bethune was also president of the National Council of Negro Women: By the early 1950s she had become an important black role model. Mrs. Bethune didn't show up for any of the matches, but she did speak at the ATA banquet (all black organizations seem to have an annual banquet), from which I recall only her rather strange comment that the tournament represented an accomplishment by blacks in their march toward progress in American society. I also recalled that as a youngster I was taken by my father to hear Mrs. Bethune speak at a highly unusual interracial meeting in downtown New Orleans during which she made a point of not sitting too close to the white male speakers. She was extremely dark skinned, buxom, and eloquent, with a deliberate and dramatic speaking style, which did not reflect black southern speech. The contrast between her shining black skin and country-church carriage and her spectacular command of language was absolutely startling. At this meeting she told a story of visiting a garden in Europe, I think in Belgium or Holland, where she came across a rare black rose, "the most treasured rose in the garden."

At the tournament the outstanding black player was Althea Gibson, but she was shunned by the black socialite tennis players because of her "street" background in Harlem. No one spoke to Gibson, and she in turn spoke to no one. That was a few years before she won the national championship at Forest Hills. Recalling these memories made me want to see Bethune-Cookman again. The few towns along the way were small and uninteresting. They looked run-down, as if there had been no development since the 1940s.

I had no trouble finding the black community of Daytona and Bethune-Cookman. Since it was June, there were no students around. The college campus appeared to be isolated from the community. What would you say of a school with a high-wire fence around the men's dorm? The old red-clay tennis courts were gone, and there were several new buildings, but it seemed they had no style or dignity. A few football players were gathered at the gym, and a basketball game was in progress at a nearby park, which appeared to be a hangout for young men.

This scene in Daytona, along with similar scenes in St. Augustine and Jacksonville, intensified my impression that, for blacks, Florida was and had always been primarily a place of migratory agricultural work, except for the few families that had resided there for generations like the Twines of St. Augustine. The economy, from outward appearances, seemed weak, so that this eastern section of Florida was a home of poor whites and blacks, abandoned dreams, festering racial resentments, abundant weaponry (more gun shops in Daytona Beach), and illegal drugs, which had become a mainstay of the economy, particularly for young blacks. The barbed wire surrounding the Bethune-Cookman dormitories, which made them look like prisons, conveyed the strong message that the school desired to keep out the surrounding community with all of its social problems, a reversal of the traditional posture of black private colleges, which sought to strengthen and buttress the old black communities economically and culturally by providing social programs and jobs. The entire corridor from Jacksonville to Daytona Beach looked as if some awesome, malevolent engine of destruction had cut a swath through it, sucking up all its energy and life-generating spirit, leaving in its wake cocaine, heroin, basketball, and a few churches.

At Gerald Eubanks's house in St. Augustine, I had met Caroline Proctor, who works in a drug abuse program with cocaine mothers. "All black," she sighed. "Drugs are overwhelming St. Augustine," she added, "and in terms of changing things, we're at a stalemate. Even our political representatives should know that."

The tourist information in the material handed out by the St. Augustine Historical Society does not mention the events of 1964. "History," for the purposes of official St. Augustine, seemed to have progressed far enough once it reached the Flagler era. Now that the Spanish were long gone, posing no threat, Hispanic-American history was "in," providing a pleasant and exotic seasoning to St. Augustine's image of itself. The events of 1964, on the other hand, were perhaps likely to arouse the curiosity of tourists who might wonder why the protests had occurred, and why the resistance to them was so bitter. And this was a curiosity the Historical Society apparently did not wish to encourage. The Historical Society *had* done a good job of restoring the Lincolnville photographs of Richard Aloysius Twine. But a history of racial exploitation, conflict, and controversy—that history is to be avoided.

I visited the Ripley's Believe It or Not! Museum. Robert Ripley was a peculiarly American "explorer" type, patterned on the European explorers of faraway places during previous centuries. "Ripley was a world traveler who visited places few people even heard of, from the temple of heaven in China to a town in Norway called Hell!" the informational brochure reveals. I remembered that Ripley's cartoons were syndicated in the daily newspapers when I was a boy. This museum, one of seventeen around the world, was perfect for St. Augustine tourists in search of the safely bizarre. "Wherever he went, he searched for the old and the unusual. In his quest, Ripley documented the customs and beliefs of many ancient and modern civilizations. Every year, millions visit the Believe It or Not! Museums to take part in a similar adventure—one in which they experience firsthand the incredible world of Robert Ripley!"

There were depictions and enlarged photographs of Ripley, in helmet photographed with a tall New Guinea "head-hunter"; crossing the Sahara by pony; pictured with physical freaks and "vaudeville artists"; holding shrunken heads from South America; bringing home to America "a genuine Tibetan skull"; pictured with "the tallest man of all time"; and so forth. After a while I gave up. This was prepackaged voyeurism for Americans who are ignorant of the world's cultures—Ripley being an accepted interpreter of the "oddities" of "others." The non-Western world, particularly the colonial third world, is presented here as a collection of circus phenomena—with Ripley as the brave hero who endured hardship to photograph the exotic, acquire unlikely facts, and return to America with unthinkable artifacts.

The old structures of the town, cast in stone, resemble the fortresses against the outside world implied by Ripley's. (Such structures exude wealth and, when necessary, display cannon as a symbol of weaponry.) If we are wealthy, we can buy anything and anyone. We can purchase the exotic artifacts of other cultures and bring them home to be placed on our walls. When we die, we can bequeath our exotic treasures to our museums. As for the masses, they identify with our wealth, our fortresses, mansions, and churches.

The shellstone fortresses and the display of ostentatious wealth also reinforce the class system, which historically reinforces the racist system in the South. For poor whites excluded from the southern gentry, the most objectionable thing about the civil rights movement and black economic and political advancement was that it deprived them of their long-standing privilege of at least being above blacks. Of course, for poor whites, the gains made by blacks in the civil rights movement were not just *psychologically* problematic: Blacks would now also be competing with them for jobs, and in cases where whites were not as qualified as blacks, those whites would lose their jobs. Though Klan demonstrations like those in St. Augustine were extremely hysterical, maybe they also were the painful expressions of a deep hurt, the result of a subconscious sensing that the era of what little privilege poor whites had always considered their birthright was now coming to an end. The Flaglers and their class, and their descendants, would go on running things in St. Augustine as before, but the opening of jobs and voting for blacks would mean, in the narrow subterranean view of poor, uneducated whites, that they were only a step away from being reduced to the status of niggers.

I was about ready to leave St. Augustine, but before I did I was referred by Cherry Eubanks (whom I didn't get to interview) to James Jackson, a person who had been very actively involved in the Youth Council demonstrations, and was still living in St. Augustine. I called Jackson and he was very cooperative, inviting me to come over the next day. I was particularly excited to meet Jackson in the wake of my inability to interview Dr. Hayling. James Jackson, as a teenager, was a charter member of Hayling's NAACP Youth Council. He was also with Hayling the night a group of them were abducted by the white mob in 1963 and almost lynched. This story, though without the details, is referred to in most civil rights histories as an example of the kind of rampant violence that existed in St. Augustine when Movement protests began.

Jackson, now forty-seven, lives in the West King Street section in a trailer home with his wife and children. While his hair is graying, he still maintains a youthful look and a soft, reflective speaking style. He responded carefully to my questions.

Jackson grew up in St. Augustine, receiving his early schooling at St. Benedict the Moor Catholic school, an institution very instrumental in Lincolnville's development. (St. Augustine has had a small but constant percentage of black Catholics.) He grew up on Dumas Street with his grandmother. "Blacks and whites lived near each other," he recalled. "All my teachers were white until I reached the sixth grade." Jackson credits St. Benedict with providing him with a good solid education.

Jimmy Jackson's father was a commercial shrimper, one of the oldest and most dignified trades occupied by blacks in St. Augustine. "Dad worked for a percentage of what he caught. In most cases, the boat owners, who were white, didn't do any shrimping themselves. Dad would stay out for months at a time, working along the Florida coast between St. Augustine and the Georgia state line. He maintained a lot of independence as long as he brought back the shrimp, which he always did. He was not someone to be a yes man to white folks; we weren't brought up like that. His skill brought him a certain amount of respect other blacks didn't have."

"Did you grow up working with him?" I asked.

"No. Dad didn't want his children involved in the shrimping business. When I was fourteen, he allowed me to begin working with him in the summers, but only, he said, if I passed my schooling. Shrimping for a living was a very difficult life. And very dangerous. Especially when you work at night, and you have to work at night; sometimes you have to deal with sharks. The shrimping industry was started by Greeks in Fernandina, just north of here. They did it the same way. Whites purchased a boat, though they knew nothing of boating, hired a black as captain, and the blacks actually did the fishing."

I asked him how the economic situation here compared to Jacksonville.

"In Jacksonville there was industry. Here, you were either in education, a domestic, a railroad man, a shrimper, or a tour carriage driver. Blacks were not allowed into the construction trades, or were deliberately kept at the bottom. It was made obvious and it hurt. For instance, there was a city tractor that mowed grass in the parks and along the streets. Whites drove the tractor; blacks were hired to walk behind the tractor cutting the grass the machine couldn't reach with a scythe. Black foremen were forbidden on the 'railroads.' Blacks were the 'rail gang,' maintenance people, or you worked in the 'barn'—it was always unskilled physical work."

"There were *no* black role models in St. Augustine?" I asked him.

"The supposed role models didn't set a good example; they didn't try to help others. I specifically remember that. There wasn't encouragement to seek higher education. Nor was there encouragement when we began demonstrations. My close friend's mother told me not to come back to their home anymore once I joined the NAACP Youth Council and began sitting in. She said, 'I got to protect my job. I don't want you to see my son again.'

"When we began demonstrations, a policeman came over to the high school to interrogate me. I was called to the principal's office. This policeman demanded that I address him as 'sir.' The principal, a black man like us, was sitting right there and he said absolutely nothing. That's the kind of role models we had."

"Well then, how did you become involved?"

"I was invited to an NAACP Youth Council meeting at Bethel Church in the spring of 1963. I was eighteen years old. The Youth Council was just getting itself together. The fact that we were talking about actually *doing* something appealed to me. After a meeting or two, Gerald Eubanks was elected youth president, I became vice president, and Dr. Hayling became our adviser. Our first action was to picket downtown stores, particularly those with lunch counters that did not serve blacks, or served blacks in segregated sections; the same kind of protests kids were making everywhere in the South. All together, there were about sixty high school youth involved, a few college students from Florida Memorial, and a tiny group of adults. Once we decided to move to the sit-in phase, expecting to be arrested and jailed, the senior members of the NAACP leadership opposed us. I was one of the first to go to jail that summer of 1963, along with several other teenagers.

"The president of the NAACP, Fannie Fullerwood, begged us to stop. She claimed, 'We didn't authorize sit-ins,' but we told her, 'We're not gonna stop.' Soon after this disagreement we were scheduled to meet at the First Baptist Church, and the minister evicted us; he put the Youth Council out of his church. We moved our meetings to the Elks Rest Lodge on Washington Street. Around the same time, President Puryear of Florida Memorial informed his students he would expel them if they participated in another demonstration. After that, most of their students wouldn't associate with us."

I asked Jackson to tell me the story of his kidnapping and close call with death at the hands of the Klan in the fall of 1963.

"By late summer and early fall 1963, there was beginning to be a lot of Klan activity in town in response to our demonstrations. This was not just St. Augustine, but people from all over this northeastern pocket of Florida—somehow St. Augustine became a magnet that attracted these crazies, brought them out of the woods. Klan rallies and wild speech-making about what they were going to do to the 'niggers' was a form of entertainment for them. In September 1963, Klan members began passing out flyers in downtown St. Augustine announcing a public rally to be held on the night of the eighteenth, in a field just south of town to the east of U.S. One. This was one of the first of their big rallies. All the key racists were supposed to be there, including Hoss Manucy, the leader of the Ancient City Hunting Club. This was just after the bombing of the church in Birmingham that killed four little girls, so the Klan and violence were active as never before. Dr. Hayling, myself, and two guys with us that day wanted to know more about what the Klan planned for St. Augustine. We decided we would try to eavesdrop on their meeting; it was Dr. Hayling, Jimmy Hauser, Clyde Jenkins, and myself.

"At first we tried to hear what they were saying from the black recreation park at the south end of Lincolnville, but we couldn't because the sound from their loudspeakers was obstructed by dense trees. So we decided to get close enough to be able to hear. We drove out to U.S. One, where we could see Klan members beckoning cars onto a road that led to the field they were using. There were no police around. We decided to try another road that we thought would take us close to the field without coming across the access road they were using. But as soon as we got back there, we discovered the Klan had posted sentries along all the roads, including the one we were on. As soon as they spotted our car, they jumped out of the bushes alongside the road with rifles and shotguns. At first they had no idea who we were, but when they saw we were black, they ordered us out of our car and marched us into their rally. It was about ten P.M. I was frightened and my overwhelming feeling was disgust that we had been caught like that.

"After we arrived at the meeting, they separated us. They wanted to know what we were doing on that road. Our story, which we quickly agreed upon in the car, was that we were going fishing and got lost. This seemed to be working, but unfortunately for us, *very* unfortunately, when they searched us they found a picture of a Caucasian woman in Jimmy Hauser's wallet. You know what that meant to those fools. Up to that point they really hadn't recognized us; they hadn't even recognized Dr. Hayling. But now they were excited. They wanted to know what this nigger was doing with this white woman's picture in his pocket. Hauser, who was nineteen and wasn't thinking, told them the woman was his sister-in-law!

"So they were discussing what to do with us. Then someone recognized Hayling. 'That's that nigger dentist!' Then they recognized me from demonstrations at the Plaza. First, they decided to beat us, separately. I weighed about one hundred forty pounds. A big white guy was hitting me with his fist. He kept knocking me back on a car. I could see that they had knocked Hauser down and they were jumping up and down on him, stomping him. I was trying desperately *not* to go down. Finally, they hit me in the head with a lug wrench. During all this, someone was holding a shotgun at my head.

"Then, after they'd beaten us half to death, they asked, 'What we gonna do with 'em now?' So someone came up with the idea 'Let's castrate 'em.' I made up my mind right then they were gonna kill me before I let them castrate me. Just at that time Hauser screamed. The man with the shotgun looked off in Hauser's direction. I took off running toward the road where they first caught us. They didn't shoot; they ran after me. But I was so foolish because I ran into the same sentries that captured us before. They were just waiting because they could hear all the commotion and see me running. I was running for my life but when I hit the road they popped out and said, 'Nigger, you *hold it* right there.' And I had actually outrun the guys who were chasing me. 'Turn around, nigger; let's go back to that meeting.' Just then I heard the word 'castration' again and I flew into the woods.

"But they were right behind me and caught me again, beat me again, and dragged me again back to the meeting. I could see they had Hayling, Jenkins, and Hauser tied together. They pushed me in with them and then I heard someone say, 'Let's burn them up. Somebody go get the gasoline.' I just knew we were goners.

"Not too long after that, really just in time, the sheriff, L. O. Davis, appeared out of nowhere and told them, 'All right, boys, that's gon' be enough of that.' He hated us, and I'm not sure he or some of his officers weren't there all along, in the background, watching everything that happened. Years later, I ran into one of the white guys who was there at the rally and he said he thought the entire kidnapping was staged until he saw us getting beat up and all the blood—saw how savage it was.

"The sheriff piled all four of us into a patrol car and drove us to Flagler Hospital. At the hospital emergency room one of the aides made phone calls for us. They stitched me up and wanted me to remain hospitalized, but by then I was so afraid I thought they might come looking for us there that night. So I went home. Hayling was more seriously injured, and had to be removed to a hospital in Jacksonville.

"The next morning I looked at myself in the mirror and became totally pissed that we had let this happen. When I told my grandmother what happened, she was just glad I was still alive. My father was away on the boat. He was so angry when he returned and heard about it he wanted to go looking for some of those men with a weapon, but we calmed him down.

"Anyway, after that beating, I was all the more determined not to let anything of that sort turn me around. I had the keys to Hayling's Volkswagen convertible. I picked up his car, lowered the top, and purposely rode all over town to make it known that what happened the previous night would not ground me. A close friend saw me and demanded that I go with him to the hospital in Jacksonville to have my head injuries more thoroughly checked out. Four of the Klan people were arrested in our case and went to trial. Their cases were dismissed, but the jury found *Hayling* guilty of assault. The judge fined him one hundred dollars."

I asked Jackson how he felt about SCLC coming in 1964.

"I agreed with it. Those of us who wanted to continue demonstrations were totally dissatisfied with the NAACP. They were holding us back. They weren't doing anything." He mentioned with particular disgust a march in Tallahassee in which a contingent from St. Augustine was asked to drive over and help, but "we had to pay our own way, because the NAACP wouldn't fund our trip.

"When Hosea Williams came in 1964, more of our young people became involved. Hosea related well to young people and we had to have young people. Elders like my grandmother were wavering and worried. She wanted me to apologize to the minister who kicked us out of First Baptist. Which I never did. Basically, our elders were negative toward marches, sit-ins, and picketing. I do remember that Miss Gracie Gardener was an older person who was always there with us."

I asked whose idea it was to conduct night marches. "Hosea's. And he was smart. Looking back on those times, the biggest mistake the other side made was to let the Klan loose on us. You never heard about St. Augustine, no matter what kind of demonstrations we did, in 1963. When the Klan came into the picture, we became national news. But it was rough out there. It was like a small war. I never knew people—men and women—could call us such names or throw so many bricks."

"What was the impact of King's appearances?" I asked. "Was it a big deal?"

"Yes. It was. For a small town like this. That was a shot in the arm." I asked Jackson how he felt when the SCLC's organizational efforts ceased immediately after passage of the civil rights bill. "I didn't mind them leaving. They couldn't stay here forever. Everyone knew that from the beginning."

Finally, I asked Jackson to drive with me to the field where they were beaten. As we drove down U.S. 1, he remarked, "None of this development [restaurants, a new hospital, a shopping mall] was here then. All of this was woods." We turned into the road they followed in 1963, only to discover it was closed off. He pointed to the field where the rally was held. Then we drove over to the former site of the Flagler Hospital on the Mantanzas River. We took a spin through Lincolnville, Jackson showing me where businesses were once located, especially those on Washington Street, which is now a ghost town. He pointed out the movie theater, nightclub, restaurants, and Elks Rest Lodge.

"Lincolnville was not all black," Jackson told me. "So many neighbors were white it made our efforts there more difficult. Whites simply could not believe blacks they had known all their lives were protesting. They blamed the whole thing on 'outside agitators.' "

Finally, we drove over to the Lincolnville recreation area, which had a surprisingly nice city park. The community center in the park is named for Willie Gallimore, a famous Florida A&M and Chicago Bears football running back, a St. Augustine native. Gallimore was killed in a tragic automobile collision in the 1950s while still in his prime with the Bears. We visited the churches that became the meeting places of 1964—First Baptist and St. Paul's—and traced the route of the 1964 marches downtown. "We marched in twos on the sidewalk," Jackson recalled.

"Rednecks congregated in the Plaza park. After they beat us, they followed for a short distance on our return trip, but they never followed us all the way into Lincolnville. We had to do the best we could; there was just no protection from the police."

As we drove on West King Street to return to Jackson's trailer home, we decided to drive out to the unoccupied campus of Florida Memorial, its decaying buildings still there, like a modern archaeological site. I noticed a cross street named for former President Puryear. "Puryear," Jackson recalled offhandedly. "He was the type of black man who made students who worked for him enter through the *back* door." When we arrived back at Jackson's trailer, I asked him why he never left St. Augustine.

"I did," he responded. "I couldn't get a job here. I was arrested *nineteen* times," though, he was quick to add, none of these were felonies. "My brother resembles me. As I became known in the Movement, he was fired from his job at the hospital. Maybe they thought he was me. I moved to New York after I married, lived in Manhattan. And I had work all the time I was there. But..." He paused awhile to reflect. "One day as I was entering my apartment house, a man behind me yelled, 'Hold the door for me, please.' Well, you know, that's how people get in your building who want to commit a robbery. I slammed the door in his face. Later, I found he actually lived on my floor. I didn't know him. I just didn't feel at home in New York. Maybe I realized I never would.

"That night I told my wife it was time for us to leave New York and return to Florida. We didn't even know our neighbors. Here, you see, despite all the problems, and there are plenty, I do know my neighbors. People speak to you, even if they don't know your name. That's the way I grew up.

"When I returned, I was able to get a job as a maintenance repair person with the telephone company. They looked past my civil rights arrest record and hired me on the basis of my work record."

"And when you returned had St. Augustine really changed?"

"Yes. And no. However, one day I was downtown and I almost bumped into an old white man. He said, 'Excuse me, sir,' and went on by. He was entering a store, I was coming out. Then it hit me who he was; it was Hoss

Manucy," the most rabid racist of the old St. Augustine Klan. "Of course, he didn't recognize me."

" 'Excuse me, sir?' What do you think that means?"

"I can't even begin to explain what that might mean." Jackson laughed. "I was just amazed. Maybe time changes everything, whether we like it or not."

# ALBANY

⌒

*Time may change everything, but the wheels of change seemed to turn more slowly in St. Augustine than in other places in the Black Belt South. It was time for me to leave. I didn't believe I would learn much that would alter my impressions of the town if I remained a year. I left St. Augustine on July 17, my next destination the southwest Georgia town of Albany, a place of legendary resonance as an early battlefield of the southern civil rights movement. In 1962, the Albany campaign waged by SNCC and Martin Luther King, Jr., and his SCLC was the first of a series of mass-movement civil rights efforts in southern towns that came to symbolize the mainstream of southern protest with its nightly meetings, marches downtown, and massive jailings.*

*The Albany campaign had operatic dimensions: powerful contending forces aligned in stark opposition, highlighted by the glare of national and international news media. A southern town surrounded by beautiful rolling fields, stained by a long history of slavery and serfdom, Albany was the site of the exhortative and plaintive music of the black churches crying out for freedom. The campaign, however, concluded in inconclusiveness and disappointment, leaving few heroes or heroic images.*

*Albany nevertheless established the pattern for subsequent mass-participation campaigns in Birmingham and Selma that would lead to undeniably concrete achievements: the Civil Rights Act of 1964 and the Voting Rights Act of 1965. Through these statutes the face of the South was changed forever.*

*The effort in Albany began in November 1961, with a planned protest challenging segregation at the Trailways bus station. These initial protests quickly broadened to include mass marches against every form of segregation, the result being mass arrests on a scale unprecedented in the history of the civil rights movement up to that point.*

*I was eager to discover the results of this sustained effort and its impact now, almost three decades later. Albany's 1990 total population was about ninety thou-*

*sand, including the surrounding subdivisions, with a black majority of about 55 percent; I felt that the impact of civil rights activity there over a longer period would be far more substantial than, for instance, in St. Augustine, so it would be reasonable to assume that expectations of black achievement were considerably higher there.*

Florida Highway 297 took me through Hastings, known as the Potato Capital of Florida. From Hastings, I drove southwestward to Palatka and from there on across north Florida on sparsely traveled Highway 20 to Gainesville.

At Gainesville, I connected with I-75, which took me north into Georgia until it intersected with U.S. 82 at Tifton. Albany is about forty-five miles west of this junction. I had driven Highway 82 many times in Mississippi; it traverses the very heart of the southeastern Black Belt. Originating on the Georgia Atlantic coast at Brunswick, U.S. 82. was a road cutting through beautiful tall pine trees. Passing the village of Ty-Ty, then Sylvester, I arrived at the outskirts of east Albany by about 7:00 P.M. I located an inexpensive motel on the highway, settled in, and called Charles Sherrod, the leader of the first group of SNCC organizers, who had ventured into Albany during the summer of 1961. Albany has since become Sherrod's permanent home; for the past twelve years he has been a city commissioner. I arranged to see him the next morning.

Strangely, I felt at home. Maybe it was the unbelievable heat, which sapped all of one's energy even at night; maybe it was the stillness, the slower passing of time, the smell of the trees and flowers, the absence of massive electricity, which made night more nightlike; or maybe it just had to do with lazy speech—a speech I both despised and recognized as belonging to "home."

I was trying to figure out why this place felt so familiar. Albany certainly has little in common with New Orleans. Maybe it reminded me of East Texas, of sections of Houston. Houston is my mother's home; we visited her parents, Doctor and Ladybelle Covington, every summer when we were children. Then I came to know Houston more thoroughly when I worked for a black newspaper there during the summers of my junior and senior years in college. What Albany had in common with Houston, I finally decided, was an air of semiurbanity—Albany gave the impression of being half-city, half-country—which is exactly how Houston felt in the 1940s and '50s.

That night, a Sunday night, I couldn't wait to explore the town. Driving westward on U.S. 82, I crossed the Flint River bridge, where in downtown Albany U.S. 82 becomes Oglethorpe Street, which is the main artery running through town. To the north of Oglethorpe is the old downtown business area; on the opposite side, in a slight valley, is the large black housing area: I didn't see signs of prosperity. I noticed a proliferation of pawnshops; apparently, the ubiquitous gun shops of St. Augustine have become the pawnshops of Albany.

After a right turn, U.S. 82 becomes Slappey Drive, a journey through fast-food joints and chain restaurants and the usual chain motels and gas stations. At a corner, a sign read: NEW AND USED RADIATORS FOR SALE (SMILE. GOD LOVES YOU). The few blacks I saw out were young people, but they were not into the flamboyant dress and hairstyles of Charleston or New Orleans—no closely shaved haircuts, no earrings. Stylish dress usually necessitates money, but black youth have invented styles without expensive clothing—any sort of garish self-assertion will do. I didn't see evidence of that in Albany.

The next morning, I met Charles Sherrod in his small, sparsely furnished office in the downtown area. I was surprised how youthful he looked, though he must be in his early fifties. He spoke so softly it was a wonder he was as effective a civil rights leader as he had been; his efforts in southwest Georgia, and the fact that he still remained there thirty years after he came as a volunteer, had made him a SNCC legend.

Sherrod was born and raised in Virginia, and had finished college there. He joined SNCC and headed south in 1961 just after graduation from divinity school. Very soon after he arrived at the SNCC headquarters in Atlanta, he was sent to Albany to begin organizing efforts.

"Why did you remain here in Albany?" I inquired.

"Because I couldn't think of a better place to go after the Movement was over. This was beautiful country, and I liked the people. As for the racial situation, there's racism everywhere. I really grew up down here. I married down here; my wife is from Baker County, just south of Albany. And I believed Albany could change for the better. At least I believed that then."

"Does southwest Georgia remind you of Virginia?" I asked.

"Some places, some churches remind me of Virginia. But there's a music here I never heard in Virginia. When the whole church opens its mouth to sing, that's something I had never heard before. That's one reason why I chose to stay. Does that make sense? It did to me."

"Did you ever become a minister of a church here, as an extension of your organizing role?"

"No. I have never had a church, though I might like to do that some day. You see, I was always critical of the church even while I was in it. However, the Movement I participated in has been *of* the church; that may sound like a contradiction." Now Sherrod works in a governmental social service program, but his main concerns are focused around his work as a city commissioner.

Thirty years ago, in the summer of 1961, Sherrod, Cordell Reagon, and Chuck Jones—Reagon and Jones were student volunteer organizers—arrived in Albany with the intent of motivating blacks to register to vote; the same sort of efforts were beginning in Mississippi at that time. Southwest Georgia, with Albany as its economic hub, was an important target because of its huge Black Belt population and its long, legendary reputation for harsh repression of its black folk. The idea was to get people activated, if possible, and to get them moving with greater self-assertion and political strength.

Despite the existence of a functioning NAACP chapter organized in the 1950s, Albany was no beacon of progress for blacks. The NAACP chapter was primarily a middle-class group of black professionals and ministers, a few of whom were inclined toward militancy, most particularly the younger sons of the Clennon King family. He was an Albany patriarch, an important black Albany businessman. His talented and energetic sons, attorney C. B. King, Jr., and businessman Slater King, were considered key leaders in whatever progress black Albany had or might make.

When Sherrod and his colleagues arrived in Albany, it was C. B. King and his extended family who provided them with encouragement and housing, breaking with more conservative members of the NAACP. That summer the SNCC organizers were able to talk a few churches into letting them hold rallies. They decided it would be best to target young people like themselves in their organizing efforts. Toward this end they canvassed Albany State College, a black school situated on the east bank of the Flint River. Though they were successful in winning some converts, the president of the college, William H. Dennis, quickly banned Sherrod, Jones, and Reagon from the campus.

The prospects for an active Movement in Albany took a dramatic leap forward in early November 1961 with the issuing of a new Interstate Commerce Commission ruling banning segregation in interstate public transportation facilities. SNCC quickly decided to stage a test in Albany. An integrated group of volunteers, including a few Albany State students, attempted to sit in the bus station's white-only waiting room. They were immediately arrested for violating the segregation statutes, and Albany was immediately in the national news. Within days marches and rallies were organized in support of those jailed, which resulted in additional arrests numbering in the hundreds. From that point on, the racial situation in Albany accelerated swiftly toward unanticipated, unprecedented, and uncoordinated events.

One of the black leaders in Albany, Dr. William Anderson, was an old friend of Martin Luther King, Jr. He invited Dr. King to come to Albany to speak at one of the nightly rallies held in support of those arrested at the bus station.

King accepted Anderson's invitation, and arrived in Albany to speak before a large audience at Shiloh Baptist Church on the night of December 15, 1961. It may or may not have been a surprise to King, but after the speech Anderson announced that King would lead a march downtown on the following morning, and asked everyone present to return to the church to march with them. On the morning of December 16 the march was held, and King, his chief aide and companion Ralph Abernathy, and Dr. Anderson were all arrested for marching without a permit. The Dougherty County jails were already full; King, Abernathy, and Anderson were taken to the county jail in Americus, Georgia.

With the arrests of the SCLC leaders, Albany had become, in December 1961, the focal point of national civil rights interest. An extensive corps of national and international press descended on the town, explaining and exposing every aspect of the Movement demands, protests, and the marches that led to even more jailings. After King declared to the press that he, Abernathy, and Anderson would remain in prison through Christmas if necessary, all three decided to bail themselves out within a few days. They were under the impression a meaningful agreement had been negotiated with the city by responsible Albany black leaders. After they read the text, they realized the "agreement" offered little that was concrete and no guarantees of implementation; it wasn't worth the paper it was written on. This fiasco left King vulnerable to criticism of having prematurely abandoned a campaign he had implored others to join, asking them to come to Albany to be with him in prison as a witness against injustice.

I believe that most historians have concluded that from this point on, the King-led phase of the Albany campaign began to fall apart. Andrew Young feels that King was "trapped in Albany," forced by the media to the forefront of a conflict he was not prepared for, had not committed himself to, and finally, had no real control over. It didn't help that the Albany campaign was plagued by vague and changing objectives. Every aspect of public-facility segregation was protested, resulting in mass jailings but few practical results. The city shrewdly exploited divisiveness and confusion among the campaign organizers and leaders.

To make matters worse, there were real antagonisms and resentments between Movement organizations in Albany. The SNCC leaders felt they were the true authors of the Albany effort, that they had been co-opted by King and SCLC (because the media focused on him rather than a group effort), and they complained personally to King about it. He heard them out, replying, in effect, according to Young, "I understand what you're saying, but I can't control the media." SNCC and SCLC were akin to younger and older brothers, but the breach between them that opened in Albany was never closed.

The local NAACP—excluding members like the Albany Kings who had already broken with the more conservative faction—was not happy with the presence of SNCC or with King and his SCLC. They must have felt their traditional leadership had been completely usurped by outsiders who were just visitors to Albany.

Given all these problems, King decided to leave Albany temporarily at the end of 1961. He hoped to limit himself to only sporadic visits until the summer of 1962, when he planned to lead a better-organized, full-scale series of demonstrations. Meanwhile, the city of Albany wasted no time in trying to keep King out altogether through a federal court order barring further demonstrations.

When a sweeping court order, which enjoined King personally, was issued by district court judge Robert Elliot in July 1962, King reluctantly decided to pull out of Albany completely. King, according to Young, was angered by Elliot's order, and protested strenuously to Attorney General Robert F. Kennedy during a long phone call (Elliot was appointed by President John F. Kennedy). Finally, however, King was unwilling to violate a federal court injunction. He well recognized that the civil rights movement must have the respect and support of the federal courts, for only the federal courts had the power to rule local segregation laws unconstitutional.

Andy Young, among others, believed that Albany was a valuable learning experience for King and SCLC, as they planned for a do-or-die campaign in Birmingham, in 1963. In Birmingham and subsequent campaigns they learned to clearly define and state their goals and stick to them at all costs until they had accomplished all or most of their demands. Albany was also a lesson in the dangers of taking on campaigns they could not control, that were fraught with internal or local disputes.

⁓

Once King's phase of the Albany struggle wound down to an unsatisfactory cessation, the town dropped from national consciousness as a place whose racial or civil rights conflict was noteworthy. No fundamental issue had arisen since then in Albany that even approaches the significance of the civil rights years.

King departed but SNCC remained and even expanded its effort to improve black voter registration. Additional canvassing was instituted in the surrounding counties—Worth, Lee, Baker, and Terrell. SCLC also contributed by hiring a local staff to assist in registration. Financial support to keep an interracial team of volunteers in the field came from the Voter Education Project in Atlanta. Sherrod decided to settle in Albany, married, started a family, and eventually entered political life in Albany.

The difficulties between SNCC and SCLC always fascinated me. I wondered how Sherrod, as SNCC leader in Albany, got along with Dr. King.

"We were good friends. I respected him, called him 'Doc.' SNCC guys called him names and made fun of him, but they wouldn't let anyone else disrespect him." He explained further: "I understand what our people were complaining about. Doc and SCLC would come in after we worked hard to get a project moving. This happened several times after Albany. Besides, SCLC made it harder for us to organize, because Doc attracted people who I would call 'onlookers.' He just did, I don't know why. I'm talking about people who came to mass meetings not to participate, but only to hear Dr. King speak. To see and hear a famous person, to be mesmerized by his melodious voice and flowing words. And then he's gone. When we call a meeting, there's a totally different dynamic. It was just very difficult for us to get anything done because we were not glamorous. We had a hard time getting back to the task we began with, because people had to face the realities of getting themselves activated without the spotlight of national attention."

"Has there been any real progress and development here in Albany since those days? However you want to define progress?"

"This town is just as racist as it has always been," Sherrod replied. "The whites are not willing to be called Klansmen or Birchers anymore—but 'conservatives' is okay. They are conscious of the right way, but they are not willing to walk that way. Everything we've achieved here has been fought for, not given. It's the same in all areas. Churches are still segregated. Until two years ago there were no black loan agents at any of the banks. Housing is still segregated. Whites are moving out of the city to the country. The new commercial development we have is toward West Albany, where whites are moving."

Whites might be moving to new suburbs, but I observed that I hadn't seen the burglar bars and protective iron gates so common now even in the small towns I had been traveling through. "But everyone here is *thinking* iron gates or windows," Sherrod replied. "It has to do with crimes associated with drugs. Now we have a movement to pull together, whites and blacks, to fight against illegal drugs. And we're winning. But that doesn't mean the town isn't racist."

I asked Sherrod on what basis he would measure progress since the 1960s, to the extent there had been any? He cited tangibles: "Paved streets and gutters in black neighborhoods, increased black home ownership, better salaries, running water in homes where none existed, upward mobility in terms of hiring and promotion of black policemen, firemen, and heads of city departments." All of these small steps, he made sure to point out, were the result of pressure and protest, not goodwill.

"Is race more of a factor in Albany than other towns in Georgia?" I asked.

"Yes," he replied. "It's a peculiarity of Albany. Albany has attracted industry, and some people have good jobs with area companies like Miller Brewing, Procter and Gamble, Merck and Company, Delco Remey Company, Mars, and Anheuser-Busch, and several Albanians work at the Marine Corps logistics base just outside of town. This is the highest retail store area in the state outside of Atlanta. People come here from surrounding counties to shop in our malls.

"Despite this material progress," Sherrod repeated, "the racial gulf still exists, with wide divisions between the white and black communities. Even among blacks themselves there are deep divisions, with roots that go back to slavery. We have increased black voting through our registration campaigns. Blacks are voting. Blacks constituted the votes to elect two white mayors, plus other local officials. Now white candidates come to the black community for a 'blessing.' Would you consider this progress?" It was characteristic of Sherrod to make statements by using questions.

"It sounds like remarkable progress to me," I replied. "But you seem to feel it's all rather illusionary."

"Yes."

"Why? What's preventing real progress?"

"Old money. I feel Albany would have undergone a really dramatic economic transformation if Interstate Seventy-five, which runs from Florida to Atlanta, had been routed through here instead of fifty miles to the east at Tifton. You see, the interstate creates business in all the little towns along its route. Old money interests stopped it from coming through Albany; they didn't want that to happen—it was a case of old money keeping out new money."

I understood Sherrod to be saying that the interstate, which would have made

Albany a far more important crossroads, would most likely have created new businesses, which might in time threaten the control of the encrusted economic elite of Albany. "Also, in Albany we don't really seek federal monies because federal dollars bring federal regulations. Our black contractors can't bid on city and county contracts because they aren't bonded. As a city, we could bond them ourselves, but we don't. Our contracts could be divided into smaller pieces so black companies could have a measure of participation. As far as the county government is concerned, it awards sixty-five million in contracts but none to black contractors. So we have limited economic gains, except for those few people who make good salaries in the industries."

I asked if Albany was losing its young population.

"Of course," he said. "Our kids go north. Go west. They come back here to look for work but too often they're kicked out. Meaningful work is limited. Unemployment is high."

I also asked about the status of school desegregation in Albany, though I had learned not to equate the extent of school desegregation with educational progress; school desegregation, and how it impacted black children, was a complicated question, I was discovering, with widely different interpretations of what constituted quality education.

"Our public schools are mostly black, about sixty–seventy percent. The racial division among teachers is about equal. The superintendent is white. But we have a strange problem: Within the so-called desegregated schools, the teachers have somehow learned how to teach white kids without teaching black kids. This is done through what they call a tracking system, and once you are tracked in a certain category you remain in that category until you quit or graduate. Too many black kids are on a nonacademic track. In the rural areas we have the same thing, only worse. There's a lot of truancy and all kinds of disciplinary problems. Maybe we need to go back to 'neighborhood choice.' This would lead to resegregation, but at least there would be a choice of what schools you want to attend, and maybe black kids would do better.

"I believe the next major black protest movement will come out of the high schools. High school kids are getting fed up with their own situation. It bothers me, for instance, that black-white teams of school administrators in effect make it difficult to teach black history and a positive sense of black culture in integrated schools. You can't say to a black youth in the presence of a white staff person, 'Son, you got to be better than them. You got to think faster, run faster.' That kind of prompting helped us through. There's no more of that."

⌒

Teaching a history of the South to black and white children in the same schools is going to be an arduous task for a long time to come, I thought, unless some sort of fictional history is invented, maybe a string of lies everyone can agree upon. The real history, or histories, are too painful and too recent to be easily digested, especially given the terribly opposing interpretations of those histories.

As far as southwest Georgia is concerned, if the Creeks were still with us, there would be a third history of the making of that part of the South; but then, they aren't with us to tell, or argue for the telling, of their story. Southwest Georgia was once their land, or rather, was once occupied by independent Creek villages that made every effort to accommodate themselves to the rapidly multiplying white villages, until they became a permanent inconvenience and were killed or forcibly removed to Indian Territory, Oklahoma, by the U.S. military. This process was completed in 1836, the year Nelson Tift, a native of Connecticut, founded the village called Albany. He chose a site on the Flint River, which he must have believed possessed much potential, once it was discovered that the Flint flowed southward until it met the Chattahoochee at Lake Seminole, then, under the name of the Apalachicola, traversed the Florida panhandle until it emptied into the Gulf of Mexico.

Albany never fulfilled such grandiose dreams; instead, it became the rough-hewn commercial hub of one of the earliest Deep South cotton kingdoms. With the Creeks "removed," enormous sections of forest were cleared and prepared for agriculture, followed by an immense importation of African slaves to work the land.

W. E. B. Du Bois describes antebellum Dougherty County in his *Souls of Black Folk* (1903) as "perhaps the richest slave kingdom the modern world ever knew. One hundred fifty barons commanded the labor of nearly six thousand Negroes, held sway over farms with 90,000 acres of tilled land, valued even in times of cheap soil at three millions of dollars."

From the time of Reconstruction until the early twentieth century, the story of Albany parallels that of other areas of the Black Belt, except for a few southwest Georgia twists—a systematic dismantling of the temporary rights enjoyed by blacks during Reconstruction; terror as a weapon of disenfranchisement; the attempt by some blacks to hold on by purchasing small areas of land, though most slipped into peonage. Those became beholden, from year to year, to the owners of large, postwar plantations as they slipped over the years into abject dependency.

During the years between 1900 and 1961, when the first civil rights workers arrived, Albany blossomed into a full-fledged commercial center of southwest Georgia, a growth made possible by its railroad, its role as a major producer and distributor of pecans, and its being the financial headquarters for the surrounding farms and plantations. The decision to locate Turner Air Force Base on the outskirts of town in 1941, however, did much to boost the economy. Because the base was a federal employer, many blacks found work there. Black businessmen developed their own small commercial area in the section of Albany called Harlem, on the opposite side of Oglethorpe Street from the major commercial district on Broad Street. This arrangement made it convenient for customers to shop in both the white and black downtown areas. Some blacks became successful businessmen and they were the ones who, along with a small, college-educated professional class, founded the fledgling NAACP chapter in the 1940s. As for black political activity that could bring about changes for the masses, it was nonexistent. As in other southern towns, pre-1960s-type voting leagues were established that registered a tiny number of voters who endorsed and voted for whatever white candidate sought their vote, if the black vote was sought at all. By the beginning of the sixties, Albany had expanded to a town of fifty-six thousand, of which roughly 41 percent were black and ready to respond to a more aggressive leadership in demanding a modicum of civil rights.

～

While I was visiting Sherrod in his office, an elderly gentleman, severely dressed in black, strolled in. He turned out to be the Reverend Samuel Wells, a native of Albany whose experiences spanned the pre-civil-rights period and who became an important local activist once the demonstrations began. Now in his mid-seventies,

Reverend Wells had grown close to Dr. King in Albany, and was later hired by SCLC as a permanent member of their staff. Reverend Wells was also a strong supporter of Sherrod. He was helping Sherrod prepare for his campaign for reelection to the City Commission, to be held in two weeks. I asked if I could take him to dinner, and he willingly accepted. We went to a chain steak house where we conversed over a heavy buzz of noise, food announcements, and Muzak.

I liked Reverend Wells. He was folksy, reflective, and philosophical. Every time I saw him in Sherrod's office he looked like an old-fashioned black southern preacher, but his ideas weren't old-fashioned. I sensed from his speech that his schooling had been limited; but, as with many elders who were essentially self-taught, Reverend Wells had a questioning sense about him and an eagerness to keep abreast of new events and ideas that too many so-called educated folk lack.

Reverend Wells said he was born in Lee County, just north of Albany, in 1916. When he was a boy, his family moved southward to central Florida, and remained there for six years, living about twenty miles from Tampa. "My father was a sawmill man; he ran around from woods camp to woods camp cutting logs. The logs were shipped to Tampa where they dried lumber and finished them."

During the Depression, in 1932, the family moved northward to Albany. "All the lumbering work went bad, so my father came on back here. My grandmother, uncles, and aunts, they all lived here. So this became home. My family goes back a long ways here in Albany. My grandmother lived to be one hundred; she died just after we returned, so she must have been here during slavery."

I asked Reverend Wells to tell me what Albany was like in the 1930s.

"When we returned to Georgia from Florida, as far as I was concerned, it was like leaving freedom to return to slavery. Southwest Georgia was that far behind time. In *every* which way. In all transactions between the races. My father found work at Reynolds Brothers Mill. We lived about five miles out of town. I walked four miles to a one-room school held at St. Paul's Baptist Church. One teacher taught all eight grades."

During World War II, Wells was drafted and sent to the Pacific theater. "We were integrated in the middle of a battle on Okinawa Island. We weren't segregated again until we were preparing to return to the United States," he recalled bitterly.

"After the war, did you choose to return to Albany?" I asked.

"I never knew the difference. I never seen a city that was really much better in terms of race. In Atlanta you might feel better but that's about it. We didn't feel we needed King to lead us—he was our helper. What he was saying in our mass meetings was already in our hearts."

Because of his prominence in the Movement, Reverend Wells and his family (he had four children) were barred from jobs in the Albany area. When he joined the SCLC staff, he and his family moved to Atlanta, where he worked in the subsequent SCLC campaigns. He continued to return to Worth County on Sundays to pastor his church, New Springs Baptist, driving back and forth from Atlanta. Finally, after his wife died in 1986, and with his children grown and on their own, Reverend Wells returned to Albany.

Now he looks back on what was accomplished by the Movement with disillusionment. "I was naive," he said. "I felt that if we demonstrated and suffered, we would melt the hearts of the whites. I even preached that in overcrowded jails. I thought all they had to know was the extent of our dissatisfaction with things as they were. It turned out that suffering and protesting didn't make any difference." He sees contemporary Albany as deeply divided, not only between the races, but among blacks themselves. I could well imagine that barriers between blacks and whites were still very real in Albany; nothing I saw led me to believe the opposite. I wondered, however, if splintering within the black community, based on class or whatever, was more severe in Albany than in Orangeburg, Charleston, or St. Augustine, where I frequently heard the same comment: Intraracial fragmentation was a precondition of weakness in the effort to achieve racial progress or group economic goals. In Albany I often heard the additional accusation, offered with derision, that the black community suffered from the near-fatal contagious disease called "plantation mentality," a condition hard to overcome.

In Albany, and other formerly heavy slave agricultural areas, it seemed to me that the above remarks, when they came from Movement veterans like the Reverend Wells and knowledgeable observers like the sociologist Elaine Baker at Albany State, represented a bitter recognition and acceptance of the history of dependency and serfdom so many blacks in that area had experienced, along with a contempt for the consequent lack of confidence such blacks possess. "Plantation mentality" as I understand it and have heard it used, refers to a condition of being controlled, not only physically, but mentally—which can be traced back to slavery. Following the logic of such a chain-bound psychological mind-set, there can be no positive future; one lives only for today. Nor will protest against oppressive behavior be rewarding, for everyone knows that the white (plantation) owners are all-powerful, have long memories, and the resulting retaliation will be brutal.

Generation after generation of this kind of thinking had become internalized into a psychology of defeat and despair. Maybe under such a condition, those few "city" blacks and individual property owners who considered themselves better off decided to construct every barrier they could to make sure they were seen as different and distinctive, and that they were in no way associated with dependent serfdom.

Even so, despair can too often lead to contempt for those less fortunate. Under such conditions, without any sort of unifying activity, divisiveness can become rampant. Anything will suffice: place of origin, income, education, church denomination, a particular church, one's Bible study group, choir, the block one lives on—anything. For Reverend Wells and Movement veterans like him—those who had worked for most of their adult lives to break down such real or imagined barriers and to instill a sense of hope—to witness again such partitions within the black community, in addition to the expected problems that come from just being black, the pain must be very great. He used the harsh term "genocide" to describe the schools; he noted ominously that a prospective new county prison was being planned for the Albany area. "What happens to our kids today begins with the school system and ends with the penal system. It's all designed to keep blacks out of the mainstream of this society, forever."

Once in Sherrod's office, Reverend Wells remarked, "God has always given us impossible tasks. It seems our impossible task is being black in America and surviving."

Reverend Wells revisited with me the Trailways bus station on Oglethorpe, the site of the 1961 sit-ins, though it looked like any other small-town bus station. There certainly wasn't any commemorative plaque. While we were there, we happened upon Mr. A. C. Searles, the editor of Albany's *Southwest Georgian*, the town's black weekly, who was shipping copies of the paper to nearby towns. Searles also looked to be in his seventies. I asked him if I could meet him at a later date in his office, to which he agreed.

When I was in college, I worked summers as a teenage reporter for a Houston,

Texas, black weekly, the *Informer*, which was owned by Carter Wesley, a crusty attorney who was a friend of my father's. Mr. Wesley didn't find law lucrative, so he turned to publishing a chain of East Texas black weeklies under the *Informer* name to keep his head above water.

Since Mr. Wesley's staff was perpetually short-handed, I had to cover every kind of story, from murder cases to the completion of a new swimming pool in Emancipation Park. As a result, I obtained a much more realistic sense of what life in the segregated world was like than I did from my schools, with their cloistered and dated knowledge, where the teachers often seemed to view school as a welcome respite from everyday reality. Newspaper people always seemed to know another twist on the truth, another version of the story, even if they didn't print it. I also learned that what we were going through then as a race was part of a much longer story, that current events we thought so unusual or odd always had a precedent in an earlier time if we only knew those earlier stories.

I called Mr. Searles, and we set a time to meet at the newspaper office in the old black downtown called Harlem. There were beauty parlors and barbershops, a record store, and a surprisingly good soul food cafeteria/restaurant. The old Ritz movie theater was under renovation, a stark symbol of hope in the midst of the older, worn-out structures that made up this Harlem.

When I arrived at his office, Mr. Searles was ready and waiting for me. Cluttered with old photographs, plaques, signs, and framed certificates, his office was decorated with the mementos of a busy past. On the window behind his desk there was a sign printed in bold type:

PLEASE

NO LOAN

COMPANY

HERE!

DO NOT

ASK US

TO LEND

MONEY

Mr. Searles turned out to be rather formal in an old-fashioned way: He spoke with the polish of education, and was quite forthcoming. He began by reminding me that there were many unsung and forgotten heroes of the Albany Movement: "Many adults went to jail here." He pointed out that his role was as a recorder of events and member of the black establishment during the Movement years, rather than as an activist who marched and went to jail himself. He left no doubt, however, as to his Movement sympathies.

Mr. Searles told me he was born in Albany, and had attended Albany State in the late 1930s when it was known as Georgia Normal, the state college for blacks. After two years he had transferred to Tennessee State for the completion of his college degree. (Georgia had no four-year state college for blacks prior to World War II.) He chose Tennessee State because it was the only black college with a journalism program. "I always wanted to be a newspaperman," he explained. "I believed newspapermen and lawyers could bring about more freedom for my people than work in other occupations. I got the journalism in school, but I wasn't able to get the law degree, even though I attended Z. Alexander Looby's [a famous Nashville NAACP attorney] Kent School of Law while I was at Tennessee State. I didn't have the money to attend law school and my mother wanted me to come home," he explained. So he returned to Albany in 1940. In 1942, Mr. Searles began working at the *Southwest Georgian*, which was owned by Clennon "Daddy" King.

I asked Mr. Searles to tell me something of what southwest Georgia was like in pre-Movement days.

"Well," he said, leaning back in his chair, "when I first started with this newspaper I wrote a series of articles about a black man named Bobby Hall being killed down in Newton, just south of here in Baker County. They'll string you up down there in a minute. This was in 1942. The sheriff lynched the man, shot him two or three times.

"Bobby Hall had a beautiful pearl-handled pistol. The sheriff stopped him on a traffic violation, searched his car, and found this pistol in his glove compartment. He said, 'Where you get this pistol from, boy?' Bobby answered, 'My daddy gave it to me.' The Halls were land-owning black folks in that awful area. The sheriff replied, 'No, he didn't. This is a *stolen* pistol. I'm going to take it to my office to see if anyone will claim it. I'm going to find out what white man you stole this pistol from.' So he took the pistol.

"About two months later Bobby Hall went to the sheriff's office and told him, 'You've had plenty of time to check out the pistol my daddy gave me. I'd like to have my pistol back.' So the sheriff got mad, reached in his drawer, pulled out Hall's pistol, and shot him and killed him right there in the office. Then he tied his body to the rear fender of his pickup truck and dragged him around the county courthouse square in Newton. I took pictures of the body...."

"You went down there to investigate?" I asked.

"Not me," he laughed. "I didn't want to be no dead hero. They sent the body up here to the funeral home across the street, which is where I took the pictures. I had to send the film to Jacksonville, Florida, to be developed. Then we sent the pictures to the *Atlanta Daily World*, which had a tremendous circulation. You see, Baker County used to have a lot of black land ownership. It was a sparsely populated pine tree area; the land wasn't worth that much. But the shooting and all of the other repression in Baker County was about taking those black folks' land. You wouldn't believe it, but compared to Dawson and Newton, Albany was considered to be liberal before the civil rights movement days. We bragged, 'Albany, Georgia, has never seen a lynching.' But I learned to my disappointment that when whites wanted to have a 'necktie party,' they took blacks down to Bad Baker or over to Terrible Terrell to kill them.

"Anyway, as a result of this Bobby Hall killing, blacks started a boycott in Baker County and I supported it editorially in the *Southwest Georgian*. After a little while the white folks here called me downtown and said, 'If you don't stop writing about this boycott we're going to stop advertising in your paper.' So I had to be careful. That's the way it was around here."

I asked him to tell me his version of the first days of the Albany Movement.

"A few of the best students at Albany State began demonstrations at the Trailways bus station by deliberately sitting in the white waiting room. This was in November 1961, just after the Interstate Commerce Commission banned segregation in interstate travel facilities. That station had a big waiting room for whites with a café and rest rooms, but only a small hole for blacks they called a waiting room.

Bertha Gober was a leader among those Albany State students. She had been recruited by Sherrod and Cordell Reagon, the SNCC workers who had been in town for a few weeks.

"President William H. Dennis of Albany State suspended the students who demonstrated. Then he expelled them. I thought that was ridiculous. So I went to Dennis to see if I could strike up a compromise. He refused to even talk with me. He had his secretary inform me I could not see him. Now, you see, we had been big buddies. We were fellow members of the Criterion Club, which was a club of all the leading blacks. I was president of the Criterion Club. Then Dennis sent word over to the paper that if I put my *foot* on his campus again, he would have me arrested for trespassing.

"So I immediately went to the campus, right to his office. When he heard I was there, he got in his car and left. Later, in a meeting, I called him 'the blackest white man I've ever seen.' The Board of Regents ordered him to kick the kids out of school, I'm sure, but he could have suspended them rather than expelling them, which meant they could never return."

"No one could talk sense to him?" I asked.

"No. All this, I believe, led Dennis to an early demise. He died of heart failure. He lasted only two more years, died in office. He was a relatively young man—his death came as a shock. He never said to me he was only doing what he was ordered to do."

"How about the members of his church?" I asked. "How did they take Dennis's role?"

"His church was small," he said. "They continued to welcome him. The local people in the Movement were not members of his church."

"And the Criterion Club? No one tried to kick him out?"

"No. Those were business and professional people. They sympathized with Dennis. Most of them didn't have anything to do with the Movement. Albany State teachers had nothing to do with the Movement. If they did, they would be fired, and those few who did *were* fired. The thought of kicking Dennis out of the club never came up. If I had brought it up, I would have lost."

After a reflective pause, Mr. Searles declared, "But we are a forgiving and forgetting people as a race."

"Maybe too much so?"

"Way too much so," he agreed. "Nevertheless, I feel very badly about Dennis's death."

⌢

Once I read the autobiography of Albany State founder Dr. Joseph W. Holley, *You Can't Build a Chimney from the Top*, in the Albany public library I was not surprised by the opposition of President Dennis to the civil rights movement. Dennis would have been following in Holley's footsteps, for the founder, though black, was a firm believer in white supremacy. He preached that Albany State, and its staff and students, should learn to accommodate themselves to the interests of the ruling white political and economic powers. In fact, such a strategy was a fundamental tenet of the school's establishment and growth in Albany, brick by brick from the bottom. When I asked Mr. Searles if he remembered Holley, he replied, "I certainly do. Don't forget, my first two years of college were at Georgia Normal under Holley. So I knew him. When I wrote those articles about the lynching in Baker County, and a couple of key downtown Albany businessmen called me in and told me I had to stop, they said, 'You need to talk to Dr. Holley. He may be able to put some sense into your head.'

"So I went to talk to Holley. He said, 'Searles, I'm going to take you under my wing. I want you to drive me when I make speeches at county farm conventions'— they were called 'ham-and-egg shows'—so for a while I chauffeured Dr. Holley everywhere he went. I even wrote those downtown merchants and told them I was being a *good* friend of Dr. Holley! You can call me Uncle Tom if you want, but the white folks downtown eased up on me."

"What was Holley's advice on the Baker County boycott?" I wanted to know.

" 'Stop it,' more or less. He would say, 'We have to recognize what money we can get out of these things.' He wanted Albany State boys to learn bricklaying, women to learn sewing, and so forth. One day, after a year or so of this, while I was driving him somewhere, I said, 'Since they ain't nobody here but us, tell me the truth. You don't believe deep down in your heart all those things you say to white folks to raise money, do you?' He said, 'I certainly do.' He said, 'The good white folks are the best friends Negroes ever had.' Can you believe that? Sometimes I wanted to puke over some of the things that man said.

"I learned to like him, but I decided I could *not* go along with his philosophy. Soon after that, I pretty much left Dr. Holley alone. But he got along with white people very well here." It would be difficult for Albany State to overcome such a strong history of caution and conservatism, I thought, no matter how hard they might try. It certainly didn't help that in the momentous struggle of the 1960s to activate the black community, Albany State had remained completely divorced from the effort.

I bid Mr. Searles good-bye, and decided to take a day or two to explore Albany more thoroughly.

The Albany of the 1960s is still much in evidence: that is, the Albany described in civil rights histories and Martin Luther King, Jr., biographies. Oglethorpe Street is still the main artery of Albany once one crosses the Flint going westward. Blacks live to the south; the north is prevailingly white. Though Oglethorpe (U.S. 82) is still a major route for east-west traffic, now there's a new expressway that circumvents downtown, a convenience for the truck traffic that has replaced the railway traffic, which had replaced the river traffic. It was the Oglethorpe Street boundary that was consistently "violated" by blacks during the civil rights marches. The marches had emanated from Shiloh and Mount Zion Baptist churches on the south side, and crossed Oglethorpe to confront the seat of city government at Broad and Pine streets, paralleling Oglethorpe to the north. Broad Street, a block from Oglethorpe, was the major downtown shopping area, but is no longer. The entire downtown area is virtually unpopulated by day except for a few shops and a couple of luncheonettes, and totally deserted at night. It reminded me of Greensboro's downtown. The new municipal auditorium, named for the late editor and owner of the *Albany Herald*, James Gray, located on U.S. 82-Oglethorpe, just a few blocks from the river, is a handsome edifice. A sign announced that Keith Sweat, the black singer, would soon be opening there.

Albany residents now shop primarily at malls in the newly developed western section of town, along Dawson and Gillonville roads. These malls made it possible for Albany to retain its retail economic strength. It seems that this area, called West Albany, has also become the location of new, fashionable homes of whites, along with a museum and city art center, trendy shops, upscale chain restaurants, and movie theaters. Because of its retail stores; pecan, peanut, meat-packing, and airplane parts industries; the large Procter and Gamble, Miller Brewing, and Delco Remey plants; and the collapse of farms in the surrounding area, a steady influx of people from surrounding rural areas has increased Albany's population from 56,000 to 90,000 in the three decades since the civil rights years. Blacks comprise more than 50 percent of this increase.

In the black community south of Oglethorpe, I saw evidence of rampant unemployment—many idle men hanging out—but the neighborhood was physically intact. It had not been butchered by expressways or redevelopment, and the housing ranged from run-down shacks and brick housing projects to quite nice homes and a tremendous number of churches of various sizes suggesting long-lasting, sustaining memberships. Toward the rear of the neighborhood there's a small but attractive recreational park named for Alice Coachman, the first black woman Olympic track champion, a native of Albany and former student at Albany State. Across Oglethorpe, about ten blocks into north Albany, there is a federal housing project near Albany High School that seems to house mostly blacks. These structures look relatively new, and seem much better maintained than the projects in most major cities.

But though the old Harlem black business district, running along Highland Avenue one block south of Oglethorpe, has, like the Broad Street business district, given way to shopping malls, I observed a solid block of operating businesses. I was delighted to come across an old-fashioned soul music record and tape store. It is owned by Jesse Boone, who was one of Albany's finest veteran musicians, I was informed by Mr. Searles and others. I called him, arranged an appointment, and in the rear of his store, I asked him to tell me about the historically rich music scene in southwest Georgia, and what Harlem was once like.

He recalled that black shoppers on the old Broad Street also patronized Harlem establishments. "They could visit our stores en route or on the way back home."

Now in his fifties, Boone was born in Sparta, Georgia. He came to Albany in 1951 when he was fourteen with hopes of eventually attending Albany State. "I was an independent youth. The blacks here," he said, "seemed more progressive. I was also interested in music. There was no band at the high school in Sparta, whereas the Albany school had one, so that was another reason why I wanted to be here."

As he came of age, Boone put together his own band, playing Albany regularly along with nightclubs in towns throughout the region. He mentioned Tallahassee, Valdosta, Dothan, Thomasville, Tifton, and Americus. "This was during the fifties and sixties. I can't remember any bad jobs. During those years people came out and really appreciated live music."

The live music scene has now become a record-hop disco scene. Why did that happen? I asked him. Boone took his time responding.

"First, Georgia passed a law where you couldn't sell liquor past midnight on Saturdays. That killed two nights, Saturday and Sunday." I could well understand his point, because in New Orleans there was and is live music until as late as 5:00 A.M. on Saturdays and 2:00 A.M. on Sundays. There is a lot of work for bands at a variety of clubs on weekends. "Secondly," Boone continued, "the club crowd started getting younger; they were teenagers. This meant the older folks began to stay home because they didn't want to be in the clubs with their children. Mature adults turned to gospel music for entertainment. Thirdly, there was and is a bad drug scene. I have friends who love the music but don't want to be near drugs, and the violence that goes along with it. Once hard drugs and guns showed up, professional people who make good money and who used to frequent the clubs stayed away.

"The disco scene revived the clubs, but killed the music," Boone concluded. "At first the clubs thought disco was a blessing. But the music is too loud; you can't talk or meet friends, which adults *want* to do. So if you don't dance, there's nothing to do. In my day, if you couldn't dance you could at least say, 'I'm a jazz freak,' and get into the music. People didn't come to dance. Besides, all of the fancy dancers are kids."

I asked him what had killed the Harlem business area.

"The black business community started to decline with integration. When people with jobs, the higher echelon, don't 'shop black,' you don't have anything. Some blacks won't even come down here. That's their mentality—they haven't been here in fifteen years. Shopping malls have hurt every town's downtown. When the white downtown on Broad Street collapsed, Harlem collapsed right along with it."

～

About nine that night, as I drove eastward across the Flint River bridge, I noticed large groups of black youths walking toward a disco operating out of a run-down mall on East Oglethorpe. The mall parking lot was jammed with many young people lounging around their cars, going back and forth to the disco, purchasing gasoline and knickknacks at a gas station "quick store." I pulled into the lot and parked. This was the largest gathering of black folk I had seen since I had been in Albany. I decided to check out the disco for a few minutes, but the music was at an eardrum-bursting level, and except for blinking lights it was pitch-dark inside; I couldn't see anything. Though I witnessed no trouble whatsoever, the disco gathering and the groups of youths hanging out in the lot presented an atmosphere that suggested potential violence. It would be no exaggeration to imagine that many of these kids carried weapons—the very situation of which adult churchgoing folk always expressed such a horror. Police were also prominently parked in the lot, waiting, I supposed, for something nasty to transpire. Yet, as far as I could see, outside church this was the only recreation and meeting place for young blacks available in Albany, other than events sponsored by the schools. The scene reminded me of a zydeco nightclub in Opelousas, Louisiana, I had visited a few years ago, where the sheriff's deputy stood unsmilingly by the bandstand, warily watching the clubbers for potential trouble, while the band played and the people danced and roared their shouting approval of the music.

East Albany, Du Bois had observed, was the domicile of the town's poorer blacks, those just in from the country. This was the area I was staying in. The area on the north side of U.S. 82 nearer the Flint consisted of generally poor housing and tight, twisting streets, as if it had "jes grew" without planning. Along the factory-lined Clark Street, a major thoroughfare running east–west, there were prostitutes working corners, including some white women. On Broad Street, which also extends across the bridge, the businesses looked worn and frayed. I did discover, however, an excellent example of the one new business blacks had recently gravitated toward, the car-wash "detail" business. At the one I patronized on East Broad Street, the polite thirtyish entrepreneur-owner had efficiently organized his business by converting an abandoned gas station into an air-conditioned waiting room, providing relief from the merciless July heat (it seemed to reach 100 degrees every single day). The youths he hired did a fantastically thorough job of cleaning my car—it had never been so clean! I found car wash businesses cropping up in many of the larger towns along my journey, but East Albany's was the best.

The next day, a Sunday, I decided to drive northward into Lee County to look for a section of land that used to be called New Communities. New Communities was established by an agricultural cooperative, the Southwest Georgia Project, which was organized first by Slater King, then managed by Charles Sherrod after King's untimely death in an automobile accident.

There was no marker to indicate where the land had been, but from Sherrod's description it comprised six thousand acres along U.S. 19 between the towns of Leesburg and Smithville.

To provide some background, New Communities was an extremely hopeful attempt to address what Sherrod and other black activists in Albany considered a prime requisite for black independence: the ownership of land. The entire southwest Georgia area was so overwhelmingly agricultural and so much of what happened there was and is determined by the control of land, I found it only natural that the ownership of land was considered to be a vital step if the poverty and dependency of black folk in the area was *ever* going to be addressed. To pursue this dream, New Communities was founded as a cooperative in 1967. In 1969, New Communities received a grant from the Norman Foundation, and using that along with contributions from area churches, national contributors, and individual donors, they were able to purchase the six thousand acres. Their concept, Sherrod explained to me, was to develop an agricultural collective based on the model of the Israeli kibbutz. A small team of organizers, including Sherrod, even traveled to Israel in the early 1970s to visit and examine collectives. They returned with luminous hopes.

"The land was farmed out but not developed," Sherrod said. "We constructed a building on U.S. Nineteen. We had a railroad coming through. We dug six catfish-growing ponds. we collected about thirteen thousand dollars per year for hunting rights. We sold smoked hams."

It seemed, however, that New Communities was faced with a continual barrage of economic obstacles virtually from conception. "An Office of Economic Opportunity grant that would have helped immensely was vetoed by Georgia Governor Lester Maddox in 1970," Sherrod recalled painfully. In 1978, heavy drought hit the area, he said, and lasted for six straight years. "All during that time the whites in the county fought little battles against us; they burned us, they shot into our offices; the banks refused to give us loans, and attempted to foreclose on us several times; we had to refinance several times. Our loan payments were over one hundred thousand dollars per year; we ended up owing the FHA over a million dollars in loans and interest. Finally in 1985, we couldn't come up with the money and Prudential Insurance Company, which had mortgaged the property, took it—every single acre of it. For a long time the loss of New Communities hurt me so much I couldn't even talk about it. If you had asked me about this in 1985, I would have smacked you upside your head."

Some of Sherrod's supporters who had been involved with the project suggested that Sherrod made fatal mistakes of management. Sherrod himself admits that most experts had advised them *not* to attempt to run the farm themselves, that it would be better to lease the land and let someone else take the risks. "But I felt that might create potential problems in the future which would be difficult to resolve," he said. "Besides, if we let someone else do our farming we would never learn. So we decided to manage it ourselves, and I had to bear most of the responsibility."

As I arrived at the crossroads village of Smithville, I reflected on the sadness of this story, which, like so many ambitious organizational and economic projects designed to further Movement ideals, ended in a disappointing failure. I thought, however, that the issues were too complex to point fingers or assign blame. I remembered that many veteran farmers lost their land to banks in the 1970s and early '80s. Doubtless, each one thought if they had just done this or that, they might have been saved. But given the difficult economic factors at play, and the forces Sherrod felt were against them, even the most experienced professional management might not have been able to save New Communities.

The next week I noticed there were more visitors than usual to Sherrod's office. Election Day was approaching. One of the visitors interested in Sherrod's reelection to a seventh term was Patricia Perry. I introduced myself; we talked briefly; and since she was interested in my journey, we set a luncheon date. She definitely got my attention when she told me she was a real estate agent who had recently resettled in town after living in California, that she was a native of Baker County, and that she was one of Sherrod's first teenage recruits when SNCC entered the area during the summer of 1962. Pat Perry was attractive, talkative, and knowledgeable. I asked her if she would ride with me down to Baker County to her parents' home, and show me around a bit; she agreed. As we drove southward on U.S. 91 toward Baker County and the town of Newton, I told her the story I had heard from Mr. Searles about the shooting of the black man with his own pistol.

"Was Baker County that bad for blacks?"

"Yes," Ms. Perry agreed. "Newton was notorious as a place where blacks were arrested and beaten, particularly on weekends. It was 'recreation.' Find a nigger on Sunday night and kick his ass. Recreation for the sheriff and his boys."

"Was there any sort of protection from this abuse?" I asked. "What did your folks tell you when you went to town, 'Be careful'?"

"Basically to be careful, not arouse them or make them angry—just accept it and take it—which was very difficult for me, that whole attitude." She mentioned the loneliness of growing up in such an isolated area, the vulnerabilities. "I spent a lot of time walking the woods, daydreaming. My parents never quite understood me; I was hearing a different drummer," she giggled. She was fifteen when the SNCC workers arrived in Baker County in 1965. "So many blacks were afraid to even talk to them, but I became involved immediately. I suppose I ended up representing the youth of Baker County in voting registration meetings. And my parents were supporters very soon after I joined up, but I can say the repercussions of their activity did affect them negatively."

"In what way?"

"Well, we owned property, but we were dependent upon white folks for work. Mother was a maid. Father was a farmer and a mechanic. One night, during the demonstration years, the man my mother worked for drove through Harlem and his car was stoned. What happened was after meetings at Shiloh and Mount Zion churches that night, some of the youth began to throw stones at automobiles driven by whites who were passing through. The next day he ended up taking it out on my mother, screaming about niggers, ranting and raving. My mother quit. After that she had to go all the way to Albany to find work. I worked in that white man's house for a while also. It was no fun."

"Who were the key SNCC workers who tried to organize Baker County?" I asked.

"Sherrod. He spent a lot of time down here, and eventually married a girl from Baker County. There were also several white kids who worked with Sherrod; they eventually lived with black families." Because of her Movement activism, Pat was expelled from school and ended up in high school in New York City in an exchange program SNCC was able to find for her.

A hard rain began to fall just as we left Albany; we were driving in and out of it. As we crossed into Baker County, I was once again struck by the beauty of the land. Land, land, land—that was what it was all about down here, for hundreds of years. We passed through a section of impressive live oaks lining the highway. "In 1985 I bought a store and ten acres of land along this highway," Ms. Perry remarked. "I tried to operate a supper club, bring in performers, and so forth. But it didn't work out. I went back to California." She didn't tell me why the club hadn't succeeded.

We turned left at the dirt road that leads to the family property. "Baker County," she informed me, "is mostly huge old plantations. My family's property is in the midst of the Mellons', the banking Mellons. Their plantation completely engulfs our land. If my father's horses or cows got onto their land, they would impound them and charge my father a fee to get them back. Or kill them. These were absentee plantations run by overseers, owned by wealthy northerners who came down only to hunt."

Pat Perry's grandmother had purchased the original tract of six hundred acres at two dollars per acre, she said. After a series of sales by members of the family, there were only ninety acres left. It was Ms. Perry's self-appointed mission to save as much of what remained as possible. "I think there's a concerted effort to buy land from blacks," she added.

We arrived at the Jones farmhouse, which was very plain, and met Ms. Perry's father and other members of the family. In this peaceful, isolated setting, the pines surrounding the house were absolutely stunning. Though the family was obviously not wealthy, they were at the same time fortunate in a way few black families are in the South, because they did own land, which offered a certain protection, not to mention a sense of home. "In our small house," Ms. Perry explained, "the living room was also a bedroom, and the center bedroom was the children's; all three of us. My grandmother lived with us. There was no privacy. I never had a bed of my own while I was growing up."

"Did your family and other blacks out here vote?" I asked.

"I was the first one to get my grandmother to vote. One of the people who lived back here had his house bombed when he tried to vote. That frightened everyone. Now they go regularly to Newton to vote."

I asked how she felt now, living again in Albany, thirty years after the demonstrations. "Albany," she laughed, "is a good community if you're ready to settle down and retire. But not if you're looking for excitement in your life." She spoke of the prominence of Bible studies, a weekly activity so many Albanians seem to talk about and love, and the love of heavy foods. "They eat a lot here. And it's nothing light. You're talking about collard greens, black-eyed peas, corn bread, fried chicken. I don't like to cook and one night my girlfriends were over and I threw together some spaghetti, salad, and wine. My friends said, 'Girl, that's not gon' do it!' "

Ms. Perry seemed undetermined about whether she would remain in Albany or return to California. She was committed to working for improvement of conditions in Albany, in continuing or resuming a thrust that would reclaim some of the old optimism, but outside of politics, I didn't see any functioning project of that type. She would have to initiate her own effort.

⁓

Carol King, the widow of C. B. King, had recently been elected to the school board. Since she had moved from Cleveland to Albany in the late 1950s to be with her husband, I thought Carol's impressions of Albany would be valuable. C. B. King was the most aggressive and successful civil rights attorney in the history of southwest Georgia, if not the entire state, and though unusual because of his formal manner and speech (according to those who knew him), he was able to relate to all the Albany civil rights factions, which is saying something. For three decades C. B. and Carol had been in the middle of every civil rights or related black political effort undertaken in Albany. I visited her at her tasteful and attractive home near Harlem on a stormy Albany night. Carol King is gracious, unabashedly intelligent, and well educated, letting you know it. After two weeks of hearing "Al-*benny*" accents, I was shocked to hear Mrs. King's unadulterated midwestern speech, every "r" pronounced as if she had arrived from her native Cleveland night-before-last instead of forty years ago as C. B. King's bride. A graduate of Case University Law School in 1963, C. B. had decided to return to the South to establish his practice. She recalled the trauma of the adjusting to living in the Deep South.

"Albany was very, very frustrating," she recalled, "*and still is.* You wonder why not just move somewhere else and *enjoy* life. I came from a middle-class black family in Cleveland. We never talked about being black. Sometimes my parents would say things like 'All those poor people down south; they're being lynched and all that; aren't we lucky to be here.' Then when I moved here, all the extended King family *ever* talked about was race. What was happening here, there, and everywhere with respect to black people."

C. B.'s father, "Daddy" King, was a career postal worker who ended up owning two supermarkets and establishing a dress shop for his wife. He founded the *Southwest Georgian*. He was founder of the Albany NAACP, and the father of seven sons, each with striking, individualistic personalities. C. B. and Slater King became particularly important figures in the Albany Movement, and later in Georgia state politics.

Carol King told the story of how, upon his return from law school, C. B. King quickly won a reputation as an aggressive defender of black rights in the courts. He became known for his mastery of the law and his stiffly proper speech. "The Albany white elite had never seen anyone like him," Mrs. King assured me. When Sherrod and Cordell Reagon first came to town in 1961, C. B. was one of those who agreed to offer support; at first Sherrod and Reagon lived in the C. B. King home. C. B. was the attorney for Sherrod's New Communities. His relentless suits against the city and county opened up new opportunities for blacks in city and county government. C. B. ran for Congress in 1964 and in 1970 for governor. He died of cancer in the late 1980s. Slater King ran for mayor of Albany in 1963. He was killed in a tragic automobile accident in 1969.

A few minutes after I arrived, the thunderstorm outside blinked the lights in Mrs. King's house, and we were in danger of losing power. It seemed as if I experienced more rain and heat in Albany than anywhere else on my entire journey; it sounded like the town was being bombed from the air.

"What would you cite if someone asked you for signs of hope in Albany?" I asked. Mrs. King mentioned Leadership Albany, a series of conferences and workshops she had recently attended. She explained that Leadership Albany was an attempt to bring together diverse community leaders in a retreat atmosphere; some blacks were included, one of the very few opportunities in Albany for meaningful biracial contacts. "But the perceptions of the whites in that group are not mine," Mrs. King was careful to add, explaining that the complexities of her roles as wife, mother, and Head Start center director in a middle-class black family devoted to the racial struggle had made her into a person few whites in Albany could understand.

Much of Carol King's conversation had to do with her concern that her husband receive posthumously the kind of recognition from blacks and whites she feels he was denied in life. But, in my opinion, it will be a long time before that happens. Having come of age in an area when blacks were tragically dependent and historically subservient to whites, C. B. King, from the stories I heard about him, was the most independent of men, the living antithesis of subservience. Since his career consisted of bringing numerous civil rights actions against the city of Albany, most of which were successful, professionals in Albany, white and black, who were on the opposing side will be just as happy to forget him, and his example.

Though racial consciousness was forever a part of their lives, C. B. and Carol King sent their children to private schools in the North, and one of their sons to school in Kenya. Mrs. King remembered that C. B. had instructed his children as they prepared to leave Albany to keep an imaginary mirror with them. "Now I want you to pull that mirror out every night," he told them. "Look into it and repeat, *I'm a nigger, I'm a nigger, I'm a nigger.*' No matter what happens during the day, I want you to never forget how you're seen here, and what you have to work to overcome."

⁓

I had heard so much about Al-*benny* that was depressing, I decided to call Rutha Harris, one of the founders of the SNCC Freedom Singers, to talk to her about black church music in the area, which everyone said was remarkable.

Rutha Harris lives south of Oglethorpe Street in a modest family home, comfortable in an old-fashioned way with its spacious living room. I sensed a space where one could sit with others but still be alone for contemplation and soft conversation. I didn't see a television set.

Now fifty, quiet, and extremely reserved, Rutha Harris said the Freedom Singers were organized in Albany in 1962 at SNCC mass meetings. Their presentations were so inspiring that SNCC decided to send them all over the South to perform where demonstrations were taking place. I saw them perform at a SNCC fund-raiser in New York in the early 1960s—they were sensational, more moving than all the speeches and orations.

Ms. Harris said she was a student at Florida A&M in Tallahassee when Sherrod, Reagon, and Chuck Jones first arrived. Home from college during the summer of 1961, she and her entire family attended the first mass meetings at Shiloh and Mount Zion Baptist churches. Her sister, McCree, and her two brothers, Emery and Alphonso, were early recruits. It did not take long for Sherrod and company to learn that Rutha, though a teenager, already had a reputation in her church as a talented singer. Shrewdly, Sherrod and the SNCC leaders asked Rutha and her brothers and sisters, along with others with outstanding voices, to lead the communal singing of hymns that were a staple at the nightly meetings. "Albany," Andy Young told me many times, "was a *singing* movement. If song could make us free, we would have been free."

It didn't take long for Rutha Harris to become completely involved. "You're sitting in one of Albany's Freedom Houses," she noted proudly, for her family had offered lodging and meals to many a volunteer from afar during Albany's days of struggle.

Ms. Harris explained that her world had always revolved around the church and music. "My father was a Baptist minister who died in 1951. We sang in what we called 'common meter,' " and she sang a few phrases of "Guide Me, O Thou Great Jehovah" to illustrate common meter. My impression was that I was hearing a scale and phrasing that were very African. A mezzo-soprano; I don't believe there's anything quite like Ms. Harris's style in commercial music, except for the singing of some gospel choirs. What she was singing could not be duplicated on the piano. I asked if her style was different from those of other singers in Albany. She didn't think so.

The "freedom songs," she explained, were the result of a suggestion by Bertha Gober, one of the early Albany State student activists, that certain church hymns be converted into civil rights anthems by changing the lyrics to convey the themes and particularities of the current struggle. For instance, the plaintive hymn "Oh Mary, Oh Martha" became "Oh Pritchard [Police Chief Laurie B. Pritchard], Oh Kelly [Mayor Asa Kelly]"—"Oh Pritchard, oh Kelly. Open them cells. Can't you hear

God's children crying for freedom?" This was probably the only time in the history of social protest that the beseechers dignified the objects of their protest with magnificent song. Lyrics like "I ain't gonna let nobody turn me around/I'm gonna keep on marching to freedom land" may not have opened one jail cell, but they did imbue the Movement with a buoyancy that even the police chief may have enjoyed. Once, Ms. Harris recalls, she encountered Pritchard inside the city jail when she herself was imprisoned after participating in a march. "He yelled, 'Rutha, sing that song 'bout me and Kelly,' so I sang it. Why not?"

Old hymns in their new garb as freedom songs quickly became popular. The first traveling freedom singers group included Cordell Reagon and also very prominently, Bernice Johnson. Bernice was one of the Albany State student activists expelled by the president; later she married Cordell Reagon. After her brilliant career with the freedom singers, Bernice Reagon developed into the foremost laureate of black folk music. Her group, Sweet Honey in the Rock, has maintained and raised to new heights the work initiated by the freedom singers in 1962.

I asked Rutha Harris if she had ever seriously considered a professional singing and recording career. "I had an opportunity to record when we were out on the road," she replied, "but I was so wrapped up in the Movement I decided not to return to Florida A&M for my sophomore year—we were doing so much traveling. But my mother made me promise I would return to finish college after all this was over." Ms. Harris held to her promise, turning down offers to record, and graduated from Albany State in 1967. She majored in music, performing often with the jazz group led by Albany State music professor T. Marshall Jones. "I should have pursued a recording career more aggressively," she admitted, "but I would have had to leave Albany to do so." She works now as a teacher of "slow learners" in the public school system.

What change, if any, had she seen in Albany through the years? Ms. Harris hesitated for a long while before answering. "Sometimes I wonder. Black folks have not come together. We're worried about who will get the praise. What's the difference if we all benefit? Sometimes all the suffering we did seems in vain to me. I don't get involved anymore, except when I'm asked to sing freedom songs."

And then she said she would have to very soon conclude our interview. The time for her weekly Bible study group had arrived, and members of the class would be coming over to her home. I asked her to sing "Amazing Grace" for me. She sang it beautifully, in her own style, leaving me with a lyric memory of Albany that lifted my spirits.

⁓

I needed to return to New Orleans for a few days. When I returned, I learned that Charles Sherrod had lost his election for the City Commission to a black opponent in his district. He had served six consecutive two-year terms. When I stopped by to see him, he was understandably depressed. "Why don't you think about leaving Albany for a while?" I suggested. He wasn't interested. "I'll never leave Albany. Leave and go where?"

I couldn't answer that question. Since 1961, Sherrod had devoted his life to Albany, raised a family there. Now Albany was his home, whatever it held in store for him.

Sherrod's defeat had also cast a pall over Pat Perry, and in the course of our discussion about the election at lunch, she introduced me to young Michael Moss, who was working as a waiter. This was Moss's summer job; he planned to return to school in Massachusetts in a few weeks. When Ms. Perry related the story of Moss's upbringing at New Communities, I asked him if he would tell me more about himself later when I could interview him.

Only twenty-one, Moss spoke without a trace of a southern accent, and was quite forthcoming with his story when we talked later. He was extremely light skinned, a rarity among Albany blacks. "I play the role of the tragic mulatto," he quipped. He explained that he is the product of a southern black woman from Fitzgerald, Georgia, and "a Connecticut white boy of Portuguese and Irish descent." His mother, Irma Moss, like Pat Perry, was a young activist in the Southwest Georgia Project. As a result, she was expelled from high school in Fitzgerald. But she was able to continue her schooling at a progressive high school in the Massachusetts Berkshires called Windsor Mountain. It was probably there that she met Moss's father, Edward Turner. "I didn't know my father until I was thirteen," Moss added.

With Michael as a baby, his mother returned home to Fitzgerald, a town about fifty miles east of Albany. Within a few years, she married Samuel Young, who was a Sherrod faithful. His family of five settled on New Communities land, which is where Michael grew up. "I loved that land," he remembers. "It was wonderful; peach trees, plums, grapes. Plenty of places to be by myself. It was like growing up in paradise." There were about thirty people living and working on the property, he remembered. Michael received his first schooling in Leesburg, a small town just north of Albany.

In 1981 the Young family moved to Stuyvesant, New York. They lived there for four years, working as caretakers of the estate of the ex-wife of actor Sidney Poitier. "I went from the country to the country," Moss laughed. Then the family decided to return to Albany, because Michael's mother wanted to be more politically active. Michael attended high school in Albany for two years, admitting that the awesome transitions were difficult. "My family was a family of political activists," he said, "but I was far more interested in music and the arts."

Once again, after graduation from high school, Michael left Albany to return to Massachusetts, where he attended Berkshire Community College. He also worked there with a theater and modern dance company. As a "child of the Movement," living back and forth between the Northeast and southwest Georgia, what did he really think of Albany? "Well, I'll tell you, the minute I hit the city limits I felt like I was entering a tomb," he began. "I was wearing my dreads and I knew I had to cut them off just to get a job. Albany is a reality check for me. Going back and forth from a largely white world to a black world is kind of difficult."

I mentioned the sense of suffocation even I was beginning to feel in this place where everyone knows everyone else, or thinks they do, and where the town seems smaller than its population of seventy-five thousand. Time stretches rather than contracts. After two weeks, I said, I felt like I had been in Albany for a year. Moss said he understood. "I don't really care about getting a job at Procter and Gamble and working all my life to be able to buy a Honda. And I'm just not into church, though my mother's father is a Baptist minister. If you're not into church around here, there isn't much else to do. I came back because my family is here. It's the only family I have."

"And your mother?" I asked. "What would she have you do?"

"Be safe and secure. Which she never was. Maybe Mother would like me to be a racial leader, but the arts are the only thing I care about." He was itching to get back to Massachusetts where he could rejoin his rock and reggae band.

"And Albany?" I asked, as I asked everyone. "Does it have a future? Does it have the potential to transcend its racial past and fulfill the promise of the Movement?"

Moss looked at me a long time, then smiled softly. "No," he answered.

# SELMA

Selma, Alabama, is a small town located at the very heart of the Alabama Black Belt. Long a commercial center of the prosperous surrounding plantations, Selma's pre-1960s black population viewed their town as a place of extreme racial repression.

In the mid-1960s, Selma was targeted by national civil rights groups, led by Dr. Martin Luther King, Jr., for a mighty, highly publicized campaign to dramatize the denial of the right to vote. Wave after wave of black citizens marched to the Dallas County Courthouse in an attempt to register, but were turned away. The SCLC campaign, buttressed by every major civil rights group and an unprecedented coalition of national ethnic and religious leaders, culminated in a massive five-day march to the state capital of Montgomery. This march produced some of the most memorable images in the history of the southern Movement. In practical terms, the Selma-to-Montgomery march was the prime catalyst for the passage of the landmark Voting Rights Act of 1965 later that summer, one of the most remarkable and lasting achievements of the southern Movement.

A quarter century later, a bitter dispute over school desegregation broke out in Selma, resulting in the termination of the contract of the new black school superintendent. I was interested, while visiting Selma, in investigating this new source of conflict, and its relationship, if any, to the advances and new opportunities created by the changes wrought during the sixties.

I left Albany and headed for Selma, Alabama, driving along the historic Black Belt Highway, U.S. 82. The term "Black Belt" takes its name from the fertile agricultural black soil of the Deep South. Much of the land, however, is red clay, as is the case in southwest Georgia and central Alabama. But many of the slave and postslavery agricultural workers were African Americans, and the phrase applies equally to areas with heavy black populations. The area covers roughly a strip of relatively flat land about one hundred miles wide beginning at the Atlantic Ocean and sweeping through southern South Carolina, south-central Georgia and Alabama, central Mississippi, southern Arkansas, and central Texas from Houston in the south as far north as Dallas, and as far west as San Antonio. Black Belt counties in Alabama, Georgia, and Mississippi were specifically targeted by civil rights groups in the hopes of dramatically increasing voter registration among their heavy black populations. U.S. 82 slices right through the heart of the "Belt." The highway follows a slightly northwestern route that passes through Dawson and Cuthbert, then crosses the Chattahoochee River bridge, to Eufaula, Alabama. It is a pleasant drive through gently rising hills, right through the heart of Lower Creek country with historical markers sprinkled along the way to commemorate the military engagements in which the Creeks and Seminoles met their fate at the hands of the American Army, and receded into history.

Despite the presence of occasional neat, prosperous-looking—at least from the highway—old towns like Eufaula and Cuthbert, this land I was driving through did not look very much different, I thought, than it must have two hundred years ago when it was Creek occupied. This impression was intensified on the Alabama side of the Chattahoochee where, after the old port of Eufaula there isn't another town of importance until Montgomery, about ninety miles west of the river.

I might have followed U.S. 82 all the way to Montgomery, but I decided to turn off at Union Springs where U.S. 82 intersects U.S. 29, and drive directly northward to the town of Tuskegee. Tuskegee is the home of Tuskegee Institute, renowned in black lore as the home and headquarters of Booker T. Washington at the turn of the century. In his time, Washington controlled virtually all of the national political patronage directed toward blacks by the White House, which admittedly wasn't much. After Washington's death in 1915, Tuskegee Institute continued to expand, and retained its position as one of the most influential black educational institutions in the country.

The later history of Tuskegee and surrounding Macon County reflects the radical and dramatic stages of social change in the Deep South in the 1960s, and the racial conflict that took place, and its story casts a shadow over the history of other Alabama towns, including Selma.

In his well-written and thorough examination of Tuskegee's triumphs and trials, *Reaping the Whirlwind,* Robert Norrell pursues the idea that Tuskegee never represented the paradigm of racial amity and economic cooperation that was projected in its myth; on the contrary, the heavy black presence in Macon County had always created a racial tension, though that tension was suppressed during Washington's time at Tuskegee Institute.

Race relations in Tuskegee underwent significant changes in the twentieth century, but those changes occurred slowly, building from unpromising origins that provided no hint of the changes to come, like a river containing revolving and contradictory currents whose main current finally veers off in an unanticipated direction.

The Tuskegee story is entwined in the dual themes of voting and education. When Booker T. Washington arrived in 1881 from Hampton Institute in Virginia to take charge of a new school to be funded by the state of Alabama, local black self-assertion and Reconstruction activism had already been effectively suppressed by local whites, through violence and the threat of violence. In 1870 two blacks were killed when armed white men shot into the main black church in Tuskegee. Members of the Zion Negro Church had been extremely active in organizing and sustaining freedmen suffrage. The whites had broken into a church financial meeting thinking it was a political meeting, and started firing at everyone. To cover up the shootings, local Democratic leaders arrested five blacks and charged *them* with the murders. There were no convictions. James Alston, the black state representative from Macon County, had to flee, barely escaping with his life.

In 1881 the Tuskegee whites who decided to back the establishment of a school for blacks were motivated by an interest in retaining the four-fifths majority black population of Macon County as field hands to work their profitable lands, thus counteracting the new migration of freedmen to newly open lands in Kansas, in an attempt to escape the raging outburst of Redemptionist oppression and terror. ("Redemptionist" is a term southern whites used to describe the period when they returned to power in 1876–1900.) Tuskegee Institute was also, and more legitimately, born out of the desire of black church leaders to build a school in an area where almost all the ex-slaves were, of course, illiterate; though they well realized that such a school could not survive if it was perceived as inimical to the interests of the local ruling white families.

Booker T. Washington established a policy of accommodation to the prevailing conditions of white political and economic domination, and from that position he attempted to move forward. The first students at Tuskegee made their own bricks; they constructed the first Tuskegee classrooms and dormitories. Extra bricks were sold to town whites. Within a few years, Washington's diplomacy and his emphasis on industrial and vocational education at the expense of voting became very popular among whites. Even during the depths of Redemption, when lynchings became common and the Klan raged unchecked, Washington achieved the status of a southern prophet.

During the years 1890–1915 several other schools for blacks were created in Tuskegee's image; for years thereafter it was quite common to come across secondary schools scattered throughout the South named for the "sage of Tuskegee." Some black schools and community institutions were also named for the eminent and reclusive Tuskegee agricultural chemist, George Washington Carver.

When Booker T. Washington died in 1915, Robert Moton, principal of Hampton Institute, was chosen as his successor. Moton followed in Washington's footsteps in terms of educational theory, but under his leadership from 1915 to 1935, Tuskegee veered toward a more liberal arts curriculum. The Institute also provided a notable service for the national press by chronicling the number and manner of lynchings of blacks each year; an antilynching campaign and the passage of antilynching federal legislation were major concerns of the NAACP and other black organizations during the 1920s and '30s.

Moton can also be credited with an extremely fortunate decision made while ostensibly adhering to the Washingtonian policy of passive education within the segregated system. Following World War I, it became known that the federal government wanted to build a hospital for black military veterans. Because of Moton's influence in the White House, inherited from Washington, he was able to lobby successfully for the hospital to be built in Tuskegee on property purchased from the Institute. The hospital duly opened in 1923. But then a bitter dispute broke out between Moton and influential local whites. At first key whites thoroughly endorsed the project, but when they realized that Moton intended to staff the hospital entirely with black professionals, they tried to get the decision reversed, and have the facility staffed by whites. But Moton stuck to his guns, and the hospital became an all-black institution. That meant that an additional group of black professionals with middle-class incomes settled in Tuskegee, creating a potential power base that the controlling white oligarchy did not welcome (even though Tuskegee banks and businesses stood to profit from the additional commerce generated by the hospital). The VA jobs were under federal jurisdiction, and not subject to the control of local whites, or the type of indirect influence whites had historically exercised over Institute personnel through Washington and Moton.

Then in 1941, under extreme pressure from black organizations and during the time in which the nation was in an intense mobilization mode, the Army decided to form a historic black Air Force squadron. The new president of Tuskegee, Fred Patterson, lobbied for the squadron to be trained at Tuskegee. Patterson was subjected to withering criticism from other black leaders, for they felt a segregated unit at Tuskegee would undermine their hopes for an integrated training program. Nevertheless, Tuskegee was chosen, and the training of the Tuskegee airmen created tremendous racial pride. The success of the black airmen, who in their first missions served as fighter plane escorts for bombers, quickly became national news. The Tuskegee airmen left an indelible impact, and forced the nation to change its views on the desirability of using black troops in combat. Most of the Tuskegee airmen were college students or graduates; they had formed yet a third pool of educated blacks in town under federal auspices. The Tuskegee juggernaut developed by Booker T. Washington in the earlier part of the century was now bearing a rich harvest of black economic strength in a very small town in the heart of the Alabama Black Belt.

From the shadows of these developments emerged one of the most unusual political visionaries of the twentieth century. Charles Gomillion, a native of South Carolina, was a Tuskegee professor of sociology who had studied under the legendary sociologists Charles Johnson and E. Franklin Frazier at Fisk University. In the late 1930s, Gomillion joined the Tuskegee Men's Club, which, among other things, had been requesting improvements in basic civic services for the black community in Tuskegee, with meager results. Gomillion immediately attributed a main cause of the impotence of the black community to the lack of voting strength—only thirty-two blacks were registered in Tuskegee, compared with eight hundred whites. The registered blacks included members of the Institute's staff, the hospital staff, and a handful of local businessmen. Poorer blacks didn't even think about voting.*

Gomillion himself wanted to register, of course, but he quickly discovered that getting registered to vote in Macon County required running a virtual obstacle course. A poll tax was a key impediment. The tax applied to whites as well as blacks, but court testimony later revealed that their poll taxes were usually paid by political candidates, or by their employers, or white landowners.

Applicants also had to pass a property and literacy test to the satisfaction of the three-member Board of Registrars. Three hundred dollars of property was required, and the literacy test was so arbitrarily applied it could be used to disqualify anyone. Sometimes black applicants were asked to copy and interpret long sections of the U.S. Constitution. In civil rights lore the favorite literacy test question was "How many bubbles are there in a bar of soap?" or "How many seeds are there in a watermelon?"

The third obstacle was the requirement that an applicant be vouched for by two registered voters; the registrars carried a list of approved "vouchers," only one of whom on the whole list was black. In effect, these requirements meant the Board of Registrars could allow or prohibit the registration of individual applicants as they saw fit. Such prohibitory devices, or variations thereof, were commonly used in other heavily black counties in the Deep South.

A fundamental principle of Booker T. Washington's theory of racial progress was that the acquisition of education and economic independence—"pulling oneself up by one's bootstraps"—would eventually lead to political power. But nothing could be clearer to Gomillion than that even in Washington's own hometown, despite the continued growth and influence of the Tuskegee Institute after his death and the presence of the Veterans Administration hospital, which had created a small

---

*These figures are from Robert Norrell's *Reaping the Whirlwind*, p. 36.

black educated and economically independent class unequaled in any other town its size in the entire nation, educated blacks still could not vote.

Gomillion had not attempted to register since he returned from his studies at Fisk in 1934, because he could find only one white man to vouch for him, a downtown Tuskegee shoe salesman. In 1939 he was able to obtain a second voucher from the white contractor who was to build his house, as a condition of the contract. That is how Gomillion finally was able to register; he paid the poll tax as a faculty leader at the Institute, and the literacy test was not applied to him.

In 1941, under Gomillion's leadership, the name of the Men's Club was changed to the Tuskegee Civic Association (TCA) to broaden its base and open membership to women. The aims of the association were still primarily innocuous civic and educational programs, but they gradually began to shift their focus to voter registration. During World War II, over the course of several skirmishes, the TCA forced the registrars to accept blacks as vouchers (though the registrars still chose which blacks would be vouchers); the association also forced the Board of Registrars to limit themselves to either using the property *or* the literacy requirement, but not both—hardly earthshaking victories.

Meanwhile, racial tension and conflict over voter registration paled in comparison with the frequent confrontations between black airmen and the town's white police, which almost turned into a miniwar within World War II. White townspeople saw the black soldiers as the enemy, and began arming themselves to prepare for the attack they were sure was coming. Under these conditions an NAACP chapter was established in 1944 by a civilian employee at the Army Air Force base.

As a result of the TCA's continual efforts and many racial conflicts in the community, Tuskegee blacks became more and more aware of the need for strong racial organization. Thus, the originally small activist black community, represented by the Institute-dominated TCA, emerged from World War II with significantly swollen ranks. What had once been a tiny stream was by 1946—with the addition of hospital and military personnel, not to mention the growth of the Institute itself due to Veterans Administration benefits—a river. The TCA and the NAACP formed a natural alliance, particularly on the issue of voting. In 1945, the voter applications of more than two hundred blacks were denied by the Tuskegee Board of Registrars. The TCA immediately filed suits in both state and federal courts.

These initial efforts through the courts failed. However, in the late 1940s, because of the appointment of a new chairman, the registration requirements were liberalized and the number of blacks registered to vote in Macon County quadrupled in little over a year. Then the liberal registrar was removed as part of a political deal, and the doors slammed shut once again.

According to Norrell, this on-again, off-again policy toward black registration reflected an indecision within opposing white political factions over whether they would try to cultivate the potential black vote. In most cases, including that of Tuskegee, the brief experiment with opening the registration books was quickly abandoned.

From 1950 on, white diehards in Macon County became extremely creative in their attempts to stem the tide of black voter registration. Meanwhile, the TCA instituted voting education classes in which blacks were taught how to deal with legitimate constitutional interpretation tests. These classes, while extremely valuable, could not, of course, change the arbitrary decisions of segregationist registrars, who continued to fail blacks left and right simply because they were black.

In 1954, for the first time since Reconstruction, Tuskegee blacks ran a candidate for public office. Jessie Guzman, an Institute educator, campaigned for a vacant school board post; though clearly qualified, she was routed by a 3-1 margin. Then, incredibly, a bill was introduced by the Macon County state representative in May 1957 that would gerrymander black Tuskegee right out of the town of Tuskegee. "What remained," according to Norrell "was the town square, the streets where whites lived, and several thin arms reaching out to take in whites residing on roads leading out of Tuskegee. In a few cases, the new boundaries ran down the middle of streets to exclude the blacks on one side. All but twelve of the twelve hundred black voters had been removed." In June this bill was passed by the state legislature without a single dissenting vote.

Gomillion and the TCA responded immediately, with tremendous support from the now thoroughly galvanized black community. They inflicted a tight economic boycott on all the white merchants in the town. The Tuskegee boycott was launched with the stirring example of the Montgomery bus boycott fresh in everyone's minds. The boycott in Tuskegee, just thirty miles to the east of Montgomery, quickly won the support and active participation of Martin Luther King, Jr., and the officials of King's Montgomery Improvement Association.

It was not long before town square merchants were trying to find their way out of a situation that was economically ruinous for them. Even so, the boycott didn't stop livid conservative whites from proposing a plan by which Macon County itself would be abolished and divided into five sections; the five surrounding counties each inheriting a piece, though this plan would not address the problem of the boycott. (Eventually, the plan was dismissed as foolish.) By the spring of 1958, half of Tuskegee's white businesses had failed, the survivors suffering a 50 percent decline in sales.

In August 1958, the TCA broadened its counterattack by filing a federal suit, *Gomillion v. Lightfoot*, against the mayor of Tuskegee, arguing that the reapportionment should be invalidated on the basis of being racially motivated. After a long and thoroughly argued hearing before the Supreme Court in 1960, the Court agreed that the law in question was racially discriminatory in intent. *Gomillion v. Lightfoot* was an important case in Supreme Court history, because the Court extended its inquiry, for the first time, to examine the *intent* of a state legislature in passing a law.

*Gomillion* was remanded to the court of federal district judge Frank M. Johnson, who was destined to play a crucial role in Alabama civil rights cases during the 1960s. Judge Johnson immediately reinstituted the old Tuskegee city boundaries, though that did not mean the question of voting had been solved. But, in March 1961, Judge Johnson also ruled, in response to a Justice Department action against the Macon County Board of Registrars, that the board "had deliberately engaged in practices designed to discriminate against qualified Negroes." In a stunning and unprecedented decree, Johnson ordered that the same standards applied to white applicants be applied to blacks, that racially applied impediments to registration be obliterated, and that sixty-four obviously qualified blacks who had been rejected be immediately added to the voter registration rolls. The result was to open the polls to blacks in Macon County to an extent surpassed only by the monumental Voting Rights Act of 1965.

Gomillion and the TCA now turned their attention to the question of public school desegregation. In the wake of *Brown*, faltering, difficult first steps toward school desegregation were being taken throughout the South under a variety of orders from federal district judges. Though Gomillion and the TCA viewed voting as their first priority and though the Institute operated its own high school of superior quality, the demand for school desegregation was no less urgent in Tuskegee than in other sections of the Black Belt, if for no other reason than to equalize the widely disproportionate funding spent on white as opposed to black schools.

In 1963, Judge Johnson, in response to a standard NAACP suit, issued a ruling that set a date for desegregation to begin at Tuskegee High School. Thirteen black students were scheduled to enter school on the first Monday of September. After years of denouncing *Brown* and defying any attempt to initiate desegregation, this time key whites on the school board, and even a few in the community, were prepared to go along with the judge's order, and were confident they could pull it off. They were tragically mistaken.

In Alabama, prosegregation forces, led by Governor George C. Wallace, had vowed never to accept desegregation, and had made resistance to decrees of the federal courts a national cause célèbre. Wallace's attempt to prevent the entrance of two black students to the University of Alabama earlier that year had turned out to be a hopeless gesture, but Wallace had made national news by "standing in the schoolhouse door" until he was forced to give way to the U.S. marshals. In Tuskegee, Wallace sent state troopers to the high school to prevent the new black students from entering. This action held up the desegregation process just long enough to discourage white parents from sending their children to the school, while plans to arrange an alternative all-white private high school, Macon Academy, were activated. Funds were raised for the new academy in an atmosphere of prosegregation hysteria; eventually, the only students who entered Tuskegee High were the thirteen blacks. The net effect of these developments was to split the minority white community of Tuskegee between those few who thought it proper to proceed with public school desegregation and those whites who, like Wallace, seemed to believe desegregation could be postponed forever. The split was so deep it destroyed relations between friends, church members, ministers and their congregations, and in some cases, members of the same family. As a result of such intense animosities, several key antisegregation whites moved away from Tuskegee with no intention of returning.

Unfortunately, the splintering within the white community paralleled a similar political division within the black community between the Institute-dominated TCA on one hand, and a new political organization, the Non-Partisan League, comprised of younger blacks who were mostly Veterans Hospital workers, on the other. For some time younger members of the TCA had believed the organization was too moderate, its historic victories notwithstanding. Once sit-ins, freedom rides, and freedom marches had become highly publicized in other places, younger blacks in Tuskegee wanted to follow suit, but Gomillion believed that marches and activist protests were counterproductive. Gomillion was also willing to support liberal or moderate white candidates for election, whereas the Non-Partisan League was bent upon running black candidates for all offices. This difference of opinion was exacerbated by a feeling on the part of new activists that the Tuskegee Institute community was inattentive to the needs of the poorer blacks in the town and surrounding county. Once Veterans Hospital staff members were registered in sufficient numbers, and ready to flex their political muscles, they were determined to elect their own people, even if Gomillion and other educated blacks thought them unqualified.

With the election of a black sheriff, Lucius Amerson, in 1966, the Non-Partisan League forged ahead as the dominant political organization in Macon County, and Gomillion and the TCA receded into the background. The cumulative effect of this election, plus the election of several other blacks to city and county offices, was an almost complete polarization of the white and black communities, a polarization complicated by the political division within the majority black community, and the bitterness of the white community as they saw blacks acceding to positions of political power.

At the same time, a new, aggressive activism emerged from the previously easily cowed Institute students. Encouraged by SNCC, they challenged not only the white establishment, but the conservative black Institute administration, including the elders of the Tuskegee Civic Association. SNCC students, with the assistance of the organization's national leaders, led marches downtown to the town square, and they launched several attempts to attend white churches, where they were angrily rebuffed.

In late 1966, the SNCC/Tuskegee contingent turned its attention to voter registration in Macon County, producing excellent results in the wake of the Voting Rights Act passed the previous summer. By 1966, twelve years after desegregation was ordered, Tuskegee High School had become all black, reflecting the total refusal of whites to deal with institutions in which blacks had an equal or predominant presence. White students continued to flock to Macon Academy and smaller all-white private academies, or to public schools where they were in the majority.

~

I had been in Tuskegee twice before. In 1951, I was there on a Morehouse College athletic trip as part of our tennis team. At that time, the feeling of a separate black world in a small town was complete. Students ventured from Tuskegee Institute only to the areas immediately adjacent to the campus, and only when it was absolutely necessary. It was as if we were visiting a protected island of blacks within a sea of the white South; venturing out to sea was undertaken only with elaborate care and preplanning, and such ventures out of familiar territory, I sensed, were brief and hurried.

Then, in the summer of 1967, I had spent a week in Tuskegee with the Free Southern Theater troupe; we performed at the Institute. The first program was poorly attended; the second night a few more people came; the third night was packed. I remember an intense discussion after a performance of poems written by black writers. After our presentation, during a discussion with the audience, a white Vista worker remarked, "I didn't know there was any such thing as black poetry; I thought there was just poetry." This opened up a rip-roaring debate among audience members, exactly what we had hoped for. The audience was primarily students, with hardly any teachers in attendance, even though we had been brought there by an Institute summer program. Poet David Henderson of New York, then in his twenties, had joined us for a few weeks and his reading was most enthusiastically received; it was as if the students had never heard the northern urban images David brought to his work, utilizing elements of black popular music, and they seemed astonished that it could be done. (This was long before David's fascinating biography of musician Jimmy Hendrix, *Voodoo Child of the Aquarian Age*. His book of poetry, *De Mayor of Harlem*, contains several poems written on this trip.) We knew Tuskegee had undergone a time of troubles, but we were excited by the fact the students were alive and interested. For black elders, 1967 must have seemed a dangerous and confusing time. For serious, inquisitive black youth, it was an exciting time.

While in Tuskegee, I had visited friends of my parents who taught at the Institute. I was taken aback by their automatically dismissive attitude toward SNCC, as if the organization carried the poisonous stigma of a Communist party cell. I didn't know then of SNCC's role in the Tuskegee story. Institute decorum was eloquently symbolized by the impressive Booker T. Washington statue at the campus entrance in which the founder is lifting the veil of ignorance from the face of a young black man—or, as some might say who opposed Washington's conservative philosophy of racial advancement, lowering it. The worn, distinctive red-brick buildings of the quite substantial campus, the dusty museum of Carver's Chemical Laboratory, and the formal dress and hearty manners of the waiters at the Dorothy Hall Guest House restaurant all bore out this decorum.

As I had driven around the town that summer, I could see the affluence of the Institute housing neighborhood—substantial homes with neatly trimmed gardens and so forth—in contrast to the run-down homes of non-Institute blacks in town and in the rural areas. No wonder the intraracial class conflict had been so bitter.

The gaping chasm between the worlds of Tuskegee whites and blacks was also startling; there simply was no kind of interracial interaction that I could see, other than that grudging interaction that derived from commerce. In 1967 there was not even the hint that these two worlds might at some time converge. Whites owned town square businesses and banks. There was a black "corner" on the square with a service station and a small restaurant.

And yet the physical beauty of the place, the stunning red clay and the bricks baked from that clay, made this part of Alabama unforgettable. It was, in effect, a western extension of rural southern Georgia, though Tuskegee was more advanced than Georgia, with its consciously designed move away from the world of the plantation and the stigma of serfdom. In this setting, the dammed-in need for black self-assertion had erupted like a volcano, drowning all the decorous tenets of Booker T. Washington under the hot lava of angry rhetoric. At that time, I could sense a searing of the collective psyche of Tuskegee, a burning so enveloping that Tuskegee would not, and could not, ever be again what it had represented at the turn of the century.

My impression upon entering Tuskegee in 1991 from the south on Highway 29 was of an all-black third world town with the memories of colonialism still evident in government buildings and city square. Despite the change in politics over the past thirty years, the statue of the Confederate soldier still maintains his stance at the center of the town square, as if to reassure white Tuskegee that no matter what is happening now, the pendulum will surely not swing too far in the direction of black control, even if it is held back only by the weight of the image of that faithful soldier, his rifle at parade rest. The statue is adorned with the engraved sign: EXECUTED BY DAUGHTERS OF THE CONFEDERACY. HONOR THE BRAVE. SOLDIERS OF MACON COUNTY.

WELCOME TO TUSKEGEE, a newer sign reads. JOHNNY FORD, MAYOR. The town's first black mayor. Almost every person I saw in the dying town square was black; the businesses resembled those of any small village, though they were not nearly as prosperous looking as those in Orangeburg, for instance.

I drove up to the Institute but it, too, looked as if it had seen its best days. The town of Tuskegee seems to have faded into a somewhat neglected museum, but its painful racial transition, from a town controlled by whites politically to one of black political control, did, or could, serve as a precursor for similar towns in the struggle for black education and voting rights. I actually only spent a good part of a day in Tuskegee while en route to Selma. Late that afternoon I hit the road again so that I would arrive in Selma before nightfall.

Leaving Tuskegee, I joined the jarring rush of heavy truck traffic on I-85 west into Montgomery, just thirty miles away. U.S. 80 on the west side of Montgomery is a spur of I-65. It passes the airport, then cuts through a section of outlying businesses—auto repair shops, shopping malls, truck stops. A mile or so later, it opens into the small hills leading directly westward to Selma.

From here the fifty-six-mile stretch of U.S. 80 to Selma traverses no towns and passes only a few farmhouses. It seemed as if I had departed from not only the city of Montgomery but the twentieth century itself, an impression made all the more real when I passed a billboard depicting a plantation mansion-house. VISIT SELMA, the sign invited. HISTORY, INDUSTRY, QUALITY OF HOPE. Really? I thought. I didn't see any industry and maybe their wish for industry constituted the "quality of hope." The landscape was *extremely* rural along this road; it was the same kind of terrain that surrounds Albany. When I reached the outskirts of Selma, I arrived at the Alabama River and crossed the awkward-looking Edmund Pettus Bridge to enter the town proper.

Selma is a town smaller than Albany but larger than Tuskegee. Selma's population is about twenty-four thousand, 55 percent black. By comparison, Albany boasts such a larger variety of businesses and places of interest it made Selma seem, initially, a disappointment.

I was interested in visiting Selma not only because of its legendary civil rights history, but also because of a flare-up that occurred there in 1990 over the process of school desegregation that led to boycotts of classes and demonstrations by black students. These demonstrations were sparked by the school board's vote to not renew the contract of the first black school superintendent, Norward Roussell. I was especially interested in getting to the bottom of this issue, because school desegregation as it had evolved during the three and a half decades since *Brown* was a matter of serious dispute in every town I had visited, from Greensboro southward. I hadn't encountered a single place in which black parents and community leaders were satisfied with the public school system in their localities. Blacks felt they were trapped in a kind of bind because they had fought so hard and long to eliminate school segregation; now they couldn't so easily denounce desegregation. The complaints were many and varied, ranging from allegations that the schools were still largely segregated, to the belief that within desegregated schools the majority of black students were being shortchanged in the quality of their education. Many southern black leaders privately lamented the demise of the old black schools, complaining that even under segregation their children had been better prepared and more carefully guided toward a promising future than is the case now.

The situation in Selma also intrigued me because the school superintendent in question, Norward Roussell, was a native of New Orleans, my hometown. Both he and his twin brother, Norman, had risen from extremely limited economic circumstances to earn Ph.D.s in education. I had heard that white residents of Selma considered Roussell arrogant and difficult to work with, but the degree of self-assertion now rather common among blacks of achievement in New Orleans would make Roussell hardly unusual; if the school board was interested in a subservient black, why had they hired Roussell? I wanted to discover a little more about this story for what I thought it might reveal about the kind of place Selma is now, almost three decades after the great 1965 campaign that led to the Voting Rights Act.

After crossing the Edmund Pettus Bridge, U.S. 80 becomes Broad Street, until the highway turns left at Highland Avenue, and leads out of town into rural Dallas County. There are large black communities on both sides of Broad Street, particularly the north side; communities with the type of aging frame houses I had seen in Albany and Lincolnville in St. Augustine. The downtown commercial area that once existed along Broad Street and to the east of Broad near the Alabama River is a relic of the past. The abandoned and boarded-up brick structures that once served as the riverfront commercial district, with the signs of their former lives still painted upon them—Associated Standards, Soul Shop, St. James Hotel, Boston Bargain Store—were perfect candidates to join the movie set of abandoned downtowns that I had first seen in Greensboro. Directly behind the old riverfront commercial area is Brown's Chapel AME Church, decorated with attractive white trimming, the main chapel flanked by twin rectangular, turreted towers. While still imposing, this historic church looks as if it has been added onto several times over the years, so that all the wings and towers don't quite seem as if they are part of the same design. In front of the church is a monument honoring Martin Luther King, Jr., with a sculpted bas-relief of King that does not resemble him at all. This monument also commemorates the three civil rights workers who were killed during the Selma campaign of 1965: the Reverend James J. Reeb, Viola Gregg Liuzzo, and Jimmy Lee Jackson. The street, formerly Sylvan Avenue, is now named for Dr. King. Brown's Chapel is surrounded by a federal housing project named for the famed Tuskegee scientist George W. Carver.

King Street is very wide and bisects the projects. Two blocks away from Brown's Chapel is the First Baptist Church, which rivals Brown's as a church of historic importance in Selma. It was along this two-block corridor, flanked at both ends by the two landmark churches and surrounded by the housing projects, that almost all the famous Selma marches were launched. From here protestors walked the approximately nine blocks to Lauderdale Street, on the other side of Broad, to the Dallas County Courthouse.

The courthouse remains today as it was a quarter century ago, a stolid background for photographs of the unforgettable sheriff-buffoon Jim Clark dressed in military attire with Eisenhower jacket and helmet—the great defender of white privilege (though he himself was hardly privileged). The courthouse is constructed of a sort of greenish stucco and glass, with high, narrow windows; a huge, modern clock sits atop its rectangular tower. It looks like a government building from the Roosevelt New Deal era.

Selma itself is sort of dominated by the Edmund Pettus Bridge spanning the fairly wide Alabama River. The map supplied by the Visitor Information Center informs us that the bridge was designed in 1938 by a native Selmian and was "acclaimed as an engineering feat never before accomplished," apparently because it could bear large loads without falling into the river. The Alabama River was the key factor in early Selma history; Selma was an important port. Selma was also a river junction for those traveling by boat to Mobile and the Gulf of Mexico.

The bridge and the courthouse are of a piece. Like so many bridges and courthouses all over the South, they were built in an age when the New South was expanding its economy and entering the American national economy more fully, a cornerstone of the Rooseveltian New Deal.

Selma High, the formerly all-white high school and site of the 1990 demonstrations, is located on Broad Street near the intersection of Highland, set back nicely from busy street traffic. It is an aging but probably adequate structure that looks to have been constructed in the 1940s.

Driving through the black section west of Broad along Lapley Street, I came across Selma University, a school created in the nineteenth century by the black Baptist Church to train young ministers. On the east side of town, hidden away in a cul-de-sac that cuts it off from the surrounding neighborhood, is Concordia College, a Lutheran school whose black students had little to do with any of Selma's protest efforts. As small as these colleges are, despite the limitations of their programs, and despite the fact that they represent sharp religious divisions within a relatively small black community, they supplied Selma a touch of a black educated elite class.

Just to the west of Broad Street, near the river, is the most prestigious white neighborhood, and the streets near the main thoroughfare of Dallas Avenue are lined with impressive mansions. A little farther from downtown are an Alabama riverboat ramp, a public park, tennis courts, and the Medical Center Hospital. Most of this older, upper-class white housing, even on the streets near downtown, boasts wide, generous porches and considerable yards. Nowhere, not even on these expensive homes, did I see burglar bars, or any other indications of an unusual fear of crime. I also did not notice a lot of "hanging out" on the streets of Selma's black communities. In fact, I did not see many people at all out on the streets, nor did I come across much nightlife, though there was a disco near the downtown area.

There aren't many hotels and motels in Selma, and I was surprised to discover that most of them were already booked for the weekend. I finally found one run by an Indian family who lived on the premises. During my stay in Selma, this motel did a brisk overnight trucking business, but there were also many black families who looked as if they might be attending family reunions in Selma or the surrounding towns. When the families arrived, the kids would head straight for the swimming pool, an unaccustomed luxury for some, and a welcome one, given the blistering heat of those summer days.

I didn't expect much from Selma's restaurants, and my low expectations proved to be justified. Along Highland there is a small mall with a Chinese restaurant and a franchise steak house—other than that, there were the usual fast-food places along the highway. It was along this commercial strip that led out of town toward western Alabama that I discovered a Waffle House, probably the most ubiquitous cheap restaurant found throughout the South in its various manifestations. I settled in there for coffee as I made notes. These places always give me a slight trepidation, because they look like Klan hangouts, because they are frequented by uneducated and/or lower-class whites, those who most resent any assertion of rights or assumption of equality by blacks. Now, even in 1991, I have a fear that I will walk into a scene of loud talk and stories about "niggers." Usually, however, on this trip, they turned out to be okay, sort of like the Greensboro truck stop.

⌒

The town of Selma was founded in 1820, probably with the hope that it would become a vital port along the Alabama River, a junction between northern Alabama, Tennessee and Georgia, and Mobile on the Gulf Coast, reachable by the Alabama and Mobile rivers. The town was named by William Rufus King, one of Alabama's earliest senators.

As it turned out, Selma did establish itself as a prosperous industrial port. When the Civil War broke out, Selma was the South's largest munitions arsenal and manufacturing center, employing ten thousand people. It didn't hurt that Montgomery, less than sixty miles away, was the first Confederate capital.

As Union armies made incursions into the South, they directed their initial attacks against towns that were key supply ports along the Mississippi River and its tributaries. By 1865 this objective was essentially accomplished. The Union armies then turned their attention to "mopping up." Selma was sacked in March by a large Union force under General J. H. Wilson, who was pursuing the Confederate calvary hero, Nathan Bedford Forrest, and a goodly portion of industrial Selma was burned by the Union forces.

During an all too brief postwar Reconstruction, Selma freedmen were apparently more successful than their compatriots in Tuskegee; they elected one of their own, Ben Turner, to Congress. But by 1874, as in Tuskegee, independent black political activity had been suppressed and whites were firmly back in control under the leadership of the former Confederate general Edmund Pettus, for whom the bridge over the Alabama is named. With the advent of the twentieth century, the black community of Selma was effectively disenfranchised and thoroughly dominated by the white elite and its police force. Selma may have been a bit better off than other towns in the Black Belt because of the presence of strong churches, and Selma University. But not much. Black Selma was a virtual colony of white Selma.

Attorney J. L. Chestnut, in his autobiography, *Black in Selma* (with Julia Cass), evocatively depicts Selma during his coming of age in the 1930s and '40s, and the dependency and vulnerability of the black community. A graduate of Howard Law School, Chestnut returned to Selma in the 1950s as the first black lawyer, performing a role that paralleled C. B. King's in Albany. Chestnut cites many examples of how the white power structure used the police as a virtual army of occupation, "overseers" who exercised great power where blacks were concerned, a power so overreaching it even extended to sexual domination. Some white policemen, Chestnut points out, from his observations and stories he frequently heard, were regularly able to force themselves upon black women, even married women, without attempting to conceal such behavior; black men, even husbands, were unable to protect their women. On the other hand, an alliance between a black male and a white woman, once the relationship became known, was a sure prescription for a criminal charge of rape, and an automatic death sentence if found guilty, particularly in Selma.

Many of Chestnut's most notable early criminal cases dealt with black men ensnared in terrible and seemingly hopeless legal binds. The black community had very little leverage in such cases, and what little there was could only be employed by the most prestigious ministers, extracting a reluctant favor here or there from white officials with whom they were on friendly terms. But such leverage never extended to altering the fundamental terms of domination. Chestnut's harrowing portraits of twentieth-century Selma helped me to understand their deep reservoir of black malcontent.

Police abuse was hardly unique to Selma; it was a problem in towns and cities across the South. In his study of Tuskegee, Norrell points out that police abuse against poor blacks was always a burning issue. To some extent, the Tuskegee Institute community was immune from these ravages; but since Selma had no black middle class of comparable size, the abuses in Selma were probably worse, and how blacks were handled by the police more telling and more meaningful.

The origins of resistance to oppression and tight dominance by a ruling white oligarchy in Selma are marked by the same sort of incremental efforts that characterized the struggle for the ballot in Tuskegee. Charles Gomillion and the Tuskegee Civic Association were the catalysts for change in Macon County; Sam Boynton and the Dallas County Voters League were their indefatigable counterparts in Selma and Dallas County. Sam Boynton was a graduate of Tuskegee Institute and a student of the brilliant agricultural chemist George W. Carver. Boynton was assigned to Dallas County in 1928 as the first county extension agent, as part of a federal program that in Alabama was deeply tied to the innovative efforts of Tuskegee Institute to improve farming conditions among blacks in rural areas. Boynton created educational conferences and fairs, and lectured local farmers in new methods of agriculture. In those days, several African students from Liberia and Sierra Leone journeyed to Tuskegee to study agriculture under George Washington Carver. Then Carver sent them to Dallas County to observe Boynton's program, because of his innovative approaches to farming, particularly methods of crop rotation. In his work, Sam Boynton was joined by his future wife, Amelia Platts, also a Tuskegee graduate assigned to Dallas County in 1929 as the home demonstration agent; while Boynton addressed the men, she assisted black women in homemaking.

Boynton also encouraged black farmers to purchase land and to more aggressively seek out and take advantage of new federal agricultural programs created by the Roosevelt New Deal. Boynton's other passion was to preach voting. County blacks had voted during Reconstruction, and supported themselves rather well in tiny villages like Bogue Chitto. They had founded rudimentary schools for their children, but as with all black settlements in the South, they suffered dramatic setbacks during the white South's Redemption. By the 1920s only a handful of blacks in the entire county were registered.

Beginning in the late thirties, Boynton dragged his farmers, one by one, into the registration office in Selma, only to achieve negligible results (other than, possibly, the amusement of the registrars). Like Gomillion, Boynton believed that blacks could only protect their land and homes if they participated actively in the political system, a conviction rooted in the bitter history of Reconstruction and its dismantling.

Boynton also realized that black voter registration was the only viable route to protect black citizens before the law, and the court system. Though no black had ever served on a jury in Dallas County, many blacks had been tried and convicted by county juries. Normally, the indictment of blacks, particularly on charges brought by whites, was tantamount to conviction.

In Dallas County the Boyntons looked to a lonely predecessor, C. J. Adams, for guidance and inspiration. Adams was a veteran of World War I, a commissioned officer who became a railroad mail clerk upon discharge. It was Adams, surely believing anything is possible, who founded the Dallas County Voters League in 1929 and, around the same time, a fledgling chapter of the NAACP. He was the only active member of the chapter. For his efforts he was subjected to harsh reprisals; he was jailed several times, charged with notarizing false birth certificates and other documents, which may have been true, according to Chestnut, and finally he gave up and moved to Detroit in the 1940s. Sam Boynton succeeded Adams as president of the Voters League. It was not long before he, too, came under pressure for his voting advocacy, and in the forties Boynton was forced to give up his job as county agent. Amelia Boynton had resigned from her job as home demonstration agent in the 1930s when she married. The Boyntons thereupon started an insurance agency, but that did not relieve the harassment. Charges were brought against them for alleged irregularities in their business dealings.

Despite the determined efforts of the Voters League in the 1940s and '50s, the results were depressing, compared, for instance, with the steady increases in registration in Tuskegee. In Dallas County, black applicants were subjected to the two-voucher requirement, constitutional interpretation tests, and various forms of economic reprisal if they did not desist. When the Voters League worked hard in 1955 to unearth twenty-nine blacks who would sign a petition requesting the school board to take the first step toward desegregation, the *Selma Times-Herald* published the names of the petitioners and their addresses, clearly inviting retaliation. Within a week all but a handful of the petitioners had withdrawn their names; sixteen of the twenty-nine lost their jobs. Boynton and the hard core of the league's faithful held fast, conducting citizenship classes and so forth, but by 1961 only 156 of an estimated 15,000 blacks in Dallas County were registered. A vigilant White Citizens Council chapter had been organized in Selma in the wake of *Brown*. The Citizens Council led the way in applying heat on blacks, and in pressuring wavering white merchants to fire black employees associated with the Voters League. They were to be denied credit if they were customers. By the end of 1961 the situation in Dallas County looked so bleak that anyone expressing the opinion that the isolated, suppressed, and spasmodic efforts of the Dallas County Voters League would within a few years become the fountainhead of the most magnificent voting campaign in the history of the American South would have been considered insane.

⌒

In 1962, Bernard Lafayette, a young black divinity student affiliated with SNCC, settled in Selma with a plan of buttressing the civil rights organizing efforts there. SNCC had earlier recognized the voting potential of the heart of the Black Belt; Lafayette's venture was very similar to the Sherrod-led effort in Albany. Lafayette was received and housed by the few Dallas County Voters League activists, who were happy to see him come to their city, but he quickly decided to focus his efforts on Selma's youth, as was consistent with the SNCC approach whenever they entered a community. In particular, Lafayette attempted to recruit students at tiny Selma University, which by 1962 was basically a Bible school. He was run off the campus by the president, but not before he was able to convert two or three student supporters.

There were no further important gains until May 1963, when Sam Boynton died after a long illness. Lafayette was determined that Boynton be properly memorialized, and after a struggle, was able to win the support of the minister of Tabernacle Baptist Church, one of the largest in black Selma, for a memorial service. The Boynton memorial was turned into a virtual mass voter registration rally, despite the intimidating presence of Sheriff Jim Clark and his deputies. From that point on the Selma Movement, as it came to be known, began to acquire a vitality marking the beginning of a new epoch in the Black Belt. When Lafayette was beaten by two white thugs with the butt of a rifle soon after the Boynton memorial—only a neighbor's response to his screams saved his life—instead of being discouraged, he used the beating and his very visible bandages to provoke the passive black community into recognizing the need for activism, thereby nurturing the field for the unprecedented events of the next few years.

~

Despite these hopeful steps, Chestnut points out, most of the efforts were limited to strengthening the Voters League, and the league's one-at-a-time approach would never have been able to register enough blacks to bring about real change. A mass-registration approach was required, and Tuskegee and other more activist southern towns provided object lessons to this effect. Lafayette had to leave Selma to return to school in late 1963; he was replaced by Worth Long, a SNCC volunteer from Arkansas. Long, an astute observer who would in post-Movement years emerge as one of the South's most learned folklorists and experts on the blues, quickly set about the task of following up Lafayette's efforts to recruit students at Selma University, working surreptitiously.

In the summer of 1964, SNCC leaders Jim Forman and John Lewis joined Worth Long in hopes of waging an up-tempo voting campaign, thus heightening Selma's profile on the terrain of civil rights activist towns. They staged a Freedom Day with fifty demonstrators marching to the county courthouse in an effort to register. Instead, they were roughed up by Sheriff Jim Clark, pushed around with cattle prods, and arrested.

~

With black activism showing no signs of abating, on July 9 state circuit judge James A. Hare, a Selma blueblood and hard-line segregationist who maintained arcane theories on black racial inferiority, apparently deciding he had seen enough, issued an order prohibiting public meetings of more than three people; an order that singled out fifty blacks by name, and specifically named fifteen black organizations, and the Ku Klux Klan.

This imperial edict was selectively enforced (used only against civil rights gatherings), and it held up for the remaining months of 1964, because of the tacit support of the sympathetic federal judge sitting in Mobile. Judge Hare's ruling did, however, make it clear to activist Selmians that if they were ever going to move past the point of a limited number of registered voters, they needed outside help. By the late fall of 1964, only 335 blacks were on the Dallas County voting rolls.

That very fall the idea of inviting Martin Luther King, Jr., and SCLC to Selma to help launch a far more intensified voting campaign began to emerge within the Voters League. Such a campaign was actually not that far-fetched. King knew that voting rights were the next big target of the civil rights movement, that the Black Belt of Alabama was a fertile field for such a campaign, and that that fertility was augmented by his personal and organizational ties in Alabama. King's wife, Coretta Scott King, was born in Marion, just thirty miles north of Selma, as was Andy Young's wife, Jean Childs Young. King had, after all, first risen to national prominence as leader of the Montgomery bus boycott. And he had raised his profile among national civil rights leaders to a preeminent position through the 1963 SCLC campaign in Birmingham, which had resulted in the passage of the sweeping new Civil Rights Act of 1964, and his winning the Nobel Peace Prize in the fall of 1964. The centrality of Selma in Alabama, with its significant but dormant black population suffering from a history of serfdom and controlled by an unyielding white elite—symbolized by Judge Hare's dictatorial court order—made Selma an inspired target for a major campaign effort.

The fact that the earlier efforts of the Voters League and the more recent probings of SNCC workers had cracked open the door a bit through marches and appeals meant that SCLC wouldn't have to start from scratch; a beachhead was already established in Selma. The Voters League formally invited Dr. King by letter in mid-December 1964. But by then King and SCLC had already decided Selma would be the site of their next major campaign, and had already drawn up elaborate plans.

On the night of January 1, 1965, one hundred and two years to the day after Lincoln's Emancipation Proclamation, the Selma campaign was launched via an eloquent, well-thought-out "give us the ballot" address by King at Brown's Chapel AME Church. In holding this highly publicized meeting, the Voters League and SCLC deliberately violated Judge Hare's order. Sheriff Clark, however, declined to enforce it in an effort to lessen cause for conflict. City officials hoped that maybe if they would just ignore "racial problems" in Selma for a while, King and SCLC would go away and look elsewhere for a more promising organizing territory. Meanwhile, the SCLC staff settled in to begin the task of canvassing and building support from the small base established by the Voters League and SNCC.

Then, in lightning succession, within a three-month period, events transpired that created indelible images of Selma as a place of classic violent repression in defense of the segregationist southern order. To the old-line faithful of the Voters League, accustomed to seeing their registration efforts move at a horse-and-buggy pace, the rush of spectacular and unforeseen happenings between January and April 1965 must have been stunning, though not unwelcome.

The old-line white Selma elite must also have been struck with awe, though awe tempered with shock and a profound sense of dismay at having been depicted, in their eyes, so unfairly. Their fine, peaceful town had somehow, through manipulation by their northern enemies, been transformed into an archetype of racism, violence, and repression before the entire world; while they knew that such a representation of them was not accurate. They must have wondered what the world was coming to as the pace of marches and demonstrations and demands quickened. Was it better to try to crush this contagious outburst of insanity with the usual police brutality, as they had always done, or better to do little or nothing and hope that the torrent of escalating protests would spend itself, and move on, leaving their beloved Selma in peace?

The first marches to the courthouse by black citizens who wished to be registered were turned away in barely suppressed rage by the irrepressible, scowling Sheriff Clark. Within weeks after the first marches, Clark had lost control. He was photographed on the grounds outside the courthouse kneeling over the fallen Mrs. Annie Lee Cooper, poised with his club ready to smash her skull in, as she tenaciously tried to resist his blows. Unfortunately for Clark, there was no photograph of her just moments earlier knocking him to his knees with a right cross, followed by a left hook which sent him sprawling. The incident had begun when Sheriff Clark pushed Mrs. Cooper while she stood in a registration waiting line.

Then, King and Abernathy were jailed for, technically, leading a march without permit; actually, for leading a march that challenged everything white Selma stood for, beginning with the denial of the ballot. King, in jail again just three months after receiving the Nobel Peace Prize, was an unsettling image conveying the uncomfortable truth of a South still fundamentally unchanged.

Even black public school teachers found the courage to march to the courthouse in Selma. Without a word spoken or chant uttered, it was made perfectly clear that these blacks, despite their being professionals, and their higher-level education, were also barred from voting.

After a few weeks, the campaign was broadened to include registration marches in the counties surrounding Dallas County, especially in Perry County to the north. In Perry County, at Marion, black education had long been advanced through the Lincoln School. Rural Perry County was dotted with unincorporated villages whose blacks, often landowners, exercised unusual independence, though few were registered to vote. Though outside their territory, these were also people cultivated by Adams and Boynton.

On the night of February 17, blacks attempted to march to the courthouse square in Marion, the county seat. As they emerged that evening from church, where they had held their premarch meeting, they were brutally beaten. The attack by the police was made more terrible by the turning off of the street lights, so that the beatings could take place in darkness. Television newsmen were also attacked, and their cameras were smashed to make sure there was no documentation; one national newsman was beaten so badly he had to be hospitalized. That night, Jimmy Lee Jackson, a twenty-six-year-old Marion resident who was participating in the demonstrations, was shot by a policeman while attempting to protect his mother. He died a week later, and the funeral, at which King and other SCLC leaders spoke and led the long march to the cemetery, became the bitter birthplace of the idea for a march to Montgomery. Jimmy Lee Jackson's body should be deposited on the steps of the Alabama statehouse, argued SCLC leader James Bevel, since Alabama's governor, George Wallace, with his growing reputation for virulent racism and his defiance of desegregation court orders, was symbolically responsible for the killing.

It was Selma's fate that SCLC decided that a march protesting the Marion beatings and Jackson's death should be initiated not in Marion, but in Selma, the central focus of their campaign. March 7 was selected as the date to depart on the long march to Montgomery, from Brown's Chapel. There was uncertainty how far the group would actually make it, and whether they needed federal protection, but no one anticipated the brutality with which the march was pushed back across the Pettus Bridge that Sunday. The marchers were heavily tear-gassed, beaten, and then chased into Brown's Chapel by troopers on horseback. Had it gone any further, no doubt the young men in the surrounding Carver housing projects would have opened fire with their weapons, causing a small war to erupt in the streets of Selma. As it was, it was all the march organizers could do to keep things from getting completely out of control.

The beatings on the bridge were captured on national television, and those images were displayed over and over as a visual testimony to what blacks were up against in Selma. From that point on, events rushed forward at a torrential rate.

King issued a call to the national religious community to join him in Selma, and Selma was inundated with volunteers responding to his call. There were several preparatory marches of various constituencies of volunteers: religious leaders of virtually every denomination, labor leaders, and representatives of other civil rights groups. Selma was being transformed into a mighty cause and symbol. One night, a white volunteer, the Reverend James Reeb from Boston, was set upon and beaten by white thugs downtown. He was turned away from Selma Hospital and died from his injuries en route to a hospital in Birmingham.

Finally, the momentous march began in Selma, covering a few miles each day until reaching Montgomery on the fifth day. The marchers were provided with federal protection by President Johnson, a level of national support undreamt of when the campaign began. The eyes of the nation watched, dazed, stunned, fascinated. On the steps of the state capitol, at the conclusion of the march, King gave one of his most memorable speeches, asking, rhetorically, over and over, *how long* blacks must wait for justice in America. "Not long," he finally answered, his voice ringing through to the huge audience in front of the state capitol that afternoon and across the nation by television:

> *For I come to say to you this afternoon however difficult the moment, however frustrating the hour, it will not be long, because truth pressed to the earth will rise again.*
>
> *How long? Not long, because no lie can live forever.*
>
> *How long? Not long, because you will reap what you sow.*

*How long? Not long, because the arm of the moral universe is long but it bends toward justice.*

*How long? Not long, because mine eyes have seen the glory of the coming of the Lord, trampling out the vintage where the grapes of wrath are stored. He has loosed the fateful lightning of his terrible swift sword. His truth is marching on.*

That very night a volunteer from Detroit, Mrs. Viola Liuzzo, was shot to death on Highway 80 as she was returning from Selma to Montgomery in the process of ferrying volunteers after the march. This murder, amid the triumph of the just-completed march, which itself was born of the death of Jimmy Lee Jackson, was a harbinger of the ambiguity and sadness of the days to come.

In the background, behind the powerful images and drama of the march, there was a growing conviction in the White House and Congress that an overriding law that would unlock the voting machines of the South to the masses was imperative, or the demands would continue and escalate until they exposed a glaring contradiction of the democratic principles in the country that considered itself the leader of the "free world." So it was that the Selma campaign became the catalyst for the Voting Rights Act of 1965, which in retrospect was a major factor in changing the face of the South forever. For the first time since Reconstruction, blacks were now able to vote in numbers proportionate to their population, though implementation occurred slowly and several subsequent legal battles were required to assure that the rights promised would be delivered.

After the march to Montgomery, with the immediate objectives achieved, all of the volunteers left Selma, and Selma receded once again into the background, leaving Selmians, black and white, to work out the denouement themselves. This was the peace white Selmians had wished for, but it was too late; Selma and the South had crossed a bridge from which there was no turning back.

The Voting Rights Act gave rise to the entrance of blacks into electoral politics in Dallas County, as well as the other Black Belt counties in central Alabama. Blacks now commenced to organize, and to run for political office in the towns and counties. These positions carried with them small salaries, but also opened the doors to lucrative government contracts. In the Black Belt, blacks became city and county commissioners, and members of school boards, and achieved the election of a state senator in Dallas County. These elections led to government contracts for the law firm of Chestnut, Sanders and Sanders as attorneys for regional governmental boards with black majorities, and a few other contracts. But blacks did not win the mayoralty of Selma. When I arrived in 1991, Joe Smitherman had, against all odds, survived for twenty-two of the twenty-six years since 1965 as Selma's seemingly perpetual mayor. He continued to enjoy massive white support, and now, the support of a few black voters who benefited from jobs and appointments awarded by the mayor.

The first people I wanted to meet in Selma were attorneys Rose Sanders and her husband, Hank Sanders. My only previous trip to Selma had been about six years earlier, for a theater conference we had called the Southern Black Cultural Alliance. Once a year theater groups from the Deep South held a meeting on Memorial Day weekend. That year Rose Sanders was our hostess. She is a Harvard Law graduate and native Alabamian who had moved to Selma with her husband, Hank, also a Harvard Law graduate, primarily, they said, because of the romance of Selma's civil rights history, the obvious need for attorneys in the Alabama Black Belt, and their own philosophical inclinations toward consciousness raising and community development. Rose Sanders had always been active in amateur theater, and with her boundless energy she created three Selma organizations designed to heighten black consciousness among youth: the Black Belt Cultural Center; the Children of Selma Theater Group; and a larger, multipurpose organization, the Twenty-first Century Foundation. Meanwhile, as an outgrowth of their political activism, Hank Sanders was elected state senator from the Black Belt area, the first black to be so elected since Reconstruction.

I was only in Selma for one day for the mid-1980s conference, and was not much impressed then with the town or its potential, but I was impressed with the number of youths Rose Sanders had involved in theater—teens and preteens. Her energy seemed to be a magnet across the generational lines, and kids gravitated toward her with great enthusiasm. It is no surprise that when the Selma High School dispute broke out in 1990, Rose Sanders was in the middle of it; she was a prime leader of the boycott. Rose and Hank Sanders are law partners of J. L. Chestnut, the Selma attorney whose autobiography, *Black in Selma*, had so effectively chronicled black life in the town.

~

When I called J. L. Chestnut on Monday morning and explained that I was visiting Selma, he agreed to see me at noon. The offices of Chestnut, Sanders and Sanders are in a one-story structure large enough for several attorneys' offices and a library-conference room. The atmosphere there was light and energetic, and totally lacking in the forced smiles I found in so many similar offices in South Carolina, St. Augustine, and Albany.

I had intended to invite Chestnut to lunch, but when I arrived he had just finished frying fish in the office kitchen. Having recently read his book, I felt I knew a great deal about him. Sometimes meeting an author whose work you like can be a disappointment, but Chestnut was no disappointment; within a few minutes he made me feel quite at home. Short, rather stocky, with graying hair, Chestnut nevertheless gives the appearance of youth and boundless energy. In fact, the entire legal office seemed to be functioning at a very high-energy pace. I sensed that this office was a legal nerve center not only for Selma, but for the entire state of Alabama.

When I asked Chestnut how he assessed the gains of blacks in Dallas County as a result of the Voting Rights Act, he replied, "Martin never said the vote would deliver thirty million black folk. He said it would get us into the ball park; we would have to learn to play the game. We argued all the time about the limitations of the vote; we've seen only limited gains. We've had ups and downs, and it's difficult to translate all that into what might be termed real progress."

"You don't think people here have made progress?" I asked him.

"It's a matter of perspective," Chestnut explained. "White folks often remind me of how far we've come. And that is true; probably nowhere in the history of the universe have people come from nowhere politically to where we are now in such a short time. But black people are still economic serfs. We consume everything and manufacture nothing. We can't have freedom until we have more economic independence. Black conventions, for instance, spend millions of dollars at white-owned hotels to argue about black poverty and white racism."

"Then economics is the key?" I asked. "Even if you have the vote?" I had heard this in every town I had visited.

"Yes," Chestnut agreed. "Serfdom seems to be an integral part of being black in Selma and in America. When you get to the money game, you get to the heart of where the problem is. You see, economics is an entirely different matter from civil rights, or even politics. For us, it must involve different strategies and different energies.

"During the sixties I was fascinated by how the attitudes of the businessmen, the real movers and shakers, differed from those of politicians. U.S. Steel of Pittsburgh *was* Birmingham. They were not on Bull Conner's side. But they had not given any thought to black people as such. They saw all people as units of labor. They were not in the business of making steel; they were in the business of making money. These owners were not hung up on maintaining the heritage of the South. Most of them weren't from the South. When Bull Conner and police violence became an economic liability, they were ready to cut him loose and they did."

The historic importance of Selma as economic hub of the Black Belt west of Montgomery was not only the reason why the town was chosen for SCLC's campaign, but the reason why Selma will have a future, Chestnut contended.

"Selma," he continued, "is, in a sense, off the beaten path. We're still pretty rural; change of any kind comes slowly. Change is frightening. We're still a small, sleepy town where everyone knows everyone else. It's just that we had our linen hung out before the world—whites and blacks both feel Selma 'got a dirty deal.' But what happened was no accident. Selma was long a central command post of the state of Alabama—the whites controlled the balance of power in the state legislature because of Selma's wealth. We always knew that if Selma fell, Alabama would never be the same again.

"That's why there was such a bitter conflict over the tactics used in opposing us. Despite the attempt to finesse the situation, there were enough of those controlling whites—not Clark, but those who told him what to do—who were certain a stand must be made here, and the Pettus Bridge became a metaphor for that wall of resistance: 'Beat them back, don't let them advance a foot further or the state will *never* be the same.'"

When I was able to get a few minutes to speak to state senator Hank Sanders, Chestnut's law partner, he enthusiastically seconded Chestnut's assessments. Sanders, in his fifties, is harried looking, soft-spoken, and overweight; he was wearing a Ghanaian Kente cloth strip over his blue suit jacket. He rolled off a score-card of achievements and failures: Blacks have won majorities on school boards and county commissions in five of the six surrounding counties where they are a majority, and significant numbers in other counties where they are not. Greene and Wilcox counties, where blacks have virtually turned the racial, and political, situation upside down, are infamous for their poverty. Circuit court judges and district attorneys "control the legal machinery of the counties, particularly district attorneys, because of their power to choose who to charge with crimes," said Sanders. No blacks occupied those slots. "Those two offices are often used against our efforts toward equal justice for blacks. Let's face it," Sanders concluded, "economic power always wins over pure political power. Or it compromises the effectiveness of political power. Economic power controls communications, which can define issues in such a negative way you can't overcome it. Folks can only base their opinion on the information they receive, information we, as advocates of change, don't control."

I asked if there would one day be a black mayor of Selma, and if so, whether it would help. "Well, in Selma it would," he answered. "Mayor Smitherman uses his office to mobilize against education, political development, and economic development that would benefit the entire population. Because Dallas County is the economic center of the region, it has been more difficult to effect change here. It's been a twenty-year fight. Of course, if we brought about *real* change in Selma it would become a national symbol of change, so the stakes are still very high."

When I spoke to Mayor Smitherman on the phone and requested an interview, he said he was tired of talking about civil rights. He suggested I speak to the town's public relations person, but I declined to do that.

Bruce Boynton, the son of Sam and Amelia Boynton, and also a former partner of Chestnut, has been county attorney for the Dallas County Commission since 1988. Boynton, a debonair gentleman in his mid-fifties, met me at the famous county courthouse.

"We won the right to vote," he began, "but it didn't mean much as long as city and county commissioners were elected via at-large districts. You might be able to elect one black who was absolutely powerless, and that was the extent of post-1965 political progress for a long time. We went to the federal courts to argue for a transition to single-representative governmental electoral districts, which at least gave us a chance, based on the concentrated pockets of black population."

The shift from at-large to district elections did not occur until 1985, twenty years after the Voting Rights Act. This crucial ruling was the result of a brace of suits brought before the federal courts by the Justice Department in support of blacks challenging city council, county commission, and local school board elections. Because of the shift to single-district elections, two hundred additional blacks were elected in the state of Alabama in just three years. During this period the number of blacks (and possibly whites also) registered was rather substantially increased by the appointment of deputy federal registrars in each county. There was no more standing in line to register at the courthouse. "Now, for instance," Boynton pointed out, "the Dallas County Commission is comprised of three blacks and two whites. Otherwise, believe me, I would never have come to be the first black county attorney."

Boynton recalled his extraordinary upbringing as the son of activist parents in a small provincial southern town in the 1950s, as we conversed softly in the county courthouse library. "I didn't feel I was better than other blacks, but I certainly felt I was better than to be treated in a segregated fashion. George Washington Carver was my godfather. I was raised to resent any kind of implication of inferiority. I didn't come into contact with whites who made me feel inferior, and I didn't have to."

I had first heard of Bruce Boynton from Thurgood Marshall when I worked as press attaché for the NAACP Legal Defense Fund in New York in 1961. Marshall spoke admiringly of him for his defiance of a segregated lunchroom in a Richmond, Virginia, Trailways station while en route to Selma from the Howard Law School in December 1958. His case went to the Supreme Court and, in 1961, *Boynton v. Commonwealth of Virginia* became the legal basis upon which interstate segregation of public transportation facilities was outlawed. Boynton was barred from practicing law in Alabama when he finished law school because of the prominence of his Supreme Court case. He therefore began his practice in Chattanooga, Tennessee, in the early 1960s.

Boynton returned to Selma from Chattanooga in 1968 as an attorney for SNCC. He spent considerable time in the surrounding counties, especially the extremely rural Lowndes to the east, where SNCC had established a beachhead in the immediate wake of the Great March, in hope of electing blacks to office.

"What was it like when you returned to Alabama?" I asked him.

"What stands out, as I look back, is the number of blacks who were not participants in the Movement who all of a sudden became spokespersons, pushing those who were active aside. Selma has had the same problems," he offered. "And there were problems of violence. I was beaten by the sheriff's deputies on the courthouse square in Camden in Wilcox County. I had to travel with bodyguards. I couldn't get much help from anyone. I was known and a target. So I had to leave Selma again." Today he finds the interracial politeness that prevails to be deceptive as a barometer of change. "The racial status quo remains the same. Business is going on as usual. Except that now there are more young blacks who don't even understand the problems they're up against."

Alvin Benn, who is white and lives in Selma, is the reporter who covers politics in the Black Belt for the *Montgomery Advertiser*. He agrees with Sanders and Boynton that blacks have used their new access to the ballot advantageously. But, as is the case in Tuskegee, whites are rarely willing to form biracial coalitions, or accept situations in which blacks dominate policies. He says that some whites feel the mass advent of blacks into politics is the result of unfair conditions imposed upon them (whites) by a hostile federal government. "When the federal government says, 'Do something,' they say 'Stick it,' " Benn laughed. "People don't like to be told what they can or cannot do."

"Well then," I asked, "will there be a massive white exodus if blacks win parity—or more political power than they have now?"

"I can't see that," Benn replied. "The economic base in the Belt is still white. If interracial cooperation doesn't work out, then they'll say, 'You go your way, we'll go ours.' They'll double-tax themselves for segregated academies if need be.

"But as for their leaving, I don't see that happening. Selma and Dallas County will always dominate the Black Belt because this is the most heavily populated county. And it is interesting to see what has happened to the black vote as registration increases: It's breaking into factions. Just like white folks. A winning black candidate now has to pick up at least a few white votes. The answer to it all in Alabama, as far as I'm concerned, is the need of both races to respect each other, and there needs to be more than just tokenism."

"More than tokenism?"

"Well, when blacks took over the Dallas County Commission [three blacks, two whites], heads rolled. Whites were fired left and right; and blacks hired. Lately, there have been some compromises."

We were conversing on a Saturday morning in the *Advertiser*'s storefront Selma office, next to the Pettus Bridge. Benn was in his late forties, I would guess, was dressed casually, and was very forthcoming. On the question of race, I would consider him an enlightened realist. I had been closely reading his excellent articles on the Alabama Black Belt in the *Advertiser*. We strolled outside to take pictures of the bridge and the state historical markers commemorating the Great March and the Selma Movement.

"Do you think that is the great fear among whites," I asked, "that blacks in black majority areas will enter the game, take over, and treat whites the way blacks were treated for a hundred years?"

"Well, that's certainly the fear in the school systems," Benn replied evenly. "Whites are saying, 'You got it, now you run with it, and good-bye. We've got our academies and country clubs, we're never going to see you people, you're not gonna get any money from us when you have a bake sale or rummage sale or for whatever you need no matter what you need.' This is what is happening in Wilcox County. That county is so poor some families give their kids toilet paper to take to school. That's a shame after all we've come through."

The road to the town of Marion in Perry County snakes slightly northwestward along a two-lane highway, passing small farms that appear as isolated as one can get in the American South. Born and raised in the city with its noises and constant, rushing stream of activity and violence, I am always amazed at how peaceful rural places can be, invoking another, earlier time.

I was going to Marion to talk with Albert Turner, the best-known Perry County organizer during and since the civil rights movement, who's now one of the three blacks on the five-member County Commission. I had called ahead, and Turner was expecting me. I followed Highway 80 west to Marion Junction, which turns out to be just a name for a crossroads. Now I was on the bumpy state rural Route 45, about to complete the twenty-mile drive from Selma.

As I entered Marion, I could see that it was considerably smaller than Selma, but it looked wealthy. There are two major well-kept white educational institutions, Marion Institute, a junior college, which I passed on my way to the courthouse, and Judson College—both pre-Civil War institutions, evidence of a long prosperity. But I also knew that Marion was home to the historic black Lincoln School, established by a Union officer during Reconstruction and maintained until the 1950s as a center of education in Alabama by the American Missionary Association of the Congregational Church.

It wasn't difficult to locate the courthouse; all roads led to it. Turner had said he would meet me in the courthouse, and told me to "just ask anyone where I am"; but he was nowhere to be found, and when I asked a black police officer, he said he hadn't seen him. When I called his home he was there, and he gave me directions for the half mile or so ride to his house.

When I arrived at Turner's home, situated on a slight hill, I had to find my way to an entrance; an addition was in construction. Turner seemed to be working his way through the inconvenience. A burly, heavyset man who exudes strength, Turner explained, as he introduced me to his wife and seated me in his den, that six years ago his home was burned in a mysterious fire, a fire the Turners believe was arson. They were just now in the process of rebuilding. Both Turner and his wife were key Black Belt organizers, who were indicted in a high-profile federal voting fraud case in 1985 over the issue of absentee ballots in Greene County. They and the others indicted with them were acquitted of all charges. It was during this time that the fire occurred.

Turner is a native of Perry County, born in 1936. He said he can trace back three generations of his family in Perry County. "This is an unusual county," he emphasized. "I believe someone said, at some point in this century there were more blacks with Ph.D.s in Perry than in all of native black South Carolina. Alabama State [the black state college in Montgomery] originated right here at Lincoln School."

I mentioned the prosperity I observed in my short drive through Marion leading to and from the courthouse. The Turners lived on a "black" street of attractive homes, though none were mansions. "Yes," he agreed. "There's been black and white prosperity here beginning with Reconstruction. But the whites *were* very oppressive in their efforts to subdue black assertiveness, because we here were aggressive and independent in Marion. Our whole struggle has been to regain what we lost after Reconstruction and protect it through the ballot.

"My activism stems from my father; he wasn't the average black person. I was not born in Marion but in the rural area a few miles west of here. My father was a little bit revolutionary. He owned his own land and so did his father. He started his own school bus system so we and other kids in our settlement could go to school in Marion. He attended Lincoln and so did his children. Lincoln was both our elementary school and high school, though after a while the high school was dropped. I went on to Alabama A&M in Huntsville, where I graduated.

"There's a difference between blacks who were raised in the plantation system, and those who owned their own land," he carefully explained, echoing the theme so elaborately developed in Albany. "Independence in your family history *means something*, no matter how oppressive people are around you. I've never seen myself as inferior. I never had to work for whites and all that. My activism through all these years comes from that family history of independence. Our family had twelve brothers and sisters, and we *all* went to college. My daddy *believed* in education and religion. You *had* to go to church and school to live in his house."

Turner related what Perry County was like when he returned home from college in the 1950s. "Number one, I couldn't vote. No blacks were registered, not one, despite the history of education in the county. So we formed the Perry County Voters League. We were faced with the same obstructions as they were in Dallas County—constitutional interpretation tests and vouchers. In Perry County three persons to act as personal vouchers per applicant were required, even if you passed the written test. When we tried to prepare people to take the test, they changed the tests on us, which made it impossible to teach the information required. The registrars made up about three hundred tests—or I should say, they were made for them since the registrars only had a sixth grade education themselves. When you came to register, they would tell you, 'Open that book.' *Wherever* you opened the book, that was your test. For ten years no one passed; no blacks were registered until 1965."

Turner was the leader of the contingent that bused down to Selma from Marion the morning of March 7, 1965, to begin the intended March to Montgomery that ended up with the violence on the Pettus Bridge. "You could trace the 1965 Voting Rights Act right here to Marion," Turner said, smiling. "It all had to do with the terrible beatings we suffered on the night of February seventeenth, and the killing of Jimmy Lee Jackson. On the Sunday morning of March seventh, three hundred to four hundred people left for Selma from Marion—by ten A.M. we were at Brown's Chapel waiting for church to end and the Selma contingent to congregate."

Andrew Young had come over from Atlanta that morning carrying instructions from a concerned Dr. King, who was scheduled to preach at Ebenezer Baptist Church in Atlanta. King told Young to cancel the march, realizing that more time was needed to adequately prepare for it. When Young arrived at the Pettus Bridge from the Montgomery airport, he was shocked to see the large number of Alabama state troopers gathered on the Montgomery side of the bridge, preparing, it seemed, to put down a major insurrection. But when he arrived at Brown's Chapel, he was equally shocked to see the large number of people waiting to march; worse, Turner told him, there was no way he could return to Marion without at least attempting a march, that is, if SCLC ever expected his people to march with them again. "I told Andy if SCLC didn't want to lead us, I would march by myself just with the people from Marion. We were crazy enough to think we were going all the way to Montgomery. We had left Marion with backpacks full of clothing and food—our people were fired up." It didn't take long for Young to gauge the mood. He put in a call to King at Ebenezer to explain the situation, and King reluctantly agreed that, under the circumstances, they should go forward.

"I knew I would be in the front line, and so would John Lewis, of SNCC, by his own choice. The question was whether Hosea Williams or Andy Young would also be in the front line. They flipped a coin and Hosea lost. By the time we started out in columns of twos for the bridge, I realized, from all the information we were receiving from our people on the other side, that we were going to get beat up. The only thing I wasn't sure about was whether we would get killed. I'll admit that the bulk of the marchers didn't know what might happen; only the leaders knew. I have never been more fearful than I was that Sunday. But we had to go."

Turner was in the second row of leaders when the marchers reached the eastern foot of the bridge and the charge by the troopers began. "I wasn't hurt," he emphasized. "I was a football player at Alabama A&M, so when I saw them charging, I went into a three-point stance, pushed forward myself, and I actually split the line of troopers. When I hit them, they parted; in fact, I bowled several troopers over. Their idea was to push everyone back into the line behind them so that our people would be knocked to the ground and easier to beat up." At this point, Turner rose from his leather seat, demonstrated his football stance, and showed me how he actually ended up behind the police charge.

"Once I got myself together, I worked myself back to the peak of the bridge where most of our people were retreating from the beatings. I was concerned that we get the women together in a circle, and protect them with an outer circle of men. The troopers didn't cross that. And they weren't going to beat the men, either. That's when they tear-gassed us. Slowly, keeping that circle, we retreated down the bridge. We were very careful, as organizers, to keep our people from panicking, running off, and getting injured or killed."

As they moved back toward Brown's Chapel, the troopers, on foot and horseback, beat them. Some of the marchers ran into homes in the Carver projects for safety, and some of the troopers actually entered the projects in wild pursuit. "Then we almost had a war, because people in the projects had shotguns. Andy helped keep the situation under control in the projects."

Out of this disaster, of course, was forged the final triumphant March to Montgomery, and the Voting Rights Act of 1965. "As a result of all this," Turner concluded, repeating the same refrain as his Selma contemporaries, "we did well in politics but we don't own a thing more than our own homes. And the whites down here want to take back the political gains we've made."

⁓

Having heard so much about the small towns surrounding Selma, and how integral they were to conditions in the Alabama Black Belt, I decided to take a weekend driving tour to view some of them. First of all, I wanted to explore Lowndes County directly to the east of Dallas County, situated between Selma and Montgomery.

Lowndes County occupies a distinct place in civil rights lore because of courageous organizing in that infamously repressive county by SNCC in the wake of the Selma marches. By 1965, Lowndes County had become so stigmatized for wanton killings and violence against blacks, it was nicknamed "Bloody Lowndes." Lowndes closely paralleled Dallas in its cotton plantation, heavy-slave-majority economy and Black Belt history during the antebellum, Civil War, Reconstruction, and Redemption periods, but its black community, of course, lacked Selma's educational institutions and large churches that after Emancipation helped break the fall into total helplessness and dependency. Independently or defiantly inclined blacks in Lowndes had to get out if they expected to live.

In 1960, Lowndes was one of the poorest counties in the nation, with a median per capita annual income of $1,364 (for blacks it was $935), the lowest in Alabama and half that of Dallas County. There was no hospital, nursing home, or ambulance services, and only two physicians and two dentists. Though 81 percent of the county population of roughly fifteen thousand were black, not a single black was registered to vote; none had been registered in the entire twentieth century. With the encouragement of SNCC workers, by 1966 and 1967, blacks had largely overcome their fear, were meeting openly, and were organizing a political effort under the names of the Lowndes County Freedom Organization, the Black Panther party, and finally, the Democratic party. The Black Panther symbol was adopted as a means of easy identification on voting machines. The name was used later by the militant California faction. John Hulett, a veteran labor and civil rights activist in Birmingham who returned to his native Lowndes in 1959, became the first black to register in April 1965. Once the gate was opened a bit, a rush of black registrants followed suit, particularly after the passage of the Voting Rights Act.

But these early efforts were not without sacrifice. The execution-style killing of Jonathan Daniels, a white theological student working with SNCC in the county seat of Hayneville in August 1965, and the quick acquittal of his murderer, was a frightening example of the extreme white reaction to the unprecedented attempt by blacks to assert themselves.

Now, twenty-five years later, John Jackson, a founding member of the Lowndes County Freedom Organization, is mayor of the village of White Hall, and blacks have won various offices in the county. John Hulett, the most prominent early black Lowndes leader, was elected sheriff in 1970, and remains so today.

I drove to Benton, where the Alabama River curves into U.S. 80, to take an offshoot back road, Alabama State Highway 40, which parallels 80 to the north. At Benton there is a sign marking the Holy Ground Battlefield, the site of a village where the Creeks were crushed in 1815 during their last-gasp rebellion, canonized as a landmark in the steady beat of American expansion. Route 40 led to a state park built along the Alabama River; a very nice one, I thought, and well used on this Saturday afternoon by picnicking blacks and whites; families using the same park in such close proximity would have been unthinkable in the old days. If there was only one park, blacks would have been excluded or a high wire fence would have been erected to "separate the races," as segregation was so delicately described.

As I drove eastward toward the village of White Hall, I was surprised by the amount of traffic hurrying along this tiny, two-lane back road. U.S. 80 did not seem to be used for local traffic; Highway 40 is a much more direct route to and from people's rural homes.

White Hall turned out to be not much more than a junction with Highway 23, which runs north and south. The city hall of White Hall is a one-story building, and it was closed. I would have liked to meet John Jackson, since he was such a key organizer in the first Lowndes County black political efforts, and is still here today providing a quarter century of continuity. I pulled into the side parking lot and peered into the windows of the white-frame building with a brick-veneered front. A small palm on the front lawn. All the city departments appeared to be in this structure—health, taxes, police.

I wondered what it was like to be mayor of a small place like this. I imagined it was like being superintendent of a large apartment building in New York—taking care of the fuel, air conditioning, water, and sundry other necessities and complaints brought to you by tenants, and collecting the rent. Not as owner of the building, but as superintendent, caught between the interests of the owner and the concerns of the tenants. Not much fun. And the salary isn't that great. Of course, now when the tenants come with their complaints, most of them can at least face someone who looks like them, and has shared their experiences. Could we say that's improvement?

The shock of seeing blacks in positions of authority in city halls of large cities is now wearing off, but in the tiny villages of the Deep South, the very blood cells of the South as we knew it, the experience is still new for both blacks and whites, including the officeholders themselves. In fact, such political offices have the danger of seeming to hold more power than they actually do. I wondered, for instance, how the whites who own and operate Lowndes County relate to this black city hall. From what Alvin Benn had told me, I gathered not at all. The new political reality does not seem to have prevented the perpetuation of two separate worlds that only rarely rub against each other. In the state park, blacks and whites were sitting right next to each other, but not interacting. In the village halls, blacks now have a few of the jobs, but the economic power structure of the region remains unchanged.

As I left White Hall, I passed a black club off to the right blaring sounds of the blues that drifted out to the highway. The music sounded great, so I circled around, crossed the railroad tracks paralleling the road, and took a gravel road to return to the bar.

"Not a jukebox," the owner replied to my question. He was alone. "Just the radio." I ordered a soft drink. He was a blues enthusiast, I deduced from the posters on the wall. "From these parts?" he asked, though of course he knew I wasn't, from the minute I opened my mouth. "From New Orleans," I answered. "Just passing through." When I finished my drink, I left, but I liked his place and I liked the fact he didn't want to know too much about where I was from or where I was going. Didn't seem to concern him.

Where Highway 40 loops back to an intersection with U.S. 80, I came upon the village of Lowndesboro. I was amazed at the size of the Greek revival homes there. The clay is beet-red, a startling image of riches in the midst of poverty and of the red dirt at the core of the Black Belt. A historical marker reveals the dry facts of Lowndesboro's saga: settled before 1820 by planters from South Carolina and Virginia; first called McGill's Hill. Incorporated in 1832 as Lowndesboro in honor of William Lowndes, a South Carolina plantation owner. Site of a brief Civil War skirmish between Nathan Bedford Forrest's fleeing troops and Wilson's raiders on April 10, 1865. Apparently the grand homes I saw are surviving King Cotton plantations from before the Civil War; it was this old-line economic strength that made any attempts by local blacks and poor whites to better their condition so unlikely, so seemingly impossible, though it was not the rich planters who stood in the courthouse door to turn away blacks. They could hire poor whites to do that.

~

I decided to skip Hayneville, south of U.S. 80, and instead return to Selma to take U.S. 41 southward to Wilcox County. Camden, the county seat of Wilcox, was where Bruce Boynton said he was beaten by a sheriff's deputy at the courthouse, where Alvin Benn said the school board, now controlled by blacks, was in charge of a school system so poverty-stricken that students have to bring their own toilet paper to school. Camden and Wilcox County were much maligned by blacks as a hellhole of racism in pre-Movement days. Like Lowndes, Wilcox County had no blacks registered before 1965.

The drive southward to Camden was extremely hilly and winding, with precariously narrow shoulders. It is a picturesque trip, the highway roughly paralleling the extremely wide Alabama River southwestward from Selma, though you cannot see the river from the road. The quality of the highway suddenly improved when I entered Wilcox County; I didn't expect that. After a drive of about forty-five minutes, I arrived in Camden. There was a white policeman sitting in his patrol car, like a sentry at the crossroads stoplight every motorist has to pass to enter into town. I braked carefully, then turned right onto the road into town, halfway expecting the policeman to follow me once he noticed my Louisiana license plates. There was no movement from the comfortable sentry post, however. This was just any old Saturday afternoon in the summer of 1991, not 1951. In 1951, I would have been followed by the policeman and probably stopped. I would have had to know someone in town or have ready an acceptable story explaining what I was doing there; then, the police still overtly thought of themselves as overseers and slave patrols when it came to blacks. Blacks "off the plantation" were considered vagrants; vagrancy was a crime.

There wasn't much to Camden, just hills and valleys along the winding drive of less than a mile to the courthouse, which also serves as jail and town library. What I saw of the black community looked poverty-stricken, but what I noticed even more was a kind of desolate isolation; isolation, possibly because Camden was so cut off from everywhere and it looked it. Maybe fifty years ago you had to drive through Camden to get to the Gulf—Pensacola or Mobile—from Selma, but not anymore. All southbound automobile or truck traffic used I-65 between Montgomery and Mobile. White Hall, for instance, seemed less isolated. After driving around Camden for a half hour or so, I didn't find anything interesting. I drove out on Alabama Highway 10 toward Greenville for a few miles. The land is rural, heavily forested, much different from the Selma area, which is flatter, cultivated farmland.

I doubled back to Camden and decided to explore a road to the Roland Cooper State Park. That park also sits along the Alabama River; it seemed to be a wonderful boating site. Unlike at the Holy Ground Battlefield, there was hardly anyone in Cooper except a few people on the riverbank; I didn't see any blacks. I parked for a while just to rest and take in the serenity and the river. I couldn't get anything on the radio; I had found a perfectly dead spot.

In fact, Selma, too, seemed to be in a dead radio spot, its AM stations dominated by church and gospel music, both black and white versions. There was almost nothing worth listening to on the FM dial. In his autobiography, Chestnut laments the cultural isolation of Selma. As a big jazz fan, it must be hard for him.

In the Sanders/Chestnut office the secretaries were listening to a station from Linden, about sixty miles to the southwest, upon one of my visits. A Marion gospel announcer, I noticed, began his morning show with prayers for everyone including baby-sitters, "that they may properly take care of their charges." One morning I was able to pick up the world news from Radio Australia on my shortwave on Band 3 at 955.

Finally, as dusk slowly set in, I returned to Selma, following the same route that brought me southward.

The next day, a Sunday, I drove westward on U.S. 80 to Uniontown and Demopolis, two Black Belt towns smaller than but similar to Selma. I was shocked by Uniontown, located in a bottom pocket of Perry County. Uniontown looks as worn-out as Camden; the mansions and cemeteries seemed to suffer from neglect. There was not a trace of economic vibrancy, not even a McDonald's or a fried chicken joint. Off the highway, south of 80, I was surprised to come across housing projects; I suppose they're everywhere. It seemed that everyone who could get out of Uniontown had left.

(When I later mentioned my impressions of Uniontown to Chestnut, he was not generous in his assessment of the town's black mayor. "He and I have totally different philosophies," he offered. "He's always thought he could work with and use whites. I've always thought at best you can reach some sort of quid pro quo with whites. His attitude goes back to slavery. There's still blacks who believe white folks have what it takes, and that blacks just don't. Some of these people are politicians. But in my opinion, if you don't really believe in your people, you don't have any business holding public office.")

I drove on toward Demopolis, a distance of about thirty miles or more, a crossroads town at the confluence of the Black Warrior and Tombigbee rivers. From Demopolis the Tombigbee snakes southward until it flows into the Alabama River north of Mobile. The drive westward is smooth and flat through luscious cultivated land, a drive not overly burdened by truck traffic this Sunday afternoon.

Demopolis appeared far more sprightly than Uniontown. It even seemed to have retained an active downtown business district. There was Greek-revival architecture similar to that of Lowndesboro, well-kept mansions with massive white columns. Demopolis is larger than Uniontown, about half the size of Selma, I guessed. I smiled at the sign advertising the LILY WHITE CLEANERS, situated across the street from worn-brick housing projects. There was a town square with the obligatory

Civil War statue, a soldier armed with musket beside a cannon and a plaque that read, TO OUR CONFEDERATE DEAD. It almost seemed as if the same enterprising salesman had worked every southern town of sufficient size, selling exactly the same monument with almost exactly the same inscription. Near the downtown square I saw a beautiful plum-colored house; someone had an imagination. I didn't see a soul downtown, not even a sheriff's deputy. I noticed the River Insurance Agency, specializing in "life, health, happiness, and prearranged funerals." Why leave anything to chance? Before heading back to Selma, I stopped for a cup of coffee in a Waffle House, this one managed by a black woman, the only franchised restaurant I came across with a black manager during my entire journey.

Demopolis looked peaceful, but it had not been hospitable to blacks in the old days, I learned later. In the 1960s it was home to the Grand Dragon of the Alabama Klan. And Amelia Boynton, in her book *Bridge Across Jordan*, tells a story of being refused lodging at a motel in 1964 after she went there to speak, and of being virtually run out of town by the sheriff.

A week or so later I visited the town of Eutaw, the seat of Greene County a few miles northwest of Demopolis, for the annual Black Belt Folk Roots Festival. Eutaw and Greene County became an organizing target of black activists from all over the South as early as the late 1960s. Economic co-ops and cultural activities were a fundamental part of the Greene County effort, as was the work of the Federation of Southern Cooperatives, in attempting to build economic strength. By 1991 blacks had achieved considerable political success in the county, electing a probate judge and several county commissioners and school board members. There was also a black sheriff. This success began in 1969, prior to the shift to single-district elections.

The idea of blacks enjoying themselves with blues and barbecues on the grounds of this former fortress of southern white supremacy was probably revolutionary in itself, I thought, as I walked around the courthouse square. The guitarist played and sang while children ran and played near the courthouse plaque, which informs us that the county was named for Revolutionary War hero Nathanael Greene. (Greensboro, North Carolina, where I began my journey, is named for the same general. Eutaw is named for Eutaw Springs, South Carolina, the site of one of Greene's encounters with the British. No doubt, a planter emigrating from South Carolina in search of cotton riches had sought to implant his memories of South Carolina firmly in the soil of west Alabama.)

Greene County became part of the westernmost Alabama Black Belt, another land of cotton richness built on slave labor. Now, for the first time, the descendants of slaves are beginning, through the availability of the ballot, to make their voices heard in Greene County.

I introduced myself to a group of friendly women sitting along a row of picnic tables and food booths; they were selling fried chicken, potato salad, ribs, cakes, colorful artificial flowers, and whatever else they had prepared for the occasion. When I brought up the subject of change in racial politics, the most outspoken lady was in no mood for self-congratulation. "We're just tryin'," she remarked. "Got a long way to go. Progress," she added, with a laugh as much for herself as for me, "is slow." Almost all the shops surrounding the town square on this Saturday afternoon were closed. "Do any blacks own stores downtown?" I asked. "Just two," she answered. "And we have a black-owned county newspaper."

Later I took a drive to the outskirts of town to see Greenetrack, the seemingly extremely lucrative greyhound racing track. It was almost time for the gates to open at 7:00 P.M.; traffic was thickening on the heavily traveled Interstate 59, which connects Eutaw with Meridian, Mississippi, to the west and Tuscaloosa and Birmingham to the east. The greyhound track is owned by the county: Blacks pretty much run it; whites and blacks come from miles away to bet on the dogs, and, like a new, brightly lit casino, it has generated a brace of inexpensive satellite stores and fast-food chains. The road leading to the track from I-59 is named Martin Luther King Memorial Highway.

Driving back into town I came across more housing projects. There was a festive air. People were happily gathered outside their compounds and in the streets, as if sharing the holiday celebration taking place at the courthouse. Actually, seeing them close up, these weren't such bad-looking projects. As I passed the county jail, I saw some youngsters who seemed to be waiting to enter; I wondered if they were prisoners released for the afternoon or if they were merely going to visit incarcerated friends and family.

I drove by Eutaw's strikingly aristocratic Presbyterian Church. Most Presbyterian and Episcopal churches in small southern towns are quite elegant—they are the bastions of the upper class. I passed the office of the Greene County Historical Society, which, I suppose, is another stronghold of the present—or former—ruling class in this time of shifting versions of what we call history. The Greene County Riding Club. Impressive homes. Leaving town, on the road southward to Demopolis, Highway 43, I passed through a black neighborhood of prosperous-looking brick homes.

Camden and Uniontown had looked decidedly run-down, as if time had passed them by. Demopolis, Marion, and Eutaw seemed to be a little better off. Even from a quick glance, unbelievably extreme racial and class income disparities were apparent in Lowndesboro and Lowndes County in general.

～

As I was returning to Selma, it occurred to me that I really did not see large numbers of people—in the fields, in front of their houses, or on the roads—in Dallas, Perry, Lowndes, and Wilcox counties. My overall impression was one of isolation. And there didn't seem to be evidence of people working, either agricultural work or factory work. Of course, that is exactly the harsh reality testified to by Chestnut, Hank Sanders, and Alvin Benn in their comments. It seems as if the initial elation over black political success in the region has been followed by the harsh, sober reality that the electorate that has brought these new politicians to office is still, nonetheless, economically impotent—under- or unemployed. But there is a startling contradiction within this depressing pattern—a few blacks, particularly those with education, training, and political contacts or contracts, are faring better than ever, while the majority of blacks, those without education or marketable skills, have slipped backward into a seemingly inflexible pattern of dependency. The unskilled or minimum physical labor jobs on the farm or in the towns that used to employ many people hardly seem to exist anymore.

In *Black Reconstruction in America*, W. E. B. Du Bois observed that "Sumner and Stevens saw that the Negro needed land and education and that his vote would only be valuable to him as it opened the doors to a firm economic foundation and real intelligence." Blacks never did acquire enough land during Reconstruction or afterward to protect themselves from the ravages of Redemption, but as Albert Turner and others pointed out, in communities where there *was* sufficient ownership of land, like the one where Turner was raised, black activism and security were much more evident. I understood Chestnut and Hank Sanders and Rickey Hill in Orangeburg to be saying that the obverse has not proved to be true—that is, the vote has not so far "opened the doors" to economic strength except for a fortunate few. The ballot alone, devoid of economic strength, has proved to be of limited value. In fact, a widening chasm is developing between the "haves" and the "have-nots" even *within* the race, a chasm already present, as everyone testified to in every town I visited beginning in Greensboro, thereby eroding the Movement concept—or myth—of one black community unified by a common interest in overcoming the barriers to full citizenship, despite differences in education or income.

What factors brought about this disturbing state of affairs? For one thing, farming by 1990 having become heavily automated has fundamentally changed agriculture in the Black Belt. Machines now do the work of field laborers at less expense. Large numbers of people working the cotton fields, despised as the work was, are now a relic of the past. The few new jobs in this region are either directly or indirectly political. Because elected political posts, appointments, and contracts are limited, it is also natural that as more blacks enter the electoral process, competition for the black vote results in a dogfight for the available spoils, as was the case in Tuskegee and Macon County. (In Macon County, Tuskegee Institute blacks and Veterans Hospital blacks fought each other for political control of the county once the door to the ballot swung completely open.) This may be inevitable, but when such intraracial political warfare occurs, who represents the interests of those on the bottom of the economic scale? Having been exposed to little education up to now, it's understandable that blacks economically trapped by the obsolescence of their skills are not capable of converting to a new, service-based, high-tech economy.

As a result of these developments, many former agricultural laborers have left the small towns for the larger towns or the big cities of the South in search of work, in a later version of the historic migration to the cities that began in the early twentieth century. It is the same process we saw on a minor but steady scale in Albany. Had large numbers of blacks remained in the fields as laborers, there is the possibility that some of them, as a result of the changes in the political order, might have become small landowners and householders. The results of the migration to larger towns, however, have been consistently unrewarding. There are few new opportunities for employment in cities like Birmingham, Montgomery, Memphis, Atlanta, or Albany for immigrants without high-tech skills. Such people either end up on governmental assistance, which is becoming ever more grudging, or become entrapped in even worse fates like the underground world of drugs and crime. Who among the new black politicians is speaking for them? What is going to happen to these people? Will the nineteenth-century idea of African colonization to solve the American race problem, so popular among northern political leaders including Abraham Lincoln, reappear in the twenty-first century as a way of dealing with blacks and other minorities who are considered economically useless? As I understand it, in several of his conversations with visitors, including Frederick Douglass, concerning the fate of the newly freed slaves, Lincoln expressed the opinion that large numbers of ex-slaves would never be accepted in America. He seemed to believe African repatriation would be the most desirable and humane solution, though Lincoln was assassinated before his policies on the status of African Americans could be fully developed.

Finally, blacks have had little success in entering the private sector even when they have adequate education and training. The only exception might be businesses that directly or indirectly serve the federal government. Other new economic opportunities would, of course, result from the creation of new black businesses. But new businesses are always a risky venture requiring available capital, not to mention education, in the broadest sense of the word.

Actually, in Selma and in the surrounding towns, I didn't see any evidence of new white businesses, either. Poor whites may be somewhat better off than poor blacks, but changes in the southern economy have also affected them negatively. It just seems to be the peculiar misfortune of blacks that at the very time they are achieving historic political gains, changes brought about by a long struggle for the ballot, the economy of the Deep South has shifted away from labor-intensive work, and away from small independent farms and businesses. It's as if, after decades of trying to get in, the door to the southern "big house" of economics has finally swung open a bit, with blacks, peeking their heads in, greeted with a "Nice to see you, but, sorry, we're just moving. It's not by choice, you understand; it's the ever-changing trends of economics. We have to stay on top of things. Sorry."

⌒

It is from this perplexing and uneven state of progress, or lack thereof, that the dispute that broke out in the Selma public schools in 1990 must be viewed. For if there is any remedy for altering the prevailing economic condition of blacks, it must come through education and training. In this increasingly technological age, education is more than ever the treasured key to employability, not only for those on the bottom who face an awful future of permanent unemployability except, maybe, as mules for the drug industry, but also for those with the most promise, if they're going to be able to maximize that promise in an age of global economics and rapid changes in the way we view the world.

It is not surprising that a conflict over schools exploded in Selma. Selma's black community has a rich history of activism, and Selma occupies a central economic and political role within the Black Belt. The law firm of Chestnut, Sanders and Sanders—called derisively "the Jeff Davis crowd" (because their office is on Jefferson Davis Avenue)—was quite willing to play the role of protagonist in the controversy, and did not hesitate to wage a bitter, contentious dispute by challenging the school board.

⌒

From the days of Reconstruction, blacks, eager for education, founded their own schools as extensions of their political, economic, and church activities. This was accomplished with the extremely valuable assistance of sympathetic whites, particularly those who saw the education of freedmen and freedwomen as an extension of their religious mission. By the early twentieth century the South had begun to establish public school systems, particularly in urban areas, to accomplish the task of primary and secondary education, replacing most, but not all, of the private church-affiliated schools. Though public schools for black southerners were terribly underfunded, such schools, which were almost all administered and taught by blacks, served to further the educational tradition begun under church schools despite the obvious drawbacks of segregation.

Today, the new desegregated public schools have inherited the historical task of educating black children. But in all the towns I visited, there were complaints expressed by blacks about those schools. The first and most common strategy after *Brown* was an attempt by whites to postpone desegregation as long as possible. When federal court desegregation orders could no longer be evaded and elementary desegregation began—in most cases between 1965 and 1970—a large percentage of white students, as many as could afford it, fled the public school systems for newly created segregated private academies. In most places, that left the public schools to blacks and poor whites. The unstated caveat was that such "desegregated schools" were hardly a priority for public tax dollars, since whites didn't want to pay taxes for schools they had abandoned to blacks. Both black and white teachers and administrators tiptoed through the first period of integration, a time fraught with tenseness, unpleasantness, and extreme uncertainty about educational policies and biracial etiquette, even when there was absolute sincerity and goodwill on the part of those involved.

It is important to remember that the problems faced by both whites and blacks in trying to effect school desegregation were absolutely unprecedented—no experience in the history of the South could have prepared these communities for what they would face with school desegregation. Nor were they prepared for the frequent complaints by black administrators and coaches that now, under the new unified system, they had been relegated to subordinate roles while their white counterparts were rewarded with the senior positions just because they were white. There were also complaints that integration too often consisted of sending black students to the former white schools. The former black high schools were then relegated to the junior high school level, and often given a new name. These changes deprived the black community of a sense of historical continuity, the continuity of memories of fellow students and favorite teachers, athletic teams, graduations and proms, and public events, all of which are part of a rich school life. It is as if the price of integration was the discontinuity of black institutions. The rationale for proceeding in this way was certainly that the formerly white schools were larger and better equipped, but blacks complained that that wasn't their fault, and it seemed unfair to them that they had to pay for being historically shortchanged with the obliteration of their schools and their historical memorabilia.

In certain cases, in the larger urban areas, as in Greensboro and Charleston, the old black schools were retained, with an almost totally black student body and staff. But in those instances a county school had also been either built or enlarged in a predominantly white area with parents, black and white, given the option of registering their children in either school. Usually the county school ended up predominantly white, since few inner-city blacks could afford to send their children to a school in the suburbs, simply because of the distances involved. This system has been deemed acceptable under current federal rules. The county schools are often newer, being funded through county bond issues that arose after desegregation. In addition, with respect to various black objections to what was happening within the school system, one could hear whites complaining on talk shows all over the South, and in letters to the editors, that they had come a *long* way to adjust to desegregation, and at great cost to their traditions and mores and racial beliefs. Now blacks were saying they were *still* not satisfied. What on earth did they want?

These vastly different interpretations of what has transpired since *Brown* framed much of the discussion about schools as I traveled throughout the South in 1991, and were painfully present in the Selma dispute. During my entire journey I did not encounter any dispute as intensely felt as the arguments over school desegregation in Selma. Whites were particularly put out, because they felt they had made a genuine effort to retain white enrollment in the high school, rather than losing whites to the private academies, and they had been largely successful.

Selma was able to successfully postpone school desegregation until 1970, sixteen years after *Brown*. Desegregation in Selma followed the familiar pattern first established in Little Rock and New Orleans, whereby a few black kids were selected and assigned the role of sacrificial lamb to absorb the insult and fury of unyielding whites (mostly adults) upon their entrance into the formerly all-white school. These black children were almost always the offspring of parents who were active in the civil rights movement and who had volunteered the names of their children in the original class-action desegregation suit.

Jo Anne Bland, now in her thirties and working as coordinator of the Sanders'

Twenty-first Century Program, was in that first class of blacks chosen to integrate Selma High School, then called Parish High. As young teenagers, Ms. Bland and her friends were swept up into the excitement of 1965, attending meetings every night at Brown's Chapel, and joining demonstrations, including the infamous march of March 7, where she fainted on the bridge when the troopers attacked.

We talked over lunch at a restaurant just a few feet from the eastern foot of the bridge, where the beatings began. "My father told me I was to be a part of the integration team," she related. "It was *awful*. It was already traumatic enough just to be going to high school for the first time. To go to a place where you're not wanted by the students and teachers because they felt we were forced upon them made everybody unhappy. There were just eight of us, and sixteen hundred and ninety-two of them, dedicated to making our lives miserable. I cried every day. One kid spit on me every day. Every day I told the principal, and every day it didn't do any good.

"I told my father, who owned his own small taxi company, and he told me to follow that boy wherever he went if he spit on me again, and report him, but when I did, the boy would always deny it. Finally, in desperation, one day I left his spit on me as proof. I realized my teacher wasn't going to do anything. So I went to see the principal, who berated me for not being in class.

"So I ran to a pay phone and called my daddy. When he arrived at school, I was hysterical. He stormed into the principal's office with me in tow and the principal said, 'Wait just a minute. You don't just walk into my office.' That made my father angry. They went 'round and 'round until the principal calmed Daddy down enough for them to talk. So the principal sends for the kid and he denies it again. Then I started crying and my father got mad again. So he beat up the kid and then beat up the principal until the secretaries called the police.

"The police came and took Daddy to jail. So I was left there alone. I called another driver to come get Daddy's taxi, and later they got him out of jail. But I noticed from then on, I *never* had the problems I had before. Whenever I had a complaint, the principal *did* something. But it was tough."

Though the really nasty experiences might have been limited to the first year or so, there was, from the beginning, a smoldering discontent on the part of the black community in Selma about the entire process of school desegregation. The complaints, according to Chestnut, centered around three issues. First, blacks had problems with the composition of the school board, which was all white in 1970, and the method by which the board was selected. Chestnut describes the board selection process as "self-perpetuating." That is, when members left the board, successors were chosen by the board, under an 1890 law. Blacks felt that new board members were chosen from the same circle of upper-class whites, so there was never anyone who identified with their interests. Sanders and Chestnut filed suit against the procedure, a case they eventually won in 1976. The legal victory didn't amount to much, however, because the new arrangement shifted the power to appoint school board members to the Selma City Council, which Chestnut, Sanders, and everyone else I spoke to in Selma feel is controlled by Mayor Smitherman. Selma school board members, they argue, are always subject to unusual political pressure.

Generally speaking, the composition of southern school boards was an early target of the black electorate as it flexed its muscles, because such boards control not only educational policy, but the allocation of school funding and the awarding of contracts and services, some of which are quite lucrative. And such contracts are almost always awarded to white firms.

The second issue of contention had to do with the naming of a white principal for the new Selma High instead of the black principal of the former black high school, who had greater seniority. In the mid-1970s Sanders and Chestnut urged the black principal to sue, and though at first he was reluctant, he finally did so and won. He served one year as principal of Selma High before retiring.

Third, and more portentous, the black community expressed unhappiness with what they perceived as a practice of "leveling," arranging students into three distinct academic tiers—high academic, general, and vocational—though this was never official school board policy. As far back as the seventies, according to Chestnut, black parents had charged that too many of their students were being assigned to the middle and lower levels, and an unjustifiably large percentage of white students were being assigned to the upper level. But until the eighties, the question of leveling was not persistently pursued, mostly because there was no easy or concrete means to get at the issue, to determine criteria.

Such was the situation in 1987 when, after a national job search, the Selma school board took what seemed to be an unusual and unexpected step in the direction of racial amity by hiring a black superintendent, Norward Roussell of New Orleans. Roussell was eminently qualified. In his mid-forties, he was a graduate of Dillard University, and had received his Ph.D. from Wayne State University. He also had fourteen years of experience as a teacher and administrator in the New Orleans public school system.

I was quite surprised to find Roussell still living in Selma. The decision of the Selma school board not to renew his contract had flared into such a contentious public issue, polarizing the community racially and bringing Selma considerable national notoriety, that I thought he and his family would have been long gone with a hearty "Good riddance" to this country place, which in every way was the antithesis of New Orleans. But he and his wife were still there, running a convenience store on U.S. 80 just after the westward turn. They both greeted me warmly as fellow travelers from the Big Easy, as we call New Orleans, though I had never met them before. Roussell quickly agreed to talk, we set a time, and I interviewed him in the back room of his store.

Roussell is short, medium-dark skinned, heavily mustachioed, unsmiling, and quite the opposite of ingratiating, though I imagined he could be friendly with people he liked. He has a slightly "Creole" look—not only the color of his skin and type of hair, but a certain swagger of self-confidence—that I associate with New Orleans. He spoke informally and gruffly, with an assertiveness that must have startled Selmians both white and black, a forget-the-niceties-let's-get-on-with-the-business-at-hand attitude.

It was very clear from Roussell's first words that he was a well-informed person. "I had never visited Selma prior to taking this job," he began. "I knew it was a small town, but I believed there was a real opportunity here to show that you can have serious quality education in a town that had been so racially torn in the sixties and had been in the forefront of the civil rights movement. The name Selma means something. So I proceeded to embark on a course of changing things without fully understanding the dynamics of what had happened here. Without understanding that what happened in 1965 had affected the politics of Selma, but it had *not* affected the attitudes and mind-set of the residents."

I described to him my drive through the Black Belt, since the onset of my journey in Greensboro, my impressions of widespread idleness and poverty, and the disappointment of other blacks with the progress of black students in the new desegregated schools, and the lack of black cultural or community impact on those schools.

"Well," Roussell replied, "one of the things that made the transition difficult here, and which bothered me when I arrived, was the absence of any memorabilia from Hudson High, the old black school. It was hard to find even a trophy, a plaque, or anything like that; only written records and documents. I didn't think you could just wipe the historical slate clean like that. The outstanding teachers and coaches of those schools were role models for black youth, and played an important part in their education."

He and his twin brother, Norman, were raised in uptown New Orleans on Magnolia Street. Their father, Edward, was a former athlete, a baseball player in the Negro Leagues, who received his education "from travel." He died when the twins were only eight years old, but Norward remembers that his dad could outrun teenagers in the neighborhood, and he demanded respect. He was a vegetable dealer, operating a truck from the French Quarter markets; he eventually managed several other truck dealers, who drove through neighborhoods selling their wares. With his death, their mother had to raise the family, and though she had only a fourth-grade education, she wrote and spoke clearly, Norward remembers, and encouraged her children to follow through with their education. Norward and Norman attended Ricard Elementary School near their home, where both were quickly identified as outstanding students by their English teacher. From there they went to McDonough 35 High (the high school at the foot of Rampart Street), which prided itself on its academic reputation established by the principal, Lucien D. Alexis. "We were taught that we could exceed," remembers Norward. "There was no acceptance by our teachers that we were in any way limited in our ability to learn. We were expected to destroy the stereotype of black inferiority." Teachers encouraged the brothers to go to college, though no one in their family had ever attended college.

The Roussell twins did not enter college immediately; they joined the military for four years, serving in Korea between 1952 and 1956. When they were discharged, they were able to enter Dillard University in New Orleans on the GI Bill, which enabled so many needy young men, black and white, to attend college. Both graduated in 1960 with degrees in education. Both brothers took master's degrees in education from Fisk University in Nashville, then earned their doctorates from Wayne State University, Norward in 1973 in educational administration, Norman a year later in higher education administration. Norward worked for fourteen years in the public school system in New Orleans as a teacher, assistant principal, and finally as an assistant superintendent before he was selected as superintendent of the Selma system in 1987. Dr. Norman Roussell now serves as a vice president for administration at Loyola University in New Orleans.

The Roussell brothers are remarkable examples of what was possible under the old black elementary and secondary schools provided there was sufficient identification of talent and encouragement to push forward.

After a year or so on the job, Roussell said, he began to make some unsettling discoveries. He found out, for instance, that the board had never hired a black contractor in the entire history of the system. "At least not one who owned his own company. There had been black subcontractors for whites who were the contracting party. There was one instance when I recommended a black roofer who submitted a legal bid, a bid which was accepted by the architect who did the plan. The night of the board meeting his was the only bid and his offer was excellent. The white board members said, 'Well, we think we should have more bids.' Now, they knew every contractor in town had had a chance to bid. I said, 'I don't see any reason not to give him the contract and I am going to make the recommendation.' In the board meeting, that became a big issue for discussion. Finally, I had to say, 'The recommendation stands, and if you refuse to accept the bid then I would have to say to the man the only reason his bid was rejected was because he is a black company. And I don't think that's the kind of message we want to send out.' At that point they voted for it. School systems are also big business," he added. "So who gets the contracts can become a political issue, particularly when blacks are concerned."

"Did you seek out black contractors?" I asked him.

"I didn't seek out black contractors, but I made sure they were not excluded when we sent out bids. There were some white companies who also had never received bids from the school system."

"So it was a good ole boys system."

"The good ole boys system, the tight-knit thing—'I'm going to help you so you can help me.' And if you were not in that circle, white or black, you didn't get any help. And it didn't help that no blacks had ever worked in the business office of the school system."

"So all the contracts were handled by whites, even after desegregation?"

"Everything. Contracts, salaries, development of the budget, decisions on instructional supplies, all of that. I found that the historically white schools were much better equipped. For instance, in the white schools there were ten students to a computer. In the historically black schools you had a hundred students to a computer. When I got there, they had old dictionaries, old books, old desks, in the old black schools. I began to change all of that. I bought new furniture, maps and globes of equal quality. Some of their maps had only forty-eight states. This was in 1987!"

The conflict that brought Roussell down, key Selma blacks believe, was his decision to attack the system of "leveling," or the tracking of students into hierarchical groupings. "The Selma policy," Roussell said, "was something I was not told about. In the New Orleans system, we may have had a class of heterogeneous kids who learned at different rates. And we might group some of them together for, say, math or reading, but we didn't place a whole group of so-called fast learners together for all classes, or a whole class of medium-fast and a whole class of slow students together like they did here. I think this was done early on to keep whites in the system. Many of the well-to-do whites did not abandon the public school system when desegregation occurred, because their experience was always one of going to class with their peers, with other wealthy children. It worked the same way with teachers. Teachers considered upper-class, from that milieu, taught Level One classes. In fact, all of the Level One teachers at Selma High were white teachers. When I inquired about it, they said that was an accident."

"An accident?"

"Yes. Level One was supposed to be the college prep track. Now, the leveling wasn't so sharply applied in the elementary and the middle schools, but it certainly was at Selma High. And there was something else interesting about Selma High. In the usual grading system, A equals four points; B, three; C, two; and so forth. But for Level One students, A equaled five points. Since only ten percent of the Level One students were black, and the grades of Level One students were assigned *more* value, in the nineteen years since desegregation had begun there had been only one black valedictorian. This in a high school which was about sixty percent black."

"I suppose that would make sense if there are more white students in a position to receive grades of higher value."

"Yes, and this variable grading system was carried out to the lowest or vocational level; on Level Three, an A was worth only three points. So this grading system had a much more penetrating effect than people realized.

"For two years I studied the test scores in English for all students. I found there were students, both black and white, in Levels Two and Three whose scores in achievement were higher, significantly higher, than the scores and achievement of some of the students in Level One." This evidence proved, in Roussell's judgment, what black parents had been saying all along. He was careful to make it clear, though, that the basic rationale for this sort of preferential placement was the economic class and status of the student's family, not race. Of course, in most cases, though not all, there was a close correlation between racial and economic class lines.

"Leveling was bad in the first place, and made worse because it was misapplied," Roussell said. "And it made a difference, because when it came time to apply for college and to take the college entrance examinations, students on Levels Two and Three who had done well on those levels for their entire high school career suddenly discovered they had not taken courses which would enable them to do well on the college entrance test. For instance, they may have taken 'General Math,' 'Business Math,' 'Everyday Math'—that kind of foolishness. But they would not have had algebra or biology, which are necessary, and they certainly weren't exposed to calculus, foreign languages, or advanced literature courses, all of which stand you in good stead if you're going on to college.

"I challenged this system. In my judgment, this was clearly denying students the freedom to pursue the best educational opportunity the system had to offer, because they and their parents had no say-so about what courses they were taking."

"Who set up these levels in the first place?" I wondered.

"As far as I could learn, when desegregation occurred in 1970, the white principal of Selma High went to the board with a proposal. The proposal was never approved by the board. But somehow leveling began anyway, and it was well entrenched when I arrived in 1987. But it was always a sort of unofficial practice. Black teachers within the system knew what was going on, they had to, but I suppose they didn't want to buck the system and take on the issue. I guess they were so happy to be there at all, they didn't want to cause trouble. Also, it was the beginning of integration, which blacks had fought for so long; they might have been reluctant to be seen as continually bringing up complaints."

In a public board meeting in the summer of 1989, Roussell proposed that objective criteria be established for class levels, and that honors classes be opened up to more students at Selma High. Around the time Roussell was hired, a group of concerned black parents had organized themselves into a group they called Best Educational Support Team (BEST) with Bruce Boynton's wife, Alice, as chairperson, to monitor the schools. In 1987, BEST had written to the board requesting that all academic levels be eliminated. In fact, in my talk with Bruce Boynton at the courthouse, he had said that their daughter, a student at Selma High, had quietly informed him and his wife at the dinner table one night that she had been placed in Level 2 on a teacher's recommendation, though she felt she belonged on the top level. She complained, and was elevated to Level 1 without the involvement of her parents, who would certainly have intervened. But how many black kids would have a sufficient sense of self-worth and determination or the parental clout to lodge an effective complaint against being placed on too low a level, especially if Level 2 was comprised primarily of other blacks, who were their friends and so forth?

Roussell's rather modest proposal for opening up class levels hit Selma with the force of a lashing, tornado-warning thunderstorm. Intense discussions and arguments broke out during six months of meetings between black and white moderates in an attempt to find common ground. "There was disagreement between white and black Selma over whether race had anything to do with the levels," Chestnut notes in *Black in Selma*. A disagreement, I discovered later, that has not abated, and which is profoundly related to the harsh national debate over the validity and objectivity of test scores and what they might mean in terms of learning potential in different ethnic groups, or whether it makes sense to attempt such broad generalizations on the basis of test scores alone. "Virtually all white people said they didn't see anything racial about learning levels ... virtually all black people saw levelling as if not racist, racial ... the white community spoke ... of concern that classes would be watered down for children on the top if more blacks were included," Chestnut says. "The black community's concern was whether children in the (two) lower levels were being adequately placed, taught, and challenged. When white parents are saying one thing and black parents something else that alone should indicate that race is a central factor—in perspective if nothing else," Chestnut argues. Obviously, the biracial discussions did not produce a solution or common basis of understanding where leveling was concerned.

While this debate over the issue of leveling was raging, Roussell incurred the enmity of some blacks working within the system by transferring to other schools a few teachers and coaches who thought they should not be transferred, a move that had nothing to do with tracking. These actions seemed, in such an impassioned climate, to create a negative perception of Roussell's personality. Most whites, it seemed, and surely some blacks, considered Roussell too abrasive and arrogant in his administrative style, aside from the merits or demerits of his educational proposals. Asked about this, Roussell says matter-of-factly, "I trained and recruited some principals and teachers that I felt could make a significant difference in the system." I asked him if he felt he had the support of the system's administrative staff for the moves he had made.

"I believe so," he argued, "but it's hard to tell. You are dealing with a mentality of 'Whoever is in charge, that's who I support.' And certain blacks had their own little arrangements with the power structure. Certain blacks had jobs with important responsibilities, but they didn't exercise them," he added. "They were merely physically present. They never challenged the system just in terms of trying to exercise the authority they should have had. This had gone on for years."

"Among both blacks and whites?"

"Right. As for blacks, there is tremendous fear here ... racism breeds an awesome sense of fear among individuals that they must go along with the system to survive. ... The ordinary person here is tied into an institutional job or private industry that's still primarily dominated by white administrators and leadership."

In the late summer of 1989, in a private school-board committee meeting to evaluate the superintendent's performance, a newly appointed white board member moved that Roussell's contract not be renewed. The renewal of his three-year contract was scheduled to come up before the full board in December 1989. His contract was to expire in June 1990. A black board member defended Roussell in the committee meeting, according to reports Roussell heard later, and the move to release him was temporarily stalled.

Already highly sensitized, and concerned over the leveling debate, activists in the black community became incensed when they heard of the move to release Roussell. BEST and its supporters began organizing community rallies in support of Roussell's superintendency. Underscoring the intensifying conflict, which had now shifted to the issue of whether Roussell should be retained, was a peculiarity in the structure of the Selma school board. In 1989 the board was comprised of eleven members—six whites, five blacks. However, six votes constituted a quorum. The majority whites, if they voted unanimously, could pass any motion they wished without the support of a single black member. Had seven votes been required for a quorum, at least one black vote would have been required to make an official board decision.

There were other problems having to do with the board. Mayor Joe Smitherman had a major voice in deciding who the City Council would choose for the board, and by everyone's account, he was no friend of Roussell's. Both Roussell and Chestnut are convinced that Smitherman tightened control over the board by using his influence to have the City Council appoint members who were opposed to Roussell during the two years he was superintendent. "There was a pro-Roussell board when I started," Roussell explained. "By late 1989 it was an anti-Roussell board, because there were six people sitting who had agreed to get me out. I understood what was going on and accepted the fact that when you come in and change the structure that has existed, and transfer and tamper with the mind-set of who is superior and who is inferior, you're going to have problems. The other thing: It's very difficult to overcome a system that has perpetuated illiteracy in the black community for so many years. For the top students the school system worked extremely well. For most black students it was a case of an education for the cotton fields."

⌒

At a board meeting on the night of December 21, 1989, the six white members voted not to renew Roussell's contract upon its expiration in June 1990. That happened at a public meeting, packed with partisan whites and blacks and members of all the community organizations that had become involved. The five black board members, all of whom voted to retain Roussell, stormed out of the meeting in protest of the majority's action.

⌒

Once word spread of the board's action, the black community exploded, Chestnut recalled. "This issue galvanized the entire black community" as no other. A one-day boycott of schools by the black community was organized.

With a tense situation at hand over the Christmas holidays and on into the new year, the board, still meeting without its black members, now attempted to dismiss Roussell without waiting for his term to expire. This effort backfired and stirred up another, much more volatile, boycott by black students. Roussell then demanded that the students return to school even though they were boycotting in support of him. Finally, the Alabama National Guard and the state police were called in. There was national television coverage as picketing and fights between white and black students broke out inside Selma High. Suddenly, Selma was once again the focus of national media attention over a racial issue, as if the events of 1965 had come back to haunt the city fathers (and mothers) once again.

⌒

During this period, attorney Rose Sanders emerged as an unremitting critic of the school board and its actions, not the least because her daughter Malika was a student at Selma High. Her husband, Hank, Chestnut, and their entire office staff, along with Alice Boynton and BEST, were constantly in the forefront of the protests, but no one was more vocal and visible than she was. In fact, she herself virtually became an issue. In her interviews, particularly with the national press, Ms. Sanders charged that the issue at hand was one of continuing racism; and that Roussell had only become unacceptable when he had proposed to alter the prevailing leveling system, a charge that made some white Selmians furious.

In February, when the board tried to terminate Roussell and replace him with a well-known black Selma leader, the Reverend Frederick D. Reese, Rose Sanders and two other attorneys from her law firm demanded to see Mayor Smitherman, because they were sure he was behind the move. This attempt at a meeting ended up in a physical tug-of-war in the mayor's office, with police arresting Ms. Sanders.

Medium-dark skinned, energetic to put it mildly, smallish though not tiny, Rose Sanders exudes youth. When I met with her, Ms. Sanders's office desk top was a clutter of papers, files, and collapsible legal-size folders. She wore an African print dress and a huge wooden and shell bead necklace. The office walls were decorated with the usual framed diplomas and certificates interposed with African sculptures and a bas-relief sculpture of Martin Luther King, Jr. As we talked, she sipped herbal tea. I asked her about her background.

"My father was an AME Zion Methodist minister. From the point of my parents' marriage—in Mobile County, Alabama, where he is from—for twenty-five years we traveled throughout the Southeast from church to church. I was born in Salisbury, North Carolina, in 1945; we lived first in several small towns in North Carolina, then Kentucky and Tennessee, finally settling for a while in Greenville, Tennessee, where I graduated from high school." Ms. Sanders attended and graduated from Johnson C. Smith College in Charlotte while her parents moved on to Birmingham, living on "Dynamite Hill" a middle-class black neighborhood that became the frequent target of fanatical Klan house bombers during the height of the civil rights years.

The peripatetic Rose Sanders visited Harlem during the summers of her college years, living with the family of a close friend and classmate. It was in Harlem that she stumbled upon her lifelong avocation and most consuming passion, theater, though she has never had any formal drama training. "All the kids on the block wrote a play—*We Grow Up Young*—with me directing, and from then on, I was hooked. We performed that play all summer long—outdoors, on stoops, in the middle of blocked-off streets, wherever." That experience, it seems, provided an early prototype for the youth theaters she would later develop in Selma.

Rose Sanders must have been an exceptional student, because from Johnson C. Smith College she was accepted at Harvard Law School, where she received her law degree in 1969. Her first job was with the National Welfare Rights Organization in Harlem. She and Hank, whom she had met at Harvard, were married in 1970 and went off to West Africa on a Ford Foundation grant to study the Africanization of the continent's universities since independence. ("There was none," she commented dryly.)

After a year in Africa, they returned to live in Huntsville, Alabama, Hank's hometown, where Hank went to work for the legal services program. While in Huntsville, they both passed the Alabama bar exam, and decided they wanted to set up their own practice, but not in Huntsville.

"How did you end up in Selma?" I asked.

"Hank chose Selma. Somebody told him that lawyers were needed in Selma; that there was a very brilliant lawyer here, but he was an alcoholic—this turned out to be Chestnut. So Hank came here and he says he drove up Washington Street and saw all those black people hanging out on the corner. From that minute he knew this was the place he wanted to be.

"I was not eager to move to Selma 'cause my family had come through Selma years ago and I didn't like it. But we agreed we would come here for five years and then I would choose where we lived for the next five years."

Once in Selma, the Sanderses formed a partnership with Chestnut. Chestnut, who discusses his alcoholism in *Black in Selma*, attributes the arrival of help in the form of the Sanders team as one factor in his recovery. Rose and Hank also established the Black Belt Cultural Center. Early on, Hank established himself in Black Belt politics, and was eventually elected state senator in November 1983. Meanwhile, Rose created a new traveling musical theater group, the Children of Selma, of which she is director-producer-writer. In the 1980s the Sanderses formed the Twenty-first Century Foundation, designed to encourage leadership among black youth through workshops and retreats, the only program of its kind, of the scale on which they attempt to operate, that I know of in the Deep South. All of these programs have an Afrocentric focus that does not shrink from stark realism. Children of Selma performed a daringly frank skit on teenage pregnancy and AIDS at the New Orleans Jazz Festival in 1991. A large part of Rose's success comes from her ability to draw young people to her, along with similar-minded adults like Jo Anne Bland and the late Jackie Walker, Barbara Pitts, and Carol Zippert, all of whom contributed to the various Black Belt Cultural Center projects. Eventually, Rose Sanders and the entire "Jeff Davis" law office became deeply involved in the school dispute, but a good portion of Rose's interest in the educational dispute was related to her prior cultural work with black youth in Selma.

"The main issue now in Selma *is* Mayor Joe Smitherman," she asserted. "Until we do something about him, it's going to be hard to raise and develop issues, because he has a way of manipulating black and white people against each other in order to maintain his position. Throughout the educational issue, you'll find, he was involved.

"We sat quietly in his outer office for forty-five minutes to an hour. He kept saying, 'I'm going to see you.' I kept getting up, going to his door, knocking very politely. 'Mayor, when are you going to see us?' 'In another minute, I'm going to see you.' The second time, I went back to my seat peacefully, no problems. The third time I made up my mind I was going in. Now, that's the truth. I opened the door. The officer who was near the police chief came up behind me, and grabbed me by the neck. My law partner, Carlos Williams, saw this and grabbed him. We had a big tussling match. I was just thoroughly disgusted.

"They arrested me, put me in a car with one of the most racist cops in the city, me alone. Took me to the back of the jail, handcuffed me, and dragged me like a dog over concrete. This was the first time I was arrested, in February. My last arrest over this protest was in August 1990. You will not believe what we went through during that period—the threats and the arrests."

Ms. Sanders was getting so many telephone calls that it was obvious I was taking up her time; I prepared to leave. Besides, as our discussion progressed, she seemed to become increasingly weary. "I'd like to leave Selma," she admitted. "But I am not going to just pull up and say, 'I'm leaving.' But this is a place where I get blamed for everything. Usually, I deal with it well, but my children have been through a lot. I just think I need to find another base, because after you've been in a place too long, you lose your effectiveness." She did seem to be slightly overwhelmed by the activities surrounding her. I guess it was her gift, or curse, to see too much what needed to be done. As I was leaving her office, she said she planned to attend the school board meeting that evening. "I'm gonna monitor 'em," she assured me, her spirit suddenly aroused again.

~

As a result of the tumult over Roussell's contract, and concern over unrest, an estimated two hundred white families pulled their children from the public schools in the spring of 1990 and placed them in private academies. During that period Selma was racially polarized to an extent not experienced since the mid-1960s. Meanwhile, Roussell continued to act as superintendent.

The board offered him an extremely lucrative settlement if he would leave immediately. To accept this offer, which he said was $400,000, he would have had to leave town virtually overnight. There was also a clause in the offer that would have prevented him from speaking or writing about Selma. "But I didn't accept it," he told me. "It was a crude attempt to just buy and sell me and to demoralize the black community by saying, 'See, you may have respected him and thought he was important, but we bought him off.' And, of course, if you can buy someone that's a significant public figure, then you break the backbone of the folk who look at black people in those kinds of situations and say, 'Here's somebody who is able to stand up to that kind of thing.' I was not going to give them that, no matter how much money they offered. My wife, my family, agreed not to do that.

"You see, Tom," he added, "I knew for some time that what was needed on the board to pull me down was being put in place. So what I did was say, 'Well, I know I have until June 1990, so given that amount of time, I'm going to bring as much equity and as much fairness and opportunity for every student as I can.' It would have been foolish to try to survive as superintendent, because in order to do that I would have had to become a part of what I knew ethically as a professional was not in the best interest of the students."

Finally, the assistant superintendent, who was also black, accepted the job of superintendent. The black school board members then returned under an agreement that there would be a majority black membership in alternating years, though, as Roussell noted, "It's not simply a matter of color. It's a matter of which blacks serve on the board.

"Without a serious economic base the black community here is extremely dependent on the white community. You don't have any blacks in positions where they can leverage; there can't be a real biracial partnership, because everybody has to bring some clout to a partnership. Here there's just one side with clout."

As of the summer of 1991, there had been no basic changes along the lines Roussell recommended to address the problem of leveling, and Roussell didn't seem to think there would be.

Several people had suggested that I speak with Alston Fitts, who was described as a "white moderate," and who had played a key role in the biracial discussions around leveling and Roussell's superintendency; discussions that unfortunately did not result in an agreement. I called Mr. Fitts at the Society of St. Edmund office, where he serves as communications director. The Society of St. Edmund is a Catholic Church order that for several decades has served the black community of Selma and the surrounding region. Fitts is also considered an expert on Selma history. Fitts agreed to see me, and I met him at his office the next morning. Fitts impressed me with his sincerity, though I found him maybe a bit too somber and intense. We talked for a while in his office. I guessed he was in his fifties. He was still clearly upset over the hostilities and anger of the previous year.

Fitts started off by saying that he found disheartening the current extremely polarized racial atmosphere in Selma, which had existed for more than a year. "The demonstrations and the closing of Selma High seemed at the time a deliberate attempt to drive the white kids out. My kids chose to stay, despite the increasing isolation and increasingly hostile environment. But what has come about in Selma High is resegregation." That seemed to me a rather severe interpretation of what had happened, and I said so.

"Yes," he explained, "by the standards of the U.S. Civil Rights Commission, if minorities are below twenty-five percent, you no longer have an integrated school.

In this situation white kids are the minority. In 1984, whites were about thirty-two, thirty-three percent at Selma High. In the fall of 1990, after all the furor, the white percentage had dropped to twelve percent. Now, for the beginning of this school year [1991], that percentage has decreased even more, to six percent.

"My children were receiving a more balanced education than I ever received in Tuscaloosa; they were reading Margaret Walker's *Jubilee*, and so forth. They weren't getting an all-white education. My kids went to school with black kids, which I think is an extremely valuable experience. I grew up under segregation in Tuscaloosa, which was a Klan town. Now, because of the hostilities, we're being driven back into opposite racial camps. To me, that's just the worst thing that could've happened."

I asked Fitts if he had been able to work with Rose Sanders, and if not, what the problems were.

"I've tried to work with Rose Sanders in the past, but found it an extremely discouraging experience. Had she used a different set of tactics during the school controversy, there wouldn't have been the massive white flight which occurred. She helped to make it a more racial issue, because Roussell did have some white support.

"My particular complaint against Mrs. Sanders is that she continues to broadcast that ninety percent of the white kids were in the advanced classes, and ninety percent of the blacks in the lowest level, when she knows these figures were inaccurate. The day after Roussell resigned, I looked at the actual figures. The levels followed economic class lines, not racial lines. My kids confirmed that forming levels by race did not exist. Now, as for the advanced placement courses [Level I], you had to pay fifty dollars down. That was a definite class bias."

Fitts also said he could not understand why Roussell had let Selma's name be "blackened." "It's a reflection on his term as superintendent," he added. "I would like to be friends with him, but all this has complicated my feelings toward him. My friends have told me it was silly of me to care about *how* the school policy was interpreted as long as there was any disproportion. To me, there is a difference between what happened and what was represented as happening."

Fitts offered the observation that whites like himself who had always sought to "do the right thing" were now befuddled. "We integrated schools," he said, "because of charges of black psychological inferiority under segregation. Now I feel like we're being forced back to segregated schools because of charges of black psychological inferiority under integration. What are we supposed to do?"

With this last question, for which I had no ready answer, our interview arrived at a roadblock. I might have offered that blacks went to court in search of improved educational opportunities, including better facilities, first and foremost. If this purpose was not being served under the new integrated schools, then blacks had a right to complain. But I didn't say that. I instead mentioned Roussell's complaint about removal of all traces of the old black school. Though they may have been inferior in supplies, facilities, and funding, they certainly were not inferior in memories, or in the accomplishments of their alumni, especially given the obstacles they were faced with. Fitts responded by telling me of his avid interest in black history, particularly in Selma, and the recent effort of a biracial group to dedicate a monument at the grave site of Benjamin Turner, the black congressman from Selma during Reconstruction.

"What cemetery is he buried in?" I asked.

"In old Live Oak on Dallas Avenue. It's a white folks' cemetery, but in the old days some blacks were buried there."

"Do you have time to take me to see it?" I asked. I promised him I would treat us to lunch afterward. So we drove off to the graveyard, which turned out to be a rather elaborately monumented and expansive cemetery located on the "white" side of town.

For Fitts, this cemetery was alive with Selma's history. "This is the resting place of Confederate generals. Many of them retired in Selma, you know."

"I've read about that," I said.

I drove into the cemetery, and onto a dirt road, passed more monuments sprouting from the ground, some of which were enclosed within rusted, embroidered fences. "We may as well park here and walk," Fitts said as I drove to a corner of the cemetery. We walked the short distance to the Turner monument. Turner's impressive vertical monument was inscribed: PLACED BY A BIRACIAL GROUP, MARCH 31, 1985. His tombstone read:

BORN A SLAVE IN HALIFAX COUNTY, NORTH CAROLINA, B. S. TURNER IN 1870 BECAME THE FIRST SELMIAN ELECTED TO THE UNITED STATES HOUSE OF REPRE-

SENTATIVES. AS THE FIRST BLACK CONGRESSMAN FROM ALABAMA, HE FOUGHT
FOR AMNESTY FOR CONFEDERATE LEADERS. CIVIL RIGHTS FOR BLACKS. EDUCATION
FOR ALL.

"Turner *deserves* to be here," joked Fitts, as he saw me staring at the reference
to "amnesty." I remembered that Du Bois had pointed out that many black leaders
backed amnesty for former Confederate leaders if they would support the Fourteenth
and Fifteenth amendments, particularly the Fifteenth which guaranteed suffrage for
freedmen. "He had been buried in an unmarked grave. We decided to do something
about that." A committee was formed, mostly members of the black Masons and
Elks clubs, as well as interested whites like Fitts, and money was raised for the new
tombstone to be dedicated in a public ceremony. "One of the guys in the club tipped
me off," Fitts remarked in an almost confessional way, as we trooped around looking
at the gravestones of prominent Selmians while I took pictures. "One of the guys
said, 'Alston, we love this project, but you talk a bit too much. Provide information.
Don't stick your neck out.'" He chuckled at that bit of biracial advice, or etiquette,
and so did I. (Ordinarily, blacks are resentful if a white person they are cooperating
with on a black historical, cultural, or social project automatically assumes the position of visible leadership. Sensitive whites know that it is better to let blacks assume
the visible leadership and determine the style of presentation, even if the participating
whites are the author of the idea. Usually, such delicate matters are never discussed;
adjustments on the part of whites without discussion are considered by blacks as a
sign of intelligence and positive commitment.)

"It was a wonderful ceremony. Fancier than anything I'd dreamed," Fitts recalled
as we headed toward a restaurant. "But Mrs. Sanders threatened to picket it because
a Republican, Senator Denton, came down to take part. She thought it was a mock-
ery of Ben Turner's memory."

I muttered something like, "Well, I'm sure Rose has her ideas about history."

"Mrs. Sanders," Fitts answered, "sees history solely in terms of the current
struggle. I think of the past as past, though shaping heroes for the present." I
suggested that though it seems Rose Sanders has been and continues to be extremely
irritating to those on the opposite side of an issue from her, and maybe even those

on the same side, people like her are crucial because they keep the process of questioning alive.

"You speak as an outsider," Fitts assured me. "Two of my friends who took their kids out of the public schools last year said they had to do it because their kids were becoming racist. They were being harassed by black kids and were becoming bitter. Though I must admit I heard this secondhand. My kids say they're leaving Selma, never to return except to visit. It's just that this whole experience with the school has been embittering for me. I feel I've lost."

We decided to eat at one of those fast-food-style steak places with a salad bar. There weren't many choices.

"You don't see what you're going through now in terms of public school integration as part of a process?" I offered as we sat down to eat. "A junction along a very long road?"

"It's just that I don't believe Mrs. Sanders intends for there to be a significant white presence at Selma High," he answered with despairing sincerity. "There's also been academic deterioration." Fitts mentioned the tendency of black students to prefer being accepted by friends rather than acquiring the oddball reputation of a good academic student. "Some black students say openly they prefer segregation. What has happened is they have taken a U-turn."

Another key white leader who was involved in the school dispute, and who also had children in the public school system, was psychiatrist David Hodo. I was told he was a steadfast supporter of Roussell throughout the dispute. I asked if I could see him, he agreed to talk to me, and we met at his office in a renovated Victorian-style house in the old white section across the street from the Dallas County courthouse.

Dr. Hodo is of Irish descent. He told me his name was originally Hodeaux, an anglicized French name. "My ancestors were probably convicts from Ireland," he joked. He looked to be about fifty, with gray hair; I found him quite relaxed, unflappable. Of course, in his profession he is hardly a stranger to the interview process.

Dr. Hodo is a native of Alexander City, Alabama, located about fifty miles north of Montgomery; however, he had relatives in Selma and Marion and had visited both towns as a youth. A graduate of Auburn University, he spent three years at the University of Alabama Medical School, then served his residency at the College of Charleston during the time of the hospital workers' strike, I was surprised to discover, where he got to know Bill Saunders. He lived in Boston for a year, then enlisted in the Navy; afterward, he returned for his psychiatric training at Tulane University in New Orleans. He and his family moved to Selma in 1975, where he set up a practice. Hodo also maintains a hospital consultancy in the Black Belt area. I asked him why, or how, he had decided to settle in Selma after having lived in such a variety of places.

"Early on, when I chose psychiatry, I pretty much decided I wasn't going to live in a small town. Then I worked in a hospital in Natchez, Mississippi, and I found it interesting. That began to change my mind. I suppose Selma was like coming home."

I wondered if his friendship with and support of Roussell had hurt his practice? "In terms of what I had to do and the patients I'm seeing, I don't see that it did."

We got right into a discussion of Roussell and the board. "I thought the board got unreasonably angry," Hodo began. "Roussell could be abrupt. And headstrong. I'll tell you the kind of person he is. He came out to my house to ride a horse. We raise horses. He said he knew all about horses; his father was a fruit and vegetable peddler in New Orleans. I told him, 'Don't gallop the horse.' The next thing I knew, he was galloping the horse. To me that was symptomatic of his problem here. People would say, 'Don't gallop the horse,' and he would do it anyway.

"Roussell had the mistaken view he was in charge. The board said, 'We hired you, but we're in charge.' The comments you heard were things like, 'Well, I always told Norward my door was open, and he never came by.' And Norward would say, 'I always told him my door was open. . . .'

"I thought Roussell was a good school superintendent, with good ideas. The white students did well; there was no exodus. It was going well until the fateful December board meeting, though he had been having problems with the board. I did anticipate there would be problems from the first day. I didn't think someone who was from New Orleans, where I had lived, would work here. I had seen the way blacks operate in New Orleans; there's just an aggressiveness and swagger that's simply not known in Selma, even though the board thought they were doing something progressive in hiring a black superintendent."

"What about the issue of leveling classes?" I asked. I agreed that the New Orleans style of black swagger, the Dutch Morial style (Ernest "Dutch" Morial was the first black mayor of New Orleans, 1976–1984), would drive the white folks crazy in Selma, but Selma blacks and Roussell believe it was really his proposal to change the policy of leveling, or tracking, that brought him down.

"But I disagree," answered Hodo, evenly. "It didn't have that much to do with tracking. It had more to do with his not dealing with the board. He probably could have accomplished his changes in a way that would have made it impossible to get rid of him, in terms of keeping his job. But that was not, and is not, his style.

"There was tracking in my hometown school in Alexander City. I've always known that. Certain people whose parents were better off were given better courses. People from less well-off families were not offered those classes. There was a social class division all the way through in my school."

"Well, what about Smitherman?" I asked. "Roussell and the Jeff Davis gang think Smitherman was a real problem, and that he controlled the school board."

Hodo thought for a while, then answered. "We think the mayor was unfairly represented as having caused all this, and I don't think he did it. Basically, he got caught in a situation and handled it to the best of his ability."

"Roussell doesn't read it that way," I said. "He said Smitherman never accepted him. The terms of board members among his supporters ended and the replacements were not supporters. All of the blacks I talked to have a problem with Smitherman."

"I don't know that I agree with all that," Hodo replied. "My guess is that members of the board complained to the mayor, and that caused problems. Maybe the mayor didn't handle it as well as he could have. He could have said, 'We had a discussion and we've resolved our difficulties,' and just announced that the controversy was over."

"Could he have gotten away with that?" I asked. "And what about Rose Sanders?"

"Rose Sanders can be provocative, but sometimes she just gets mad. She got mad at me last year over something I thought wasn't that important. I don't care to be battered by Rose. In my experience, if you wait a little while, it will be all right. And I think she's stretched thin, with all she has going on. A lot of trouble in the world is not over the issues, but people getting into personality disputes. Of course, as I said, to me it would have been a miracle if Roussell had worked out at all in Selma."

⁓

During my earlier discussion with reporter Alvin Benn, he had expressed much the same opinion as Dr. Hodo. "The school board should have extended Roussell's contract, at least for a while," he remarked. "It was more of a personality conflict than anything else. If they had tried, they might have been able to work with him.

"He was used by the Jeff Davis crowd. To come in from New Orleans and try to tell the aristocracy here how to run 'their' school system wasn't going to work. No one could do that. Had Roussell used more sugar than vinegar, things would have gone a lot smoother. A little more diplomacy, input from the board members, etc. He was just a little too overbearing.

"There *was* a problem with Smitherman," he continued. "The mayor looked around and saw Roussell was making more than he was, even though he had been there thirty years."

Once again I asked about the leveling/tracking issue. "I have my doubts about the tracking," Benn replied. "My daughter was in Level One. She did fine. My son was in Level Two. Now he's got his master's degree."

I persisted: "A big complaint is that the school advisers and counselors aren't recommending kids on the low levels for higher levels if they can do the work. You don't think this is an issue?"

"I'm not sure the levels even exist!" Benn replied somewhat testily. "Have you talked to the present superintendent?" I admitted I hadn't. "Well, they [the Jeff Davis crowd] think he is an Uncle Tom. Is he an Uncle Tom or an independent educator? As I understand it, now if you ask, you can take the courses you wish. As I see it, when three hundred white kids left and didn't come back, that was the end of the public school system. It was not about tracking; at the bottom line it was about pure political power. For two hundred years whites ran things; now blacks want power. So somehow, both races are going to have to get together. The gap is going to have to be bridged.

"There's no other town like this in the world, believe me," he added. "Little ole ladies tell me, 'People *love* to come to this town to look at our lovely homes.' I say, 'Come on! People come here for one reason—to look at the *bridge!*' But when the twenty-fifth anniversary of the Selma march came, a biracial committee was established by the mayor, and it was opposed by the Jeff Davis crowd."

As we walked out of the *Advertiser* office to take pictures of the bridge, I said, "Obviously, they resented such a committee because it came from Smitherman," I offered. "They probably feared he would co-opt the Memorial."

"Maybe so," said Benn. "But *nothing* happens in this town unless it comes from Smitherman. He has a solid white block. All he needs is a five or ten percent black vote, which he maintains because he's appointed blacks to jobs."

I asked Benn for his opinion of Rose Sanders. "I've seen her do fine work," he said. "I've seen her do fine work for white candidates; I've seen her do great work with black kids. But I think she goes overboard on some things, I really do. She's *very* aggressive. Hank is just the opposite; that's their natures. There's no doubt they helped people when there was no one else to help them. But now they've become a power unto themselves. And that's a problem."

⌒

The intensity of the concerns, and the rumbling of discontent expressed by the black community over the status of education in contemporary public schools since *Brown*—not just in Selma but throughout the South—is deeply rooted in the immense historical role education has played in racial advancement since Emancipation. As I had seen and heard on this journey alone, touching only a few towns, schools and schooling have had as much to do with the benefits brought about by the civil rights movement as have historical black churches. This broad tradition of reverence for education has to do with the passing on from generation to generation, not only of information, but of cultural history and heritage, particularly in the South, and focuses on group rather than individual achievement. What happens to schools in the post-*Brown* period should be judged, I can hear black elders saying, in the context of the historical role of education for blacks prior to *Brown*—that of expanding opportunity. And that consistency of the role of education is more important than whatever value may lie in racial integration itself. If desegregated systems don't serve to *expand* opportunity for blacks, then why shouldn't they be rejected, and abandoned for some better system?

~

When I started my journey, not really knowing whether it would turn out to be a full odyssey, I had begun my descent from Washington down through Charlottesville, Virginia, where I visited friends, and on to Durham, North Carolina, driving alone while listening to radio reports of the bombing of Baghdad. In Durham, I took the time to lay out my plans for the forthcoming trip with Barbara "Nayo" Watkins, an old, close friend and fellow cultural worker who had just recently returned to the South to be director of the Chuck Davis Dance Company. A native of Atlanta, Nayo is a poet and playwright, and has worked as coordinator of black cultural groups and festivals in Mississippi—difficult work with no financial rewards or recognition. In the mid-1980s, Nayo was named director of a feminist theater in Minneapolis, At the Foot of the Mountain. This job, as Nayo expected, turned out to be an enormous change from black cultural work in Mississippi, a real challenge for Nayo. During this period we remained in touch, as we tried to analyze our separate but somewhat similar experiences. (I was serving as director of the New Orleans Jazz and Heritage Foundation, which presents the annual Jazz Festival.)

As we sat in an upscale restaurant in a renovated mall of small shops and galleries, bringing each other up-to-date on our assessments and projects, Nayo mentioned that one of the first problems she had faced upon resettling in Durham was which high school to choose for her teenage son, Hollis. There were three choices, she said: the integrated, formerly white high school, now 70 percent black; the county high school, 70 percent white; and the formerly black high school, which somehow never desegregated (maybe it had a handful of white students). "When I first arrived, everyone said, 'Put your kid in the county school, it is better,' but when I looked at the new subdivision housing I would have to live in to qualify, I said, 'I really want to live in the city, if I can get something decent.'" She found something decent and chose the all-black school for Hollis. "When I checked it out, I found all it had done over the years was produce leadership. I don't see why it can't do it now." Her son took well to the school, graduated, and is now attending Morehouse College.

As I worked my way southward, I often reflected on Nayo's decision. I'm sure there are others, but she was the first black parent I knew who deliberately went against the grain of integration to enroll her child in an old black public school, when other options were clearly available.

This brings up a question, from the perspective of almost forty years after *Brown*, that perhaps now needs to be asked: What, exactly, was wrong with the old black public schools that for years served their constituencies so well despite deprivations and the isolation of segregation? Those schools produced the generation that launched protests against segregation in the South and brought down the FOR WHITES ONLY signs.

Of course, we know about the underfunding, the deplorable lack of books in rural areas, and the absence of transportation to and from school, which was at the core of the *Briggs* v. *Elliott* case in rural South Carolina (one of the five suits combined to form *Brown* v. *Board of Education*) and many others. Nevertheless, there is an inescapable irony in the fact that those old schools provided much of what is absent in today's postsegregation schools: the desperately needed psychological support that black children must have to progress into areas of accomplishment of which they otherwise would have no knowledge. Somehow, that sense of support, the presence of great possibilities, even in the most meager of circumstances, was the one factor that made it possible to overcome all the well-known material obstacles.

Maybe it also had to do with the fact that school was not then a compulsory obligation, but an opportunity. There is no doubt that the students' self-worth was enhanced by seeing a large number of black teachers, coaches, and principals, who provided them with positive role models, and who often became mentors of particular students.

Finally, the old schools, no matter how dilapidated or deprived, provided black children, sometimes directly, more often indirectly, with a sense of the historical continuity of the educational experience of their race through the existence of the school itself or its antecedents. Despite the social and cultural isolation from mainstream political and economic society, and the stigma of inferiority created by racial segregation, black public and church schools in the South did offer undeniable psychological advantages, as so many of the people who related their stories to me had testified. It was as if the very visible barriers of segregation itself, which affected teachers and administrators as well as students, created the motivation to burst past the barriers, to jump over them through knowledge and skill, so that the very limitations of opportunity became a catalyst driving us forward. It is a paradox that once visible and legal segregation fell, and racism became more nebulous and less concrete, the corresponding group motivation to overcome racial obstacles flagged, and achievement became more of an individual matter.

The first black schools, from the time of Reconstruction, were predominantly church affiliated; then in the twentieth century, with the opening up of municipal and county schools for blacks, meager as they were, the church-related schools gave way to public schools. Du Bois points out that black Reconstruction legislators were the first and most consistent advocates of public school systems in the South, as they had realized most acutely the benefits of education.

The high school I attended in New Orleans, Gilbert Academy (the history of which I mentioned when I met Dr. Warmoth T. Gibbs and John Kilimanjaro in Greensboro), was a school that, looking back over four decades, was an exemplar of the best old black schools in the days of racial segregation.

Every morning I embarked on an hour-and-a-half journey from downtown to uptown—two buses and a streetcar—to arrive at the academy, which operated out of the old New Orleans University campus on luxurious St. Charles Avenue, the only black institution on the mansion-lined avenue. After school I returned home by the slower St. Charles Avenue streetcar route to Canal Street, even though I would have had a shorter ride by bus. The buses, which were not air-conditioned, spewed out nauseating exhaust fumes from their rear engines, enveloping those sitting in the back of the bus—a special poison reserved for those of color.

I always preferred the back of the clanging, rocking, screeching streetcar as it crawled toward the central business district, looking out at the vista of the city's extremely variegated life and its stately manifestations of past sugar plantation wealth. It was as if I was riding a very slow train passing through an old, prosperous town separated from the city. This view revealed a past of unshakable certitude. In comparison, school, my reason for these journeys, was an immense speculation, if not a hopeful creative fiction, based on the belief that a change in our status would soon occur.

When we arrived at the streetcar's terminus, Canal Street—the major interurban spine of the city and the dividing line between downtown and uptown—I walked the three or four blocks along Canal to the bus stop where I would catch the bus that would take me downtown to my home in the Gentilly area. Almost everyone traveling across town had to change at Canal Street, making it not only the city's main shopping area, but the major intersection and transfer point. When people got off from work at 5:00 P.M., Canal resembled a huge moving, crisscrossing bus and train station. The stores and shops and display windows along Canal never failed to excite me, not that I could purchase anything. The ubiquitous WHITES ONLY signs, indicating stores we could not enter, stores we could enter but not try on clothes within, sandwich shops and restaurants that served whites only, water fountains and bathrooms we could not use, movie theaters we could enter only from the side in order to climb to the designated "Colored" section in the balcony, constituted a virtual steeplechase of obstacles to maneuver through and around, which I had to master so as to avoid making a fateful racial mistake. The endless variety of restrictions and specifications (in the rear, in the front, upstairs, or from the side only) made us aware, even as youngsters, that someone had gone out of their way to create this mess. The segregation system, if we could call it that, was clearly artificial and man-made, based on the laughable fiction that this maze of special arrangements was necessary because of our natural inferiority, a color-drenched failing that would contaminate white civilization upon close contact.

Never in a hurry to rush home, I frequently wandered over to South Rampart Street, a tributary of Canal Street, where the sepia world unfolded in full bloom. South Rampart Street was a fascination of color, movement, and style; sounds and scents. Here were the stores for blacks: clothing stores, tailor shops, rooming houses, and a decent hotel sprinkled among pool halls, endless pawnshops, bars, fish fry joints, barbershops, beauty parlors, a photography studio, and, at the foot of the district, a black weekly newspaper, a high school, and railway station. It was along this strip that jazz and the New Orleans forms of black popular music were born and nurtured and where record stores that sold the most up-to-date music were located. South Rampart rocked with the sounds of trumpets and saxophones and the cries of southern black music, particularly the story-laden songs of early rhythm and blues great Louis Jordan. Flamboyant dress was the order of the day, any day, not just Saturday or Saturday night.

Really, South Rampart was a black colony of Canal Street. The FOR WHITES ONLY signs were absent and the insults of not being allowed here or there were not as graphic, but it was still a land of economic dependency where blacks spent their hard-earned dollars but owned very little. This situation was most strikingly symbolized by the pawnshops on every block where personal possessions were hocked for a few dollars, the beginning of a descent into the dizzying vortex of debt that culminated in losing everything. Despite the joys of the music and nightlife, it was a proscribed and insular world. I was both attracted to its fabulous intensity of life and repelled by its limitations.

Our education at Gilbert, as Mrs. Bowen wore us out repeating, was designed to take us beyond the limitations of the South Rampart Streets—this was its reason for being and its enduring hope. Our real education, however, was the world of the academy's uplift ethos, tempered by what we observed every day on the streets of New Orleans traveling to and from school, which served to define for us how we were viewed by mainstream white society.

At school we were inundated with a million extracurricular activities, almost as if school was designed to be more than school; it would become a world unto itself. In our English class, Miss Marie Blakely introduced us to Shakespeare's plays, her response to the outside world. Trim, in her mid-forties, unmarried, dark skinned, and unhumorous if not downright prudish, Miss Blakely seemed insufficiently aware of the theories of our "natural inferiority"; therefore, we were dragged through the exotic and grave worlds of *Hamlet, Macbeth, King Lear,* and *Julius Caesar,* as we tried our best to discern their plots. There was no extraneous talking in her class, or you were sent to see Mrs. Bowen, something, believe me, no student looked forward to.

Then there was Aaron Dutton, our chemistry, math, and physics teacher. Medium-brown skinned, with slick hair, then in his early forties, and formerly on the staff of New Orleans University, Dutton treated us as if we were an unreasonable burden, and it was up to us to stretch our minds to reach a standard of learning he could respect. Blessed with a superior mind, Dutton today would no doubt be working in a highly technical industry, not teaching school. He taught science from experiments and principles (we almost blew up his chemistry lab); anyone could understand the basic laws of the physical world, he unsmilingly seemed to think, and when he gave vent to his scorn at our failures of comprehension, we strove to prove we were not hopelessly stupid. You-can-do-it rhetoric was not Dutton's stock-in-trade; he sort of believed we could do it and when we did do something right, we received half a smile. After school hours he taught those who were interested the elements of photography—developing, printing, enlarging—before we ever took a photograph.

I never heard Dutton say anything about launching an attack against segregation. I do remember him saying, during one of his frequent digressive meditations, "I don't know about you, but I don't want to be white. I *like* being Colored." I had never heard anyone say that, and I never forgot it.

⌒

The question still remains: What was so lacking in the old black schools that made the black leadership find it preferable to aim for integrated public schools at all costs, even if superior black schools were sacrificed in the process? One answer would be that the problem of legal segregation and discrimination was a far larger issue than education itself. Basic inequities in the South were so firmly entrenched that had all the black schools been on a level with the very best in America, sufficient education itself could not have brought about the necessary changes. Even with the best education, blacks could not hold certain jobs, be elected to office, or in most cases even vote, or compete on a level playing field with whites.

Second, a sense of one's worth must, to a great extent, be proven through comparison and competition. We *thought* Gilbert was a good school, that our athletic teams, in particular, were superb, but how could we possibly know if we were not allowed to compete against all the other schools in the city? Even the good black schools could not allay a feeling of isolation from the center of things. Such forced isolation, despite the official creed of uplift, had the deleterious effect of fostering feelings of inadequacy and inferiority, and reinforcing self-doubt in a million small and subtle ways. Even with some of our best teachers, I sensed an oft-suppressed but occasionally expressed suspicion that ice frozen by whites was undoubtedly colder, no matter how much we said it wasn't, that *something* must be wrong with black people to have constantly suffered such abuse from the non-African world virtually throughout history—there must be some hidden failing, some awful and unmentionable sin. There were all kinds of corrective theories: If we could just change this or that one thing, we would improve our condition—every leader had a magic solution. Fears were often expressed through devastating self-deprecatory racial humor blacks indulged in among themselves—humor that sought ways to adjust to defeat, victimization, and discouragement.

This deep-rooted lack of racial confidence led to various forms of protective compensatory behavior, like pretentious titles brandished by those who considered themselves or wished to be considered important, overly proper speech by those who wished to appear educated, formal dress for all occasions by those who feared they would otherwise be insufficiently clothed—we saw this every day in our schools.

A better sense of the history of African Americans, of slavery and racism, and a familiarity with the works of black writers or with the history of Africa, might have helped, but courses in these subjects were virtually forbidden. Considered unnecessary. Our education instead consisted of attitudes, allusions, and dispositions from elders in reaction to the racial condition without us (or possibly our elders) knowing the roots of such attitudes or strange compensatory behavior. African-American history and literature would have provided us with a more concrete sense of who we were and how we had come to where we were. Maybe we thought so little of ourselves that we believed our story was not a legitimate subject of study; there was far more interest in what was happening on the *other* side of the river.

Had such courses in black history and culture been included as part of our curriculum and been taught with real knowledge, blacks would have been far more reluctant to leap toward the vague euphoria of a desegregated future without guarantees that such knowledge would be included in the new schools.

Third, we shouldn't forget that schools like Gilbert and McDonough 35 (attended by the Rousells) in New Orleans were not the norm; they represented the cream of black secondary schools in the Deep South. The majority of black segregated primary and secondary schools were vastly underfunded and poorly equipped, and teachers were often substandard in their own educational backgrounds, even though the inspirational factor may have overcome all these obstacles. We should also mention obvious problems like the need for available transportation, which were cited so prominently in the *Brown* v. *Board of Education* Supreme Court case.

Then, too, as a private school run by the Methodist Church, Gilbert, like all secondary schools started by supportive churches in the wake of Reconstruction, was, by the mid-twentieth century, in deep financial trouble, and hanging on by a thread. Blessed with a large but aging facility, there was nevertheless a need for new equipment, books, and supplies that the Methodist Church in the New Orleans area could hardly afford. Teacher salaries were but a pittance. The tuition of $17.50 per semester per student (though not that easy to come by for most students) could not even begin to cover school expenses. Academies like Gilbert all over the South were closing; it was obvious their students would have to transfer into the public school systems.

For the above reasons—inadequacy of facilities in a dual system, the inability to compete in an open system that would hopefully bring blacks into the mainstream of southern societies, and the isolation, and all the psychological problems created by isolation—the national black leadership concluded there was no alternative other than to demand full school desegregation. Hopefully, integrated schools would lead to a more racially and class integrated society. The black leadership was not sure *how* desegregation would work and what it would mean, but there was a strong belief that if desegregation meant a general betterment of conditions for blacks, and most important, a removal of the legal stigmas of inferiority, then the rather vaguely viewed future on the other side would be a definite improvement. Separate schools in those days before 1954, to them, equaled inferior conditions imposed by others from outside. "Separate but equal" in public institutions was *always* a fiction, they knew, and in fact, was an impossibility, as the black leadership (and the white leadership) also knew.

❡

So far, so good. The leaders, however, were so intent upon fighting segregation, then tokenism once the grinding, painful machinery of school desegregation began, that they neglected to create a mechanism to monitor the process in terms of fairness and quality of education, a costly mistake. It was a major problem, in my opinion, that civil rights attorneys were still calling the shots throughout the initial period of desegregation, whereas what was required was more than litigation—a broad-based leadership in educational policies and administration was desperately needed. It was all new territory anyway, with southern federal judges improvising desegregation plans, trying to figure out how to proceed. The Supreme Court said "desegregate"; the district court judges had to decide how to "activate." Almost always blacks found themselves reacting to what had happened rather than participating in the early decision-making or creating proposals as advocates, as they had done so effectively in the legal battle to destroy the constitutional basis of segregation.

For instance, once token school integration began (which meant a few blacks entering all-white schools, as we heard over and over from the towns I had just visited), who was prepared to speak for black students, teachers, or administrators who felt they had been mistreated during the process of forming a unitary system? The local NAACP chapter? They were hardly educational specialists. Veteran black teachers? Sometimes, but they risked their jobs if they rocked the boat too much, and they rarely spoke as a group. Schoolchildren themselves? Not hardly. Not even if they were able to recognize and articulate the problems facing them.

Meanwhile, segregationist politicians and educational officials, acting as if they were under siege from the federal courts, were busy creating devices and stratagems designed to circumvent meaningful school desegregation. Blacks were made to pay a heavy price for demanding integration, not only by forcing their children to walk through the gauntlet of "those who don't want us," in the words of Jo Anne Bland, but by the closing of formerly black schools, or their designation as junior schools, by the demotion of black principals and coaches, and by the letting go of black teachers deemed "unqualified."

In the Black Belt South areas like Tuskegee, where heavy black majorities exist, whites fled to seg academies, leaving the schools virtually all black with a reduced tax base and the strong resistance of whites to bond issues designed to improve the public schools they don't attend. This process created, in effect, a full circle of change back to de facto segregation—now with the approval of the federal courts because, on the surface, those systems had been subjected to desegregation orders.

⌒

This is about where the situation rests now, and the problems are many. Maybe, in leaping forward toward school desegregation, we forgot that no real remedy for our societal marginality could be the result of biracial education alone, unless basic changes were made in American society, in terms of increased opportunity, particularly for those on the bottom rungs who suffer the most from lack of education and opportunity.

⌒

Maybe blacks also forgot that achieving such an open society would entail a continuing and changing struggle and still does, for if we conclude that public school desegregation has not worked smoothly, we have to also admit that the process is a genuinely difficult one, presenting new and unprecedented problems. Attempting to integrate students across the racial gulf, not to mention the income gulf, was bound to raise inevitable problems. Sharing classes and school activities with the children of parents your parents worked for, or perhaps still work for, is not easy. Black teachers teaching white children, and whites teaching blacks is an admitted challenge, one no previous experience in the history of the American South would have prepared any of them for.

And there is a problem teaching large numbers of indigent children, some with social and family problems so severe they are virtually dysfunctional. In such cases, teachers can become overwhelmed with the problem of behavioral management, and unable to focus on teaching. It is also difficult for such children—how can they discard their everyday problems at the drop of a hat once they enter the school door? Those problems are not eased by the newness of integration, with its long history of conflict.

Cultural differences and the debate over curriculum in integrated schools are the issues that inevitably flared into a source of conflict in Selma. But these conflicts are and will continue to be present in every school system that achieves a substantial biracial presence. How do we teach the history of the United States, especially the history of the South? What sort of music does the band play? What songs should the choir sing? What are the standards of beauty if a racially integrated school is foolish enough to hold a beauty contest? In what manner are black achievements celebrated, or defined as achievements, and how are such celebrations presented without antagonizing or alienating white students? Can such material be presented without challenging the beliefs and prior learning of white students? How do we *really* measure intelligence and ability, once we accept that standardized tests are not reliable measures? Is it even necessary to have a uniform measure of intelligence and ability?

⌒

In Norward Roussell's view, Selma's story is the story of a town that was not sufficiently prepared to sustain equitable and meaningful school desegregation, even if that failure only came to light because Selma, to some extent, actually attempted to go through the motions of progress toward that ideal. To Alvin Benn, the school dispute was really about political power, not education. I would agree with both; the two matters are profoundly related, since the ability to control the educational process, and all that effort entails, cannot be achieved without some measure of political and economic power.

As I left Selma on U.S. 80 headed toward Mississippi and the conclusion of my journey, I reflected that it has been Selma's particular fate to play the unhappy role of precursor on the battleground of race relations in the South, and this is no accident. In Selma the three themes of African-American political rights, economic sustenance, and education had wound around and around each other for more than a century. In fact, the hundred-mile corridor traversed by U.S. 80 from Selma through Montgomery to Tuskegee was not only the heart of the Deep South's Black Belt, but the heart and soul of the struggle to achieve full citizenship for black Americans, marked by extraordinary leaders, from Booker T. Washington to Martin Luther King, Jr.

In this area of inspired conflict and leadership, we might see Selma in terms of its extremity of need. No other town has a right to look down upon Selma's struggles with the problems of race in America; for Selma's travails, painful as they have been, should serve as a beacon, a signpost along the long road toward a more racially equitable South.

# MISSISSIPPI

~

*For black southerners, Mississippi was always considered a place of dread. NAACP attempts to organize in the state were met with repression and violence. In the early 1960s, SNCC organizers were considered extremely brave when they launched a campaign in McComb to attempt voting registration and to protest downtown segregation.*

*By 1964, in an effort to expand demonstrations throughout the state, many white youth of conscience responded to SNCC's calls for support; this became Freedom Summer. Bob Zellner, the most legendary white SNCC leader and a native of Mobile who now lives in New Orleans, remembers that "Mississippi and its evils were a centrality for all of us. We had to crack it if there was ever to be meaningful change in the South."*

*Efforts to break through Mississippi's wall of white power basically took the form of innovative projects spotted throughout the state designed to bring blacks into the political life of the state, and at the same time, improve their economic condition. Now, years later, it was my intention to visit some of the places where such projects existed to see what had happened to them. I was particularly interested in the fate of Canton, West Point, Philadelphia, and several towns in the Delta.*

*The Delta, I decided, was a fitting place to conclude my ten-month-long journey which began in Greensboro. Yes, the legendary Delta, which has served as the end and the beginning for so many southern journeys.*

I departed Selma on August 27 heading for the state of Mississippi, where I planned to visit several small towns of particular civil rights significance, beginning with the very small town of Canton, twenty miles north of the state capital of Jackson. Even if I had remained in Selma another year, I don't really think it would have altered my sense of what had transpired there. It was time to move on.

I drove through Uniontown and Demopolis, then as U.S. 80 joined I-20 and I-59, swept westward to Meridian, Mississippi. Then, after skirting Meridian, drove ninety miles through rolling hills, heavy forest, and no towns until I reached the Jackson confluence of highways, I-55, north and south; I-20, east and west. These highways, and the railroads that follow the same routes, make Jackson the largest metropolitan center between New Orleans to the south, and Memphis to the north.

From the Jackson intersections I drove northward on I-55, bypassing the old city but cutting right through the "new" city, the booming commercial and housing area called North Jackson. Then into the countryside again for a few miles as I crossed into Madison County, until I reached the Canton exit.

Canton is not one of the best-known towns on the 1960s civil rights maps. However, the effort to register black voters that occurred there during 1963 and 1964 was so bitter, so hard fought that the struggle there nurtured fears that white Mississippi would *never* progress, never yield an inch willingly.

Canton also happened to be the town in Mississippi where several New Orleans Movement volunteers ended up working. The Movement in New Orleans was organized by the Congress of Racial Equality, and so was Canton.

⁓

I was raised to think of Mississippi, from the relatively safe distance of New Orleans, as truly a Heart of Darkness. Every person I knew considered Mississippi an unfortunate place, and one to be avoided if at all possible. I still recall an early childhood nightmare: the lynched body of a black man hanging by rope from the Pearl River bridge, his body swinging slowly as traffic flowed on the bridge above. The traffic above was everyday life as we knew it; the body below represented the horror of an intemperate and irrational violence lurking just underneath everyday life. That is the way I came to understand the nightmare. Why were "Colored" people so hated, the objects of such vilification and violence? And it was *violence* that was associated with Mississippi; racial flare-ups of the most mundane kind could end up in death; death without remorse or punishment.

I learned later that the image of the hanging man was not just my imagination. It was apparently based on a photograph I must have seen in a regional black newspaper of a lynching that did occur at Pearl River in the late 1930s or early '40s. The Pearl River forms the boundary between Louisiana and Mississippi; somehow I assumed that this murder took place in Mississippi, not Louisiana.

We thought racism and violence in southern Louisiana were minimal compared with Mississippi. Even as a child I was aware of the evil, grotesque-looking, white-suited Senator Theodore Bilbo who filibustered and raged against antilynching legislation in Congress. Presumably, in his view, all blacks were candidates for the funeral pyre. And then there were the stern admonitions from our young summer camp counselors when our New Orleans YMCA group traveled to Waveland on the Mississippi Gulf Coast for a week of summer camp: "Be careful, now, you in Mississippi. This is *not* New Orleans. You better behave."

Fears of irrational Mississippi as an evil place for black folk were substantiated by rather stark facts. Between 1880 and 1940 nearly six hundred Mississippi blacks were lynched, with no convictions. The lynching of fourteen-year-old Emmett Till in 1955 in Tallahatchie County and the refusal of a jury to convict his killers, who later admitted they committed the murder, were both startling and a symbolic archetype.

In the 1940s, only five thousand blacks were registered to vote, reports John Dittmer in his superb *Local People: The Struggle for Civil Rights in Mississippi*. In 1949 the median income for whites was $1,614; for blacks, $601. Between 1940 and 1950, three hundred thousand blacks left Mississippi in the hope of finding better conditions elsewhere; in 1950 blacks constituted 45.3 percent of the state population, down from 53 percent in 1940. In 1950 there were only five black attorneys in the entire state. Only 3 percent of the black population had completed high school. Mississippi spent $122.93 per pupil per year for the education of whites, $32.55 for blacks. The average yearly salary for white teachers in 1948 was $1,861, more than double the figure of $711 for black teachers.

With this stellar record of white supremacy, it is not surprising that Mississippi officials were leaders in the effort to defy the Supreme Court's *Brown* decision of 1954. The Citizens Council was organized in Indianola in the fall of 1954 to formulate a plan for the maintenance of segregation. Citizens Councils quickly spread to other areas of the state, winning wide support among state officials. Blacks who had been active in organizing voter registration drives and who spoke out in favor of school desegregation were threatened, and the Reverend George Lee of Belzoni was shot and killed in cold blood in 1955. Dr. T. R. W. Howard of Mound Bayou, a prominent physician and a voting rights organizer, was run out of the state. The minuscule, virtually underground NAACP was rendered almost totally ineffective because of terrorist threats and economic reprisals.

In addition, many blacks who were registered to vote before 1954 were actually dropped from the rolls because of a new policy requiring "reregistration" and the centralization of registration procedures through each county courthouse. Finally, in 1959, there was a frightening reminder of Mississippi's violence when Mack Parker, a black man charged with the rape of a white woman, was snatched from the jail in Poplarville by a mob and lynched, his body thrown from the old Pearl River bridge of my childhood nightmares. If racial change and justice meant anything anywhere, change in Mississippi, to the degree it existed, would be, I thought, the surest barometer of progress in the American South.

The first Mississippi civil rights demonstrations began in Jackson in 1961 with sit-ins by Tougaloo College (a black private college on the outskirts of North Jackson) students on March 27 at the city library. They quickly spread to downtown lunch counters in the style of student sit-ins throughout the South. I followed these developments with avid interest from Harlem where I was living while working for the New York City welfare department. Would it be possible to sustain demonstrations in Mississippi, that bastion of violent resistance? I wondered. Possibly in Jackson, I thought, but certainly not in the isolated rural areas. I was therefore all the more impressed with the courage of Bob Moses and his first SNCC attempts to organize voter registration efforts in McComb, in southwest Mississippi, in 1961–1962, where protection for civil rights workers was virtually nonexistent. If Moses was able to win converts among young native black Mississippians, I knew it meant a new day was possible in Mississippi, no matter how loudly state officials shouted their defiance and threats. I also knew that black activism was absolutely necessary if real change was going to occur.

My own initial trips to Mississippi in connection with civil rights activities also had begun in the early 1960s while I was living in New York. In the spring of 1961, Thurgood Marshall offered me a job as press attaché for his NAACP Legal Defense Fund. "Civil rights is getting to be big business now," he said. "We need someone on a full-time basis. You can start next week." I had just finished interviewing him for a story I was writing for *Jet* magazine on a northern school desegregation case. I jumped at this opportunity, as I was eager to get away from the Welfare Department. In the fall of 1962, I was in Mississippi, along with the Legal Defense Fund staff, as part of the massive and highly publicized effort to enroll James Meredith as a student in the University of Mississippi.

The hysteria in Jackson during those days was unlike any I ever experienced; white Mississippi was being whipped into a state of frenzy by Governor Ross Barnett and the Mississippi media over the "integration threat."

During those weeks of Mississippi madness, I spent quite a bit of time with Medgar Evers, the state field coordinator for the NAACP. Our staff, led by the inspiring and unrelenting Constance Baker Motley, set up temporary headquarters in Medgar's tiny one-room office on the second floor of the Masonic Temple building on Lynch Street. Myrlie, Medgar's wife, was also his secretary. My job was to answer the constantly ringing phone—calls were coming in from everywhere—while trying not to give out too much information. Caught in a thunderstorm of excitement and racial conflict, we did the best we could. Meredith, who could be distant or friendly depending on his moods, also pitched in and helped.

The bulldogish Evers was a World War II Army veteran who had served overseas. While attending Alconn A&M, a black state college near Port Gibson on the Mississippi River, on the GI Bill, Medgar served as captain of the football team. A doer rather than an orator, Evers played the role of NAACP master sergeant in Mississippi, though his troops were few and far between. In retrospect, I'm sure Medgar realized how dangerous his situation was, and how much he angered the extremist segregationist fringe in Mississippi. But he also knew he couldn't allow himself to worry about the dangers and still function in his chosen role. While I was working in his office, he often received nasty, profane, threatening calls. Those calls bothered him, of course, but he gave as good as he got: "You may as well do what you gonna do because we not going to stop protesting," he would shout into the telephone. Then he would slam down the receiver. Even so, Medgar was a pleasant, fun-loving person; he could express anger, but I never detected bitterness.

Because the racial situation in Mississippi was so desperate, Medgar Evers was one of the few southern state NAACP officials who welcomed the entrance of SNCC and CORE activists into Mississippi. He would have probably preferred that they operate under the flag of the NAACP, and he had to be careful with the NAACP national office, but he told me once when we were discussing NAACP policy, "Let's face it. We're in such bad shape down here we need all the help we can get; we're not in a position to pick and choose."

While I was in Jackson, in January 1963, for a second time in connection with the Meredith case, Medgar asked me to ride with him to the University Hospital to pick up Clyde Kennard, who was scheduled to be released from the hospital and prison that day. Kennard, who was in his mid-thirties, had been jailed on trumped-up charges when he attempted to enter the University of Southern Mississippi in Hattiesburg in 1959. A military veteran who had lived in Chicago for a while after his discharge, Kennard had attended the University of Chicago and had sought to continue his education when he found it necessary to return to Hattiesburg on family business that year.

Mississippi officials were extremely nervous about Kennard's application and tried to persuade him not to go through with it. Kennard persisted. Finally, instead of rejecting Kennard's application, which might have brought about a federal deseg-regation suit, Hattiesburg officials decided to jail him, hoping that his fate would act as a deterrent to other blacks who might wish to enter Mississippi's all-white state educational institutions.

Kennard was charged with masterminding the theft of five bags of chicken feed from a white man's farm, a charge so ludicrous it would have been laughable if the outcome had not been so serious. He was convicted in less than a half hour, and sentenced to seven years in prison. Since 1959, Kennard had been incarcerated at the Parchman Penitentiary farm. In 1962 he was diagnosed as terminally ill with cancer and hospitalized. Apparently, state officials had decided it was wiser to quietly release him than to have him die in jail on their hands.

Knowing the full story from the beginning, Medgar was in a bad mood when we left for the hospital. When we entered the gloomy for-Colored-only waiting room and discovered that Kennard's release had not been processed, Medgar became very angry. He denounced everything from the inefficiency of the hospital staff to the segregated waiting room itself, which he promised would *"come to an end!"* The white hospital staff tiptoed around pretending they didn't hear him and the blacks sat patiently waiting to be called on, tensed up with fear. I searched for a dime to call Connie Motley to meet us at the jail to bail us out, since I knew that's where we were headed. If the hospital called the police to arrest Medgar, I wasn't going to just stand there and do nothing.

After an hour or so that seemed like a month, Kennard appeared looking frail and worn, and we finally left. We brought him to a friend's home, where his pastor was to pick him up for the drive back to Hattiesburg. It was here that Kennard told me the story of what had happened, though he was too weak to speak above a whisper. He died in Chicago before the year was out. It is ironic, but not totally unexpected, that Medgar died from an assailant's bullet before Kennard succumbed, shot in the back at night in June 1963.

After returning from New York to live in New Orleans in 1965, I traveled to Mississippi many times in conjunction with my work with the Free Southern Theater, which was founded at Tougaloo College by Doris Derby, Gilbert Moses, and John O'Neal in 1964. My job with the Legal Defense Fund had of necessity restricted me to meeting only local civil rights leaders and those involved in Meredith's court case. Now, with the Free Southern Theater, I was becoming more of a participant in the Mississippi freedom effort.

In 1968, through Free Southern Theater contacts, I was offered a part-time job teaching African-American literature and creative writing at Mary Holmes Junior College in West Point, Mississippi. West Point is in the northeastern part of the state, near Columbus; I arranged to teach both classes on Wednesdays so that I could spend the bulk of the week in New Orleans with the theater. Sometimes I flew, but most of the time I commuted by automobile, a drive of five hours from New Orleans.

Mary Holmes was a Presbyterian school I had never heard of; the small student body was drawn from throughout the state, along with a few from Alabama and Georgia. I quickly discovered, to my surprise, that both Mary Holmes and the town of West Point were buzzing with activity. This tiny school was in 1968 the non-profit sponsor for federal Head Start programs in the state of Mississippi. The Child Development Group of Mississippi was one of the first and most innovative Head Start programs to receive a grant from the Office of Economic Opportunity. As a result of being at the center of Head Start activity, the Mary Holmes student body had tripled from roughly a hundred students in 1960 to more than three hundred by the time I arrived in 1968. As for West Point blacks, I soon discovered that they possessed an aggressiveness, confidence, and sense of style, in contradiction to the image of Mississippi black docility. People were open, friendly, and loud, qualities I finally learned to appreciate.

One of the first people I met in West Point in 1968 was John Buffington, the chief organizer of numerous economic developmental projects in the surrounding Clay County. A native of Buford, Georgia, Buffington had come to West Point from Chicago as a SNCC volunteer during the heightened campaign of 1964, named Freedom Summer. In his late twenties, Buffington had spent two years at Morehouse College before moving to Chicago. Assigned by SNCC to Columbus, twenty miles to the east of West Point, he experienced little success there, but discovered, to his surprise, much more fertile organizing ground in the smaller West Point. From a Georgia town of about the same size, Buffington quickly mastered the racial dynamics of West Point. He took a liking to it, settled, and had married there by the time I arrived. We quickly became close friends.

Buffington's Clay County Development Corporation, among other things, was operating a post-Freedom Summer attempt to produce jobs through craft cooperatives in the county. There were sewing and farming co-ops in Una, a candle-making project at White Station, and woodworking, mattress-making, and catfish pond projects in West Point.

These economic co-ops were part of a statewide effort called the Poor People's Corporation. The PPC, headquartered in Jackson, was the most ambitious of several innovative economic cooperatives attempted in the state in the wake of the collapse of the plantation economy, which, meager as it was, had provided people with a modicum of economic support. Since Clay County produced more small co-ops than any other area in the state, several talented and committed SNCC-oriented workers had gravitated to West Point. I especially remember a weekly newspaper and a cultural arts festival, which produced a lot of excitement, and the establishment of one of the state's first legal services offices under the direction of attorney Jesse Pennington in 1969. Previously, there had been no black attorney in the entire northeastern section of Mississippi. Meanwhile, the Poor People's Corporation hoped to market the Mississippi products by locating and developing national retail outlets. Some Poor People's crafts were sold through Liberty House stores in major cities. Marketing, however, turned out to be a nightmare. Marketing difficulties also cast a pall over the future of the Clay County projects, a problem Buffington and his assistant, Frankie Free, were already tussling with when I was there during 1968–1970. Production was no obstacle, and the workers were delighted to be laboring under humane conditions they could control, and where they could demonstrate pride in their efforts. But production meant little if the products could not be sold.

During the summer of 1970, Mary Holmes hosted a summer program to upgrade the educational standards of Head Start teachers, which I participated in as a teacher. In an attempt to build reading and writing skills, poet Primus St. John and I used readings from the works of black Mississippi authors, particularly Richard Wright, a writer with whom the Head Start teachers were not familiar. We also had them write stories about their own communities and life experiences. What they lacked in technical ability was made up for in the beauty and realism of their stories, for many of the Head Start teachers in Mississippi, mostly women, were also key Movement activists in their communities.

Listening to them read their autobiographical papers gave me a much better sense of how the civil rights movement was structured from the bottom up, and a new appreciation for the silent, generally unknown legions of people who risked everything in the struggle to bring themselves and their communities into full citizenship.

Stories I heard in the Head Start classes, and the Movement leaders I met in the course of my friendship with Buffington, were the origins of the idea that it might be very worthwhile for me to begin an oral history of activists in the Mississippi Movement, realizing that if their stories were not soon recorded they would be forgotten as memories dimmed and elders died. In the mid-1970s, I dived in and began taping Mississippi activists, driving up from New Orleans for the sessions. For ten years I continued with this project, taping about forty life stories altogether.*

The first person I interviewed in 1976 was Annie Devine of Canton, one of the most extraordinary women of the Mississippi campaign. I can thank veteran SNCC leader Ed Brown for sending me to Mrs. Devine, for I had only previously known of her through Annie Moody's classic autobiography, *Coming of Age in Mississippi*, much of which tells the story of the painful effort to register blacks to vote in Canton.

Annie Devine was an insurance saleswoman and the mother of four children when the first Congress of Racial Equality organizers arrived in 1963. Canton was and is the seat of Madison County, which has a 75 percent black majority population, the same conditions that made Albany and Selma ripe for organizing. Except that in Albany, because of its professional class of blacks, and in Selma, because of the efforts of the Voters League, a handful of blacks had voted in each town. Madison County had no Voters League and a virtually nonexistent black professional class—people of color had not voted since Reconstruction. To make sure they didn't, the county courthouse was protected by a mean sheriff, Billy Noble, who apparently had a free hand in dealing with blacks who got "out of line." His antagonist, and leader of the CORE project in Canton, was a youth from New Orleans, George Raymond. Annie Moody, who was then a student at Tougaloo, just down the road a bit from Canton, was the organizer who recruited Mrs. Devine.

In 1963, Mrs. Devine was well into her middle age, divorced, caring for her children, and living in a housing project. A former schoolteacher, she knew the value of voting and full citizenship, though she never voted. It didn't take her long to decide to join in with young folk; she could help them a lot through her church contacts, and through her encyclopedic knowledge of the black community acquired from insurance canvassing. When she declared in church, "You don't have to whisper about me, I'm in it. I'm in the Movement," it opened the door for other adult black Cantonians to commit themselves. And commitment was necessary. George Raymond was jailed endlessly, and beaten numerous times. The names and addresses of

---

*The Mississippi Civil Rights Oral History Collection is in the Amistad Research Center in New Orleans, and the Tougaloo College Archives in Jackson, Mississippi.

blacks who attempted to register were printed in the local newspaper just as in Selma. Nevertheless, they persisted.

Extremely dark skinned (her skin practically glows), deliberate and meditative rather than exhortative, Mrs. Devine put me through the third degree back in 1976 before she would be interviewed. When she decided to trust me, I was amazed at her power of reflection and quality of analysis. When I asked about choices of actions, she replied, "If we had done something else, it might have been better, but we didn't know that then." In her view, the 1960s was an effort by struggling human beings to come to grips with their situation and at least attempt to do something about it, provided they could define their situation. Mrs. Devine was not capable of the salable lie, or the romanticization of the Movement. I never forgot her statement as she joked while making me coffee in 1976: "I don't know. All we may have done through the civil rights movement is open Pandora's box."

Mrs. Devine had praised C. O. Chinn, a black Canton club owner, also one of the first converts, who provided support and sustenance for Raymond and other CORE organizers. Chinn himself became a key organizer and was jailed as a result of his efforts. "If George needed a ride, Chinn drove him; if he needed food, Mrs. Chinn fed him; if he needed a bed, the Chinns provided it," explained Matt Suarez, the New Orleans former CORE leader, when I interviewed him on the Canton-Madison County 1963 effort.

Annie Devine quickly became well known within Movement circles; by 1964 she served as a statewide spokesperson, traveling to other towns to make speeches, often in concert with Fannie Lou Hamer of Sunflower County in the Delta, and Victoria Gray of Hattiesburg, two other great local leaders who emerged literally from the fertile earth of the Mississippi Movement. Mrs. Devine, Mrs. Gray, and Mrs. Hamer were chosen in statewide elections to represent the Freedom Democratic party in the challenge to unseat the all-white Mississippi Democratic party delegation during the presidential election in 1964. This historic effort, much analyzed by civil rights historians, ended in predictable political defeat but set a precedent that fore-shadowed the opening of the Democratic party to black participation in the state in the following three decades.

I returned to Canton to talk with Mrs. Devine several more times during the 1970s and '80s, and to learn from her wisdom. My interviews with her led to others and others, so that the totality of the interviews and my experiences in Mississippi gave me a special feeling for the place; not only the people, but the starkly diversified terrain, the physical beauty of the state, which stood in contrast to its history of racial grief. Because of its reputation, I came to believe that the conflict in Mississippi was more fundamental, the issues were clearer, the need greater, and the people more grateful for whatever help they received. Through its warriors for justice, male and female, white and black, I came to like the people of Mississippi and to appreciate them for their genuine belief in hope for a better future.

Now, in 1991, twenty-seven years after Freedom Summer, blacks have clearly won the ballot, though that was more the result of the Voting Rights Act of 1965, which appointed federal registrars to monitor recalcitrant areas of the South, than a capitulation by Madison County officials. Now, in the 1990s, black voters pretty much control Canton, though not Madison County, as was explained to me by Community Action Program director Walter Jones; Board of Supervisors member Karl Banks; and attorney George Nichols, a former Canton Board of Aldermen member. A deep cleavage has developed between two new black political organizations in Canton, over the few elective offices in town. There's so little private-sector work for people in Madison County, the struggle for control of political patronage and the jobs that might flow from political office has created a nasty battleground. As a result, the potential impact of a unified black vote has been substantially diluted. Meanwhile, the expansion of young white upper-middle-class housing and businesses in North Jackson has, in the seventies and eighties, flowed well across the Hinds-Madison county line into southern Madison, increasing the population and property values in Ridgeland and Madison (the town). Canton, the largest town in the county, while embroiled in its own intrablack political squabbles, has suddenly become the poor northern and primarily black relative of south Madison County. Even so, Canton is growing, Calvin Garner, a Tougaloo graduate in his thirties and an administrator for the Community Action Program, assured me during a tour he graciously gave me of the town. It didn't look like it was growing, though it did appear to be making an effort to renovate itself. There is an effort to spruce up the town square. I was happy to see a couple of black-run clothing stores a block from the square for those customers who don't shop in Jackson, and a small restaurant that sells wonderful fried catfish. The problem is, with a large shopping mall and several smaller malls, full of every sort of retail business imaginable in North Jackson, most Cantonians do their heavy shopping there. The old square, which was lined by thriving all-white businesses in 1963 and 1964, was then the main Canton shopping area for blacks, said Garner. Square business became the target of intense retaliatory boycotts when blacks were turned away from the county registration office at the still-dreary courthouse. At least those days are gone, and maybe black political officials, if they can get themselves together, will modernize the town center. "It's just that," confessed attorney George Nichols, "we're a generation behind every other place in Mississippi."

Canton doesn't seem to be a generation behind when it comes to the destructive presence of hard drugs, a fact everyone attested to. This was a completely post-1960s phenomenon in small Mississippi towns. I didn't expect to see evidence of hard drugs in places like Canton. In the sixties, the small towns still had an innocence about them; you could concentrate on worrying about the police. Movement volunteers, who were virtual strangers, could enter a town and organize in pool halls and cafés, places frequented by black youth, without encountering suspicion. That couldn't happen now. Suspicions involving drugs, along with the violence associated with drugs, not to mention undercover police work, would discourage conversations with strangers.

Garner told me that after graduating from Tougaloo College, he had moved to Detroit to find work. But then the violent crime in Detroit worried him so much he decided to return to his Canton hometown, which he thought would be safer. Canton probably is safer, but "it's not the same town I grew up in," Garner admitted. "In the old days you could leave your house doors unlocked. Not anymore."

By 1991, Mrs. Devine, now in her eighties, was living in Michigan with her daughter, Monet. I did talk with Jewel Williams, Mrs. Devine's intelligent, and exuberant, protégée, now in her fifties and a ten-year veteran on the Board of Aldermen. She also hosts a radio talk show.

Jewel Williams first met Mrs. Devine when she was known as "the insurance lady. When she dropped insurance to work with CORE's project in Canton, it made a difference." Ms. Williams was then working at Madison Furniture Company making $1.05 per hour. She quickly became a younger convert to the Movement, a member of a group Mrs. Devine called "the girls," and when she joined an attempt to unionize the factory in 1965, she was fired. Finally, she and Mrs. Devine were able to find work in one of the Head Start programs. "I took home forty-five dollars per week in the furniture factory. Head Start paid one hundred eighteen dollars a week. We were happy to get that work."

Ms. Williams confirmed the political splintering in Canton—"No one seems to be able to ride over it; you're either in one camp or the other. Our troubles really began," she added, "way back in the sixties with the competition for Head Start jobs. For people who had been involved in protest demonstrations, there was no work after the Movement except for federal programs. No white man was gon' hire us to work in his business, and people like Annie Devine and myself weren't gonna pick anybody's cotton, or work as domestics in any white man's house." Those days were over. So those few federal antipoverty program jobs had to make up the difference, but there simply weren't enough even though the Mississippi Head Start program was the largest in the nation by 1970 (more than one hundred centers served more than ten thousand children). I remembered when I was working in the Mary Holmes Head Start program how jealously the workers guarded their jobs, even though their salaries would have been considered a pittance by national standards. But federally funded jobs were the only ones these black Mississippi women were going to get in Mississippi. Those meager salaries provided a degree of theretofore unknown independence for staff members. The program itself provided educational advantages for its participating children, which, over the years, motivated many of them toward college.

Because Head Start was so economically crucial, bitter disputes emerged over who would control the program in the state. Since the Canton center was the largest in the state, it quickly became a political football. The entire story, as it was explained to me, is enormously complicated, but to give some indication of the depth of the bitterness, C. O. Chinn and George Raymond, those two staunch allies in the Canton voting struggle, became enemies in the late 1960s over their competition for a Head Start job, a dispute that must have been terribly demoralizing to those who knew them in the Movement. "That got us off to a *very* bad start," bemoaned

Ms. Williams. Eventually, Raymond took sick and left Canton for good in the early seventies, returning to New Orleans. In 1973 he died in New Orleans at the age of thirty. His close friend, Matt Suarez, observed that George Raymond's entire "adult life was devoted to Canton. When things didn't work out for him there, you could say he died of heartbreak." In Canton, one could almost draw a straight line from the struggle to win the ballot to competition within Head Start over jobs to warring political factions within the black community, an amazing dissipation of the unity and dogged determination represented by the Freedom Democratic party.

To provide some background, during the unforgettable summer of 1964 the civil rights groups in the state together decided, in a moment of inspired brilliance, that they would dramatize voting barriers against blacks by staging their own state-wide elections. Though the votes didn't count, the well-publicized process demonstrated the potential strength of the black vote, and in the same stroke, the extent of the denial of the ballot in Mississippi.

It may have been anticipated that once blacks acquired the ballot in a heavy black majority area, they would compete with each other for the available spoils, but too often the benefits from black electoral victories have been limited to the few. Most of the people to whom I spoke, from Greensboro to Canton, have this belief. This makes me wonder if blacks have not expected too much in terms of the potential social and economic changes that would result from merely electing black political officials.

First, as everyone pointed out along my journey, political office without economic strength usually becomes only a celebratory window-dressing; some black person has acquired a title and salary. That new official, however, is *very* vulnerable to lures and deals from those who *do* have money to offer in exchange for votes, or contracts—a phenomenon all too painfully obvious in the years since blacks have been electing their own officials.

Second, in a multiparty open system, electoral politics is by its very nature divisive, tending to break up blocs of voters, unless there is some overwhelming unifying issue to bind the bloc together. Anyone who qualifies and can win enough votes can be elected. Where the candidate stands on the issues may be of no consequence whatsoever.

The problem here is that the rationale for blacks acquiring the vote in the first place was, hopefully, to empower people to address issues and concerns that they felt were neglected because they were excluded from the political system. Maybe now, as we approach the twenty-first century, a new black political think tank, or political action committee, is needed to identify and address national political issues affecting all black communities, since too many individual politicians are primarily concerned with holding office no matter what. The NAACP once performed the community spokesperson role, but it simply doesn't or cannot fulfill that function anymore. New realities have created new issues that require specialized and sophisticated study. Canton's problems were but a symptom, I thought, of the larger picture of mixed results from black electoral success in the South and the nation.

⌒

I thought it time to leave Canton, and move on to West Point, in the northeastern part of the state. I drove back to Jackson, then over to Meridian on I-20, then took the mostly two-lane U.S. 45 north to West Point, as the temperature dropped into the 60s and 70s; it was now mid-September. This was the route I usually followed in the old days when I was commuting from New Orleans to Mary Holmes to teach. I was immediately struck by the town's economic strength: A huge Babcock and Wilcox plant; Bryan's Meats, one of the largest meat-packing companies in the South; and Fitz Lumber Company were the largest businesses. West Point was deliberately chosen in 1857 as a railroad depot; today goods headed for Mobile and Chicago travel through West Point. Small as it is (population ten thousand), the town is a crossroads. Location is just about everything in determining whether a town thrives or dies, I was learning.

West Point blacks may not have the top jobs at these factories, but they have jobs to an extent rare in any southern town. The resulting prosperity evidences itself today in nice brick homes with neat lawns, new automobiles, and lifted spirits. I drove past a black man mowing his lawn while he hummed, loud enough to override the lawn mower motor. In the white community, there are magnificent homes; some are truly mansions. At 4:00 P.M. there was a traffic jam on Main Street, a congestion that could only have been caused by a change in factory work-shifts.

Sitting in a restaurant on U.S. 45, I am struck again by how loudly West Point blacks speak and laugh, as if they are shouting to one another across fields, or all the way down the block. People were gregarious and open—as I remembered the town when I was working in Mary Holmes.

I arrived on a Saturday, which was an election day. When I went to see Sylvester Harris (who was suggested to me by one of the best-known SNCC veterans, Hollis Watkins, originally of Summit, now of Jackson), Harris was deeply involved in campaigning at his office across the street from the courthouse for a white candidate his political group was supporting. In his late thirties, medium-dark skinned, a former athlete and schoolteacher, and openly friendly, Harris is a native of White Station, one of the West Point satellite towns. Blacks and whites were stationed around the courthouse (respecting the proper distance from the polling booths) handing out flyers for their candidates. Here, too, blacks (51 percent of the population in Clay County but less than 40 percent of the registered electorate) had come into the political process, selectively backing white candidates depending on what they were offering the black community.

When John Buffington ran for mayor in 1970, it was the first time blacks had been politically active in the county on a major level since Reconstruction. Buffington lost the first primary and the election by an *identical* vote count, as I remembered it. During the campaign, Buffington's driver, Johnnie Thomas, was shot dead at a busy West Point intersection on a Saturday morning while he sat in his truck waiting for his wife to complete her shopping.

John Buffington left West Point in the early 1970s, and now lives in Atlanta. When I drove down Cottrell Street looking for Buffington's old Clay County Development Cooperation office, there was no evidence of the site—even the huge oak tree across the street from the office that was the communal gathering place for youth was gone. When I asked Harris and attorney Bennie Turner, a black West Point native and Mary Holmes graduate, about the economic co-ops, they remembered them, but none of the co-ops succeeded past the mid-seventies. Turner has done well, however. After graduation from Ole Miss Law School he joined the private firm organized by former legal services director Jesse Pennington in 1974. When Pennington departed, Turner inherited the firm. Conservative, soft-spoken, and orderly, Turner is now county attorney and serves as board chair for Mary Holmes, his alma mater. On Cottrell Street I looked for the old pool hall, bar, fish fry joint, funeral home, dry cleaner, and sandwich shop—but they were all gone also.

Buffington and I had been close friends. I decided to drive over to Atlanta to ask him why the seemingly promising economic co-ops didn't work out. Working now as a manager in a chain store, Buffington was far removed from his former civil rights milieu. It was painful asking him to go over the story of the failure of the Clay County projects, but I persisted and eventually he agreed to do it.

"First, we never had enough money to do things we were trying to do," he began. "We started with nothing. Secondly, CCDP, our mother ship, was designed to provide basic social services; that was its reason for being. Then when we decided to try to produce goods for external markets, that required another motion—and these two basic motions were in conflict. We just couldn't do both successfully. We never solved or resolved, that conflict.

"Also, like a lot of new black businesses, we lacked expertise and managerial experience. Our co-op managers were political-oriented activists, not businesspeople. Inevitably, political disputes spilled over into business matters.

"I feel there was just a general lack of know-how. Our co-ops produced quality items, but we could never achieve quantity. A little help from banks might have made a difference, but they wouldn't loan us money because they knew our limitations."

"Was it at all worth it?" I couldn't help but ask.

"Sure," he said without hesitation. "In terms of the long-range benefits to people who worked with us, it was worth it. The co-ops brought people together for crucial discussions over how best to proceed now that the Movement was over; and even if there was no agreement, the discussions themselves were worthwhile because the debates were serious. Finally, our economic experiments were innovative and they influenced other statewide efforts, some of which were very successful, like Mississippi Action for Community Education in the Delta, which loans money to help develop businesses, and creates small businesses on its own. Most of the people went on to other situations, and have been able to live productive lives. That's a kind of success, don't you think?" The fate of the Clay County co-ops did evoke memories of New Communities in Albany, and its demise. I didn't know of a single business venture that was an outgrowth of the Movement that survived, if it in any way differed from the prevailing capitalist mode.

West Point was doing okay, but as for Mary Holmes, it seemed to have receded back into a shell. When I drove onto the campus and walked around, I had no desire to introduce myself or speak to anyone; I realized there probably was no one who was there twenty years ago, or who knew what a live wire this school had been during the immediate post-Movement period. The community meetings, statewide Movement activities, and school affairs, which had been so frequent and exciting when I was there from 1968 to 1970, now seemed to have been only a mirage. If I hadn't known those things happened in that place, I would never have believed it.

After a couple of days in West Point, I headed back toward Jackson where I expected to meet Secretary of State Dick Molpus, hook up with Hollis Watkins again, and see my old friend Jerry Ward, who is professor of literature at Tougaloo College. But first I wanted to detour over to Philadelphia in Neshoba County, where I had never been before, to see if I could meet Mr. Cornelius Steele, one of the charter members of Mount Zion Church in Longdale, a satellite town of Philadelphia. Mount Zion was one of two churches that had been receptive to visits by CORE workers Michael Schwerner, James Chaney, and Andrew Goodman during Freedom Summer, 1964. They were murdered while in Neshoba County in June 1964 and buried in an unmarked grave near Philadelphia. Their bodies were finally found, proving that the murders had actually happened; key whites in Neshoba County insisted that since the three had "just disappeared," there were no killings. The FBI finally discovered who the murderers were through informants—but it was not until 1967 that seven men were tried and convicted (including a Neshoba County deputy sheriff, Cecil Price) of violating the federal "civil rights" of the civil rights workers. They served a little jail time, and were out in no time. But recently (in 1989), a commemoration of the sacrifices of the three martyrs was held in Philadelphia— and the grave of James Chaney, the Meridian black youth who was a CORE volunteer, was upgraded and cleared off. In addition, a movie about the killings, *Mis-*

*sissippi Burning*, had had a strong run, though the movie distorted the role of the FBI investigators by making them into heroes committed to racial justice, which they weren't, and by evidencing no understanding whatsoever of the civil rights movement and its constituent workers.

⌒

I drove southward to Meridian, then over to Philadelphia on Mississippi Highway 19, the same route Schwerner, Goodman, and Chaney had followed. It was an extremely forested drive of forty miles up and down hills on roads with no shoulders, though there were cutoff roads. There were more lumber trucks on the highway than I expected. It wasn't an easy drive; a two-lane highway just about the entire distance. I felt like I was steadily climbing a large red-clay hill. This drive created a weird sense of isolation, all the more so for me because there was no evidence of an African-American presence living along the road, or driving cars or trucks. The tall pines were browning, and in the early October afternoon there was just a hint of coolness in the air.

As I neared Philadelphia, I noticed several winding cutoff roads and I remembered that Matt Suarez, who had set up the CORE project in Meridian and recruited James Chaney, was famous for his daredevil driving. When there was trouble, he was the one chosen to be at the wheel; I could see from these roads that knowing the shortcuts was an essential part of security. Chaney was driving the Sunday they were caught; I wonder what would have happened if he'd decided to race as fast as he could for the relative safety of Meridian. Then I remembered the car had a flat tire; he wouldn't have gotten very far.

Pretty soon I arrived at the crest of a hill and I was in Philadelphia. It wasn't much, a 1940s-looking town with tall water towers, faded brown brick buildings, railroad tracks at the bottom of the town hill where the blacks lived, a Kentucky Fried Chicken joint, and an architecturally uninteresting courthouse and square dominated by businesses that seemed to have occupied the same spots for half a century. There weren't many people downtown.

I learned from reading a comprehensive study of the murders, *We Are Not Afraid* by Seth Cagin and Philip Dray, that Cornelius Steele and the Mount Zion Church were not actually in Philadelphia, but in an unincorporated village called Longdale on the outskirts of Philadelphia. I had no idea how to get there. At a gas station, I found a young black man who did know; in fact, he was headed that way. So I followed him, driving eastward on Mississippi 16, and after a couple of turns, entered a rock road. After driving a mile or so, my guide pointed out Mr. Steele's frame house set a few feet back from the road.

Both Cornelius Steele and his wife, Mamie, were home. In his seventies now, tall, and extremely polite and pleasant, Mr. Steele agreed to show me Mount Zion Church and Longdale sites if I returned the next day. I asked him about possible dangers in driving to Longdale from Meridian. "No. It's not as violent now," he replied. "At least not as open. Back in the old days, my home was burned. It was awful then." But the soft-spoken Mrs. Steele interjected, "It's better if you don't drive up here at night." Before I departed, their grandson, Benson, sixteen, arrived home from his Philadelphia High School basketball practice, dropped off by his white coach. Benson is a string bean with an ebullient smile. "Everything okay at school, Benson?" I asked.

"Yes," he answered cautiously.

"But we don't allow girls to call him," his grandmother volunteered again. "Some of them simply don't have any sense."

The next day I drove back to Longdale, taking a shortcut the Steeles told me about that allowed me to avoid going through Philadelphia. Mr. Steele took me over to his church, Mount Zion, a very substantial red brick church, with its cornerstone stating the church was first built in 1893 (probably the period when the community was organized) and rebuilt (after it was burned by racists to lure Schwerner back into the area) in 1965. It was rebuilt again after another fire in 1971. Mr. Steele is chairman of the board of trustees.

Recently, as part of the 1989 twenty-five-year commemoration, a beautiful marker had been placed in the yard honoring the memory of the three murdered civil rights workers. Mr. Steele and I drove to the spot where their car was pulled over by police in 1964, and to the road where they were killed, and to the farm where they had been buried until the bodies were discovered.

Two things were bothering Mr. Steele. One was the recent arrest of his son after what he described as an altercation with police at his son's place of business on Longdale Road. His son had been charged and convicted and was presently incarcerated in Parchman State Penitentiary. Mr. Steele felt his son did not receive adequate legal defense. He was also extremely disturbed over the recent hanging of a black youth in the Philadelphia jail. The death was ruled a suicide. Mr. Steele (and apparently many other blacks in the Philadelphia area) believed it was not suicide. Mr. Steele asked me to return to Meridian and contact undertaker Obie Clark, the regional NAACP leader, about these cases.

I decided to do so, but when I spoke to Mr. Clark he was already aware of the Philadelphia cases, though he hardly knew what to do. Both situations obviously needed to be thoroughly investigated by attorneys. It seemed that Mr. Clark, now in his late fifties or early sixties, a former football coach and high school teacher and currently owner of a funeral home, *was* the NAACP in this area of Mississippi and he was simply overwhelmed. I called the Legal Defense Fund in New York seeking help, explaining that I once worked there. I was told they only had time for capital cases, to try someone else, which I did, but I was never able to get to the bottom of these complaints. They do illustrate the continuing isolation and vulnerability of blacks in today's South. The complaints also illustrate the need for a more up-to-date racial organization, which can examine cases of abuse, particularly by police. The kinds of stories I heard from Mr. Steele are common all over the country, but each one is handled separately as an isolated incident. "Calling the NAACP," which is overwhelmed and hardly equipped to perform investigations, will no longer suffice.

My Philadelphia detour had now stretched to three days, but I decided to stay another day and drive over to the village of Harmony, an unincorporated black community in Leake County just west of Neshoba County and a few miles east of the town of Carthage. I planned to visit Mrs. Winson Hudson, my favorite among the old Mary Holmes Head Start teachers whom I met in 1970. Light skinned, assertive, and outspoken, Mrs. Hudson reminded me of Ladybelle, my maternal grandmother in Houston. People who got on Ladybelle's bad side were in for trouble; I sensed the same quality in Mrs. Hudson. Ladybelle not only had her say; she had no compunctions about invoking the Lord on her side. I thought Mrs. Hudson was a little bit like that, though maybe not quite as excessive.

In our classes at Mary Holmes, Mrs. Hudson wrote and spoke about her tiny, rural lumberjack community of the 1960s, and how they were forced to protect themselves by setting up armed guards once they tried to vote. She spoke with pride about their old Rosenwald School, their only school, and the Head Start Center, which, once established, became a sort of spiritual descendant of the school.

Harmony, like so many other primarily or entirely black southern hamlets, was an oasis of black independence and even defiance in the midst of the oppression and victimization that characterized the surrounding areas. Many of these people had owned their own land since the nineteenth century when blacks were buying land, and were able to maintain themselves as independent farmers. This was quite an achievement—surviving the terrors of Redemption, family migrations northward in search of work, and the awful Depression of the 1930s. When I visited Harmony Head Start Center in 1970 with our Free Southern Theater troupe, I had observed a community pride and sense of self-worth that were indeed rare in the South—I thought of it as the pride of a community of landowners.

Later, upon returning to Meridian, I asked Obie Clark to take me to James Chaney's grave site. Chaney is buried in a cemetery on the outskirts of Meridian. As Clark said, and I had discovered for myself, "You can't find it, I have to show you." After several twisting and turning roads, we arrived at the graveyard to discover, to our dismay, that someone had defaced Chaney's new gravestone. The drawing of black and white hands clasping an encased half-bas photograph of the deceased was damaged by a bullet fired into the head of the photograph, so that the picture was chipped. The inscription on Chaney's gravestone nevertheless remained intact:

THERE ARE THOSE WHO ARE ALIVE

YET WILL NEVER LIVE.

THERE ARE THOSE WHO ARE DEAD

YET WILL LIVE FOREVER.

From Meridian, I once again took I-20 to Jackson, having arranged an appointment with Secretary of State Dick Molpus. Molpus was recommended to me by Mississippi SNCC veteran Hollis Watkins as "the most progressive white politician in the state." Molpus, Watkins added, had appointed blacks to more than "show" positions on his staff, including attorney Constance Slaughter Harvey of Jackson, as assistant secretary of state. What really caught my attention was the fact that Molpus was a native of Philadelphia, where I had just visited the sites of the 1964 killings. When events were organized in 1989 to commemorate the sacrifices of the slain workers, and a historical marker dedicated at Mount Zion Church, Molpus was the only major Mississippi official to attend, and he even offered an "apology," in the name of the state, to the families of the deceased, a gesture that Watkins took to be genuine if somewhat awkward.

My interest in Molpus was further piqued because he is a founder of Parents for Public Schools, a new organization designed to stop the flight of white students to segregated academies. Organized in Jackson in 1989 at Molpus's home, Parents for Public Schools has now grown to twelve chapters within the state of Mississippi.

We talked at Molpus's secretary of state office in Jackson. I asked Molpus what had brought him to support integrated public schools when the opposite position had long been so politically popular in Mississippi. A rather short man in his mid-forties, immaculately dressed, and very smooth, Molpus impressed me with his intelligence and candor. "My wife and I," he replied, "and about two dozen other white families decided all the seg academies do is divide the resources of Mississippi. We are already the poorest state in America. Besides, the academies are not better academically than the public schools; that's just a myth. In fact, our public schools have steadily improved since the early attempts to comply with desegregation orders in the seventies, particularly since passage of a state educational reform act in 1982. Public school facilities have also improved, and public school teachers make about twice what academy teachers earn.

"Our group found a public school we liked. The school was eighty percent black; but we sent our kids there, and now we have a more racially balanced school that we're *very* happy with. This was a school the Jackson system was thinking about closing. Reversing white flight is a touchy issue, but it's one of those things that simply has to happen. When I was growing up, blacks were totally excluded from the power loop. Now, in Mississippi, which is forty percent black, blacks have entered the power loop. There's no way that's going to reverse itself in the twenty-first century. The only way we can all progress is to transform this state, given our racial realities, into something positive and creative."

I asked Molpus if his Neshoba County origins had induced a soul-searching that was a catalyst for his enlightened Mississippi racial perspective. "I'm not sure," he replied. "I was only fourteen when the murders occurred. I had no consciousness of what was happening in town racially. My father owned a very successful lumber business. I pretty much accepted everything my parents and their well-to-do set said.

"I do remember that when the civil rights workers disappeared, the white leadership of Philadelphia said the whole thing was a hoax, a ploy by civil rights activists to attract national attention to Mississippi. There was no banding together to say, 'This is wrong, we need to deal with it.' Then, when the bodies were discovered, they were all surprised. I was surprised. But we shouldn't have been. The Klan had threatened my father, threatened to burn his lumber business down if he didn't fire his black workers who attended NAACP meetings. My father told them he wouldn't do it, and had to place an armed guard out to protect his property. But I'm not sure any of that is the sole cause of my present position on schools. What I've come to see is that we as whites must finally face racial reality in Mississippi."

The Parents for Public Schools initiative for the support of integrated public schools is one of the most hopeful developments I encountered during my journey. It doesn't bother me that the group is limited to just a few people, or that there will surely be problems down the road over the question of curriculum or conflicts like those in Selma over class and racial stratifications—at least it's a beginning. Whites have to support the public schools, and support bond issues to improve schools. If their children attend those schools, there's a chance they will do that. If not, they probably won't support a taxation they feel does not benefit them.

The problem of poor educational standards and its negative effects on employability is clearly affecting the Mississippi Delta. Dick Molpus estimates that the Delta lost forty thousand people in the 1980s, people who migrated to northern urban centers in search of work.

It was early October when I left Jackson headed northwestward for the Delta. I decided to travel on U.S. 49, one of my favorite highways. U.S. 49 runs from Gulfport on the Gulf Coast northward through the heart of the Delta, then crosses the Mississippi and winds its way to north Arkansas. From Jackson, it is mostly a two-lane rising and dipping road, with very little traffic. The only town of any size whatsoever between Jackson and Indianola is Yazoo City, about forty miles north of Jackson. En route to Yazoo, U.S. 49 flows through pleasant foothills, making long, lazy curves; the visibility is excellent this October afternoon. For miles ahead I can see the few cars and trucks crawling my way.

Near Yazoo City there is, on the western ridge of U.S. 49, an expansive spread of kudzu vine, a luscious vibrant green bush that grows quickly, and is both attractive and symbolic of nature growing wild in Mississippi. When I see this stuff, I feel like I'm entering a more primeval land, a land not ruled by towns or urban centers.

At Yazoo City, a town about the size of Selma, U.S. 49 splits into two roads, 49 East going to Greenwood, and 49 West winding its way up to Indianola. I'm going to Indianola. The two branches converge again in the Delta at a village called Tutwiler.

A half mile or so inside Yazoo City on 49 West, the highway undergoes a tremendous downhill descent, a drive that requires excellent brakes. At the flat bottom is downtown Yazoo City. This is the entrance into the Mississippi Delta; there are no more hills for perhaps 150 miles. I cross the railroad tracks, and there is the main black neighborhood.

When I reached the village of Louise, I realized I was on a new section of the road, a bypass that takes one around the town. I decided to detour over to the old highway that cuts through the heart of town, the heart of town being no more than three or four blocks long. Dusk was steadily approaching and a full moon was rising, gigantic in its seeming closeness to the earth.

From the old highway I took a turnoff to another road leading across the railroad tracks to a huge cotton gin, at least I thought it was a gin. On this two-block street, there were several parked cars and quite a few people milling about, apparently just off from work, intoxicated by the excitement of the glorious rising moon as if there was no more fascinating or wonderful place on earth at this moment in history.

~

Leaving Louise, heading still northward toward the slightly larger town of Belzoni, I was struck by how denuded the cotton fields on both sides of the highway are—no workers, no worker housing, no plantation shacks, no sharecroppers. Those were images of the past based on photographs and earlier trips along this road. Somehow I expected to see some of this in 1991. Or remnants of the former plantation life. The only remnants were of recently picked cotton, strewn along the edges of the highway, residue from the huge trucks that transported cotton from the fields to the warehouses and gins, and woe to the driver caught in traffic behind one of those crawling trucks.

~

Most of the cotton along U.S. 49 has been picked. Now the process is thoroughly mechanized. The cotton pickers pick the cotton, then a worker follows in another machine that grinds up the plants in order to ready the field for the alternative crop—usually soybeans. During the day, midget crop duster airplanes perform acrobatics, swooping low above the earth to spray the fields with insecticide.

Belzoni is slightly larger than Louise, and the seat of Humphries County, which I am driving through. Belzoni is the place where NAACP leader George Lee was murdered in 1955; his successor, Gus Courts, was shot later that same year, just barely escaping with his life. He quickly moved to Chicago.

~

From Belzoni to Indianola is only twenty-five miles. Now I am passing huge catfish farms, Mississippi's new agricultural industry for which high hopes are held (the state catfish industry brings in an estimated annual income of $300 million).

Approaching Indianola from the south on U.S. 49, I could see on the right the huge Delta Pride catfish-processing complex, the largest such plant in the world. In 1986, Indianola had been in the news because of a strike by women workers, almost all black, at Delta Pride against poor working conditions, and also because of an extraordinary effort by its blacks (about 60 percent) to force the school board to appoint a black superintendent. Though the Delta Pride strike ended inconclusively, it did create an awareness of the many hand injuries suffered by low-level workers, which may have resulted in improved conditions. As for the public school issue, after a tight boycott of downtown businesses for thirty-seven days, which cost them an estimated $3 million, the white business community endorsed the appointment of Robert Merritt, a veteran black teacher and principal. Since that time Merritt has been credited with turning the public school system around and winning the active financial support of the white business community. According to Merritt, when we talked in his school board offices, a biracial task force of business leaders has now adopted certain schools. They support them through scholarships, and so forth. This business-section support was the catalyst for the passage of a $5 million school bond issue in 1988, the first in thirty-seven years. Indianola was one of the few towns in the Delta that felt like it was on the upswing. Even its two-block downtown business area looked alive and well.

Black Indianola is also one of the few Delta towns that has a thriving nightlife, most prominently the Club Ebony on Church Street, "the blues street" (there is also a street named for blues musician B. B. King, an Indianola native). The Club Ebony attracts a young-to-middle-age crowd from as far away as Greenville. Now a disco, in the past this club has attracted national artists. Unfortunately, I didn't discover any Indianola club featuring live blues.

The Reverend Michael Freeman of Indianola is a young Methodist minister and native of Monroe County in northeastern "hill county," north of West Point and south of Tupelo. ("Hill county blacks are more independent than Delta blacks," he asserted.) Freeman cited the activism displayed by black women during their long, difficult community-supported strike against Delta Pride in the mid-1980s as a psychological reason for the current upbeat mood in Indianola. The results of both the school campaign and the strike brought long-range positive results, according to Freeman. "The strike helped to break down class stratifications within the race;

people had to unify. Secondly, the workers themselves, for probably the first time in their lives, began to understand their own strength; they felt good about themselves." Freeman's words echoed as a lesson learned all along my journey. Those towns with an active, issue-oriented and engaged black community, supported by those in the white community who shared the concern with issues, were alive towns. They were the places that were most conscious of their Movement heritage, and saw themselves as continuing a change that began in the sixties or even before then. Indianola, for instance, had been an awful place for blacks; the White Citizens Council was born there. Its large black community fought hard for rights and the ballot. Now, in 1991, white business leaders were supporting the funding of the predominantly black public schools as an "investment" in their town's future. As a consequence, there was a feeling of hope and potential at that particular spot in the Delta.

Attorney Carver Randle and the Reverend David Mathews, two prominent Indianola blacks, felt so good about Indianola that they asserted that Indianola had "passed Greenville by." Greenville is Indianola's larger and better-known neighbor, situated thirty miles to the west on U.S. 82 at the Mississippi River. Indeed, it did seem as if Greenville had come upon hard times. A city of forty-five thousand, five times the size of Indianola, and Mississippi's most important river port (though it doesn't actually sit on the Mississippi, but a cutoff called Lake Ferguson), Greenville has long served as the Delta's banking and commercial center. It was only natural that key black and interracial organizations working to improve conditions in the Delta sought to establish their headquarters there. The Delta Ministry, Mississippi Action for Community Education, and the Delta Foundation are the most prominent of these groups.

The Delta Ministry was established by the Commission on Religion and Race of the National Council of Churches during Freedom Summer, 1964, to assist the impoverished black community and to help foster better racial relations. MACE, as it is called, was organized by SNCC leader Ed Brown and indigenous Delta activists in 1966 to enhance community education in impoverished areas through workshops, and so forth. Funded by the Ford Foundation, MACE now sponsors the Delta Blues Festival, which was organized by folklorist Worth Long in the mid-1970s. The Delta Foundation was created by MACE in collaboration with the Delta Ministry to stimulate economic development. Delta Foundation, now run by former Delta Ministry director Harry Bowie, was developed into a potent regional force by the late Charles Bannerman, who created a spin-off organization, Delta Enterprises. Delta Enterprises was designed to assist small businesses with supportive loans, and itself has created several small businesses, like Fine Vines, a jean factory in Greenville that employs about a hundred workers. So there have been post-Movement efforts to address the serious economic problems in the Delta.

"The problem," said Owen Brooks, who served in 1991 as legislative aide to then Congressman Mike Espy, "is the poverty in this area is so overwhelming our economic development projects don't even scratch the surface in terms of what we need." When I drove around Greenville, the town appeared almost deserted, in contrast to the place I remembered when I visited the Delta in the sixties and seventies. Obviously, there was little work for the unskilled former field workers, people who had migrated into town from the now mechanized surrounding fields. It was the story of Albany again, but Albany at least had factories for those who were determined to acquire skills. Greenville had nothing.

"Greenville has steadily lost good, solid small businesses to other communities," continued Brooks, as we conversed in a restaurant. Now in his late sixties, Brooks came south to Greenville to work as a volunteer with the Delta Ministry in 1966. An engineer in his native Boston, he had long been a black leader in civil rights activities there. Once he saw the Delta, he fell in love with it and never left. He also never lost his New England accent, which makes him sound permanently displaced in the Mississippi Delta.

"There have long been problems with the educational system in Greenville," Brooks said, "and it's gotten worse and worse. There is no effective interracial coalition here, despite the town's former liberal reputation."

When I spoke to Congressman Espy in Greenville, he readily agreed that the town was suffering from a leadership vacuum, one of "a myriad of illnesses." In his late thirties, suave, almost boyish, well spoken, and a member of a prominent black funeral home family, Espy was able to command enough white support to become in 1986 the first black Mississippi congressman since Reconstruction. He easily won reelection in 1988 and 1990 in his 52 percent white Second Congressional District. Representing an area that is progressively losing population and jobs, he sees the catfish industry as one of the prime hopes for recovery. The Delta was full of new catfish ponds where once were cotton fields.

⌐

I decided to head for the tiny, all-black town called Mound Bayou, on U.S. 61 in the heart of the Delta, to see L. C. Dorsey, who was administrator of the Delta Health Center. Ms. Dorsey, now in her fifties, the mother of six children who has recently earned her doctorate in social work—L. C. Dorsey is truly a child of the Delta. Short in stature, but passionate in her convictions, she is one of the great Mississippi success-through-struggle stories. "I grew up living in four counties," she told me, "Bolivar, Washington, Sunflower, and Leflore. I went to high school in Drew, but never graduated." Eventually, she ended up at the Stony Brook branch of the State University of New York, and enrolled in a social welfare program, where she wrote a paper on women incarcerated in Mississippi's Parchman Penitentiary, the huge, infamous state prison. Back in Mississippi for a period, she worked in Head Start, attended the University of Mississippi Law School for a year, wrote articles for Charles Tisdale's black weekly, the *Jackson Advocate*. I first heard of L. C. Dorsey when she worked for the Lawyers Committee for Civil Rights, monitoring complaints at Parchman Penitentiary, a job she held for eight years and performed with such tenacity that her investigations and the legal suits that ensued virtually transformed the brutal Mississippi prisons into an acceptable modern system. Her doctorate is from Howard University, her dissertation on prisoners who had killed their mates.

I drove the fifty miles to Mound Bayou on U.S. 61 from Leland, just a few miles east of Greenville, passing through Shaw and Cleveland. By now most of the cotton was picked and the plants were cleaned from their fields.

"We're suffering," Ms. Dorsey began, as we talked in her health center office, "from the demise of a sense of community. What used to hold us together was apprehension—churches, families, and extended families offered help to people in need. These were the units of community survival. The last time I remember this kind of support system existing was during the civil rights movement. Somehow our sense of family has broken down, felt all the more painfully in desolate areas like the Delta. Welfare was destructive because it forced women into a dependency role. Then there was housing built outside the inner cities, which broke up neighborhoods. Recently, I moved back to the town of Shelby [just north of Mound Bayou]. But I don't know people on my block. All this is new.

"Now I worry about crime in a way I never did before. Crime is directly connected with unemployment, but there is also an alienation among young people—a concern with the materialistic: cars, sneakers, clothes. Drugs have accentuated this process by clouding and obscuring concepts of success.

"What we have is a new group of people who have become dross. The prisons are their intended future, new and ever more glorious prisons, especially for young black males. Once," she remembered, "I was visiting Parchman, just a few miles from here on U.S. 49. These visits were always difficult because it was so painful I hated to go, and I heard prisoners laughing, enjoying themselves. It made me mad that they were laughing, when I felt maybe they should be crying. I asked Dwight Presley, who is now an associate warden, 'Why are these people so happy in here?' He answered, 'You don't realize. There's whole families in here; they're happy when they see each other.' They're also happy when they have a certified role in society, as criminals or prisoners, the natural conclusion to how they have been treated all their lives."

"I agree with all that, L. C.," I said. "Everything I've seen on this trip confirms those impressions. But what can we do to change some of this?"

"All I can see," she replied, "is that our salvation has to come from looking back at what we've done in the past that worked. We've got to do something for ourselves; those of us who see what's happening have to take more initiative. For one thing, we have to put money back into the black community. And we've got to do a better job with the education of our youngsters, both in and out of the public schools."

⌒

As I drove back down U.S. 61 headed for Greenville, then over to Mississippi I and the Mississippi River, southward to Mayersville, where I would meet Unita Blackwell and bring this nine-month odyssey through the South to a conclusion, I reflected on the issues L. C. Dorsey had brought up. I felt there was a need for new, specialized organizations to deal with today's complex issues of education, unemployment, drug abuse, and crime, and to monitor political officials, white or black. Relying on the NAACP as a catch-all was passé. It seemed as if the black community in the South, which had been the brave protagonist for change in the 1940s, '50s, and '60s, had now fallen behind, become less aggressive, and less able to assess what had happened after the momentous changes, or exchanges, of the '70s and '80s, had occurred. It was now time to take account.

As I drove southward into the waning day, I could see the moon rising above the fields; in the Delta the land is so awesomely flat. U.S. 61 parallels the railroad tracks, the same railroads that helped make so much of the agricultural South profitable, the same railroads that carried people away from these lands once they were no longer profitable. I flipped on the radio and picked up a blues music program from Clarksdale, twenty-five miles north of Mound Bayou. Somehow, through the force of that music, so much of it about parting and leaving, and the wistful sound of train whistles, the roaring rhythm of train wheels, I could feel the spirit of the people who had once worked this land and have left, splintering families and memories.

In my own family, on my father's side based in Georgia, I could hardly trace my ancestors back beyond my father's mother. My mother's Texas roots were torn up, too. There was nothing left of her mother's old village of Cheapeside, on the outskirts of Gonzales. Sure, some of the same structures were still there, the wind blowing through them, but there were no people. They had all died or left— endlessly searching for the ever-illusory betterment of conditions—to California from Cheapeside, to Chicago from the Mississippi Delta. On my mother's side there was the legendary figure of my great-grandfather, Ben, the furthest we could go back into our hazy past. We had heard he was a stagecoach driver between Oklahoma and Mexico. It was his spirit, I had come to accept, that had possessed me, and was driving me along all these southern roads—from North Carolina to the Mississippi River. I shared with Ben a compulsive yearning for wandering. Now, amazingly, these fields I was driving through gave me a feeling of security, of at least temporary rest, as they have for so many others, particularly those of African descent. Can any of those people ever really *be* from Chicago, Detroit, or New York City? I didn't think so.

Mississippi 1 south of Greenville is one of the most isolated highways in the South. After about fifty miles I reached the Mayersville turnoff, a westward turn on Mississippi 14 that goes straight to the Mississippi River. There was not a soul in sight, hardly a farmhouse and no cars coming the other way. Suddenly, a village appeared a mile or so ahead, a mirage it would seem. When I reached it—all one quarter of a square mile of it—with its population of 475 persons—it was Mayersville. Behind the town is the Mississippi River levee and after a half mile or so of batture, the river itself.

The town exists because of the river. Before the Civil War Issaquena County was one of the most prosperous areas of cotton and slave plantations, with huge numbers of slaves per owner, more than any other area of Mississippi. In 1851 Issaquena was home to the largest plantation in the Delta, with more than 700 slaves, according to James C. Cobb in *The Most Southern Place on Earth*. A river port was built to export the abundance of cotton.

One hundred years later the population of Issaquena County is only 1,730, of Mayersville only 475, the port forgotten. The town consists mostly of blacks and a tiny number of whites. The county courthouse is still in this settlement.

In the early 1960s when SNCC workers showed up in this forgotten place, one of the first blacks they talked into attempting to vote was Unita Blackwell, then in her late twenties, a cotton picker married to a native of the county, with not even a high school education.

Despite her lack of education, Mrs. Blackwell was brilliant and aggressive. Turned down when she first attempted to register, she appeared at the courthouse again and again, along with a few other independent blacks who braved the inevitable threats, until they were added to the rolls. For her impertinence she was told she would never again work in the cotton fields, which was about the only work available. Tall, dark skinned, full of wit and using her own unique version of English, which is more expressive than standard English, Mrs. Blackwell decided to go to work for SNCC. She became one of their most effective organizers, a younger protégée of the "three great women."

During the post-Movement years, she worked with Owen Brooks and Harry Bowie under the aegis of the Delta Ministry to incorporate Mayersville. This they did in 1976. The following year she was elected the town's first mayor.

I met Unita Blackwell and her family at her new brick home located not far from the cotton fields where she used to pick.

"All we need now," she said, "is some *work* here in this place. We're trying to lure a factory."

"Where do the people work?" I asked. There were no businesses in town except for two service stations, two stores, one owned by a black, the other owned by a white, and a new sandwich shop owned by a black man. City hall was a converted church.

"In Greenville, unless they own their own land, or wherever," she sighed.

"But still you like it here?"

"Yes, indeed. I love it. So peaceful this place. And then there is the river. Who wouldn't want to live by the river? I can go anywhere in the world and return here and feel at home by this river."

I loved it, too; Mayersville is the most beautiful, isolated, and out-of-the-way place in the entire South, for sure; Mrs. Blackwell had become mayor of a dream town.

"I'm only mayor," she reminded me. "I can't work miracles." She certainly can't be expected to, though she herself was something of a miracle. As we spoke, I thought about how her story was like so much of what I had seen in my travels these past ten months: During the civil rights years blacks had achieved the miraculous by kicking open the doors—but once inside, well, there was hardly anything there. It was almost laughable, a kind of special blues truth.

"Let's go drive over to the river," I suggested to her. We got into my car and headed for the gravel road that would take us over the levee. As we were passing the county courthouse, I asked Mrs. Blackwell if she had ever discussed the old days with the county registrar, the woman who had denied her the right to vote until Unita wore her out, and who also lived in Mayersville.

"Oh, yes. I talked with her. She said, 'That's the way we were brought up, Unita. That's the way things were then.'"

As we approached the river, a perfectly pristine scene, I asked, "What did it all mean, do you think?"

"Well, we didn't gain *much*," Unita admitted. "We changed positions. The river changes positions; it's constantly moving, you know, taking on new routes, cuttin' off old ones. It may not look like it, but it is. Any powerful force will make a change. I suppose what we really gained is the knowledge that we struggled to make this a decent society, because it wasn't. And maybe it still isn't now, but at least we tried. That's history."

# AFTERWORD

⌒

It has been five years since I visited the towns along the route of my journey. I thought it worthwhile to telephone one or two people I interviewed in each town to see if, in their opinion, anything has occurred since 1991 that has dramatically changed conditions.

In Greensboro, public school teacher and community activist Lewis Brandon cited the opening of Emily Mann's new documentary play on the Klan shootings, *Greensboro: A Requiem*, as an event of particular significance. "As you know," Brandon reminded me, "neither white nor black Greensboro had come to terms with the shootings, even though five people lost their lives. People here said it had to do with the Klan and the Communist party, and Greensboro had nothing to do with either of them.

"But in February 1996, forty people from this town, blacks and whites, chartered a bus to see the play at the McCarter Theater in New Jersey. That was important, and a kind of first for us. The script, which takes the form of an investigation, is based on interviews conducted by Emily Mann with both surviving marchers and Klansmen. None of the Klansmen ever went to jail for their actions. An actor portraying Nelson Johnson, who was a leader of the marchers, and an actress portraying Emily Mann, acted as narrators in the script.

"Our delegation included Nelson; our new mayor, Carolyn Allen; and members of the City Council and the County Commission. I think the play helped bring about an acceptance of the unpleasant fact that the Greensboro police were implicated in the killings. One of the Klan leaders was an undercover policeman. It was obvious they could have prevented the shootings if they had only been there. They knew what might happen.

"The fact that a few people in Greensboro cared enough to relive this terrible experience, to face up to it, to try to understand it, is hopefully a basis upon which we can build a degree of racial reconciliation.

"The bad news," continued Brandon, "is that the recent Supreme Court decision [of June 1996] eliminating a primarily black congressional district in North Carolina, represented by Mel Watt, cuts away a good part of black Greensboro. So we'll have to see what that means in the coming years."

Hal Sieber thoroughly endorsed Brandon's comment on the positive impact of the bus trip to see *Greensboro: A Requiem*. Sieber left the *Carolina Peacemaker* in 1993. He is now working with the Community Development Corporation on their Project Homestead, which is designed to document the sites of early-nineteenth-century African-American neighborhoods in the country.

The Woolworth of the early sit-ins has closed. There is a project afoot, Sieber mentioned, to convert the site into a civil rights museum.

～

In Orangeburg, Dr. Rickey Hill of South Carolina State reported that little has changed worth mentioning, other than that Orangeburg County surprisingly, has elected its first black sheriff, James "Poppa" Johnson, a retired policeman.

～

In Charleston, Steve Hoffious of the state Historical Society cited the closing (because of national military downsizing) of the Charleston Naval Base in 1995 as a momentous economic setback for Charleston, with grave consequences for those who for a long time depended on the military institutions for contracts and jobs. "The naval base [actually several military institutions that have clustered in Charleston since World War II] was not only the county's major employer; those jobs paid the highest hourly wage rate in the area.

"Now the city is pushing service jobs as the solution, but all that does is place more eggs in the already filled-to-the-brim tourist industry basket, with the hope upon hope that tourism will expand."

"How does the loss of the military institutions impact the black community?" I asked Hoffious.

"Badly. The naval base did hire quite a number of blacks, and paid them the same wage as whites for the same work. So now, what are these people going to do? It won't be so easy for them to find employment in private industries and tourist businesses; certainly not at comparable salaries."

Myrtle Glascoe, who resigned from the directorship of the Avery Research Center in 1993 to join the College of Charleston faculty, commented in the same vein. "The overdependence on the military bases in Charleston has worked as a detriment to public education in the area," she asserted. "As long as people had those jobs, there was no push to improve educational standards, or to train people in the kind of sophisticated skills they would need to compete in the new international corporations. In addition, South Carolina is a 'right to work' state; unions, and whatever progressive programs they might have brought with them, have been discouraged, as was the case with the hospital strike of 1969. So Charleston is in a bad way. On the other hand, in the Greenville-Spartanburg area of the state, the power structure has modified that stance. They are more hospitable to incoming industries."

Hoffious and his wife, Susan Dunn, mentioned another alarming development. The Medical School Hospital, where the 1969 strike began, is being leased to a private corporation. "As a result," said Hoffious, "all of the nonprofessional workers stand to lose their benefits. Almost all of these people are black, as they were in 1969 when they struck. The Medical School is a major employer of blacks."

Susan Dunn of the Carolina Alliance for Fair Employment added, "Under the new plan, all academic employees will remain employees of the state, so they won't lose their seniority or their benefits. Nonacademic employees will have to go back to scratch, as if they're beginning an entirely new job with a new employer. The failure to win a union really hurts here. The new employer would have to honor a union contract. Now they don't. A cook, for instance, who has worked for twenty years will have to be rehired. The new company will have the right not to rehire. And there is no guarantee that the worker will derive any wage or other benefit based on his or her two decades of service."

"Why is the Medical School Hospital being contracted out to a private corporation?" I asked.

"They say this is a cost-saving move, that this will ensure a good income flow. Meanwhile, the Medical School will be insulated from future protests or attempts to unionize. What it amounts to, as far as I can see, is the people on the bottom who have the least protection, who lack clout, will now be very vulnerable."

In St. Augustine, I was able to reach the Reverend Fred Richardson, the pastor of the St. Paul Methodist Church. "Not much has happened since you were here in 1991," he reported. "We lost Mr. Twine, who died in 1994. We're still losing our young talent; they move elsewhere as soon as they can. On the political front we've made some gains. Moses Floyd, the first black county commissioner, has been re-elected. And we've elected a county school board member, James Tucker."

Albany suffered a devastating flood on July 7, 1994. Days of heavy rains in central and south Georgia inundated the rivers and creeks, including the Flint River, which flows through Albany. "We didn't fully realize how serious the situation was," said Carol King, when I called her. She had planned to drive to the Atlanta airport that afternoon. "I just made it over the Flint River bridge before it closed."

Emory Harris, the brother of singer Rutha Harris, remembers that "the Flint River rose so fast and burst its banks so quickly people living in the low areas of the south side had to run to escape the water. The south side, where blacks live, suffered most of the flooding and devastation." That was an understatement. From news accounts the flooding was so extensive it destroyed Albany State University, which was situated flush on its west bank; shot through Albany's largest cemetery on the west bank, unearthing caskets and sending them floating down the avenue of the newly created lake; and wreaked devastation on homes, churches, and automobiles in its path. Homes near Slappey Avenue, a white neighborhood, also suffered extensive flooding. "It was the kind of disaster you read about in the Old Testament," Harris said.

In the days immediately following the flood, remembered Harris, "whites and blacks joined together as never before" to help those who had suffered losses. People came from outside Albany to help. Emergency funds from the federal government paid for housing for displaced residents in surrounding motels and shelters. Others lived with relatives or friends in surrounding towns until the water receded and they could return. The state provided trailers and temporary buildings for Albany State, which enabled them to reopen in September for the school year.

"But then, after a while, Albany drifted apart; the early spirit was forgotten; and two years later racial hostility in this town, I'm sorry to tell you, is as bad as ever, and that's pretty bad," Harris lamented.

"The crux of the problem," according to Carol King, "is deeper than just blacks and whites. Albany has received about eighty million dollars in federal funds to repair flood damage, but to this day we haven't seen much of anything but arguing and bickering within the City Commission over how this money should be used. Except for what people have done themselves, nothing has been repaired. We now have a majority black City Commission [4–3] that has disappointed us." Mrs. King has declared her candidacy for a seat on the City Commission for the election to be held in July 1996. "Given the enormity of the disaster," Mrs. King continued, "the commission should have moved expeditiously. The federal money was really all we had; most people in Albany didn't have flood insurance. Instead, almost twenty million has been spent on studies about how to proceed. That's ridiculous.

"Unless we can do something in Albany to bring people together, to bridge the awful racial gulf, and to address our problems, I don't know what's going to happen to this town."

~

In Selma the racial polarization which was so palpable in 1991 has eased somewhat, according to Jo Anne Bland, who now directs the new Voting Rights Museum on

Water Street near the Pettus Bridge. "But that doesn't mean whites have returned to the public schools," she quickly added, "because they haven't." Selma High School is about 90 percent black. The majority of white students have moved to area academies, and to Dallas County schools. Dr. James Carter, who succeeded Norward Roussell as Selma superintendent, is still in place, as is the novel school board plan, which alternates a 5–4 majority between blacks and whites each year. "Nineteen ninety-six is a black year," Ms. Bland drily informed me.

"We still have two kinds of high school diplomas—general and advanced. The advanced diploma prepares one for college. The students decide which track to pursue; most prefer the easier general diploma. We're [the Sanders legal firm group that led the 1990 school boycott] fighting for a core curriculum for everyone."

Alvin Benn, the reporter who covers the Black Belt for the *Montgomery Advertiser*, observed that there is more "racial working together" than there was in 1991. He concurs that whites have not returned to the public schools. Instead, they attend "two academies and the county school."

Norward Roussell has, since 1992, served as superintendent of the Tuskegee public schools. "Our system," he reported, reflecting Tuskegee's history since the first federal desegregation orders, "is virtually entirely black. That doesn't bother me, except for the insufficient funding coming from our local city and county tax base. Despite the obvious talent here, we don't have the resources to do those things we should be doing to better our schools. Whites simply will not invest in a school system which educates black children."

Roussell did enthusiastically note that the Alabama legislature has recently (1995) mandated the elimination of tracking and leveling in state public school systems. "We are working toward a statewide core curriculum, which we've needed for a long time."

⁓

In Mississippi, Obie Clark of Meridian reported, sadly, the death of Cornelius Steele of Longdale, who invited Goodman, Chaney, and Schwerner to their burned church in 1964, which eventually led to the murder of the three civil rights workers by Klansmen that summer. When I called Mr. Clark in June, he was then investigating a fire that had destroyed St. Paul Primitive Baptist Church in nearby Lauderdale County on Easter Sunday, 1996. "These burnings," he offered, "are not the work of the type of segregationist conspiracies we knew in the sixties when churches receptive to Movement activists were destroyed. Now, I think it's the result of just some kind of perpetual hate in the South that never seems to go away."

In the Delta, Congressman Mike Espy, the state's first black congressman since Reconstruction, was appointed secretary of agriculture by incoming President Bill Clinton in 1992. He resigned that post in 1994 under pressure of allegations of improprieties. Espy has not reemerged in Mississippi politics. Bennie Thompson of Bolton, a town at the southern tip of the district, won a special election in the spring of 1993 to succeed Espy. Thompson appeals to about the same constituency as Espy, though Thompson is probably a little stronger with black voters. Espy enjoyed stronger white support. The district is now about 52 percent black, since reapportionment based on the 1990 census. Attorney Johnny Walls of Greenville was elected to the state senate in 1992; he is chair of the state Democratic party.

Owen Brooks of Greenville has revived the Delta Ministry, his old organization. He was not as enthusiastic as I was in 1991 about Indianola's support-the-public-schools spirit. "Generally," he says, "as far as the entire Delta is concerned, we're still talking about totally separate school systems. These are ninety-five percent black public schools on one side; all-white academies on the other. The Parents for Public Schools movement started by Dick Molpus and his friends in Jackson hasn't impacted the Delta." Brooks cited former SNCC leader Bob Moses's Algebra Project, designed to innovatively teach mathematics to black kids, as a positive contribution in the public schools where Moses and his assistants are working. Brooks also notes the donation of supplies to selected Delta public school systems by the Educate the Children Foundation. "Separate schools are the reality, however. Any improvements in the level of education will have to be made within that framework."

The most telling disappointment for black voters since 1991 was the poor showing of former secretary of state Dick Molpus in the gubernatorial election of November 1995. Blacks backed Molpus with enthusiasm, but he lost by a solid 55–45 percentage to incumbent Republican governor Kirk Fordice, who is considered an extreme reactionary not just by blacks. Fordice's victory hurt all the more because every other Democratic candidate for state office in November 1995 won.

"Molpus remained aloof from his black constituency," Brooks complained, as did other blacks I spoke with. "Then when he did embrace his natural base of support, and when he became more aggressive in attacking Fordice, it was too late."

Bill Minor of Jackson, still the senior political reporter in the state, added with disgust, that no matter what strategy Molpus might have adopted, "he had no chance," given the current conservative mind-set among white voters, at least as far as the governor's race was concerned. "There is a certain streak of meanness in Fordice," Minor added. "He represents a retreat from a succession of Mississippi governors who had moved the state ahead, bit by bit."

"Did Fordice use Molpus's support for integrated schools against him?" I asked.

"He didn't have to. Everyone knew Molpus's record. I also think Molpus was too decent and too polite to really go at Fordice and try to get his goat, which would have made the race nasty because Fordice is so rude and vulgar. Molpus just couldn't do that."

Finally, in Mayersville, Unita Blackwell reports that she retired as mayor when her term was up in 1993. "It was getting to the point where a few people were jealous of me, and I was made into a target. So let someone else do it for a while. I'm still busy," she assured me. "We've set up a port commission in the hope that one day we can have a port like we had in the nineteenth century. Of course, that was when this county was full of huge cotton plantations."

"Any results from efforts to pull a factory in here?" I asked.

"Well, no. What we got was a prison."

"A prison?"

"Yes. A county prison. Right here in Mayersville. It will have two hundred fourteen beds and sixty jobs, with a preference for residents of Mayersville, those with low and moderate incomes. I don't *love* it, but that's what we got."

"And the river," I asked with a smile in my voice. "How's it doing?"

"The river's fine. Just fine. There was a delegation from China in here recently and I took them over the levee to look at our river. They said it was awesome."

# ACKNOWLEDGMENTS

~

First and foremost, I must express my appreciation to the persons who so generously shared their life stories with me. Quite obviously, these personal narratives compose the foundation of the larger stories as I saw them during my tour of 1991. Several interviewees succinctly understood what I was trying to do and urged me on to completion with a passion that I will never forget.

My only regret is that I was not able to utilize in the manuscript all of the interviews I conducted. Each person I spoke with at length, however, did help to sharpen my sense of place and history as I worked my way southward, adding valuable strokes to the total portrait.

For various kindnesses along my way, I wish to thank Skunder Boghossian of Washington, D.C.; Leonard and Rhoda Dreyfus and Charles Rowell of Charlottesville, Virginia; Nayo Watkins of Durham, North Carolina; Anna Simkins of Greensboro, North Carolina; Worth and Corrin Long of Atlanta; and Roger T. Saucier of the Waterways Experiment Station, Vicksburg, Mississippi. I am indebted to Cecil Williams, James Summers, and the Reverend H. D. Harvey of Orangeburg, South Carolina; Jack McCray and William Saunders of Charleston, South Carolina; Henry Twine and James Jackson of St. Augustine, Florida; the Reverend Samuel Wells and Pat Perry of Albany, Georgia; Jo Anne Bland and Alston Fitts of Selma, Alabama; Hollis Watkins of Jackson, Mississippi; Calvin Garner of Canton, Mississippi; Cornelius Steele of Longdale, Mississippi; Sylvester Harris of West Point, Mississippi; the Reverend Michael Freeman of Indianola, Mississippi; L. C. Dorsey of Mound Bayou, Mississippi; Unita Blackwell of Mayersville, Mississippi; and Jewel Sloan of San Antonio, Texas, for their informative driving tours.

David Garrow of New York; Jane Logan Poindexter of Philadelphia, Pennsylvania; Vernon Jordan and James Early of Washington, D.C.; Kim Lacy Rogers of Carlisle, Pennsylvania; Jerry Ward of Jackson, Mississippi; and poet Keorapetse Kgositsile of South Africa encouraged me to pursue this project in the early days of its conception, when I needed encouragement. I would also like to express my gratitude to Dr. Wesley A. Hotchkiss, of the American Missionary Association of the United Church of Christ, for his continued interest and support, which enabled me to complete my Mississippi Civil Rights Oral History, copies of which are housed in the Amistad Research Center in New Orleans and the Tougaloo College Archives in Jackson, Mississippi. I also wish to thank Marita Rivero, station manager of WGBH radio in Boston, and WGBH producer Bob Lyons for their interest in converting some of the *Southern Journey* interviews into radio programs on the contemporary South.

This manuscript would never have been completed without the dedicated stenographic assistance of Corinne Nelson of Jersey City, New Jersey, in the latter stages, and Nilima Mwendo of New Orleans, who worked on the early drafts. I am grateful to Janet Hulstrand of New York for her editorial assistance and her valuable and thoughtful questions, which were of immense help in developing the manuscript. In this vein, Kamau Brathwaite of New York University, Myrtle Glascoe of the College of Charleston, and Jerry Ward of Tougaloo College read portions of the manuscript and wrote extremely helpful criticisms and suggestions. Attorney Eugene Kidd and poet Saddi Khali of New Orleans helped with fact checking, though I must assume all responsibility for mistakes. Carl Jefferson and Roland Freeman advised me on photography. I depended on Wayne Coleman, now archivist of the Civil Rights Museum in Birmingham, Alabama, for all sorts of research assistance when he was with the Amistad Research Center; I owe a debt of gratitude to the entire Amistad staff. I must also thank Karen Rogers of New Orleans, who assisted with travel, and Marian Martin and the staff of peaceful Gulfside Assembly in Waveland, Mississippi, where I did a lot of work on this book. My close friend, attorney Lolis Elie of New Orleans, helped to ease my passage from conception to execution.

In fact, there are more friends in New Orleans who have been interested and supportive of this book than I can possibly name. I *would* like to mention the longtime members of our Congo Square Writers Union: Kalamu ya Salaam, Chakula Cha Jua, Raymond Breaux, and Quo Vadis Gex-Breaux. I am also grateful for the continuing interest and expressions of support from the staff and board of the New Orleans Jazz and Heritage Foundation and Festival, particularly George and Joyce Wein.

This volume also provides an opportunity for me to express my gratitude to J. Max Bond and Jean Carey Bond, the anchors of my New York family, for their unwavering hospitality and encouragement. They've lived with the trials and tribulations of this book from beginning to end. So have the members of my Umbra Workshop family, now scattered to the winds, though they remain with me wherever I go, whatever I do: David, Ishmael, Calvin, Joe, Brenda, Askia, Steve, Jane, Lorenzo, and the gang. Artist Gilbert Fletcher and film maker St. Clair Bourne have always been ready and eager to help. For their graciousness and hospitality in 1991 and several times before that, I wish to thank my Gambian family: Dr. Gabriel Mendy, Patrick, Edward, Alphonse, Jimmy, Daniel, John Gomez, and Mother Ya Kinta.

In a very real sense, the idea for *Southern Journey* evolved from my work with Andrew Young on the early drafts of his autobiography, *An Easy Burden*. I want to thank Andrew, my close friend since childhood, for providing me with the opportunity to work with him, which heightened my interest in the southern Movement and greatly enhanced my appreciation for the sacrifices of so many people, many of them unknown, who worked for the transformation of the South into a more just society.

I began working with literary agent Lawrence Jordan in the early 1980s when he took on the Andrew Young autobiography. It was with Lawrence's help and valuable experience that I fine-tuned the concept and proposal for *Southern Journey*. I have treasured his advice and his invaluable assistance in the business aspects of this project; his role has far transcended the usual work of a literary agent.

From the moment my editor, Claire Wachtel, called me at the Jazz Festival office in 1990 to say she liked my proposal and wanted to publish the book, she has never wavered in her enthusiasm, despite the numerous twists and turns of the often unsure road to publication. Certainly *Southern Journey* would not have been possible without Claire's faith, and without the diligent work of her assistant, Tracy Quinn.

And finally, I want to thank my family, which has been steadfast in supporting me throughout this process. I especially want to thank my mother, Jessie Covington Dent, who has always been there for me since the beginning. My appreciation goes to my brothers, Ben and Walter, and their families, who have endured me while I worked on this project. The memory and spiritual presence of my father, Albert W.

Dent, and the example of his lifetime of work building institutions for the betterment of conditions of people in the South, always remain with me.

It is with extreme regret and sadness that I note the deaths since 1991 of Dr. Warmoth T. Gibbs, Sol Jacobs, Elizabeth Gibbs Moore, Angelina Smith, and Samuel Cooper Smith of Greensboro; Modjeska Simkins of Columbia, South Carolina; Bernice Robinson of Charleston; Henry Twine of St. Augustine; Cornelius Steele of Longdale; and Wilma Falls and John Buffington of West Point. They have departed this life, but it is my fervent hope that their voices continue to live.

# LIST OF INTERVIEWEES

## Greensboro

Ms. Alma S. Adams

Dr. Claude Barnes

Mr. Lewis A. Brandon III

Ms. Carolyn Q. Coleman

Dr. Carl O. Foster

Dr. Warmoth T. Gibbs

Mr. Sol Jacobs

Rev. Nelson Johnson

Atty. Walter Johnson

Mr. John Marshall Kilimanjaro

Ms. Elizabeth Gibbs Moore

Dr. Japhet H. Nkonae

Mr. Hal Sieber

Dr. George Simkins

Mrs. Angelina Smith

Mr. Samuel Cooper Smith

Ms. Barbara Watkins

Mr. Jimmy Williams

## Orangeburg

Ms. Marjorie B. Hammock

Rev. H. D. Harvey

Dr. Rickey Hill

Dr. Barbara Williams Jenkins

Mr. Dean B. Livingston

Dr. M. Maceo Nance, Jr.

Mr. Cleveland L. Sellers, Jr.

Ms. Modjeska Simkins

Mr. James Sulton, Sr.

Mr. Cecil Williams

## Charleston

Mr. Isaiah Bennett

Rev. James G. Blake

Ms. Millicent Brown

Mr. Azikiwe T. Chandler

Ms. Mignon L. Clyburn

Ms. Miriam DeCosta-Willis

Ms. Susan Dunn

Sen. Herbert U. Fielding

Mr. Robert Ford

Dr. Myrtle Glascoe

Ms. Ethel J. Grimball

Mr. Stephen Hoffious

Mr. Jack A. McCray

Ms. Mary A. Moultrie

Ms. Arleen B. C. Reid

Ms. Bernice V. Robinson

Mr. William Saunders

Ms. Henrietta Snype

Mr. Mike Vanderhorst

Ms. Naomi M. White

## St. Augustine

Mr. James Allen

Mr. Moses Floyd

Mr. James S. Jackson

Rev. F. D. Richardson, Jr.

Mr. Henry L. Twine

## Albany

Ms. Elaine Baker

Mr. Jesse Boone

Ms. Juanita Sanders Cribb

Mr. Jeffrey Haile

Mr. Emory Harris

Ms. Rutha Harris

Dr. T. Marshall Jones

Ms. Carol R. King

Mr. Michael Moss

Ms. Patricia J. Perry

Mr. A. C. Searles

Mr. Tom Searles

Mr. Charles M. Sherrod

Rev. Samuel B. Wells

Mr. Curtis L. Williams

## Selma

Mr. James Anderson

Mr. Alvin Benn

Ms. Jo Anne Bland

Atty. Bruce Boynton

Atty. J. L. Chestnut, Jr.

Mr. Alston Fitts

Dr. David W. Hodo

Mr. Kevin Ladaris

Dr. C. N. Okoye

Dr. Norward Roussell

Atty. Henry Sanders

Atty. Rose Sanders

Mr. Albert Turner

## Mississippi

Mr. Karl M. Banks

Ms. Unita Blackwell

Mr. Harry Bowie

Mr. Bob Boyd

Mr. Owen H. Brooks

Mr. John Buffington

Mr. Obie Clark

Ms. Annie Devine

Dr. L. C. Dorsey

Mr. Mike Espy

Ms. Wilma Falls

Rev. Michael W. Freeman

Mr. Calvin Garner

Mr. Clarence Hall

Mr. Sylvester Harris

Ms. Betty Jo Hines

Mrs. Winson Hudson

Mr. Walter C. Jones

Rev. David Mathews

Dr. Robert L. Merritt

Mr. W. F. Minor

Hon. Dick Molpus
Atty. George C. Nichols
Mr. Charles Pernell
Mr. Dwight Presley
Atty. Carver A. Randle
Mr. Oliver C. Rice
Mr. Roger T. Saucier
Atty. Mike Sayer
Ms. Shirley Simmons
Mr. Cornelius Steele
Mr. Frank S. Street
Mr. Matteo Suarez
Mr. Charles W. Tisdale
Atty. Bennie L. Turner
Atty. Johnnie E. Walls, Jr.
Mr. George Washington
Mr. Hollis Watkins
Ms. Jewel Williams
Mr. Robert Zellner

## General

Dr. John Hope Franklin
Mr. Harvey Gantt
Ms. Vertamae Grosvenor
Mr. Worth Long
Ms. Barbara Watkins
Hon. Andrew Young

# BIBLIOGRAPHY

## Greensboro

### Books

Chafe, William H. *Civilities and Civil Rights.* New York: Oxford University Press, 1980.

Haynes, Robert V. *A Night of Violence: The Houston Riot of 1917.* Baton Rouge, La.: Louisiana State University Press, 1976.

Meier, August, and Elliot Rudwick. *CORE: A Study in the Civil Rights Movement.* Urbana, Ill.: University of Illinois Press, 1975.

Raines, Howell. *My Soul Is Rested.* New York: G. P. Putnam's Sons, 1977.

### Articles and Pamphlets

Beal, M. Gertrude. "The Underground Railroad in Guilford County." *The Southern Friend* (Spring 1980): 18–29.

Bryant, Pat. "Justice vs. the Movement." *Southern Exposure* (Summer 1980): 79–89.

Hatcher, Susan Tucker. "North Carolina Quakers: Bona Fide Abolitionists." *The Southern Friend* (Autumn 1979): 81–99.

————. "North Carolina Quakers: The Freedman's Friends." *The Southern Friend* (Spring 1981): 25–37.

Loggins, Kirk, and Susan Thomas. "The Menace Returns." *Southern Exposure* (Summer 1980): 50–54.

Pfaff, Eugene. "Greensboro Sit-ins: Interviews with William Thomas, Elizabeth Laizner, Clarence Malone, and Willa Player." *Southern Exposure* (Spring 1981): 23–28.

## Orangeburg

### Books

Bass, Jack, and Jack Nelson. *The Orangeburg Massacre.* Macon, Ga.: Mercer University Press, 1984.

Mays, Benjamin E. *Born to Rebel.* New York: Charles Scribner's Sons, 1971.

Mebane, Mary. *Mary, Wayfarer.* New York: Viking Press, 1983.

Sellers, Cleveland. *The River of No Return.* New York: William Morrow and Company, 1973.

### Articles and Pamphlets

Watters, Pat, and Weldon Rougeau. "Events at Orangeburg: A Report Based on Study and Interviews in Orangeburg, South Carolina, in the Aftermath of the Tragedy." Southern Regional Council. Atlanta, Georgia. February 25, 1968.

## Charleston

### Books

Beifuss, Joan. *At the River I Stand.* Memphis: B&W Books, 1985.

Carawan, Guy and Candie. *Ain't You Got a Right to the Tree of Life?* Athens, Ga.: University of Georgia Press, 1989.

Clark, Septima. *Ready from Within,* ed. Cynthia Stokes Brown. Trenton, N.J.: Africa World Press, 1990.

————, with LeGette Blythe. *Echo in My Soul.* New York: Dutton, 1962.

Fields, Mamie Garven, with Karen Fields. *Lemon Swamp and Other Places: A Carolina Memoir.* New York: The Free Press, 1983.

Frank, Gerold. *An American Death*. Garden City, N.Y.: Doubleday and Company, 1972.

Fraser, Walter J., Jr. *Charleston! Charleston!: The History of a Southern City*. Columbia, S.C.: University of South Carolina Press, 1989.

Killens, John, ed. *The Trial Record of Denmark Vesey*. Boston: Beacon Press, 1970.

Kluger, Richard. *Simple Justice*. New York: Random House, Vintage Books, 1977.

Lofton, John. *Denmark Vesey's Revolt*. Kent, Ohio: Kent State University Press, 1983.

McPherson, James M. *Battle Cry of Freedom: The Civil War Era*. New York: Ballantine Books, 1988.

**Articles and Pamphlets**

Bass, Jack. "Strike at Charleston." *New South* (Summer 1969): 35–44.

Cotton, Dorothy. "CEP: Challenge to the New Education." *Freedomways* (Winter 1969): 66–70.

Fink, Leon. "Union Power, Soul Power." *Southern Changes* (March–April 1983): 9–22.

Hoffious, Steve. "Charleston Hospital Workers' Strike, 1969." *Working Lives: The "Southern Exposure" History of Labor in the South*, ed. Mark S. Miller. New York: Pantheon, 1980.

O'Dell, Jack. "Charleston's Legacy to the Poor People's Campaign." *Freedomways* (Summer 1969): 197–211.

Woodruff, Nan. "Esau Jenkins: A Retrospective View of the Man and His Times." The Avery Institute of Afro-American History and Culture. Charleston, S.C. February 1984.

## St. Augustine

### Books

Colburn, David R. *Racial Change and Community Crisis: St. Augustine, Florida, 1877–1980.* Gainesville, Fla.: University of Florida Press, 1991.

Katz, William Lorenz. *Black Indians.* New York: Atheneum, 1986.

### Articles and Pamphlets

*Ripley's Believe It or Not!: A Guide.* Ripley Entertainment, Inc., and Ripley's Believe It or Not!, a division of Jim Pattison Industries. 1991.

"St. Augustine and the Beaches, Events." *The St. Augustine Record* (July–August 1991).

Waterbury, Jean Parker, ed. "Richard Aloysius Twine: Photographer of Lincolnville, 1922–1927." *East-Florida Gazette* (February 1990).

## Albany

### Books

Branch, Taylor. *Parting the Waters.* New York: Simon and Schuster, 1988.

Carson, Clayborne. *In Struggle: SNCC and the Black Awakening of the 1960's.* Cambridge, Mass.: Harvard University Press, 1981.

Du Bois, W. E. B. *The Souls of Black Folk.* New York: William Morrow and Company, 1961.

Garrow, David J. *Bearing the Cross.* New York: William Morrow and Company, 1986.

Holley, Joseph. *You Can't Build a Chimney from the Top.* New York: William-Frederick Press, 1948.

Lewis, David L. *King: A Biography.* Urbana, Ill.: University of Illinois Press, 1978.

Powledge, Fred. *Free at Last?: The Civil Rights Movement and the People Who Made It.* Boston: Little, Brown and Company, 1991.

Watters, Pat, and Reese Cleghorn. *Climbing Jacob's Ladder.* New York: Harcourt, Brace and World, 1967.

## Selma

### Books

Boynton, Amelia Platts. *Bridge Across Jordan.* New York: Carlton Press, 1979.

Chestnut, J. L., with Julia Cass. *Black in Selma.* New York: Farrar, Straus and Giroux, 1990.

Eagles, Charles W. *Outside Agitator: Jon Daniels and the Civil Rights Movement in Alabama.* Chapel Hill, N.C.: University of North Carolina Press, 1993.

Fager, Charles E. *Selma, 1965.* New York: Charles Scribner's Sons, 1974.

Garrow, David J. *Protest in Selma.* New Haven, Conn.: Yale University Press, 1978.

Henderson, David. *De Mayor of Harlem.* New York: E. P. Dutton, 1970.

————. *Voodoo Child of the Aquarian Age.* New York: Doubleday and Company, 1978.

Norrell, Robert J. *Reaping the Whirlwind: The Civil Rights Movement in Tuskegee.* New York: Random House, Vintage Books, 1986.

Oakes, Jeannie. *Keeping Track: How Schools Structure Inequality.* New Haven, Conn.: Yale University Press, 1985.

### Articles and Pamphlets

"Because No Man Can Live Forever," a special section of the Sunday *Montgomery Advertiser* (March 4, 1990).

"Just Schools," a special issue of *Southern Exposure* (Summer 1979).

Logsdon, Joseph. "A History of Gilbert Academy, New Orleans, La." Unpublished paper. Department of History, University of New Orleans, 1984.

Vivian, Octavia, ed. Twenty-fifth Anniversary Program Booklet, Selma to Montgomery March. Published by 21st Century Leadership Training Project. Selma, Alabama. March 1990.


## Mississippi

**Books**

Cagin, Seth, and Philip Dray. *We Are Not Afraid.* New York: Macmillan Publishing Company, 1988.

Cobb, James C. *The Most Southern Place on Earth.* New York: Oxford University Press, 1992.

Dittmer, John. *Local People: The Struggle for Civil Rights in Mississippi.* Urbana, Ill.: University of Illinois Press, 1994.

Dollard, John. *Caste and Class in a Southern Town.* Madison, Wis.: University of Wisconsin Press, 1988.

Dunbar, Tony. *Delta Time.* New York: Pantheon Books, 1990.

Lemann, Nicholas. *The Promised Land.* New York: Random House, 1992.

McAdam, Doug. *Freedom Summer.* New York: Oxford University Press, 1988.

Moody, Annie. *Coming of Age in Mississippi.* New York: The Dial Press, 1968.

Morrison, Minion K. *Black Political Mobilization.* New York: The Free Press, 1996.

Payne, Charles M. *I've Got the Light of Freedom.* Berkeley, Calif.: University of California Press, 1995.

Salter, John, Jr. *Jackson, Mississippi.* Hicksville, N.Y.: Exposition Press, 1979.

Von Hoffman, Nicholas. *Mississippi Notebook.* New York: David White Company, 1964.

### Articles and Pamphlets

Bates, Eric. "The Kill Line." *Southern Exposure* (Fall 1991): 23–29.

———. "Parting the Waters." *Southern Exposure* (Fall 1991): 34–36.

———. "Something as One." *Southern Exposure* (Fall 1991): 30–33.

Dent, Tom. "Portrait of Three Heroes." *Freedomways* (Spring 1965): 250–265.

———. "Annie Devine Remembers." *Freedomways* (Spring 1982): 81–92.

Schweid, Richard. "Down on the Farm." *Southern Exposure* (Fall 1991): 14–22.


## General

### Books

Brathwaite, Kamau. *Roots.* Ann Arbor, Mich.: University of Michigan Press, 1993.

Cash, W. J. *The Mind of the South.* New York: Random House, Vintage Books, 1969.

Dent, Thomas, Richard Schechner, and Gilbert Moses, eds. *The Free Southern Theater by the Free Southern Theater.* New York: Bobbs-Merrill, 1969.

Du Bois, W. E. B. *Black Reconstruction in America.* New York: Atheneum, 1992.

Egerton, John. *Speak Now Against the Day.* Chapel Hill, N.C.: University of North Carolina Press, 1995.

Foner, Eric. *A Short History of Reconstruction.* New York: Harper & Row, 1990.

Killens, John Oliver, and Jerry W. Ward, eds. *Black Southern Voices.* New York: Penguin, 1992.

King, Mary. *Freedom Song.* New York: William Morrow and Company, 1987.

Moon, William Least Heat. *Blue Highways.* New York: Ballantine Books, 1984.

Nabokov, Peter. *Native American Testimony.* New York: Penguin, 1991.

Olmsted, Frederick Law. *A Journey in the Seaboard Slave States.* New York: Negro Universities Press, 1968.

Quarles, Benjamin. *The Negro in the Making of America.* New York: Collier Books, 1987.

Selby, Earl and Minion. *Odyssey: Journey Through Black America.* New York: G. P. Putnam's Sons, 1971.

Young, Andrew. *An Easy Burden: The Civil Rights Movement and the Transformation of America.* New York: HarperCollins, 1996.